The Israeli–Palestinian Conflict

Also by Raja Halwani

VIRTUOUS LIAISONS: Care, Love, Sex, and Virtue Ethics

SEX AND ETHICS: Essays on Sexuality, Virtue and the Good Life

Also by Tomis Kapitan

PHILOSOPHICAL PERSPECTIVES ON THE ISRAELI–PALESTINIAN CONFLICT

ARCHAEOLOGY, HISTORY, AND CULTURE IN PALESTINE AND THE NEAR EAST

The Israeli–Palestinian Conflict

Philosophical Essays on Self-Determination, Terrorism and the One-State Solution

Raja Halwani
School of the Art Institute of Chicago

and

Tomis Kapitan
Northern Illinois University

palgrave
macmillan

First published 2008 by
PALGRAVE MACMILLAN
Houndmills, Basingstoke, Hampshire RG21 6XS and
175 Fifth Avenue, New York, N.Y. 10010
Companies and representatives throughout the world

PALGRAVE MACMILLAN is the global academic imprint of the Palgrave Macmillan division of St. Martin's Press, LLC and of Palgrave Macmillan Ltd. Macmillan® is a registered trademark in the United States, United Kingdom and other countries. Palgrave is a registered trademark in the European Union and other countries.

ISBN-13: 978–0–230–53537–4 hardback
ISBN-10: 0–230–53537–2 hardback

This book is printed on paper suitable for recycling and made from fully managed and sustained forest sources. Logging, pulping and manufacturing processes are expected to conform to the environmental regulations of the country of origin.

A catalogue record for this book is available from the British Library.

A catalog record for this book is available from the Library of Congress.

10 9 8 7 6 5 4 3 2 1
17 16 15 14 13 12 11 10 09 08

Printed and bound in Great Britain by
CPI Antony Rowe, Chippenham and Eastbourne

To my mother, Nora Halwani, and to Khadijah al-Khateeb, the two women who taught me the importance of justice and hope.

Raja Halwani

To my mother, Ruth Kapitan, whose positive influence has been greater than she might realize.

Tomis Kapitan

Contents

Acknowledgements

We wish to thank Salman Abu Sitta, the Foundation for Middle East Peace, and the Palestinian Academic Society for the Study of International Affairs (PASSIA) for allowing us to use their maps, Ali Abunimah for helpful advice, Maureen Clare Murphy for providing the photograph that made its way to the cover of this book, Steven Jones for his help in designing the cover, Vidya Vijayan at Palgrave Macmillan for her tireless editorial help in copy editing and seeing the book to its completion, and Dan Bunyard at Palgrave Macmillan for helpful advice, encouragement, and editorial feedback.

Raja Halwani wishes to thank Malik Moubayed, the owner of Café Latakia in Chicago, for his hospitality and generosity, when Halwani was writing and revising his chapters at his café; Ali Abunimah and Syrine al-Hout for help and advice; and all those with whom he discussed the issues of this book over the years and who made important suggestions; the list is too long, but special thanks go to Issa Abu Nimah, Roxane Assaf, Celeste Friend, Nora Halwani, Kathy Havens, Bayan al-Hout, Steven Jones, Tomis Kapitan, Maureen Clare Murphy, Richard Rubin, Eli Ungar, Rachel Weiss, and the members of Not In My Name. Special thanks go to Tomis Kapitan for his insightful comments on earlier drafts of Halwani's two chapters. Special thanks and gratitude also go to Steven Jones, who read the penultimate drafts of the chapters and provided incisive and humorous comments on their substance and style.

Tomis Kapitan expresses his gratitude to several people who, in one way or another, have helped him understand the various issues discussed in this book, notably, Abdul Aziz Aluwaishiq, Ali Abunimah, Robert Ashmore, Rejae Busailah, Roger Heacock, Rima Kapitan, Selma Mahdi, Georg Meggle, Roy Pearson, Glenn Perry, Igor Primoratz, Erich Schulte, Jeffrey Snapper, Herman Stark, Khaled Taha, Ghada Talhami, and, above all, Orayb Najjar. A tremendous thanks is due to Raja Halwani for his conception of this project, his instructive comments on drafts of Kapitan's chapters, and his marvelous attention to detail.

Maps

A

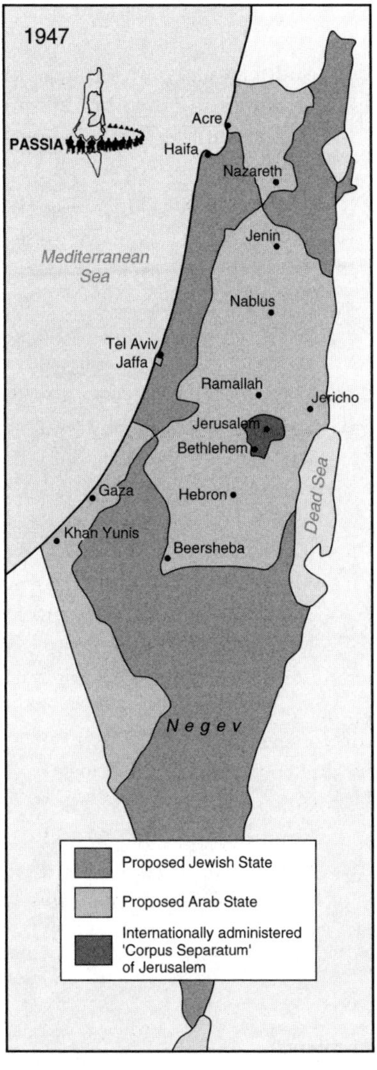

Map A United Nations 1947 Partition Plan
Source: Reproduced from PASSIA's web site (www.passia.org)

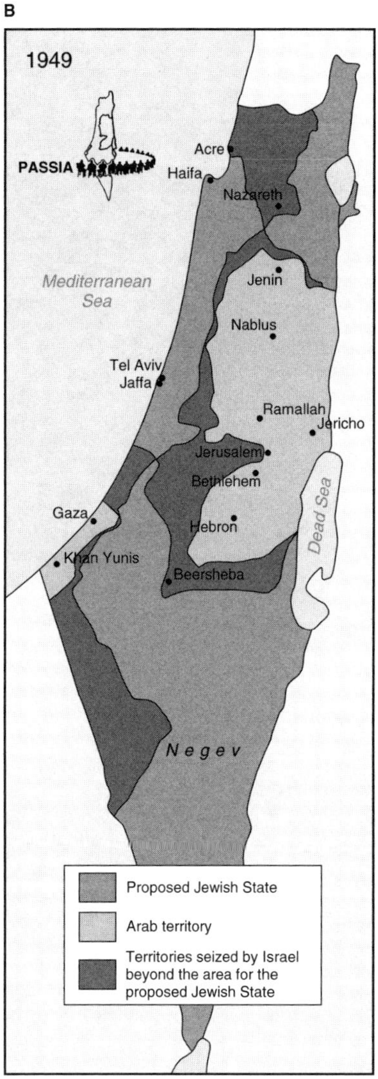

Map B The Rhodes Armistice Lines
Source: Reproduced from PASSIA's web site (www.passia.org)

C

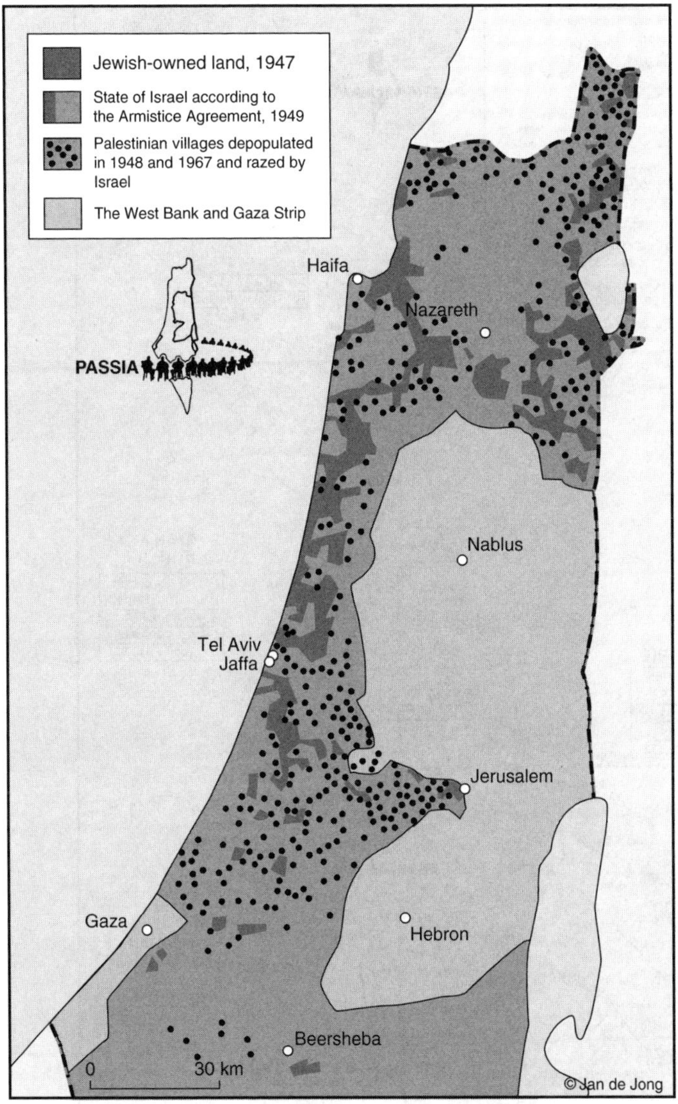

Map C Depopulated Palestinian Villages
Source: Reproduced from PASSIA's web site (www.passia.org)

D

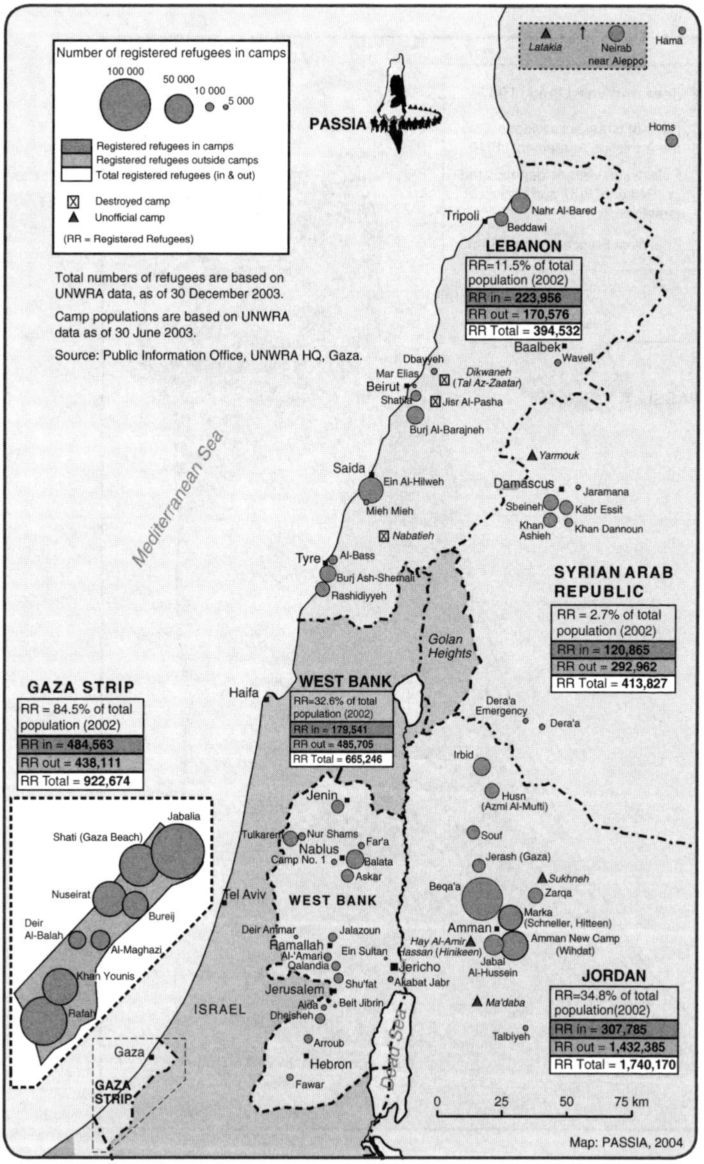
Number of registered refugees in camps
100 000
50 000
10 000
5 000
Registered refugees in camps
Registered refugees outside camps
Total registered refugees (in & out)
Destroyed camp
Unofficial camp
(RR = Registered Refugees)
Total numbers of refugees are based on UNWRA data, as of 30 December 2003.
Camp populations are based on UNWRA data as of 30 June 2003.
Source: Public Information Office, UNWRA HQ, Gaza.
PASSIA
LEBANON
RR=11.5% of total population (2002)
RR in = 223,956
RR out = 170,576
RR Total = 394,532
SYRIAN ARAB REPUBLIC
RR = 2.7% of total population (2002)
RR in = 120,865
RR out = 292,962
RR Total = 413,827
WEST BANK
RR=32.6% of total population (2002)
RR in = 179,541
RR out = 485,705
RR Total = 665,246
GAZA STRIP
RR = 84.5% of total population (2002)
RR in = 484,563
RR out = 438,111
RR Total = 922,674
JORDAN
RR=34.8% of total population(2002)
RR in = 307,785
RR out = 1,432,385
RR Total = 1,740,170
Latakia
Neirab near Aleppo
Hama
Homs
Tripoli
Nahr Al-Bared
Beddawi
Baalbek
Wavell
Dbayyeh
Mar Elias
Beirut
Shatila
Dikwaneh (Tal Az-Zaatar)
Jisr Al-Pasha
Burj Al-Barajneh
Yarmouk
Mediterranean Sea
Saida
Ein Al-Hilweh
Mieh Mieh
Nabatieh
Damascus
Jaramana
Sbeineh
Kabr Essit
Khan Ashieh
Khan Dannoun
Tyre
Al-Bass
Burj Ash-Shemali
Rashidiyyeh
Golan Heights
Haifa
Dera'a Emergency
Dera'a
Irbid
Husn (Azmi Al-Mufti)
Jenin
Tulkarem
Nur Shams
Far'a
Nablus
Camp No. 1
Balata
Askar
Souf
Jerash (Gaza)
Sukhneh
Zarqa
Beqa'a
Marka (Schneller, Hitteen)
Amman New Camp (Wihdat)
Tel Aviv
WEST BANK
Deir Ammar
Jalazoun
Ramallah
Al-'Amari
Qalandia
Ein Sultan
Jericho
Hay Al-Amir
Hassan (Hinikeen)
Amman
Jabal Al-Hussein
Aqabat Jabr
Shu'fat
Jerusalem
Aida
Beit Jibrin
Dheisheh
Arroub
Hebron
Fawar
Dead Sea
ISRAEL
Ma'daba
Talbiyeh
Jabalia
Shati (Gaza Beach)
Nuseirat
Bureij
Deir Al-Balah
Al-Maghazi
Khan Younis
Rafah
Gaza
GAZA STRIP
0
25
50
75 km
Map: PASSIA, 2004

Map D UNRWA Palestinian Refugee Camps
Source: Reproduced from PASSIA's web site (www.passia.org)

E

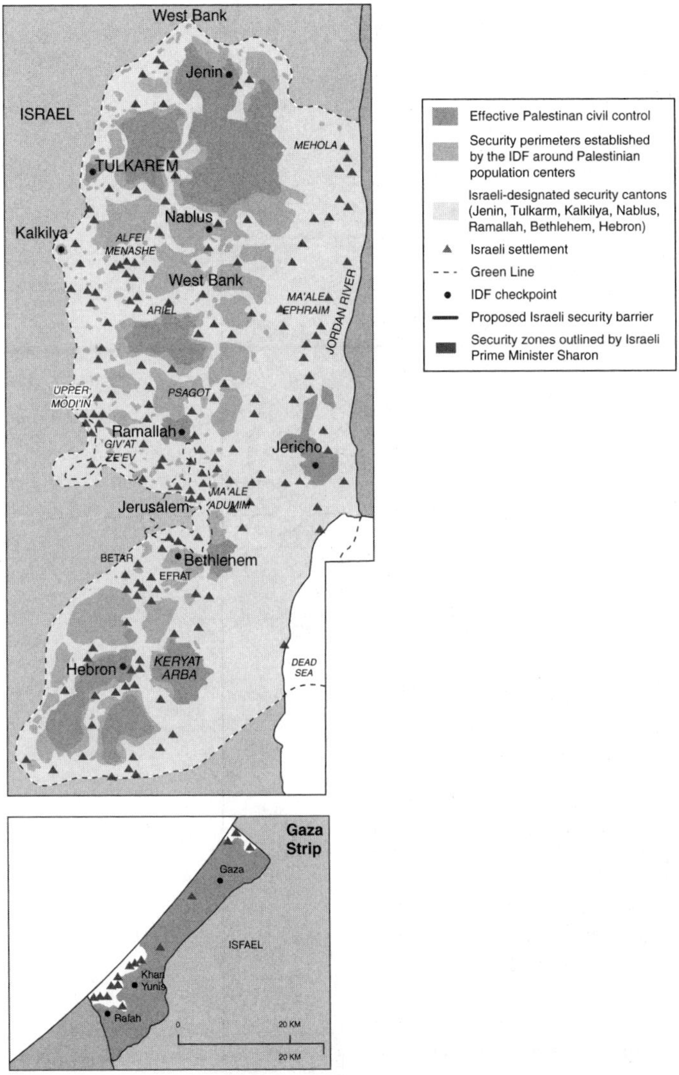

Map E West Bank Jewish Settlements
Source: Reproduced from The Foundation for Middle East's web site (www.fmep.org)

F

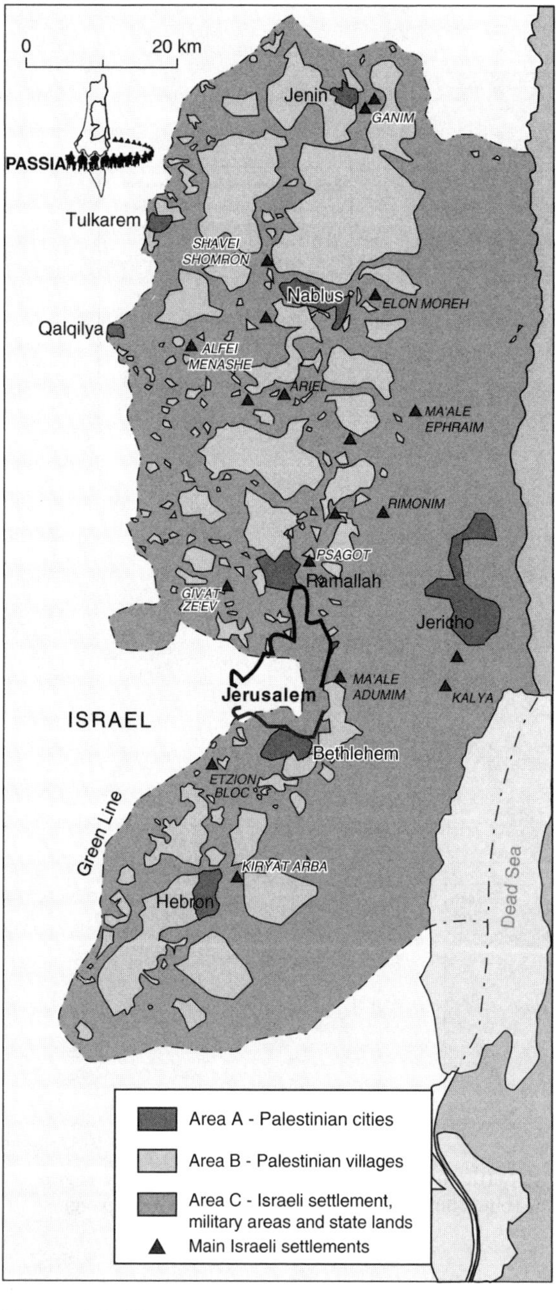

Map F Oslo II
Source: Reproduced from PASSIA's web site (www.passia.org)

G

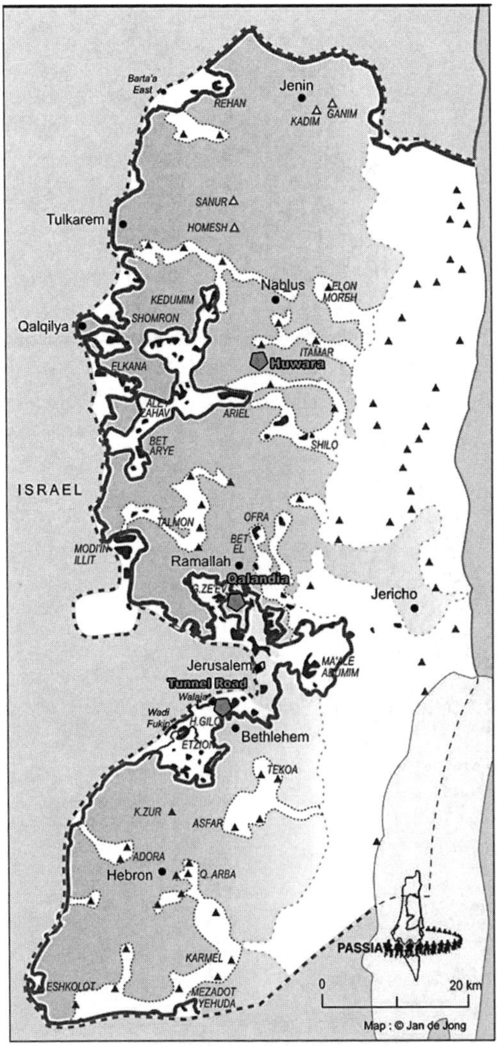

Map G The Israeli Barrier in the West Bank
Source: Reproduced from PASSIA's web site (www.passia.org)

H

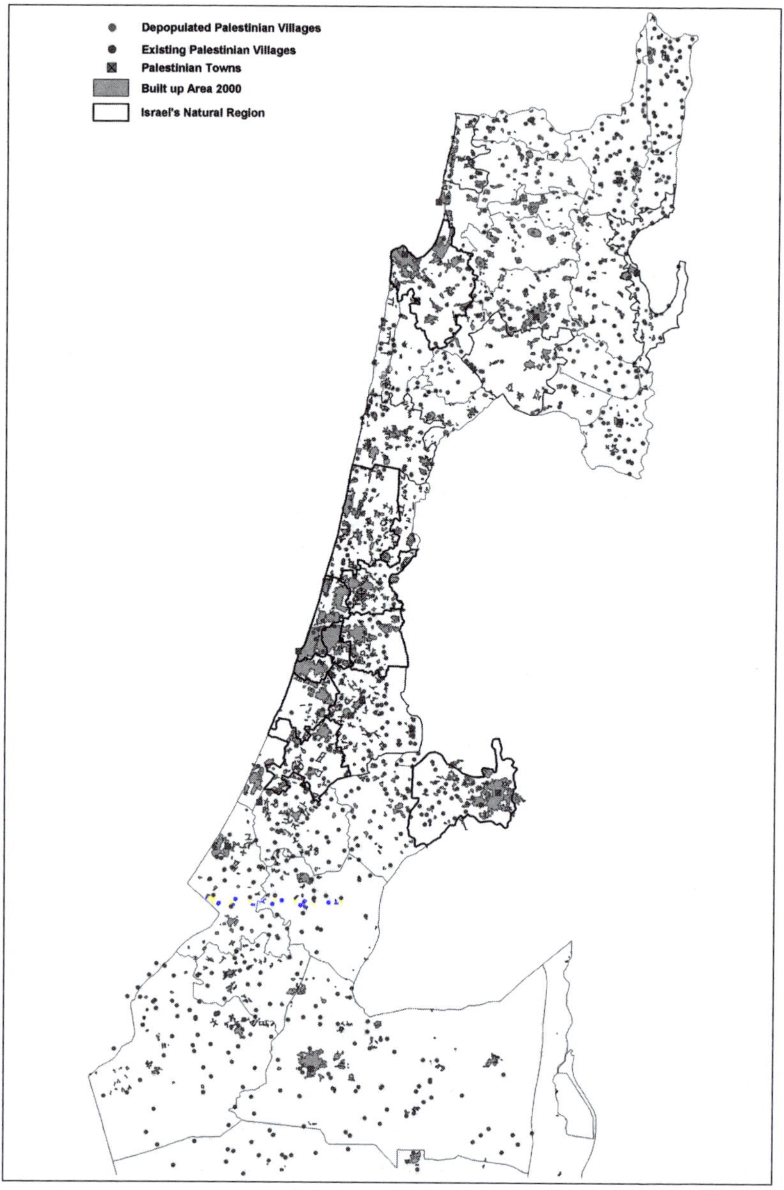

Map H The Feasibility of the Palestinian Refugees' Return
Source: Reproduced by permission of Salman Abu Sitta
Notes: The location of the present built-up area shows that over 90% of the sites of Palestinian villages remains vacant. Thick black lines define high Jewish density 'natural regions.' Medium and thin lines indicate corresponding lesser Jewish density (Salman Abu Sitta).

Introduction

Tomis Kapitan and Raja Halwani

1. The sources of the Israeli–Palestinian conflict

At the core of the conflict between Israeli Jews and Palestinian Arabs is a struggle over land; over who is to reside in, own, and possess sovereignty over the 10,000 square mile territory identified as *Palestine* in the 1922 League of Nations Mandate. Currently, this region is home to approximately 11 million people, including 5.4 million Israeli Jews, 1.4 Arab citizens of Israel, 3.9 million Palestinian Arabs in the West Bank and Gaza, and 300,000 who are presently classified as neither Arab nor Jew. Outside this area, up to 4.8 million Palestinians refugees and their descendents live.[1]

Anyone familiar with their struggle knows that more land is at stake; both Israeli Jews and Palestinian Arabs are conscious that their very identity as a distinct people is bound up with the region's terrain, cities, villages, monuments and history. As a consequence, both have been jealous in their attachments and have frequently denigrated the claims of the other. The reasons for these mutual attachments reach far back into the history of both peoples. From the standpoint of many Jews, an end to centuries of dispersion, discrimination, persecution and threats to their survival as a distinct people require that they reconstitute themselves as an independent political entity in Palestine, the birthplace of Jewish culture. For their part, the Arabs of Palestine claim an equally long historical and cultural connection to the land, not so much as a distinct *Palestinian* people, but as the resident Muslims and Christians who dominated the landscape for centuries, built its cities, established its agricultural system and tenaciously defended their homeland throughout centuries of foreign onslaught.

Despite the ancient attachment of both groups to the land, the political conflict between them is relatively recent, stemming from competing political developments in the late nineteenth and early twentieth centuries. On the one hand, there was an emerging Arab nationalism, occasioned by a gradual weakening of the Ottoman Empire and oriented towards political independence for the Arab people in the Arab heartland. On the other hand, the *Zionist* movement arose among European Jews calling for the establishment of a Jewish state in Palestine, at the very center of the Arab world. Yet a third factor was the competition among Western nations to achieve a greater influence in the eastern Mediterranean and in the oil-rich regions of the Middle East. These distinct developments were destined to overlap in various forms of cooperation and conflict.

2. The Palestine mandate

According to some estimates, in 1890, at least one-half million people lived in Palestine, of which 92 percent were Arab (89 percent Muslim and 11 percent Christian) and eight percent were Jews (Bachi, 1974). These same proportions still stood by 1914 when the population reached 657,000 (McCarthy, 1990, p. 26). Faced with this demographic imbalance, the early Zionists advocated Jewish immigration to Palestine, institution building, raising the national consciousness of Jews, and diplomatic initiatives aimed at gaining the support of the great powers for the establishment of a Jewish state with a decisive Jewish majority. While a few Zionists accepted the fiction that Palestine was 'a land without people' waiting for 'a people without a land,' most were aware of an indigenous population, but argued that Jewish needs and rights to a homeland that Jews had been unjustly deprived of 1900 years earlier outweighed the claims of the Arabs. Despite what was certain to be indigenous opposition to their project, the Zionists pressed ahead on every front, and by 1922, the percentage of the Jews living in Palestine had increased to at least 11.1 percent.[2]

It was on the diplomatic front, however, that the Zionists gained their most significant victories. In late 1917, as British forces were poised to enter Palestine, the British Government pledged to facilitate establishment of a Jewish national home and open the doors of Palestine to Jewish immigration. The pledge came in the form of a letter to the Zioinist financier Baron Edmund de Rothschild from the British foreign minister, Arthur Balfour. Its critical paragraph stated:

> His Majesty's Government view with favour the establishment in Palestine of a national home for the Jewish people, and will use their

> best endeavours to facilitate the achievement of this object, it being clearly understood that nothing shall be done which may prejudice the civil and religious rights of existing non-Jewish communities in Palestine, or the rights and political status enjoyed by Jews in any other country.

This statement—the Balfour Declaration—was the product of extensive Zionist diplomacy (Khalidi, 1971, chap. 15; Vereté, 1982; Sachar, 1989, chap. 5). Overt reference to a Jewish state was avoided in favor of the euphemism 'national home' for fear of inflaming Arab passions against the Jewish minority, though the British Prime Minister Lloyd George subsequently acknowledged that a Jewish state was intended. The Arabs, the vast majority of the population, were referred to as members of 'non-Jewish communities,' and while their 'civil and religious rights' were recognized nothing was said about their political rights or their national aspirations. On the other hand, explicit reference was made to the 'political status' of Jews in other countries. Boundaries had not been fixed, though Zionists lobbied for a Jewish state on both sides of the Jordan (Vereté, 1982, p. 77).

Over the objection of the Arabs, the terms of the Balfour Declaration were subsequently incorporated into the terms of a 1922 League of Nations decision that granted Britain Mandatory control over Palestine. The British authorities immediately opened the gates of Palestine to Jewish immigration. As a result, Jews went from 11.1 percent of the population in 1922 to 20 percent by 1931. In the 1930s, immigration jumped dramatically, reaching nearly 62,000 in 1935 and raising the percentage of Jews to 31 percent of the population by 1939 (Shaw, 1991, p. 185).

The Jewish Agency was founded in 1929 to settle the new immigrants with whom came funds and agricultural expertise that allowed Zionist settlements to flourish and expand. Land purchases were supervised by the Jewish National Fund (founded in 1901) whose charter specified that land once acquired becomes the inalienable property of the Jewish people (Smith, 2004, p. 31). In 1923, nearly 75 percent of the land worked by Arab peasants was owned by absentee landlords who lived in cities (Smith, 2004, p. 84). Of the land Zionists purchased by 1945, sales by Palestinian peasants accounted for 9.4 percent, sales by Palestinian large landowners were 24.6 percent and sales by non-Palestinian Arabs (Lebanese and Syrians) were 52.6 percent (Stein, 1984, pp. 226–27; Khalidi, 1988). The policy of redeeming the land with Jewish labor resulted in large numbers of Arab farm workers turned out of lands they had previously worked and forced to seek employment in cities. In 1933, the Arab Executive Committee declared that Jewish immigration 'has terrified the country' (Khalidi, 1984, p. 90).

These developments severely dampened hopes for Jewish–Arab reconciliation. Leaders on both sides continued to seek rapprochement though others were convinced that a negotiated agreement was impossible. The discovery that Zionists were smuggling arms into the country caused men like Sheikh Izz ad-Din al-Qassam, a religious leader in Haifa, to advocate open revolt against British rule and Zionist Colonialism. He was killed in November 1935 during a battle between his guerilla group and British forces, but his 'martyrdom' was a call to action that inspired the newly formed Arab Higher Committee to organize a general strike to press demands for halting Jewish immigration, prohibiting land sales to Jews and forming a representative government. The strike evolved into a revolt (1936–39) with Arabs arrayed against both the British military and the Jews. The superior armaments of the British prevailed; by the time violence ceased, 101 British soldiers, 463 Jews and over 5000 Arabs had lost their lives (Hirst, 2003, p. 217).

Yet, the Arab revolt altered British policy. Realizing that Arabs would never peacefully acquiesce to the imposition of a Jewish state in Palestine, the Peel Commission of 1937 recommended a partition of the country into an Arab and a Jewish state, despite objections by the former High Commissioner for Palestine, Herbert Samuel, that two states with interwoven territories would be bound in an endless struggle. The plan was rejected by both sides. In 1939, after exiling Palestinian leaders, Britain issued a White Paper calling for the establishment of a single state within ten years in which Arabs and Jews would share authority in government. Jewish immigration would be limited to 75,000 persons within the next five years, and thereafter, no immigrant would be admitted without Arab approval. The High Commissioner was empowered to regulate, delimit or prohibit transfer of Arab land to Jewish ownership, and Palestine was to be partitioned into Arab, Jewish and neutral zones under one administration (Khalidi, 1971, chap. 47).

3. The partition of Palestine

In the aftermath of the World War II, the question of Palestine was the topic of intense political debate and maneuvering. In November 1947, with the support of both the United States and the Soviet Union, the UN General Assembly voted to partition Palestine into two states; a Jewish state on 56 percent of the mandated territory, an Arab state on 43 percent, and Jerusalem internationalized under UN control (see Map A and Map B). Zionist reaction was mixed, but the Arabs rejected the recommendation outright, arguing that the United Nations had no right to set aside any portion of Arab territory for a Jewish state, and that the Western world was making them pay for the suffering of Jews during the war and after (Cattan, 1976, pp. 75–89; Laqueur, 1976, pp. 94–104; Shlaim, 2000, p. 25; Pappe, 2006a, pp. 31–7). There were no negotiations between the two communities—neither Jew nor Arab would acknowledge the existence of the other—and fighting immediately broke out. By April 1948, the better equipped and organized Jewish forces established a clear superiority, securing their recommended allotment while capturing territory assigned to the proposed Arab state.

On May 15, the day after Israel declared its independence, forces from Egypt, Syria, Lebanon, Jordan and Iraq entered the fighting. Despite population differences, Israelis placed more soldiers in the field and had the advantage of working in familiar terrain under unified control (Flapan, 1987, pp. 192–9; Hirst, 2003, p. 259). By the time an armistice was signed in 1949, Israel controlled over 77 percent of Palestine, Jordan moved into the West Bank, and Egypt into the Gaza Strip. Jerusalem was divided between the Israelis and Jordanians. No Palestinian Arab state was created, and approximately 750,000 Palestinians who had fled or been expelled from what was now Israel became refugees living in camps established in the West Bank, the Gaza Strip and the surrounding Arab countries.

4. The 1967 war and the occupation

The defeat of Arab forces in the 1947–49 War fostered revolutionary movements in the Arab world, notably in Egypt, where Gamal Abd'l Nasser assumed power in 1952. His resolve in the face of the Anglo–Franco–Israeli invasion of 1956, and his insistence that Israel is an alien presence created and sustained by Western imperialism eliminable only through a unified Arab front, made him one of the more prominent figures in the Arab world for over 15 years. Yet he miscalculated when he blockaded the Gulf of Aqaba, replaced UN troops in the Sinai with two divisions of Egyptian soldiers and concluded a defense treaty with Jordan in late May 1967, unwittingly providing Israel with a *casus belli*. Israel's attack on June 5 destroyed Egypt's air force and routed the exposed Egyptian forces in the Sinai, most of which it captured within three days. After fighting broke out in Jerusalem, Israel quickly overpowered the light Jordanian forces, occupied East Jerusalem and the West Bank by June 8, and the Golan Heights by June 11. Nearly one-fifth of the West Bank population fled, finding borders sealed upon attempting to return.[3]

The real victory for Israel was not damage to Arab military capacity—this was quickly restored—but capture of territory later used for political and economic ends, a public relations bonanza bringing increased Western support and Jewish immigration, and defeat of a popular brand of Arab nationalism. Security Council Resolution 242 (November 1967) called for mutual recognition of all states in the region and Israeli withdrawal from occupied territories. But Arab countries were unwilling to negotiate after the humiliating defeat, and Israel has continued to deny that the resolution requires withdrawal from all the territories.

Since 1967, Israel has maintained a military occupation in the West Bank, the Golan Heights and East Jerusalem, though it evacuated its troops and settlers from the Gaza Strip in 2005. In the eyes of the world community, its presence in the occupied territories is subject to the provisions of the Fourth Geneva Convention of 1949 (see, e.g., Security Council Resolution 446 of March 1979). Allowing for measures of military necessity, the Convention forbids alterations of the legal system, forcible transfer or deportation of the resident populous and resettlement by the occupying power of its own civilian population in the occupied territory. Israel has violated these provisions, contesting their application on the grounds that the West Bank (in particular) is 'disputed' or 'unallocated' rather than the occupied territory of a nation that is party to the Convention.

The most contentious aspects of the Israeli occupation are the expropriation of Palestinian land and the establishment of Jewish settlements. Though initially confined to sparsely populated areas and large neighborhoods around East Jerusalem, civilian settlements were soon established near heavily populated areas in the West Bank, a tendency accelerated by the Likud government of Menachem Begin. In 1979, the Israeli Supreme Court ruled that requisition of Arab-owned land for civilian settlements was lawful if it furthered the security of the occupying forces and occupied areas (Quigley, 2005, pp. 175–6). There are currently over 140 Jewish settlements in East Jerusalem and the West Bank, home to over 400,000 Israeli Jews.[4]

5. Palestinian resistance

The Palestinian refugees frequently attempted to gain access to the homes and lands from which they had fled or been driven during the

1947–49 war. Perhaps as many as 5000 Arabs and 250 Jews lost their lives in clashes on either side of the 1949 Armistice lines (Morris, 1993, pp. 137, 415). Palestinian resistance to Israel became more organized with the establishment of the Palestine Liberation Organization (PLO) in 1964, but it was not until after the 1967 war that many Palestinians became convinced that if their homeland was to be liberated then it was they who must do it. No match for the Israeli military on the open battlefield, they resorted to guerrilla tactics from staging grounds in the occupied territories, Jordan and Lebanon. Organized resistance in the territories was short-lived, but cross-border raids, airplane hijackings and hostage-takings by Palestinian commandos operating from nearby countries in the late 1960s and early 1970s brought the Palestinian question into the international spotlight, no incident more so than the kidnapping of Israeli athletes during the 1972 Olympic Games in Munich. Israel's response was not only to pursue PLO activists abroad, but to bomb targets in Jordan, Syria and Lebanon, causing far more civilian casualties than the incursions that prompted them.

Recourse to arms brought mixed results. On the one hand, in targeting Israeli civilians as well as soldiers, Palestinians were branded as 'terrorists' in the Western press, and accorded little sympathy after Israeli reprisals. On the other, their resistance not only restored a measure of self-respect and confidence among the Palestinian people, but it publicized their grievances after 20 long years of neglect by the world community, and gained them official recognition. At the Rabat Conference in 1974, Arab leaders affirmed that the PLO is the sole legitimate representative of the Palestinian people, and later that year, the UN General Assembly recognized the Palestinians' rights to self-determination, national independence and sovereignty.

These diplomatic gains reinforced Palestinian willingness to accept a two-state solution of the conflict, but successive Israeli governments during the 1970s and 1980s opposed any compromise with the PLO. In the summer of 1982, Israeli forces invaded Lebanon with the aim of crushing organized Palestinian resistance. After devastating Palestinian population centers in the south of Lebanon, forcing a large exodus of Lebanese northwards, and besieging West Beirut for two months, the United States brokered a truce which led to the evacuation of nearly 12,000 PLO fighters in late August to Tunisia. This marked an end to over three decades of cross-border violence that had marked Israeli–Palestinian relations.

The center of Palestinian resistance shifted in the 1980s to the Palestinians within the occupied territories. Under Israeli occupation, this population of Palestinians had been denied any meaningful exercise of political self-determination, their economic development had been stifled, their resources placed under Israel's control, their land had been steadily confiscated and the quality of their lives dipped below the standards enjoyed by people in Israel and neighboring Arab countries. The pattern of land confiscation and road networks has unfolded a type of 'Bantustans' arrangement with pockets of Palestinian populations surrounded by Israeli-dominated territory. As the pace of land confiscation and settlement building increased, Palestinian protests escalated. The Israeli military responded with force, using detention without charge, deportation, torture and targeted assassinations of Palestinian activists. The unrest in 1981–82 in which over 40 Palestinians were killed was a prelude to the more widespread protests of the *Intifada* (1987–93) when opposition to Israeli occupation was expressed not only by daily demonstrations and stoning of Israeli soldiers, but also by commercial strikes, non-payment of taxes and boycott of Israeli products. Over 1300 Palestinians lost their lives in the process (see Chapter 3, Section 5).

6. Peace negotiations

The results of the Intifada were numerous. The spectacle of Palestinian youths being beaten and shot at by heavily armed soldiers revealed that the Israeli occupation did not possess the 'benign' character its supporters had formerly claimed. A political split within the Israeli public widened. Citing security concerns, a sizeable number felt the Israeli response was justifiable, but others called for negotiations with the Palestinians, and homegrown human rights groups such as B'tselem and the Israeli League for Human and Civil Rights joined their Palestinian and international rights organizations in documenting the brutality of the Israeli military.[5] Yet, the Intifada was a step that moved the parties towards the first formal negotiations in nearly a century of conflict.

In 1988, the Palestine National Council declared a Palestinian state in the occupied territories and its willingness to live side by side with the Jewish state. In 1991, at the urging of the United States, Israelis and Palestinians sat down to the negotiating table for the first time. The results were a series of agreements in 1993, 1995 and 1998 which brought hope to many Palestinians, Israelis and outside observers that there was a genuine chance for a negotiated settlement of the conflict. Yet, sporadic violence from both sides continued, the

Palestinian economy suffered because of Israel's policy of checkpoints and closures that limited movements of goods and people and, most important, Israel expanded its settlement network, extending the road system to connect the settlements to Israel and nearly doubling the number of Israeli settlers on the West Bank. Besides uprooting some 80,000 olive and fruit trees to permit construction, the Israeli military established various mechanisms of control to isolate Palestinian 'self-rule' pockets from each other by means of fencing, checkpoints and other fortifications (Halper, 2002, pp. 36–7).

These developments placed an enormous strain on the peace process. By 2000, the peace agreements were not bringing greater freedom, prosperity or genuine self-determination to the Palestinians of the territories, but only economic deterioration, political frustration and a steadily tightening noose of Israeli control. When the two sides could not reach agreement on a final solution in the summer of 2000, and when, on September 28, 2000, Ariel Sharon and 1000 armed police visited the Haram al-Sharif in Jerusalem, violence between Israelis and Palestinians in the territories broke out on an unprecedented level. During the next six years, over 5000 Palestinian Arabs and 1000 Israeli Jews had lost their lives. This time, Israel received more political support and less criticism from the world's superpower, the United States, itself busily engaged in a 'war on terror.' Despite the U.S. Administration's 2002 'Road Map for Peace' which called for establishment of a Palestinian state in the occupied territories, U.S. President Bush reassured the Israeli Prime Minister Sharon that the U.S. stood behind Israel's military efforts in combatting Palestinian violence, and that it would not oppose the major Jewish settlements in the West Bank. Despite the periodic flurries of commissions, UN Resolutions, proclamations and diplomatic activity, the situation in Palestine and Israel remains at a political impasse.

7. Normative issues

The Israeli–Palestinian conflict is partly fueled by rival normative claims that challenge our philosophical thinking at a more general level. When does a group of people have a right to govern or possess a certain territory? Under what conditions are people entitled to political self-determination? What rights accrue to those who have been the victims of territorial aggression? How do political institutions, states or resistance organizations gain moral legitimacy? Is a state ever entitled to territorial expansion and conquest of foreign territory? When is violent resistance to military occupation justified? Can recourse to terrorism ever be legitimate in the context of political struggles?

These are critical normative questions that are not easily answered and that challenge the best political philosophies. Those who accord no place to normative assertion and debate outside the bounds of positive law might find that philosophical discussion of these questions, especially when applied to particular political conflicts, is hopelessly inconclusive. Yet, a moment's reflection reveals that every system of law emerges from an underlying level of normative thinking that differs from legal adjudication and interpretation. Such basic philosophical reflection need not be viewed as having access to a separate system of 'natural law' standing in competition to existing legal codes. Its conjectures are the creatures of our thinking, informed by our accumulated experience, and it is through them that legal provisions are appraised and statutory changes recommended. No legal system is the final word about how humans and societies ought to behave, and to restrict normative thought to enactment would immunize positive law from rational evaluation. At the same time, the statues, conventions and legal systems that are in force are immediately relevant to the philosophical and moral debate for two simple reasons. First, they are the products of centuries of normative reflection on human experience, and, second, the very fact that they have been enacted is reason for recognizing their prima facie binding force.

The following essays address a number of normative issues centered on the topics of self-determination and territorial sovereignty, terrorism and the legitimacy of violence in the pursuit of political ends, the rights of refugees to return to the territories from which they have fled or been driven and a just solution to the Israeli–Palestinian conflict. Chapter 1 takes up the right(s) of self-determination, discussing the role of the principle of self-determination in the historical development of the Israel–Palestinian conflict while attempting to ascertain whether it is still relevant to a just resolution. Chapter 2 examines the right of refugees to return to the homes, cities and lands from which they fled or were driven. It aims at formulating this right, establishing its existence, and arguing for its implementation concerning Palestinian refugees. Chapter 3 focuses on both the rhetoric and reality of terrorism in the evolution of the political struggle between Israeli Jews and Palestinian Arabs. It argues that the rhetoric of 'terror' is an impediment towards understanding and resolving the conflict, while also addressing the contentious issue whether acts of terrorism on either side against the other have ever been justified. Finally, Chapter 4 discusses various solutions to the Israeli–Palestinian conflict, arguing that a single democratic and secular state is the only solution compatible with the demands of justice.

The normative claims made are not put forward as the conclusions of legal arguments, but of moral arguments that draw on general considerations about how people are to coexist all things considered. No attempt is made to embed the proposals or arguments within a single, comprehensive normative theory. Instead, use is made throughout of a collection of mid-range normative principles that are widely accepted by political philosophers and recognized by a vast body of international conventions. Among these are the following familiar precepts, here stated in very general terms:

1. The doctrine of *popular sovereignty*: political legitimacy and obligation derives from the consent of the governed.
2. The *rights of collective self-determination*: there are collectives that possess rights of being self-governing without interference from external agents.
3. The *right of collective self-defense*: people who are the victims of unjustified aggression have a right to take collective measures in defense of their human rights and their rights of self-determination.
4. The *human rights* of life, political participation, due process and equal protection from the law, freedom from slavery, torture, arbitrary detention and deprivation of property, rights to reside in and return to one's home, native territory, and country, freedoms of opinion, expression, and assembly.

Sharper formulations of each of the relevant norms will be given in the course of developing the arguments below.

The arguments and proposals offered in this book will not be to the liking of every reader. Discourse on moral issues is controversial almost by its very nature, and when it is focused upon an emotionally charged topic like the conflict between Israeli Jews and Palestinian Arabs, normative assertions are bound to inflame some readers and the ensuing debate is likely to be vociferous. We are fully aware of the contentious nature of our essays, neither expecting nor seeking universal agreement. We ask only that our arguments are examined carefully and that criticisms be developed with a sense of philosophical responsibility rather than the polemic and ridicule that has too often characterized attempts to discuss the Israeli–Palestinian conflict openly and rationally.

We offer no magic formula for resolving the conflict. We speak as philosophers—not political strategists—who have learned enough about human history and witnessed enough of the brutal edge of contemporary political reality to know that ignoring the demands of morality in international affairs, as in our daily lives, is a recipe for bitter struggles whose consequences are often far-ranging and difficult to predict.

Notes

1. These estimates are based on figures listed by the Israeli Central Bureau of Statistics (ICBS) http://www.jewishvirtuallibrary.org/jsource/Society_&_Culture/newpop.html and the Palestinian Central Bureau of Statistics (PCBS) www.pcbs.gov.ps/Portals/_pcbs/PressRelease/endyear2006_E.pdf. The ICBS figure of 5,393,600 Israeli Jews by the end of 2006 is at odds with the CIA Factbook estimate of the number of Israeli Jews 4,853,000 by July 2006 (http://www.cia.gov/cia/publications/factbook/geos/is.html). The PCBS figures and methodology have been challenged by the American–Israel Demographic Research Group, which claimed that several errors artificially inflated the total number of Palestinians outside Palestine by a figure of 1.3 million (as reported in Wikipedia en.wikipedia.org/wiki/Palestinian_people#Palestinian_demographics).
2. The 1922 census conducted by the British Mandate Government in Palestine indicated a population of 752,048 of which Jews constituted 11.4 percent. Figures from the Palestine National Authority place the percentage of Jews in Palestine in 1922 at 11.1 percent, http://www.pnic.gov.ps/english/geography/geography-Population.html. See the following websites for more information about the population of Palestine, http://www.mideastweb.org/palpop.htm and http://www.israelipalestinianprocon.org/populationpalestine.html.
3. There is a debate about whether Israel's pre-emptive strike could be morally justified. According to Michael Walzer (1977, p. 85), Israel's existence was imperiled by Egypt's military build-up making its anticipatory strike a 'clear case of legitimate anticipation.' However, there is little to support the charge that Nasser was preparing an invasion which justified Israel's strike. U.S. intelligence reports to Israelis in late May indicated that Egypt had no plans for attack and that Israel would prevail in any case, an assessment subsequently confirmed by Israeli Generals Yitzhak Rabin, Matiyahu Peled and Ezer Weizmann (Lilienthal, 1982, pp. 557–8).
4. The Israeli Defense Minister in 1967, Moshe Dayan, was one of the sponsors of Israeli settlement in the territories. He argued that 'there is nothing sacred about the previous map from 1948,' and that settlements are important in contributing to the creation of 'a new psychological reality' (Lustick, 1993, pp. 357–8).
5. The Israeli philosopher Yeshayahu Leibowitz referred to the sponsors of repression as 'Judeo-Nazis' and urged Israeli soldiers to refuse service in the occupied territories, subsequently comparing the Israeli undercover agents who killed Arab teenagers with the members of the Islamic movement Hamas (*Chicago Tribune*, January 25, 1993).

1
Self-Determination

Tomis Kapitan

1. Disputes over territory

Disputes over territory are among the most contentious in human affairs. Throughout the world, societies view control over land and resources as necessary to ensure their survival and to further their particular life-style, and the very passion with which claims over a region are asserted and defended suggests that difficult normative issues lurk nearby. Questions about rights to territory vary. It is one thing to ask who owns a particular parcel of land, another who has the right to reside within its boundaries and yet another to determine which individuals or groups have political rights of citizenship, sovereignty, and self-determination within it. It must also be asked how these rights—if 'rights' is the correct term—are acquired.

When attention turns to the territorial rights of communities, national groups or states, sovereignty is the principal concern. Within international law, *de facto* power over a territory, say, of occupying forces or trustees, is insufficient to possess or acquire sovereignty (Brownlie, 1990, p. 111). The central conceptions underlying modern democratic thought are that sovereignty over a politically demarcated territory is vested in the resident population, and that governmental authority is derived from the consent of that population. It is simple enough to identify the latter with the citizenry of a state, but demographic and political flux makes this a loose criterion. States come and go, and sometimes a territory is stateless. Also, large-scale demographic shifts during upheavals and peacetime immigrations change the assessments of who belongs where. Does everyone residing in a place at a particular time have a right to share in its governance then? What about illegal immigrants? Presumably, sovereignty rests with the established population or legitimate residents of a territory, the most obvious candidates being those inhabitants who were born and raised to adulthood therein and whose discernible ancestors were equally indigenous. Those born and living on the outside, lacking historical, cultural or legal ties to the region, are the clearest cases of non-residents. In between is a significant gray area consisting of expatriates, exiles, refugees, voluntary emigrants and immigrants, each with varying degrees of entitlement to residency depending upon the conditions under which they entered or left the territory. One thing is clear, a person does not lose the right to reside in a territory and participate in its governance simply because he or she has been forcibly removed from that territory.

Which individuals or groups have the right to inhabit Palestine? Who owns its fields, cities and seaports? Who has the right to determine which legal and political structures are to prevail therein? Most importantly, who are its legitimate residents, and who possesses sovereignty? Answers to these questions depend upon the time frame; the considerations offered in late 1917 or 1947 could draw upon factors absent in 1897, and the same holds for the interval between 1947 and 2007. Differences in population distributions, in prevailing institutions and in political developments are all relevant in approaching these difficult questions.

In the aftermath of the World War I, both Arabs and Jews claimed political legitimacy in Palestine. Zionists then argued as follows. There is a historical connection of Jews to Palestine that extends over three millennia, maintained by a 'thin but crucial line of continuity' (Eban, 1972, p. 26). The cultural roots of Jews in Palestine are universally acknowledged, and having never established a state elsewhere, there is no other place to which they can claim an original organic link (Shimoni, 1995, pp. 352–9). Palestine is also the center of the Judaism and owes 'the luster of its history' to the Jewish connection (Jewish Agency for Palestine, 1947, p. 105). Despite having been unjustly exiled from Palestine since Roman times, Jews have a unique claim to the land that they have never abandoned, one which implies that their political reestablishment would not be a matter of conquest and domination by an external entity, but of restoration (Eban, 1956) or return (Fackenheim, 1988) of a people to what was originally theirs.

By contrast, the Zionist argument continued, Arabs have other centers of culture and religion, and the region including Jerusalem was never as monumental to them as were the holy cities of Mecca and Medina, or their traditional capitals of Damascus, Baghdad and Cairo. Nor did Arabs ever establish an independent state in Palestine and, hence,

Palestine's Arabs did not constitute a political unit with an entitlement to sovereignty in Palestine (Gorny, 1987, p. 145, pp. 213–4). They are part of a larger Arab entity with ties to the entire Arab world, not themselves a distinct people with claim to Palestine as such. Jews, on the other hand, currently constitute a single identifiable nation in need of a territory to further its culture. Moreover, their right to establish themselves as a political community in Palestine is not simply a matter of their preference. Finally, in late 1917, the *de facto* ruler of Palestine, Great Britain, issued the Balfour Declaration (see Introduction) in which it committed itself to establishing a Jewish national home in Palestine, a promise that was incorporated into the League of Nations Mandate for Palestine in 1922. For these reasons, Zionists concluded that historic title to Palestine and sovereignty over its territory belongs to the Jews.

In response, the Arabs argued that their right to dwell in Palestine, to possess and establish dominion over its territory, derived from the fact that they constitute not only the majority of its current inhabitants but have maintained this majority during the 13 centuries since the Islamic conquest—if not longer given their descent from ancient Canaanites, Hittites and Philistines. The predominant language and culture of the country have remained Arabic throughout this period, including under Turkish rule. Even if Jews have a 'historical connection' to Palestine, the inference that they have an exclusive 'historic title' which gives them the right to return, establish a state and possess it forever 'contains more of poetry in it than logic.' By that reasoning, 'Arabs should claim Spain since once upon a time they conquered it and there developed a high civilization.'[1] All systems of law include a statute of limitations by which a legal title expires after a considerable duration; without it, the world would face a cacophony of irresolvable claims and counter-claims. Jews native to Palestine are entitled to reside there and share in the determination of its future (Porath, 1974, p. 61), but sovereignty belongs to the predominantly Arab indigenous population.

Arab spokesmen insisted that the Balfour Declaration was invalid, and that the Mandate for Palestine violated Article 22 of the League of Nation's Covenant which dealt with newly liberated territories. Its fourth paragraph stated:

> Certain communities formerly belonging to the Turkish Empire have reached a stage of development where their existence as independent nations can be provisionally recognized subject to the rendering of administrative advice and assistance by a mandatory until such time

> as they are able to stand alone. The wishes of these communities must be a principal consideration in the selection of the Mandatory.[2]

Exceptions were specified in subsequent paragraphs of the Article, and since Palestine was not mentioned by name, the presumption is that it was covered by this paragraph. More importantly, when an existing state power is removed from a territory, as was the Ottoman Empire from Palestine in 1917, then sovereignty reverts back to the established population. Arabs insisted that the fact of British military occupation neither transferred sovereignty to the occupying power nor removed it from the legitimate residents. Nor did Britain have a right to give Palestine as a 'gift' to anyone and, therefore, its commitment has no binding force. If any credence is to be given to promises made by external powers then it must be remembered that Britain had also pledged its support for Arab independence throughout the Middle East prior to issuing the Balfour Declaration, and reiterated it again in 1918.[3] Since this pledge was made with an established monarch, it was superior to the Balfour Declaration which was given to 'an amorphous body lacking political form and juridical definition' (Porath, 1974, p. 52). Britain countered that Palestine was a special case, though in a 1922 White Paper it was careful to qualify its position by stating that the Jewish national home is to be in Palestine and that there would be no disappearance or subordination of the Arab population or customs.

2. The principle of self-determination

> ...once you appeal to the principle of self-determination, both Arabs and Zionists are prepared to make every use of it they can. No doubt we shall hear a good deal of that in the future, and, indeed, in it we may find a solution of our difficulties.
>
> Lord Curzon in 1918 (reported in Lloyd-George, 1939, pp. 739–40)

Towards the end of the World War I, a 'principle of self-determination' was proposed as a foundation for international order. In the words of its chief advocate, U.S. President Woodrow Wilson, it specified that the 'settlement of every question, whether of territory, of sovereignty, of economic arrangement, or of political relationship' is to be made 'upon the basis of the free acceptance of that settlement by the people immediately concerned and not upon the basis of the material interest or advantage of any other nation or people which may desire a different settlement for sake of its own exterior influence or mastery' (Wilson, 1927, p. 233). The principle played a significant role in deliberations about lands newly liberated by the World War I, and, in the aftermath of the Second, it was enshrined within Article 1 of the United Nations Charter which called upon member nations 'to develop friendly relations among nations based on respect for the principle of equal rights and self-determination of peoples.' Its status within international law was further heightened by the 1966 Covenants on Civil and Political Rights and on Economic Social and Cultural Rights, whose first articles specify the following: 'All peoples have the right of self-determination. By virtue of that right they freely determine their political status and freely pursue their economic, social, and cultural development.' In 1970, General Assembly Resolution 2625 added that, 'every state has the duty to respect this right in accordance with the provision of the Charter.'

Upon its emergence in international diplomacy, both Arabs and Jews appealed to the principle at once, each group claiming the prerogative to be self-determining in Palestine. Zionists claimed that the Balfour Declaration and the Palestine Mandate constituted recognition of the Jewish right to self-determination in Palestine. Arabs countered that those who actually owned and long inhabited a territory had the right to self-determination within it, and in Palestine this could only be the Arab majority. This clash of claims requires a closer look at what is packed into the concept of self-determination and into the moral status of the so-called principle of self-determination. The basic philosophical issues are the following:

- What is the content of a request or demand for self-determination, that is, what is it that an entity possesses in being a self-determining unit?
- What are the relevant moral norms concerning self-determination, that is, is self-determination to be construed as a right, a privilege, an ideal, a recommendation, a regulative principle, a maxim of diplomacy, and so on?
- Who are the proper beneficiaries of self-determination, that is, who or what is entitled to be self-determining?

In general terms, self-determination is nothing more than an entity's autonomy, viz., managing its own affairs as it sees fit independently of external interference. It is not surprising that people should seek to be self-determining, and the desire of entire societies to gain or preserve autonomy has often been the occasion for conflict, war, migration, peaceful separation, and inspiring literature, from ancient times to the present. Individuals almost never gain complete self-rule, unless, perhaps, they achieve the status of absolute dictators, or absolute hermits. But societies can achieve significant measures of autonomy within limited areas. In the strict sense usually intended, self-determination is a matter of statehood (Copp, 1997, p. 278), that is, of a political community's possessing and exercising sovereignty over its territory. This is how self-determination is conceived when established states are taken to be the self-determining units. There are lesser degrees of autonomy that fall short of state sovereignty, however, and these might take various forms of localized autonomy, whether we are speaking at the level of provinces, municipalities, neighborhoods, or culturally or economically defined minorities (Tamir, 1993; Buchanan, 1997a, pp. 306–7).

The normative importance of self-determination is indisputable within modern democratic thought given its doctrine of popular sovereignty. The moral imperative is that institutions of governance within a territory must be responsive to what its established inhabitants take to be in their legitimate interests. People exercise autonomy by voluntarily binding themselves to a social-political arrangement, and in so doing, they impose upon themselves a moral obligation to abide by its terms. In this way, chances are heightened that the arrangement will conform to what they perceive as just, if not to what actually is just, thereby enhancing prospects for stable peace and orderly development. By contrast, imposing an arrangement upon the inhabitants against their will, or independent of their will, is likely to create resentment that promises future instability, whether domestically or internationally—regardless whether the source of that imposition is an internal tyrant or an external power. In this way, not only is the observance of self-determination the crucial mechanism for legitimizing governmental authority and the rule of law within a given territory, it is also fundamental in promoting orderly international relations.

Whether the principle of collective self-determination is best conceived as formulating a legal right, a moral ideal, or a maxim of political prudence is a more difficult matter. Wilson spoke of 'an imperative principle of action which statesmen will ignore at their own peril' (Wilson, 1927, p. 180), in which case the principle is envisioned as a maxim binding upon those who possessed *de facto* control over 'unsettled territories,' namely, to allow the people 'immediately concerned' to determine their own future. Yet, this norm is difficult to separate from the claim that such peoples are entitled to be self-determining, and since World War II, the language of a 'right' to self-determination has increasingly appeared in documents codifying international law. These facts have not ended the debate (Philpott, 1995; Kapitan, 1997, p. 43; McKim & McMahan, 1997; Dahbour, 2003, pp. 63–8), and some argue that a call for self-determination is not so much a single principle as a 'placeholder for a range of possible principles specifying various forms and degrees of independence' (Pomerance, 1984, p. 337; Buchanan, 1991, p. 50).

Restricting ourselves to the strict political meaning of 'self-determination,' different entitlements jump to the fore. Perhaps the most obvious holder of a right of self-determination is a state, that is, a politically organized collective with a delegated authority controlling territory inhabited by that collective. The simplest and most straightforward instance of a right to self-determination is the following:

> ***Self-determination of states***: Each state has a right to exercise rule in its territory through the operations of governmental institutions without external intervention.

This is a claim-right placing a demand upon all other states, groups, and individuals—including its own citizens—for recognition of its sovereignty over its territory and non-intervention in its internal affairs. It is limited in three ways. First, it can be overridden if the state is exclusionary, that is, if it does not accord citizenship to some of the legitimate residents of the territory it governs. Second, the right of sovereignty can be overridden whenever intervention by external agents is called for, for example, when a state engages in rampant human rights abuses within its own territory. For both of these reasons, some confine the right of self-determination to legitimate states, viz., non-exclusionary states with effective institutional safeguards of human rights, thus, not engaged in systematic social, economic, legal, or political discrimination over a segment of its population, and not pursuing a campaign of belligerent aggression against external populations (Rawls, 1993, pp. 68–71; Copp, 1997, 1999; Buchanan, 1997b). But even a legitimacy restriction does not overcome yet a third limitation stemming from a people's right to reconstitute the political institutions under which it exists (Copp, 1997, p. 281), whether by replacing the existing constitution or basic laws, dissolving the state into separate sovereignties, or merging with a larger political entity. The 'people' in question consists of the legitimate residents of the territory in which the state is constituted.

This third limitation on a state's right to be self-determining is derived from the doctrine of popular sovereignty and, hence, from a more general right of self-determination, namely,

> ***Self-determination of legitimate residents***: The collective consisting of the legitimate residents of a politically independent territory has a right to establish, maintain, and alter the political institutions under which it is to live and be governed, (viz., sovereignty belongs to the people and is to be exercised collectively).

When this collective is already organized into a state in that territory, then this right of self-determination may also be spoken of as a right of the citizenry of a state to be self-determining. A state has its right to be self-determining only when the legitimate residents in the territory—ideally, its citizenry—are exercising their right of self-determination. As such, when an external agent violates a legitimate state's sovereign right it thereby violates the right of the citizenry—a people—to constitute and maintain itself as a self-governing political entity in that territory (Simmons, 2001, pp. 307, 313). Obviously, by definition, this right of collective self-determination is not limited in the first or the third way, though it remains subject to the second limitation.

Does a collective's right of self-determination derive from anything more basic? One source is the fact that a collective's self-determination is the best means for protecting the human rights of its members and, thereby, improving the quality of their lives. Also, if a collective's right over its members derives from the latter's consent, then an individual's right to self-governance provides a further basis for the collective's right. This does not mean that each individual is entitled to sovereignty over a territory, but, minimally, that he or she has a right to meaningfully participate in decisions about sovereignty over the territory in which he or she resides. Insofar as individuals exercise autonomy at the political level only through voluntary participation in a self-governing collective, then violating a citizenry's right to self-governance is *ipso facto* denying individual citizens the right of political participation. In this way, an established citizenry has a right of collective self-determination only because individuals have the right to be self-governing in the sense specified.[4]

The issue of how collective self-governance is to be implemented is another matter, and it is left unspecified by both the mentioned international covenants. A citizenry's right of self-determination requires that governing institutions are to derive from the consensus of the entire community, not by the preferences of internal minorities or agencies, or by external communities or nations. But once the decision is effected, the precise mode of subsequent citizenry participation in the governing institutions is open to debate. While it has become customary to expect that institutions regulating public life be freely determined through popular consent and operate on democratic principles, it is less clear that the notions of 'popular consent to' and 'free determination of' a particular political order require democracy (MacCallum, 1987, pp. 50–2; Moore, 2001, pp. 214–7). For example, a society might have an established and widely supported tradition whereby significant political decisions are deliberated upon and made by an unelected council of elders. Although decisions are not made within a democratic system characterized by universal suffrage, so long as the society enjoys freedom from external intervention, there is no automatic violation of the mentioned rights of self-determination.

3. The problem of exceptional beneficiaries

While the principle of self-determination confers a right 'to acquire or continue to possess the status of a state' (Copp, 1997, p. 278), existing states and their peoples are only its default or standard beneficiaries. In debates about international law and morality, self-determination has also been taken as a prerogative of yet other agents, if not principally of other agents, for instance, indigenous people under colonial rule (Bhalla, 1989). The most contested appeals to the principle have concerned exceptional applications to non-autonomous groups desirous of self-governance, whether recently liberated from previous rulers as a result of war, de-colonization, or the break up of a state, or, currently engaged in secessionist struggles.

How do we demarcate the class of exceptional beneficiaries? Speaking of *peoples* helps little, for either this is just another name for a collective (thus, Rawls, 1999a) or it is ambiguous (Michalska, 1990, pp. 72–4). Plainly, not just any such group qualifies. Individual families do not, nor do business organizations, sports teams, professional associations, religiously affiliated convents, or social clubs, even if they aspire to political autonomy. At least two minimal conditions must be met. First, a beneficiary must be politically coherent, that is, it must be an intergenerational community capable of political independence whose members share adequate means of communication and enough normative moral ideals capable of sustaining their adherence to the same political and legal institutions.[5] Second, a beneficiary must have an appropriate connection to a territory that is both geographically unified—where any point in it is accessible from any other point without having to pass through foreign territory—and politically integrable—that is, a region in which the exercise of normal state functions (e.g., maintaining a police force) would not violate the sovereign rights of existing states in distinct regions outside its boundaries. Geographical unity might not be necessary for political integrability, but departures from it weaken an aspirant's claim for self-determination (Berg, 1991, p. 214).

Yet, even this is not enough to single out a viable class of exceptional beneficiaries. If every politically coherent collective residing in a politically integrable region claimed a right of self-determination in that region, the world would be faced with a bewildering justification not only for conflicting claims between populations and sub-populations, but also for the fragmentation of virtually all existing states. There must be a mean between such extreme liberality and the restriction to standard beneficiaries, but attempts to locate it are complicated by a significant divergence of opinion about how to demarcate exceptional beneficiaries. The problem stems from the two historical sources of the principle of self-determination, namely, the doctrine of popular sovereignty on one hand and the nationalist sentiments underlying national liberation movements on the other. According to the former, the right of self-determination is a demand of self-governance on the part of the communities of legitimate residents of politically defined territories. According to the national source—a view popularized under the nineteenth century call for the *Selbstbestimmungsrecht* (sovereign right) of peoples (Umozurike, 1972, p. 3)—the right of self-determination is predicated on the idea that cultures or nations are worth preserving, and that the furtherance and protection of cultures is the very purpose of the principle. Here, the appropriate claimants of a right to self-determination are nations or national groups, that is, collectives whose members share various objective characteristics such as language, history, religious and moral beliefs, and distinctive cultural traits, and, perhaps, subjective features, for example, recognition of one's own cultural identity, a desire to live with others of one's group, and so on.[6]

A given collective might be both a community and a nation, in which case the regional and the national versions of self-determination would converge when a culture is 'preserved' through the exercise of popular sovereignty by a population consisting of members of a single national group. But convergence is the exception. Typically, not every regionally identifiable population is a single people, and not every national group is a regionally identifiable population. Moreover, just as state preservation of a culture can occur without popular sovereignty of its population, the converse is equally true. Failure to distinguish these two distinct interpretations of beneficiaries is partly due to the common perception that while the principle of self-determination calls for national autonomy, the terms 'nation,' 'national,' and 'people' are ambiguous between a purely political interpretation and a cultural interpretation. In the former sense, rights of self-determination are nothing beyond what is accorded to states and their citizenries, while in the latter sense, autonomy is mandated for culturally defined groups.

Are there, then, two further rights of self-determination, one calling for popular sovereignty within any region, the other for self-governance for any nation or national group? Admitting this would generate conflicts of rights, especially since a 'nation' cannot be self-determining except in a 'region.' A national group's bid for self-determination in a territory might be insensitive to the interests of the established majority of that territory or of a larger territory of which it is a part, just as a demand for regional autonomy might be oblivious to the cultural diversities and rivalries that prevail within a given region. Rather than speaking of two conflicting principles under the same title, it is better to avoid contradiction by adjudicating between rival interpretations of a single principle.

Before attempting this, however, it must be observed that neither the notion of a community or of a national group, as such, suffices to demarcate the remaining class of beneficiaries. Granting a right of self-determination to every people, under either interpretation, would generate the problems of conflict and fragmentation noted above. Plainly, not every regionally defined population merits self-determination and not every national group, or sub-group, can claim a privileged connection to territory that would warrant being self-determining *qua* that group.[7] Regardless of which interpretation we take, we still need a specification of the precise conditions under which a non-standard collective is deserving of self-determination. This is the problem of demarcating exceptional beneficiaries.

4. A regional interpretation of exceptional beneficiaries

Perhaps we can make some progress by inquiring into what conception of beneficiaries was operative in Wilson's own conception of his principle. As indicated in Section 2, he maintained that the required mechanism for settling questions of sovereignty, boundaries, economic and political institutions, and so on is the free acceptance of the relevant proposals 'by the people immediately concerned,' not by the interests of external parties. Unless Wilson was merely reiterating the doctrine of popular sovereignty, then the emphasis should be that 'free acceptance... by the people immediately concerned' is the deciding factor whenever there is a question to be 'settled,' specifically, when territories have been liberated from previous rulers and political structures are yet undetermined. Wilson's focus on such regions in the aftermath of WWI shows that he was concerned with more than standard beneficiaries when it comes to self-determination.

Still, the question remains: in any given instance of an outstanding question about the political settlement in a region, who are 'the people immediately concerned'? Many have construed Wilson's principle along nationalistic lines (e.g., Cobban, 1945, pp. 19–22; N. N. Feinberg, 1970, p. 45; Bassiouni, 1978, pp. 2–3; and, more recently, Amstutz, 1999, p. 59; Moore, 2001, p. 143). But there are others who find a regional interpretation to be the most accurate rendition of Wilson's intent, especially in relation to the question of Palestine.[8] To illustrate, in 1919, Wilson dispatched a commission to the Near East to report on the political situation there. At the Paris Peace Conference on August 28, 1919, its commissioners, Dr. King and Mr. Crane, claimed that only a 'greatly reduced Zionist program' would be compatible with the principle of self-determination. The British government, as if in agreement, decided to deliberately ignore the principle (Lloyd-George, 1939, p. 750; Khalidi, 1971, p. 208).

While Wilson's language was unclear, what is certain is that he viewed observance of this principle as both a natural extension of democratic theory and an essential measure for preventing future wars and 'making the world safe for democracy.'

> ...no peace can last, or ought to last, which does not recognize and accept the principle that governments derive all their just powers from the consent of the governed, and that no right anywhere exists to hand peoples about from sovereignty to sovereignty as if they were property. (Pomerance, 1976, p. 2)

The easy transition from 'the governed' to 'peoples' in this passage together with the occurrence of 'freely accepted' suggests that he was stressing the importance of popular sovereignty rather than the preservation of cultures. This same orientation is conveyed in an earlier speech in 1918 when Wilson first employed the term 'self-determination' in public:

> People are not to be handed about from one sovereignty to another by an international conference or an understanding between rivals and antagonists. National aspirations must be respected; peoples may now be dominated and governed only by their own consent. 'Self-determination' is not a mere phrase. It is an imperative principle of action, which statesmen will henceforth ignore at their peril. (Wilson, 1927, p. 180)[9]

Despite the reference to 'national aspirations,' the contrast he drew between being 'handed' from one sovereignty to another and self-determination suggests, once again, that he conceived of the latter it as a moral precept rooted in the ideal that political institutions gain legitimacy only from the consent of the governed. Wilson opposed the notion that a community may take any direction that its then dominant or ruling voices might demand, and urged, instead, that the community must follow the preferences of its significant majority. While not quite a call for the establishment of liberal democratic institutions, it is an unmistakable endorsement of popular sovereignty for every group constituting a 'governed.'

Two final points are relevant in determining what Wilson's intent might have been. First, he wrote as though his principle were more of a political maxim, designed to guide those 'statesmen' entrusted with making decisions about the future status of given territories, rather than a 'right' of peoples. Second, despite use of terms like 'peoples' and 'national,' Wilson spoke in regional terms in commenting upon the role of the principle in securing a peace treaty at the Paris Peace Conference of 1919:

> ...the principle underlying the treaty was that every land belonged to the native stock that lived in it, and that nobody had the right to dictate either the form of government or the control of territory to those people who were born and bred and had their lives and happiness to make there. (Wilson, 1927, vol. II, p. 49)

If we underline the phrases 'the native stock that lived in it' and 'born and bred,' then the principle is that self-determination must be accorded to the inhabitants of territories under discussion. The 'territories' he was speaking about were those that are 'unsettled' by recent conflict or 'newly liberated' from foreign domination, and the very occurrence of the phrase 'by the people immediately concerned' suggested a regional democratic emphasis rather than a national or cultural one. It was regional concerns that prevailed in the Paris Peace Conference, and the applicability of the principle of self-determination was contested in certain 'unsettled' regions, e.g., Alsace-Lorraine, Upper Silesia, and Palestine, because of nationalistic pressures. Again, after World War II, it was in circumstances occasioned by international conflict and colonial breakup that the paradigmatic applications of the principle occurred, often oblivious to various national and tribal distributions (Umozurike, 1972, p. 14; Espiell, 1980, pp. 46–8). Thus, the historical record does not substantiate the common perception that Wilson had national self-determination in mind, but suggests, instead, that a regional criterion was foremost in his thinking.

Here, then, is one way of demarcating the remaining class of beneficiaries along regional lines. They key is to define the relevant regions and populations in political terms. There are two types of exceptional beneficiaries. In the first, self-determination applies to the populations of politically defined regions that are *unsettled*, namely, regions where issues of sovereignty and the nature of the governing political, economic, social, and cultural institutions are as yet unresolved. Such regions include those that (i) were formerly dominated by another community but are currently free from that domination, due to wars or decolonialization; (ii) are currently under some form of internationally sanctioned trusteeship; (iii) have been accorded the right of secession by a larger state of which it is presently a partl or (iv) are presently under the control of an illegitimate state. The legitimate residents of such territories have a right to be self-determining in those territories, though they might choose to exercise that self-determination in different ways, for example, by becoming an independent state, merging with a neighboring state, or dissolving into separate states.[10]

This way of describing exceptional beneficiaries of the right of self-determination does not address the concerns of those who are anxious to press secessionist demands but do not meet any of the conditions, i–iv, for unsettled regions. Of course, a mere demand does not create a right to secession, especially if secession would violate the self-determination rights of existing legitimate states, as Buchanan (1991, 1997b) has persuasively argued. But when the existing sovereign is unable to protect the rights of a given population under its control, for example, through weakness or negligence, or, it threatens those rights through severe discrimination, persecution, or other forms of injustice, then the region may be classified as *endangered* and its inhabitants constitute the second type of exceptional beneficiaries. Their right of self-determination is a prerogative of a population to take steps to protect the human rights of its members, steps that may go beyond the measures of political and legal redress allowed within that state. This right derives from the right of individuals to appeal to collectives to which they belong, and whose other members might face similar abuse, to take collective action in the defense of individual rights. When the collective is regionally defined, then it may decide, on behalf of its members, to seek (i) political independence in the form of a politically autonomous region within the state or as a separate state, (ii) political dissolution into smaller states, or (iii) political merger with another state. Unlike the right of populations in unsettled territories, this right is not absolute or unconditional; its exercise gains legitimacy only when there is a clear and present danger to the human rights of its members.

Combining these two considerations—that of endangered regions under an ineffective or threatening sovereign and that of unsettled regions under no present sovereignty or under some form of trusteeship—we obtain a general description of a right of self-determination for exceptional beneficiaries understood in regional terms:

> ***Self-determination of exceptional beneficiaries***: The legitimate residents of an unsettled or endangered region have a right to determine their political future either by constituting themselves as an autonomous political unit, or by merging with another state, or by dissolving into smaller states.

In the case of endangered regions, merger and dissolution would imply secession from an existing state, though political independence falling short of strict sovereignty would not. Secession is not the issue in the case of unsettled regions.

Once again, this right of self-determination is derivative from individual human rights, both the right of political participation and other human rights whose observance and protection is recognized within international law. Moreover, since human rights are the chief moral constraints upon the exercise of governmental authority, the exercise of self-determination in troubled regions is justified to the extent that it complies with these constraints.[11] Thus, the right of self-determination is never a *carte blanche* for majorities to establish objectionable forms of discrimination and, therefore, it is not the sole or overriding norm relevant to decisions concerning the political status of disputed territories. For example, a community has no overriding right to constitute itself as a slave-holding society; other societies have the right to intervene to stop the practice in the interest of protecting human rights (see Emerson, 1971, pp. 466–7; Umozurike, 1972, p. 192; Pomerance, 1984, pp. 332–7; Etzioni, 1992–3, p. 34). Respect for individual human rights is one of the most essential features of the liberal democratic philosophy that has been developed over the past four centuries, and, as John Stuart Mill pointed out (*On Liberty*), such respect means protection from the 'tyranny of the majority' as much as from the intrusion of government. No matter how vigorously a community presses its bid for autonomy or self-rule, both its justification and its limitations are rooted in those human rights that have emerged in the developing system of international justice.

The three rights of self-determination present a philosophical interpretation of what the principle of self-determination calls for. The questions with which we began are now answered: self-determination is a matter of right to self-governance on the part of (i) existing states, (ii) the legitimate residents of politically independent territories, and (iii) the legitimate residents of unsettled or endangered regions. The philosophical and historical considerations raised above give reason why these rights should be recognized as norms governing international relations. This said, it remains that a right of self-determination cannot be appealed to in establishing objectionable forms of discrimination and, therefore, it is neither the sole nor the overriding normative principle relevant to international order (Emerson, 1971, pp. 466–7; Umozurike, 1972).

5. An argument for a right of national self-determination

Can a case be made for an additional right of national self-determination within a viable framework of international justice? The traditional nationalist argument for the existence of a nation-state, say, in Fichte's famous 'Address to the German Nation,' derives from the importance of survival and protection of national cultures. But in recent years, an additional consideration has been made that appeals directly to the rights of individuals to enjoy the fruits of membership in national cultures, and it is for this reason that national cultures are worth preserving. So understood, arguments for national self-determination can be given that are also based on the human rights of individuals.

I have already cited the conventional skepticism about a blanket right of all national groups to strict self-determination. Since different national groups and subgroups are interspersed throughout nearly every region, however small—the 'Russian doll phenomenon' (Tamir, 1993, p. 158)—then any attempt to accommodate the world's 5000 or so national groups through the principle 'a state for every nation' would lead either to massive population shifts or to a series of smaller and smaller states to satisfy the demands of each national group that dominates a given sub region. Moreover, as Alan Buchanan (1991, pp. 22–80, 151–62) has argued, such a program would conflict with the self-determination rights of standard beneficiaries, specifically, the principle of territorial integrity—one component of the right of self-determination for existing states. This being said, the question is open whether a national construal of exceptional beneficiaries might not replace, or be added to, the foregoing regional demarcation.

Several writers have stressed that every individual has a moral right to determine for himself or herself the sort of person he or she wants to be, in particular, to identify with certain cultural traditions. This is so because having a cultural identity is a vital human interest worth preserving (Tamir, 1991, 1993; Moore, 2001). There is a public dimension to this right; individuals need not conceal the national self-identification they have a right to possess, but, instead, are entitled to express it publicly in order to reinforce it, enjoy its full benefits, and receive recognition for who they are. In turn, each of these requires being allowed to participate publicly in the cultural life of one's nation within a 'shared public space' (Tamir, 1993, p. 73). Moreover, an individual's public expression of cultural identity is best protected when the cultural group or nation to which the individual belongs enjoys a sufficiently high degree of cultural autonomy, that is, when the members of that group have as much freedom from external interference as possible to develop their cultural life. Accordingly, from the right of an individual to seek, develop, express, and enjoy a cultural identity, we derive a right to seek participation in a culturally autonomous group with which he or she identifies.[12]

Since the very existence of culturally autonomous groups is the product of coordinated collective efforts, and since an individual's enjoyment of a moral right of participation in a culturally autonomous group implies some such collective efforts, then such efforts are themselves morally legitimate. Thus, the developing and sustaining an autonomous culture is itself a moral right of culturally defined collectives. Whether this right is reducible to the rights of individuals within that group is a distinct matter; the point is that the normative status of the group's collective effort is based on the rightness of individual actions. As with any right, correlative duties are imposed upon other agents, whether individuals, groups, or states, to respect and tolerate a group's seeking and exercising cultural autonomy.

Turning to the political dimension, Margalit and Raz (1990) have argued that since there is value to membership in a national or 'self-encompassing' group, including participation in the political activities of that group, then there is an inherent value in that group's being self-governing (Chen, 1976; Margalit & Raz, 1990, p. 451; Khatchadourian, 2000, chap. 2). As Yael Tamir (1993) stresses, this is not an argument for strict self-determination or sovereignty, but it is the basis for urging, at least, a limited political autonomy sufficient for achieving and sustaining cultural autonomy. That is, the likelihood of a national group's sustaining an autonomous culture and in achieving prosperity, self-respect, and respect from other nations is greatly increased when that nation has adequate political autonomy within the region to which it has the best claim. Will Kymlicka adds that this consideration is especially important when the group's self-esteem had previously been damaged (Kymlicka, 1989, chaps. 9, 10). So, given that a group has a right to seek and sustain cultural autonomy and that cultural autonomy is best achieved and preserved when that group has political autonomy, then the group has the right to adequate political autonomy within the region to which it has the best claim. Again, having a right of political autonomy is not unconditional or overriding, and within the present order of existing states, it is not necessarily a right of sovereignty. Culturally demarcated groups have been able to achieve degrees of local political autonomy, for example, the Inuit people of Canada, even if it falls short of complete political independence.

Establishing a claim for strict self-determination—territorial sovereignty—is the last step in the argumentation. The substantial claim is the familiar nationalist principle that in some cases a national group's cultural autonomy is endangered unless it possesses sovereign power. This can occur if external agents wish to subordinate that group's culture or even eliminate it and have the resources to do so because existing sovereigns are either unwilling or unable to protect the group. Let us call this an *existential threat* to the group's culture. In that case, the political autonomy sufficient for a national group's maintenance of its culture would involve control over the mechanisms for its own protection, specifically, over the police and the military, and this requires territorial sovereignty. If it had no right to establish sovereign political control over its own future and no right to develop and maintain effective means of protection, then the demand that other national and political groups 'tolerate' them is likely to be ineffective since intolerance would have little political price (Moore, 2001). The more political control the better, that is, when a national culture is under an existential threat, then the adequate political autonomy needed by the national group to achieve and maintain cultural autonomy and, thereby, preserve its culture, is territorial sovereignty in the region to which it has the best claim.

It follows that when a national culture is under an existential threat then the group's right to political autonomy, sufficient to turn back that threat, is a right to territorial sovereignty in the region to which it has the best claim. Here, by 'best claim' is meant a better claim than any competitors. Margalit and Raz place further conditions upon a national group qualifying for strict self-determination, namely, that independence can only be justified when that group (i) forms a substantial majority in the territory in question, (ii) the new state is likely to respect the fundamental interests of its inhabitants, and (iii) that measures are adopted to prevent its creation from gravely damaging the just interests of other countries (Margalit & Raz, 1990, p. 457).

This argument is no justification of the blanket nationalist principle, 'a state for every nation,' for the condition of a severe existential threat is crucial. Similarly, there may be national groups that cannot claim any territory as their own, or, at least, to which they do not have a 'best' claim. Thus, a national group's right to have sovereignty over its territory is not intended to satisfy the demand that each nation possesses territorial sovereignty, but only that there are cases where the right of self-determination can reasonably be interpreted in nationalistic terms.

6. A response to this argument

That there is an inherent value in national self-determination cannot be disputed, but whenever we consider a proposed practical principle, we distinguish what it might yield if people were perfectly impartial from what it is likely to produce in practice. By definition, a nation-state is constituted for the sake of a specific national group, and inevitably, its institutions, laws, and policies reflect the culture and interests of that people. Here is where the dangers lie; since few areas of the world are culturally homogenous, and since human beings are unlikely to abandon the habit of identifying with groups to which other collectives are unfavorably compared, then the *de jure* favoring of one group's cultural values is bound to be feared and resented by other groups who see it as a threat to their interests.

Let us develop these reflections in examining the nationalist argument. Everything flows smoothly up through the claim that a cultural group has a right to achieve and sustain cultural autonomy, but problems emerge with the subsequent inferences to a right of sovereignty. First, a blanket right to national self-determination would generate inconsistent demands for sovereignty in culturally heterogeneous regions. Within them, there is always cultural competition and a fear of culturally based discrimination, for when one group within such a region makes a bid for national self-determination, other groups become fearful. By the logic of the nationalist argument, they have the prerogative of raising their own claims for self-determination. But, plainly, not all these conflicting claims could be satisfied. For this reason, even if political autonomy enhances a national group's cultural autonomy, it does not follow that it has a right to political autonomy, and even less that it has a right to sovereignty.

Second, a state that institutionalizes the values of a particular culture and not those of others invokes the dual risk of intolerance and officially sanctioned discrimination within any culturally diverse region. Even if assurances are given to protect the human rights of cultural minorities, international law has not evolved to the point where there are reliable mechanisms to ensure such protection. Those individuals who are outside the favored group are in real threat of being disenfranchised or, at least, discriminated against in the distribution of benefits and privileges. For this reason, a national state can easily become non-democratic and non-representative by undermining equality and threatening the exercise of other individual rights.[13] We see this happening even when the state prides itself on its supposed democratic character. Israel, for example, proclaims in its Declaration of Independence that the state 'will uphold the full social and political equality of all its citizens without distinction of religion, race, or sex.' But Israel remains a *Jewish* state—by law it is a state *of* the Jewish people—even though nearly 20 percent of its citizens are non-Jews. Its official symbols are Jewish religious symbols, and statutes governing land ownership and the Law of Return explicitly favor Jews over non-Jews.[14] Successive Israeli governments have discriminated against Arabs in areas of education, municipal funding, and economic development (Jiryis, 1976; Lustick, 1980). The concern for keeping the state predominately Jewish is the primary reason why it has not annexed the West Bank, with the result that the Arab population in that area have been subject to four decades of a debilitating military occupation. Democratic safeguards prove hollow if a majority supports the notion that the state exists for the sake of a single national group.

Third, almost a century ago, Lord Acton pointed out that a multinational pluralistic state affords the best protection for the liberty of individuals, including their freedom of cultural expression because different cultural groups provide a system of checks and balances upon the political ambitions of the others, and will jointly act as a deterrent for excessive governmental intervention and the institutionalization of culturally specific values (Acton, 1967). Moreover, a state is more stable when it pursues the common good, that is, if 'it gives all its citizens a political stake in its stability and can count on their collective pride and gratitude' (Parekh, 1999, p. 321). If a group is treated unfairly, its allegiances to the country are damaged and potential sources of dissent and weakness emerge within the body politic. Infusing politics with competing nationalist ambitions is the surest way to divide people along national lines, and adding this layer of competition can poison relations among these individuals and groups in both the political and social arenas. Tolerance and respect for cultural diversity are better promoted if nationality is kept from having any legal or political status for, typically, groups have discriminated unfairly against each other when politics is influenced by nationalistic sentiment and one group finds itself with an upper hand politically. The more that laws and institutions abstract from cultural, ethnic, and religious identifications, the greater the assurance that nationality of another poses no threat and that the state apparatus will protect individual rights regardless of national organs. There is no reason why cultures cannot flourish under the mantle of state neutrality and freedom from fear of subordination. Cultural diversity does exist and flourish within some pluralistic states. The chances of officially sanctioned cultural suppression are lowered in the truly liberal democratic state, yet raised significantly when nationalist sentiments are at their strongest.

Fourth, to divide cultural groups into separate states will generate new interstate political rivalries. The threat of national determination to world peace must also be considered, not only because a proliferation of claims for self-determination threatens world order, but because the call for national self-determination has often been coupled with nationalistic chauvinism, persecution of minorities, ethnic cleansing (Petrovic, 1994), and interstate belligerency, for example, with Nazi Germany during World War II and, recently, in the Balkans.[15] In today's world, there is an increasing need for individuals to identify themselves as members of the global community, to work for the common interest, and to recognize that the world and its resources belong to peoples of diverse cultural backgrounds. Too frequently, the demand for national allegiance is exclusivist, pointing an individual in an opposite direction, threatening both the prospects for global cooperation and the very existence of weaker national groups.

Fifth, the marriage of government to culture also threatens to inhibit the freedom of individuals within that culture who might choose alternative expressions of that culture or seek alternative sources of identity. This danger is nicely expressed in a passage from James Joyce's *Portrait of an Artist as a Young Man*:

> The soul is born, he said vaguely, first in those moments I told you of. It has a slow and dark birth, more mysterious than the birth of the body. When the soul of a man is born in this country there are nets flung at it to hold it back from flight. You talk to me of nationality, language, religion. I shall try to fly by those nets.[16]

The principal human rights agreements that emphasize the importance of individual liberty call for limits upon social as well as state intervention. Participation in the cultural life of a nation can limit freedom, as does participation in almost any social endeavor. This is not to speak against such participation, obviously, but to insist that it be as voluntary as possible, and this is further reason to limit the legal authority of purely cultural institutions.

In sum, there is an alternative for protecting cultures and achieving cultural autonomy, namely, democratic pluralistic states with constitutional guarantees for the protection of human rights—constitutions that abstract from culturally specific values. It is through observance of such a legal framework that national groups as well as individuals stand to receive their best protection. If adhered to then even though a right to national self-determination might seem appropriate, for example, when the nation in question is an overwhelming majority, national sovereignty is not only dangerous but unnecessary. When such a constitutional safeguard is lacking, then any existential threat to a national group might call for drastic protective action in the form of international sanctions, humanitarian intervention, or, if feasible, regional secession. The principle of self-determination, therefore, is not to be interpreted as giving a collective a right to sovereignty *qua* national group; to do so is to threaten the autonomy of cultural minorities, the rights of individuals, and interstate harmony. The argument that attempts to generate a national group's right to sovereignty from the importance of cultural identification and cultural expression is a *non-sequitur*.

7. The mandate for Palestine, 1917–47

In 1917–18, combined British and Arab forces ended over 400 years of Turkish administration in various parts of the Arab world, including Palestine. The nationalities in these territories, stated Wilson in his famous 'Fourteen Points' speech of January 1917, 'should be assured an undoubted security of life and an absolutely unmolested opportunity of autonomous development.' Yet nothing of the sort took place in the Near East; in the aftermath of World War I, the newly formed League of Nations placed much of the region under mandatory rule by the British and French, Palestine going to the British. The terms of the Palestine Mandate typified the extent to which the international community has been willing to consistently ignore the rights of self-determination for the past eighty years.

At the end of World War I, there was uncertainty in Western capitals about the precise borders of historic Palestine. It was generally agreed that the region extended at least to the Mediterranean on the west, the Jordan River on the east, the southern Golan Heights in the northeast, and the Negev and Sinai deserts in the south, but there was dispute concerning the northern and eastern borders, fueled partly by Zionist aspirations.[17] The area today referred to as 'Palestine' is that classified as such by the terms of the League of Nations Mandate for Palestine granted to the British in 1922. There were approximately 750,000 inhabitants in that region by 1922, with Jews constituting 11.4 percent of the population. Ownership of approximately half of the land was in private Arab hands, 2.6 percent was privately owned by Jews, while the remainder was state property under the Ottoman law, though much of it had been farmed by generations of Arab villagers.[18]

By Wilson's principle, Palestine, either in itself or as part of a larger geographical unit, was a region to which the principle of self-determination should have been applied. Yet, despite Arab expectations, this never occurred. Political decisions by the great powers, notably, the British Government in 1917 and the American Administration in 1946, were in the interests of Zionism and eventuated in actions taken by international bodies that entailed a denial of self-determination in Palestine (Cattan, 1976; Bassiouni, 1978; Mallison & Mallison, 1986; Quigley, 1990). The Balfour Declaration (see Introduction) promised Palestine—a land which had been peopled by an Arab majority for centuries—to the Jewish people, not to the established Jewish minority in Palestine, but to the Jewish people *per se*. Although it did not define the crucial phrases 'civil and religious rights' and 'political status,' it is significant that the document contrasted civil rights with political status while avoiding reference to the political status of Palestinian Arabs, viz., the 'non-Jewish communities' which comprised the substantial majority of inhabitants.[19]

The principle of self-determination was explicitly ignored by the British Government at this time; it had no intention of granting the largest segment of Palestine's inhabitants the right to participate in the making of a decision which was to have a monumental impact upon their future. They were not consulted; no referendum, no plebiscite, was ever held, no approval from Palestinian representatives ever secured. From the outset, the Palestinians repeatedly voiced their opposition to the provisions of the Balfour Declaration, and the governments of both Great Britain and the United States were apprised of Arab opposition (Khalidi, 1971, pp. 213–21). In reporting to the Paris Peace Conference on August 28, 1919, Wilson's King-Crane Commission expressed concern about the future of Palestine, claiming that if the principle of self-determination is to rule,

> ...then it is to be remembered that the non-Jewish population of Palestine—nearly 9/10 of the whole—are emphatically against the entire Zionist Programme. The tables show that there was no one thing upon which the population of Palestine was more agreed than upon this. To subject a people so minded to unlimited Jewish immigration, and to steady financial and social pressure to surrender the land, would be a gross violation of the principle just quoted, and of the people's rights, though it kept within the forms of law.

The commissioners also noted that none of the British officers consulted felt that a Jewish National Home could not be established except by the force of arms, and, citing Article 22 of the League of Nations Covenant, that the inhabitants preferred that the mandate for all of Syria, including Palestine, go to the United States.[20]

The recommendations of the King-Crane Commission fell on deaf ears. They became no part of the policy of either the United States or Great Britain, and they were ignored by the League of Nations committees which drew up the terms of the mandates for the Near East. In March 1919, and again in April 1919, Wilson reiterated his earlier approval (October 1917) of the Balfour Declaration (Lilienthal, 1982, p. 30; Heckscher, 1991, p. 340) and in 1922 the U.S. Congress concurred

(Stone, 1981, pp. 151–2). Wilson was apparently not pressed upon the apparent conflict of this vision with his principle of self-determination (Lansing, 1921, pp. 104–5; Khalidi, 1971, p. xxxii), and the British took the view that he fully supported Zionism (Lloyd-George, 1939, pp. 734–5). The British Government had already ruled out settlement of the Palestine question by appeal to the principle of self-determination. Lord Balfour was particularly blunt:

> ...in Palestine we do not propose even to go through the form of consulting the wishes of the present inhabitants of the country...The Four Great Powers are committed to Zionism. And Zionism, be it right or wrong, good or bad, is rooted in age long traditions, in present needs, in future hopes, of far profounder import than the desires and prejudices of the 700,000 Arabs who now inhabit that ancient land. (Khalidi, 1971, p. 208)

An official memorandum of the British Foreign Office Department at the time to the British Cabinet contained an equally explicit suspension of the principle:

> The problem of Palestine cannot be exclusively solved on the principle of self-determination, because there is one element in the population – the Jews – which, for historical and religious reasons, is entitled to a greater influence than would be given to it if numbers were the sole test. (Lloyd-George, 1939, p. 750)

These statements underscore the regional interpretation of the Wilsonian principle and proclaim Britain's willingness to ignore that principle. No mention of self-determination was made in the terms of the Mandate for Palestine and, against the wishes of the Arab majority, the gates of Palestine were opened to Jewish immigration so that the percentage of Jews had climbed from less than ten percent in 1918, to 11.4 percent by 1922, to 17 percent by 1931 and to 28 percent by 1936 (see note 2 of Introduction). Even at the height of World War II in 1942, Winston Churchill, echoing the sentiments of Balfour and Lloyd George, expressed concern about the self-determination clause of the Atlantic Charter since it might obstruct Zionist settlement in Palestine (letter to President Franklin Roosevelt, quoted in Khalidi, 1971, p. 49).

At the end of 1946, Jews constituted almost one-third of the Palestine's population of approximately 1.9 million people—'by the might of England, against the will of the people' (Toynbee, 1954, p. 306). The majority of Jews had immigrated since 1919, yet only in the district around the city of Tel Aviv did Jewish numbers exceed that of the Arabs. Most of the land was privately owned by Arabs, save in the southern desert region. Jews had acquired roughly six percent of mandated territory, though their percentage was higher in the agricultural areas along the coast and in the Galilee (W. Khalidi, 1997, pp. 12–3). By 1947, despite explicit assurances from Zionist leaders like Weizmann that Jews had no intention of turning the Arabs out of their homes and land, Zionist political rhetoric in the streets and exclusivist policies on Jewish-owned land revealed other intentions.

For their part, the Palestinian Arabs requested the establishment of a democratically elected legislative council and the eventual establishment of an independent Arab state.[21] In 1937, the British Peel Commission, noting that turning Palestine into a Jewish state would mean withholding self-determination from the majority, indicated that the Arabs wished 'to emulate their successful fellow nationalists in those countries just across their northern and southern borders' (*Palestine Royal Commission Report*, London, 1937, p. 94). Committed to the terms of the Mandate, the British Government rejected the Peel Commission's recommendation of partition as impractical. Only after the Arabs resorted to armed insurrection in 1936–39 did Britain finally change its policy. In the 1939 MacDonald White Paper, the Government renounced the Balfour Declaration, restricted further Jewish immigration, and advocated establishment of a singular secular state throughout Palestine in which Arabs and Jews would share authority in government (Khalidi, 1971, pp. 461–75; Khalidi, 2006, pp. xx–xxi). This met with approval among many Arabs (though not all), but was angrily rejected by the Zionist movement (Laqueur, 1976, pp. 76–7; Gal, 1991; Hirst, 2003, pp. 220–1).

With the onset of the World War II, Zionists shifted their diplomatic efforts to the United States. In August 1946, they secured their the most significant political victory since the Balfour Declaration as President Truman endorsed Zionist proposals, setting in motion American diplomatic efforts to secure a partition of Palestine into a Jewish and an Arab state (Khalidi, 1971, p. lxiv). In the meantime, the political situation in Palestine had grown more intense. With greater international sympathy for the establishment of a Jewish state and increased demands for Palestine to be opened to Jewish immigration, British authorities came into direct conflict with Jewish underground militias, the Irgun Z'vai Le'umi and Lehi groups. Assassination, hangings, and bombings—the most spectacular of which was the

Irgun's demolition of British headquarters in 1946—marked the conflict. Britain responded by applying a stringent set of Defense Laws, initially devised to counter the Arab Revolt, and accusing the Jewish Agency of condoning terrorism. Opposition of Palestinian Arabs to Zionism remained as strong as ever, their hopes lifted by the 1945 formation of the Arab League which supported their aspirations. However, the Palestinian militia had been largely disarmed by the British during the 1936–39 revolt, Palestinian leadership was fragmented, and a leading spokesman, the exiled Al-Hajj Amin Husseini, had discredited himself by backing Germany during the war—though Palestinians leaders had generally favored Britain (Najjar, 2003; date of access: January 15, 2007). The Palestinians were decidedly less successful than the Jewish Community in preparing for future conflict.

8. The debate at the United Nations

In May 1946, an Anglo-American Committee of Inquiry recommended that until Arab–Jewish hostility diminishes, the government of Palestine should be continued under mandate pending execution of a UN-sponsored trusteeship agreement. It added that Palestine should be neither a Jewish nor an Arab state, a recommendation that satisfied neither party. When the Truman Administration renewed calls for immediate immigration of 100,000 Jewish refugees into Palestine, Britain, exhausted by war and frustrated by opposition, announced it would end its administration of Palestine by May 1948. Foreign Secretary Ernst Bevin declared that there was no prospect for compromise between the two communities. In 1947, the problem of Palestine was taken up by the United Nations which created a special committee (UNSCOP) to make recommendations to the General Assembly. A number of arguments were heard that continue to be relevant to on-going normative debates and are worth rehearsing.

The Zionists advanced a number of considerations in favor of a Jewish state. The argument from 'historical connection,' mentioned above, was reiterated, but now additional factors were relevant. Of central importance was the Zionist contention that the Palestine Mandate constituted legal recognition of Jewish national rights in Palestine: 'The Balfour Declaration became a binding and unchallengeable international obligation from the moment when it was embodied in the Palestine Mandate' (Feinberg, 1974, pp. 75–6; Feinberg, 1979, p. 242). This 'right' to establish a 'national home' in Palestine, the Zionists argued, was preserved by the UN Charter whose Article 80 stipulates nothing be done to alter the rights 'of any states or any peoples' in territories currently under mandate. Hence, the world community is obligated to honor the commitments of the Mandate. Weizmann added a balance of justice argument. While both Arabs and Jews have a legitimate claim to Palestine, in depriving the Jews of a state you deprive all the world's Jews of independence and nationhood, whereas in refusing to create an Arab state in Palestine you do not deprive all Arabs of political independence. According to N. Feinberg (1970, p. 53), this reasoning 'turned the scale in favour of the Zionist solution of the Palestine Problem,' for the minute territorial allocation that a Jewish state entailed would not be a hardship placed upon Arabs in the context of the Arab Middle East. Moshe Shertok (Sharett) added that its Arab citizens would not only retain their association with the Arab world but would enjoy the rights of citizenship in a Jewish commonwealth as 'there is nothing inherent in the nature of either the native Arab or the immigrant Jew which prevents friendly cooperation' (Robinson, 1947, p. 213). When the Arab claim is weighed against the international promises to Jews, the achievements of 50 years of Jewish settlement, recurrent anti-Semitism, and the current plight of Jewish refugees, then the route of least injustice favors establishment of a Jewish state.[22]

But an older argument resurfaced with greater weight than ever before. The Nazi persecution of the Jews strengthened the moral case for the Zionist insistence that as perpetual outsiders without sovereign power of their own, the survival of the Jews will continually be under threat. 'Hitler is gone now,' argued Shertok 'but not anti-Semitism... Anti-Semitism in Germany and in many other parts of Europe is a rife as ever and potentially militant and fierce.... The very age of European Jewry serves only to accentuate the basic historic insecurity of Jewish life in the dispersion' (Robinson, 1947, p. 212). Since it is a matter of 'life or death' that Jews be allowed into Palestine (Jewish Agency for Palestine, 1947, p. 514), and since the Jewish community there has proved itself capable of political and economic independence, then Palestine is the natural place for a sovereign Jewish state. This state would be able to absorb an influx of some 400,000 Jewish refugees from Europe and soon become a 'pillar of progress in the Near East' (Robinson, 1947, p. 214).[23]

For their part, the Arabs repeated that no credibility can be given to the argument for historical title on the basis on distant historical connection. Aside from the statue of limitations consideration, most modern day Jews cannot claim descent from the Jews of biblical times and, hence, have not inherited a claim from those who were previously dispossessed.[24] Before the General Assembly, Arabs like Henry Cattan

(Palestine), Faris al-Khouri (Syria), and Fadhil Jamali (Iraq) argued that appealing to historical connection in settling international issues,

> ...would mean redrawing the map of the whole world. It has been said you cannot set back the hands of the clock of history by twenty years. What should then be said when an effort is made to set the clock of history back by twenty centuries in an attempt to give away a country on the grounds of a transitory historic association? (Robinson, 1947, p. 227)

If historical connection is relevant at all, it is certainly the Arabs who have the stronger case since they have been the established majority in Palestine during the more recent centuries. No amount of propaganda, said Cattan, can alter the Arab character of Palestine's history and culture. Arabs have done the greater part in developing the land, establishing its citrus and olive groves, and building its terraces, its villages, its cities. The assumption that they had let its land lay fallow and the country undeveloped is as much a distortion as the earlier myth that the land was 'empty.' Even if Jews have done well with the sectors they own, the argument that development grants title could be used to justify any aggression of a technologically advanced society against a more 'backward' people.

As for the lesser injustice, while it may be true that Jewish refugees need a home, this is not to be granted at the expense of those who were not responsible for Nazi actions. That the refugees be settled in Palestine against the wishes of Arab residents would be an injustice to the majority and a violation of a 1946 General Assembly resolution concerning resettlement of displaced persons. In measuring the injustice of alternative proposals, Arabs would stand to lose more by creation of a Jewish state since they outnumber Jews by two-to-one and hold the bulk of its property. The 1919 King-Crane commission had correctly predicted that the pressures of Jewish capital would result in the displacement of many poorer Arabs, while others would find economic and political opportunities blocked. 'No room can be made in Palestine for a second nation,' concluded Albert Hourani in 1946, 'except by dislodging or exterminating the first' (Smith, 1996, p. 130). Not only would Palestinian Arabs be affected; the Anglo-American Committee emphasized that a Jewish state in Palestine would give a non-Arab power control of the only land bridge between the western and eastern halves of the Arab world, disrupting the latter's communications and territorial unity.[25]

The most significant argument of the Arabs appealed directly to the principle of self-determination. Sovereignty is an inalienable possession of the inhabitants of a territory and a Trusteeship only temporarily suspends its exercise (Cattan, 1969, pp. 252–3). The 'commitments' and 'guarantees' of the Balfour Declaration and Palestine Mandate cannot override the rights of the indigenous Palestinian inhabitants which derive from more fundamental principles. Neither Great Britain nor the League of Nations had any moral authority to 'give' Palestine to a non-indigenous group and thereby deprive the original inhabitants of their right to exercise self-determination therein. In 1946, Akram Zuaiter, a prominent Palestinian politician, appealed to self-determination as a moral principle, insisting that Palestinians have a 'natural right' to self-governance that is not dependent upon the promises of the British, the Americans, or international bodies (Zuaiter, 1994, p. 272). The philosopher W. T. Stace argued in the same vein: self-determination provides 'the only "abstract" or "moral" principle which is needed for the adjudication of the Palestine controversy,' and it 'will not be outdated a year from now or in fifty years' (Stace, 1947, p. 83). It is 'aggression' for an external agent to neglect the wishes of the majority and their 'natural right of self-determination' in favor of an alternative arrangement. The Arab Higher Committee added that Jews legitimately entitled to reside in Palestine have every right to share in its self-determination, but,

> ...foreign residents of diverse nationalities, mostly of the Jewish faith, can under no legal or moral justification, be entitled to a say in the formation of this government...This, in short, is our legal position in Palestine. As the overwhelming majority, we possess the unquestionable right of sovereignty over the country. (1948, pp. 11–2)

Since Palestine's legitimate residents opposed both the Balfour Declaration and the Mandate provisions from the very outset and have persisted in their opposition to the present day, then imposition of a Jewish state upon them would be an unmistakable denial of self-determination.

Yet, the appeal to self-determination was double-edged. At times, Ben-Gurion argued that the right of self-determination may be overridden (Jewish Agency for Palestine, 1947, p. 384), but other members of the Jewish Agency maintained that it is a misconception to view the Palestine Mandate as violating the principle of self-determination. Any beneficiary of self-determination must demonstrate itself to be a viable political unit, and unlike the Arabs of Palestine, the Jews have been recognized by the international community as having achieved this status. Echoing earlier arguments of Jabotinsky (Shimoni, 1995, p. 367), the Agency contended that the right of self-determination should not be looked upon as applying to static populations alone, but as a mechanism for rectifying ancient wrongs and giving dispossessed peoples a share in the world's land and resources.

> If there was justice in the general concept of self-determination, there was also justice in the particular expression of that concept in terms of the 'historic reparation' to Jewry. No man of liberal spirit could deny that it was justice long-delayed. Nor could he gainsay the right of his people to find its way once more into the society of nations.[26]

The Zionist argument for self-determination can be summarized as follows: (i) Jews, as a people capable of political independence, meet the necessary and sufficient conditions for being a beneficiary of self-determination. (ii) The Zionist demand for a Jewish state can now more poignantly than ever given that Jews have once again been singled out for persecution. (iii) Palestine is the only territory to which Jews as such have historical, cultural, legal, and moral ties. (iv) Palestine is not the only area to which Arabs have such linkages (Gorny, 1987, pp. 213–4). (v) There is (in 1947) 'no identifiable Palestinian Arab people' who have emerged as a viable political unit with international recognition whose own national aspirations for independence would suffer upon creation of a Jewish state (Jewish Agency for Palestine, 1947, pp. 325, 384). Therefore, by the principle of self-determination, Jews are entitled to a sovereign state in Palestine.

Is this argument convincing? The first premise of the argument is plausible only on a principle of national self-determination, that is, only if a deserving beneficiary in Palestine is to be described in national or cultural terms. On a regional interpretation, the premise is false since self-determination is not a right of cultural groups but, instead, of resident populations. In Palestine in 1947, that right belonged to the entire community of legitimate residents and at that time the Jewish inhabitants of Palestine—barely one-third of the population at best—were not the exclusive beneficiary. In fact, the claim for regional self-determination in Palestine by the majority of Palestine's inhabitants had been strengthened during the period of the Mandate. In 1919, it was by no means clear that the inhabitants of Palestine were entitled to self-determination *qua* inhabitants of Palestine rather than being part of a larger regional unit. The effect of the British Mandate was to isolate Palestine, keeping it under trusteeship while the rest of the Arab world gradually gained political independence. Since the vast majority of Palestine's population contested the Mandate's provisions, Palestine remained a paradigm case of an *unsettled* area for the next quarter century. If a regional interpretation of deserving beneficiaries is to be upheld, not only is the first premise false, but the argument is invalid due to the presence of a majority of Arabs who would have turned the vote against a Jewish state.

Yet, even if one insists upon a national reading of the exceptional beneficiaries, by 1947 the Arab inhabitants of Palestine had acquired 'national aspirations' of their own (Muslih, 1988; R. Khalidi, 1997) and were as capable of other Arabs of political independence. This discredits the fourth premise of the argument even if the logic of national self-determination is retained. Moreover, it renders the third premise inoperative, for Jews were not the only nationality with unique and distinctive claims to Palestine that they had to no other region. Given their longer and more recent presence in that land, the Palestinians had the stronger claim. Thus, in 1947, the proposal for making Palestine into a Jewish state could not be justified on either interpretation of the right of self-determination.

9. The partition resolution and its aftermath

In the autumn of 1947, UNSCOP issued both majority and minority recommendations. The minority proposal, claiming that the provisions of the Mandate were inconsistent with the League of Nations Covenant, called for a binational state. That proposal was rejected by both Arabs, who denied any parity between Arab and Jewish political claims, and by the Jewish Agency (the political arm of the Zionist movement in Palestine) which argued that a binational solution would result in constant political deadlock and reliance upon external parties (Jewish Agency for Palestine, 1947, pp. 130–5, 345, 549). The majority proposal recommended partition of Palestine into two states; a Jewish state on approximately 55.5 percent of the mandated territory and an Arab state on little more than 43 percent, with Jerusalem to be a *corpus separatum* under international administration (see Map A and Map B). Arabs would lose control of the rich costal plain which produced their most valuable export, citrus fruit, as well as the interior plains, while the central highlands would be excluded from the Jewish state. Approximately 500,000 Jews would be within the boundaries of the proposed Jewish along with 438,000 Arabs, excluding 71,000 Arabs in the Jaffa enclave that was to be surrounded by the Jewish state. In no administrative district did Jews own a majority of the land, and only in the Jaffa-Tel Aviv district did they constitute a majority of the population. Even though Jews owned but 5.8 percent of the land at the time, the majority of the land was to be incorporated into the Jewish state, including the most fertile lands along the coast and in the central plains (see landownership percentages in Khalidi, 1997, pp. 11–4).

The Jewish Agency accepted the Recommendation's provision for a Jewish state, though some Zionists rejected its partition of Palestine (Flapan, 1987, pp. 32–3). Arabs overwhelmingly rejected its provisions, arguing that the United Nations had no right to grant any portion of Arab territory to the Zionists, and that the Western world was unfairly making them pay for the suffering of Jews. Palestinian leaders urged that the legality of the plan be tested in the newly found International Court of Justice, but this never happened (Pappe, 2006a, p. 34). It was, at the time, unreasonable to expect Arabs to accept what they regarded as a 'grotesquely skewed misallocation' (Khalaf, 1991, pp. 245–6; Ball & Ball, 1992, p. 21; Pappe, 2006a, pp. 34–5) whereby the minority would acquire control over the bulk of the territory, and thus, implementing the plan would be a gross violation of the rights of the Arab majority in Palestine. While Great Britain abstained in the voting, the United States led the fight for approval, resorting to pressure diplomacy to secure the necessary votes (Khalidi, 1971, pp. 709–30). The plan was adopted by the General Assembly on November 29, 1947 as Resolution 181 (II) with a vote of 33 in favor, 13 against, and ten abstentions.

The immediate effects of the partition proposal were dramatic. After its passage of the proposal, there were no negotiations between the two communities in Palestine—neither Jew nor Arab would acknowledge the existence of the other (Cunningham, 1948, p. 481)—and fighting immediately broke out. By April 1948, the better equipped and more numerous Jewish forces established a clear superiority, securing their recommended allotment while capturing territory assigned to the proposed Arab state. Civilians on both sides were targeted, but massacres of Arab villagers by Jewish irregulars precipitated an exodus of some 300,000 Arabs from their homes and villages.

On May 15, the day after Israel declared its independence, forces from Egypt, Syria, Lebanon, Jordan, and Iraq entered the fighting. Despite population differences, Israelis placed more soldiers in the field and had the advantage of working in familiar terrain under unified control. UN-sponsored truces in the summer provided belligerents the opportunity to re-arm, while the UN mediator, Count Folke Bernadotte of Sweden, recommended immediate repatriation of the Arab refugees as a condition for any just and lasting peace. His assassination in September by members of the Jewish underground was followed by renewed fighting in October which lasted until early 1949. When the last armistice was signed in July, the Israel Defense Forces (IDF) had taken approximately 78 percent of mandated Palestine, including the western part of Jerusalem and the Galilee. The remainder was occupied by Jordan (West Bank and East Jerusalem) and Egypt (Gaza Strip). Despite the fact that Resolution 181 called for a partition of Palestine into a Jewish state and an Arab state, Palestinian Arabs were not permitted to establish a state, neither in the portion of Palestine allotted to them in Resolution 181, nor in the remaining 22 percent of the territory that remained outside Israeli control.

At least 750,000 people—70 percent of the Palestinian Arab population—became refugees through flight or expulsion by Israeli forces.[27] The long-debated 'transfer' alternative (see Chapter 3, Section 3) had now become reality, and for Israeli Jews, it was the crucial opportunity for Judaizing the country. For the majority of Palestinian Arabs, the massive dislocation meant the loss of a homeland and destruction of a community: it was, quite simply, their Catastrophe (*al-Nakba*). A General Assembly Resolution 194 of 1948 stated that refugees 'should be permitted to return to their homes and live at peace with their neighbors,' and Bernadotte added: 'It would be an offence against the principles of elemental justice if these innocent victims of the conflict were denied the right to return to their homes, while Jewish immigrants flow into Palestine' (UN Doc Al 648, 1948). Chances for such peace in 1949 were lost when Israel refused Arab demands for withdrawal to the partition plan boundaries and return of refugees.[28]

In the area that fell under its control, Israel destroyed hundreds of Palestinian villages—531 by some estimates (Pappe, 2006a, p. xiii). Vast stretches of Palestinian land—nearly one quarter of the territory of Israel—were expropriated under the Absentees' Property Law (1950) which allowed the government to confiscate land vacated by owners after passage of the UN Partition Plan and transfer it to the control of the Jewish National Fund (Jiryis, 1981, pp. 83–7). Half the Palestinians who remained under Israeli control but were separated from their property as a result of hostilities were classified as 'present absentees' and lost their land in this fashion.

There can be little doubt that the political decisions of 1946–47 prohibited the legitimate residents of Palestine from exercising their right of self-determination, for the majority opposed a Jewish state on any part of Palestine. Even if one favors a national interpretation, it is arguable that the Palestinian Arabs had the better claim in 1947 since they constituted a two-to-one majority, had developed a national consciousness (Muslih, 1988; Khalidi *et al.*, 1991), and had a firmer and more recent historical association with the territory than the Jews, most of whom had only recently immigrated. The claim that General Assembly Resolution 181 conformed to the principle of self-determination because it recommended a partition with both sides receiving sovereignty over a portion of Palestine ignores the fact that the wishes of the majority of the population in 1947 were opposed to that plan, regardless if that majority is defined regionally or nationally. Although the International Court of Justice declared in 1950 that the Assembly was the legally qualified successor to the League of Nations with a right to carry out supervisory functions over the mandated territories, it emphasized that mandates were created in the interests of the inhabitants of the mandated territory (Toynbee, 1961–62, pp. 10–11; Brownlie, 1990, p. 567). Lacking sovereignty over Palestine, and lacking even the power to convey sovereignty, the recommendations of the General Assembly concerning Palestine are not binding (Brownlie, 1990, pp. 172–3). Resolution 181, like the League of Nations Mandate before it, violated the principle of self-determination (Cattan, 1969, 1976; Bassiouni, 1978; Mallison & Mallison, 1986)—one of the few mechanisms for establishing states by law rather than force (Crawford, 1979, pp. 84–5). At the very least, adherence to that principle would have called for a referendum or plebiscite on the partition proposal by the entire population of legitimate residents (Kapitan, 1995).

One cannot rightly argue that the moral claims of the opposing sides balanced each other out, and that while one group did not receive its due the other side did. Justice is a global property of a system, whether that system is a society, a social or political institution, or a solution to an outstanding dispute. It is not a distributive property of the parts, and it cannot be partial, attending to the interests of one party alone while ignoring the remainder. Resolution 181 did not conform to the demands of justice by granting one side in the dispute over Palestine its 'due,' because so doing entailed that the other side would not receive its 'due.' Without the consent of the majority of inhabitants, this skewed allocation of benefits laid the groundwork for Middle East tensions that have endured to this day.[29]

10. The expansion of Israel

> The acceptance of partition does not commit us to renounce Trans-jordan. One does not demand from anybody to give up his vision. We shall accept a state in the boundaries fixed today—but the boundaries of Zionist aspirations are the concern of the Jewish people and no external factor will be able to limit them. David Ben-Gurion (Flapan, 1987, pp. 52–3)

The first century of the Israeli–Palestinian conflict was marked by explicit violations of the principle of self-determination. The same pattern has been perpetuated throughout the next six decades as well, despite negotiated agreements and the passage of numerous United Nations resolutions calling upon the world community to recognize the Palestinians' right to self-determination.[30]

By contrast, in the years since Israel's declaration of statehood, the Jewish citizens of Israel have enjoyed a considerable measure of self-determination: they have constituted themselves as a nation-state with membership in the UN, they are self-governing in the territory controlled by that state, and they enjoy democratic rights of political participation. Similarly, the Palestinian Arabs who became citizens of Israel—now constituting almost 20 percent of Israelis—have gained rights of political participation and legal representation within the Israel political and legal systems. However, the Palestinians lack many of the privileges and benefits allowed to the Jewish majority, and their status as citizens is not as secure as that of Jews. By law, Israel is a state *of* the Jewish people, and on January 24, 2007, the Knesset passed a law allowing the Israeli government to revoke the citizenship of citizens considered unpatriotic to the Jewish state of Israel, a measure that the Israeli Attorney General called 'a drastic and extreme move' that harms civil liberties and that violates international law ('Jewish State Passes New Racist Law against Arab Israelis,' January 22, 2007, 'Israeli Knesset passes law to revoke citizenship of unpatriotic Israelis,' http://www.palestinecampaign.org/archives.asp?xid=1878; date of access: July 23, 2007).

Nothing approaching sovereignty was gained by a Palestinian community either inside or outside Israel. The refugees from the 1947 to 1949 war lost their land and homes and political rights in their homeland, and no Palestinians have been incorporated into a state governed by Palestinians. Some individual Palestinians gained political prominence in neighboring Jordan, and from 1967 to 1982, the PLO exercised some measure of political power in selected regions of Jordan and Lebanon, but in neither case did this occur through the exercise of equal political participation or popular sovereignty. Despite the establishment of a Palestinian Authority in the occupied territories in 1993, Palestinians have been largely excluded from governing themselves apart from limited municipal control in their cities and villages.

During the 1967 war, the area under Israel's control expanded as the Gaza Strip, the Golan Heights, the West Bank, and East Jerusalem came under Israeli military occupation. The occupation of the West Bank and Gaza Strip ushered in a new era of restrictions upon the Palestinian residents of these areas and an ever-increasing loss of control over their own destiny. While Israel has justified its occupation in terms of security, it has effectively amounted to a series of steps towards Judaizing the entire territory of mandated Palestine. Some of the more apparent features of this occupation illustrate how it, thereby, constitutes a further denial of self-determination for Palestinians in their homeland:

- Confiscation of Palestinian land, both private and public. As of 2006, over half the land of the West Bank is directly controlled by Israel and reserved for exclusive Israeli use.
- Destruction of Palestinian private property (e.g., houses, business establishments, and trees).
- Establishment of Jewish settlements. Over 42 percent of the West Bank is part of the settlement network containing over 210,000 Jewish settlers with at least another 180,000 living on the outskirts of Jerusalem. The settlement network is served by an extensive road system that Arab residents are prohibited from using.
- Control over resources; Israel obtains one-third of its water from West Bank aquifers which also supplies its settlement network, while restricting the availability of water for Palestinian use.
- Restrictions on the Palestinian economy.
- Restrictions on movement by Palestinians within the territories.
- Human rights abuses in the form of extra-judicial killings, torture, deportations, collective punishment, and imprisonment without trial.
- Taxation without representation.
- Restrictions on Palestinians' rights to equal political participation in deciding upon the political and legal institutions and policies that determine their own future.[31]

The policies and practices that constitute Israel's occupation stand in direct violation of international humanitarian law, specifically, the Fourth Geneva Convention dealing with the rights of civilians in wartime, instituted to criminalize formally the sorts of crimes committed by the Nazis in occupied Europe. Israel has denied that the Convention applies to the occupied territories because the legal status of these 'disputed territories' is *sui generis* and Palestinian residents there are neither partners nor beneficiaries of the Geneva conventions (Hajjar, 2006, p. 26). Yet, its applicability to the Israeli-occupied territories has been repeatedly affirmed by all other states that have indicated a view on the matter (Quigley, 2005, p. 170) and by UN Security Council resolutions, for instance, 446 (1979), 465 (1980), and 1322 (2000).

With its extensive settlement network, its refusal to withdraw to the 1949 armistice lines, its hostile treatment of the Palestinian residents, and its reluctance to enter into meaningful negotiations with the Palestinians (see Chapter 3), Israel shows every intention in remaining in the West Bank. The real question is the extent of the territory it will attempt to incorporate into the Jewish state. One political faction has traditionally supported the Alon Plan which involves retention of up to 40 percent of the West Bank, while the other plan is to incorporate all the territory into Israel and work for the eventual 'transfer' of the Palestinians to locations outside the country, thereby completing the ethnic cleansing that began in 1948 (Reinhart, 2002, p. 197). But aside from ultimate intent, the net effect of Israeli occupation policies has been to perpetuate the systematical denial of the rights of self-determination belonging to the Palestinian residents of the territories.[32]

11. The façade of self-determination

On November 15, 1988, by the Palestinian National Council, the legislative body of the PLO, prompted by the outbreak of the Intifada in the Occupied Territories, unilaterally declared a Palestinian state, an acceptance of the UN Partition Proposal, and a readiness to recognize the State of Israel. Ten years later, the PLO Central Council reaffirmed Arafat's earlier pledge to the American President Clinton that 'all of the provisions of the [PLO] Covenant which are inconsistent with the PLO commitment to recognize and live in peace side-by-side with Israel are no longer in effect.' (Abraham, 2006, pp. 120–1). In 1991, under American pressure, the two sides faced each other across the negotiating table, and the first tangible compact was the Declaration of Principles signed in Oslo in 1993, followed by subsidiary agreements within the next five years. These agreements set forth a framework that to some observers, represented a genuine change in the opportunities for self-determination by Palestinians in the occupied territories. Palestinians were granted increased autonomy over their own local affairs, specifically, over the day to day matters of local government, economy, education, police, and so on. As Israeli troops were redeployed outside the Palestinian population centers, Palestinians gained direct control of 17.2 percent of West Bank and 60 percent of Gaza, and another 23 percent of West Bank fell under joint Israeli–Palestinian control. Most importantly, there was a call for a five-year period of negotiation on a final settlement.

The promise of progress towards a peaceful resolution of the conflict soon turned sour. The Oslo agreements of 1993 and 1995 guaranteed nothing concerning the removal of Israeli settlements, the establishment of a Palestinian state, or the return of Palestinian refugees. Israel, the stronger party, fully backed by an even stronger party, the United States, was able to determine how the Oslo principles were to be realized, if at all. It retained control over half the West Bank and a third of the Gaza Strip it had already confiscated, and during the years 1993–2000, it strengthened its settlement network, nearly doubling the number of settlers, expanding the road system connecting the settlements with each other and Israel, and approving the construction of new settlements outside Jerusalem. By controlling movement between the areas governed by the Palestinian Authority, Israel was able to restrict the movement of goods—in violation of the Oslo accords (Pappe, 2004, p. 246)—with the result that Palestinians' freedom of movement, access to markets, and overall economy diminished significantly during these years (Roy, 2007, chaps. 5, 10, 15). The percentage of Palestinian living below the poverty line increased, and because a fewer number of Palestinians were allowed to work in Israel and the Palestinian work force grew, unemployment rates tripled. The gross domestic product in the territories declined while in all surrounding countries it increased. In effect, the Oslo Accords gave Palestinians in the territories limited control over their internal affairs while allowing the Israelis to consolidate their hold on the West Bank, expand their settlements, and stifle the Palestinian economy. As one observer put it, the 'lasting legacy of the Oslo process is that far from advancing the two-state solution, it in fact laid the groundwork for the fragmentation of the occupied territories' (Abunimah, 2006, p. 67).

It is significant that the Oslo Accords did not mention a right of self-determination for Palestinians. According to Shlomo Ben-Ami, former foreign minister of Israel, neither Yitzhak Rabin nor Shimon Peres want a Palestinian state (Ben-Ami, 2006, p. 220), and Rabin 'never thought this will end in a full-fledged Palestinian state' (interview in *Democracy Now!* February 5, 2006). To use the words of Israeli Prime Minister Ehud Barak, the agreements were a recipe for Israeli establishment of a 'permanent neocolonial dependency' (Chomsky, 2003, p. 215).

In July 2000, U.S. President Clinton brought the two sides together at Camp David in an ill-prepared attempt to achieve a final agreement. According to some reports, Israel offered the Palestinians limited sovereignty in approximately 86 percent of the West Bank and Arab neighborhoods surrounding East Jerusalem, but insisted on keeping the major settlements in place and retaining security control over those settlements, the roads connecting them, and the borders (Swisher, 2004, pp. 318–9). In principle, this would mean that Israel would continue to control all movement in the territories to and from the regions under the limited Palestinian sovereignty. The Palestinians rejected that plan. While much of the English-speaking media declared that the Palestinians blew the very 'generous' Israeli offer, in truth, there was no way that the Palestinians could have accepted that plan, for the degree of control that Israel would have retained would have prohibited the establishment of a viable, contiguous Palestinian state. The West Bank territory that Israel insisted on annexing would completely surround East Jerusalem, effectively splitting the West Bank into two main cantons with access between them and to Jerusalem under Israeli control. Thus, the 'state' that Palestinians were offered would be characterized by,

- no territorial contiguity;
- no control of external borders;
- limited control of its own water resources;
- no full Israeli withdrawal from occupied territory as required by international law;
- no sovereignty over East Jerusalem;
- a right of Israeli forces to be deployed in the Palestinian state at short notice;
- the continued presence of fortified Israeli settlements and Jewish-only roads within the heart of the Palestinian state.

As John Mearsheimer wrote, 'it is hard to imagine the Palestinians accepting such a state. Certainly no other nation in the world has such curtailed sovereignty.'[33] President Clinton's assistant for Israeli–Arab affairs, Robert Malley, who was present at the talks, blamed Israeli Prime Minister Barak for the failure, claiming that 'Barak's tactics helped to ensure that the parties never got there' (Malley & Agha, 2001, Section 7). In an article entitled 'Fictions About the Failure of Camp David' (*The New York Times*, July 8, 2001), Malley wrote:

> Many have come to believe that the Palestinians' rejection of the Camp David ideas exposed an underlying rejection of Israel's right to exist. But consider the facts: The Palestinians were arguing for the creation of a Palestinian state based on the June 4, 1967, borders, and living alongside Israel. They accepted the notion of Israeli annexation of West Bank territory to accommodate settlement blocs. They accepted the principle of Israeli sovereignty over the Jewish neighborhoods of East Jerusalem—neighborhoods that were not part of Israel before the Six Day War in 1967. And, while they insisted on recognition of the refugees' right of return, they agreed that it should be implemented in a manner that protected Israel's demographic and security interests by limiting the number of returnees. No other Arab party that has negotiated with Israel—not Anwar Sadat's Egypt, not King Hussein's Jordan, let alone Hafez al-Assad's Syria—ever came close to even considering such compromises.

Talks between the two sides continued until the end of January 2001. Some progress was made, as the Israelis and Palestinians edged closer to a negotiated settlement. The principle of a return of the equivalent of 100 percent of the territory captured in 1967 was agreed upon and the Palestinians agreed that major West Bank settlement blocks could remain in exchange for land in Israel. The Palestinians would recognize a Jewish state on 78 percent of mandated Palestine, far beyond the 56 percent allotted in 1947 UN Partition Resolution, and would agree that their own state, with limited arms, would be established in Gaza and at least 92 percent of the West Bank. Both sides would have capitals in Jerusalem, with Palestinians having sovereignty over Arab neighborhoods in East Jerusalem and Israel retaining control of Jewish neighborhoods. Both sides agreed that a just settlement of the refugee issue was essential (Moratinos, 2001; date of access: March 4, 2007). However, before any agreement was reached, the Israeli Government withdrew from these talks on January 27, 2001, and two weeks later, the Likud bloc, which had been opposed even to the concessions of the Oslo Accords, unseated Prime Minister Barak's government in Israeli elections.

There are competing accounts of what happened during the negotiations that lasted from the summer of 2000 to January 2001 (see, e.g., the contrasting descriptions in Ross, 2004; Ben-Ami, 2006, on one hand, Malley & Agha, 2001; Reinhart, 2002; Swisher, 2004 on the other). But in the end, despite the agreements during the decade of negotiations that began in Madrid in 1991 and ended in Taba in 2001, the facts remain that (i) the Palestinians expressed a willingness to recognize a Jewish state within 78 percent of Palestine in exchange for a Palestinian state in the remaining 22 percent, and (ii) the Israeli Government has steadfastly refused to allow Palestinians to establish a viable state throughout the occupied territories. Bent on territorial expansion, Israel has always been a 'reluctant partner to peace' (Moaz, 2006, p. 479 and chap. 10, *passim*), Oslo or no Oslo.

Some have seen signs of Israel's willingness to allow Palestinian self-determination with its evacuation of its settlements and troops from the Gaza Strip in 2005. But this observation must be balanced against facts on the ground. For one thing, Israel continues to control the borders, airspace, and territorial waters and has not allowed the international airport in Gaza to open. It retains control of the Palestinian population registry enabling it to determine who is a resident of Gaza and who can come and go. Israel manages most elements of the taxation system and regulates the goods that go in and out of Gaza, and its frequent closures of the main cargo terminal at the Karni crossing point have had a devastating impact on the Gazan economy. By mid-2006, more than half of Gaza's population was on emergency food aid. Israel regularly shells and conducts armed incursions into Gazan neighborhoods, killing over 400 Gazans in 2006 alone including 88 children.[34]

More significantly, the withdrawal of 8500 Jewish settlers from Gaza was paralleled by expansion in the West Bank as the Israeli Government seized more land, enlarged some existing settlements, and moved some 14,000 Jewish settlers into the West Bank (*Guardian*, October 18, 2005). Since 2002, Palestinian self-determination in the West Bank has been further eroded by the construction of a massive eight-meter high wall, the bulk of which is within the West Bank—not on the Green Line (the border between the West Bank and Israel)—that will eventually extend for some 720 kilometers. Israeli officials portray the wall as a defensive measure for separating the two communities and protecting Israeli citizens from terrorism. In actual fact, it is another intensification of colonial control. By 2005, over 200,000 dunums of Palestinian land had been confiscated for construction of the wall and 100,000 trees destroyed (Finkelstein, 2005, p. 292). When completed, 14.5 percent of West Bank territory will be carved off, and 274,000 Palestinians will live in a 'closed area' that they cannot move in or out of without special permits, though Israeli settlers living in the same area will be free to move to and from the area without a permit. This is not a 'separation fence,' as sometimes called, since there will be Israelis on both sides of it. It is more akin to a prison wall, with guard towers, having the effect of enclosing centers of Palestinian population within increasingly smaller bantustan-like regions (Carter, 2006, chap. 16). Already, the town of Qalqiliya of some 40,000 people is completely surrounded by this wall, with only one gate that the Israelis can close at will, and Bethlehem is enclosed on three sides. Both communities have been affected by the closure of hundreds of shops and businesses within the proximity of the wall. It is accompanied by permanent checkpoints and sporadic travel bans that severely curtail freedom of movement throughout the West Bank (Amira Hass, 'IDF Cantonizes West Bank, sealing 800,000 Palestinians,' *Ha'aretz*, January 13, 2006). According to reports by B'tselem, the Palestinian economies in these regions will suffer even further as the West Bank becomes increasingly Bantusized and it becomes impossible to move goods without permits. In January 2005, the Israel Knesset agreed to allow the Absentee Property Law to apply to East Jerusalem, allowing the State of Israel to seize land owned by Palestinians who live elsewhere or who are cut-off from their own land by the construction of the wall. This precedent means that the Law could be used to seize land all along the new border being created by the construction of the Wall.[35]

In 2004, emphasizing the 'inadmissibility of the acquisition of territory by war' and the illegality of Israeli settlements, the International Court of Justice ruled that the wall is 'a violation of the legal principle prohibiting the acquisition of territory by the use of force' and that 'the de facto annexation of land interferes with the territorial sovereignty and consequently with the right of the Palestinians to self-determination.' Moreover, as it contributes to the departure of Palestinians from certain areas, the wall severely impedes the exercise by Palestinians of their right to self-determination and, therefore, constitutes a breach of Israeli's obligation to respect that right.[36] Yet, Israel rejected the Court's ruling. and the Israeli High Court upheld the 'legality' of the wall on security grounds (Lynk, 2005).

The settlements, the army bases, the roads, and the wall will allow Israel to annex half of the West Bank by 2010. If the past four decades of occupation are any indication of the future, Palestinians within those areas are likely to be subjected to 'daily abusive and dehumanizing mixed mechanisms of army and bureaucracy' which are 'as effective as ever in contributing its own share to the dispossession process' (Pappe, 2007). It is neither surprising nor inaccurate, then, to see Israel's colonial rule in the West Bank described as a system of apartheid.[37]

12. What the principle of self-determination calls for

> Israel at fifty is undoubtedly one of the greatest success stories of the twentieth century. Communism, fascism, socialism, and so many other 'isms' have crumbled into dust. But Zionism, the national liberation movement of the Jewish people, the one true liberation movement amidst so many false ones, has far from crumbled. It has achieved its central purpose of securing Jewish independence in the Jewish land, and it can look to the future and its challenges with confidence.
> Benjamin Netanyahu (2000, preface)

> The decision to partition Palestine by the creation of the Jewish state is one of the most considerable mistakes of contemporary politics. Some very surprising consequences are going to result from an apparently small thing. Nor is it offensive to reason to state that this small thing will have its part to play in shaking the world to its foundations.
> Michel Chiha (1969, p. 52)

The systematic violation of the principle of self-determination in Palestine has been both a failure to observe a recognized moral norm and a continuing source of the conflict between Israelis and Palestinians, Jews and Arabs, and the West and Islam. What some see as 'one of the greatest success stories' of the twentieth century, is arguably one of its major political mistakes, for the decision to create a Jewish state in the Near East against the will of the vast majority of people who live in that region, has not only fueled the conflict between Israeli Jews and Palestinian Arabs, it has contributed to tensions between the Western and Islamic worlds that threaten global stability. In this sense, Wilson's warning of the 'peril' of ignoring the principle of self-determination was prophetic; if a political arrangement or settlement of a political conflict is to endure, then the people immediately affected must not view it as unjust, and if imposed from the outside it too easily falls prey to the allegations of injustice. As Wilson said, self-determination is not a 'mere phrase' or an idle expression of an utopian ideal. Deliberately ignoring the consent of a collective can be disastrous as evidenced by a recent study of Robert Pape that concludes that 'suicide terrorism is mainly a response to foreign occupation' seeking control over 'the territory the terrorists view as their homeland' (Pape, 2005, pp. 23, 79).

> suicide terrorist campaigns are directed toward a strategic objective: from Lebanon to Israel to Sri Lanka to Kashmir to Chechnya, the sponsors of every campaign—18 organizations in all—are seeking to establish or maintain political self-determination. (Robert Pape, 'Blowing Up an Assumption,' *The New York Times*, May 16, 2005)

In view of Pape's data, respecting a right of self-determination is as much a matter of prudence as it is of morality.[38]

While ignoring the principle of self-determination has exacerbated the Israeli–Palestinian conflict, the question now to be considered is whether it is still relevant to resolving this conflict. To an extent, what has been done cannot be erased; the clock cannot be turned back to 1947, nor to 1917, nor, perhaps, to 1967. But despite the League of Nations Mandate, the General Assembly Resolution 181, the creation of the state of Israel, and 40 years of military occupation, there remains opportunity for remedy and repair. There are those on both sides of the conflict that are interested in a just and peaceful compromise. In this respect, the principle of self-determination remains as relevant as ever for the simple reason that denying legitimate demands for self-determination by either party is guaranteed to perpetuate the struggle into the foreseeable future. Even if the principle does not entail a particular solution—for example, various types of two-state solutions or a single binational state (Tilley, 2005; Young, 2005; Abunimah, 2006; Yiftachel, 2006)—it nevertheless places a constraint on what counts as a just solution. No state, institution, or law is legitimate unless it can be anchored within the consent of the people it governs. No solution to a political conflict within a territory is either just or secure unless it is responsive to the wishes of the legitimate residents of that territory. For these reasons, the maximalist proposals for either a Jewish-only state or an Arab-only state throughout Palestine are objectionable, since either would entail a denial of self-determination to substantial numbers of legitimate residents of the region. And, as is patently obvious from the preceding sections, the observance of self-determination is also incompatible with the *status quo* in Palestine.

In what precise region is the principle to be applied? This question is more sensitive. The evidence shows that the West Bank and

Gaza qualify as both unsettled and endangered regions whose residents are non-standard beneficiaries of the right of self-determination distinguished in Section 3 above.[39] The situation regarding the rest of Palestine is less clear. One might argue as follows. The rights of self-determination are being realized in what became the state of Israel in 1948–49, for both the Palestine Mandate was itself an application of the principle of self-determination and the General Assembly Resolution 181 merely confirmed the 'natural and historic right' of the Jewish people in Palestine (N. Feinberg, 1970; Stone, 1981). That the Arabs of Palestine later distinguished themselves as a national group with a claim for self-determination—and not until the 1960s according to these writers—is 'neither a juridical nor moral basis for undoing that initial application of President Wilson's self-determination principle after World War I' (Stone, 1981, p. 58). That the agreements leading to the establishment of Israel have received international sanction, quite apart from their moral merits, creates a *prima facie* obligation to respect them. For another thing, the citizenry of Israel and hence, its government, do exercise rights to self-determination insofar as enfranchisement, popular sovereignty, recognition, and non-intervention are observed. Any political solution that would deny Israeli citizens their right to determine their political future, or curtail the sovereignty of their government, would violate their rights of self-determination as standard beneficiaries. For this reason, it appears that it is an exceptional application of the principle of self-determination at best that is relevant to the Israel–Palestinian conflict, and this only in regards to the occupied West Bank and Gaza Strip, not to the whole of historic Palestine.

There are at least three shortcomings with this argument. In the first place, it sidesteps the fact that Israel exists only because Palestinian Arabs have been systematically denied self-determination ever since 1917—and Palestine is the only territory placed under a League of Nations Mandate in which the established inhabitants were not granted this privilege. Given the Palestinians' persistent attachment to their ancient homeland, their outstanding grievances, the unresolved status of Palestinian refugees, and the repeated international recognition of their entitlement to self-determination in Palestine, then the *status quo* in the largest segment of historic Palestine cannot be sanctioned by appeal to a default application of the principle of self-determination to standard beneficiaries. To do so would be a mockery of that principle. Because the Palestinians Arabs constitute a politically coherent group with an acknowledged connection to Palestine as such, and not just to the West Bank and Gaza, then they retain an entitlement to being self-determining in that region—again, not *qua* Palestinians, but *qua* legitimate residents. That force was used against them has not erased the fact that they are, and are recognized as being, a legitimate unit entitled to participate in their own self-determination (Crawford, 1979, p. 117; Cattan, 2000, chap. 34).[40]

Second, in assuming that the only unsettled or endangered region containing exceptional beneficiaries is the remaining 22 percent of mandated Palestine, the argument ignores the fact that between 3.2 and 4.8 million Palestinians live outside the territory of mandated Palestine, yet, remain as interested parties to the conflict (see Chapter 2). Most of these individuals have no claim to be legitimate residents of the West Bank or Gaza since they either were expelled from the 78 percent of Palestine that became the state of Israel or are the descendents of those refugees. Because expulsion does not remove one's right of residency, then these Palestinians also retain residency rights in those territories from which they were expelled. Since the original General Assembly Resolution 194, numerous other resolutions have recognized the Palestinians right of return, for example, Resolution 3236 (1974) which asserted the 'inalienable right of the Palestinians to return to their homes and property from which they have been displaced and uprooted,' and Resolution 52/62 (1997) stating that 'Palestine Arab refugees are entitled to their property and to the income derived there from, in conformity with the principles of justice and equity.' Rights of leaving and returning to one's country are also affirmed in Article 13 of the Universal Declaration on Human Rights and in Article 5 of the International Convention on the Elimination of All Forms of Racial Discrimination (1965) which stipulates that states must guarantee a right to return to one's country 'without distinction as to race, colour, or national or ethnic origin.' There may be degrees of such legitimacy, and priorities might have to be set to the disadvantage of those who have comfortably established themselves elsewhere, but the time gaps are not significant enough to deny the claims of dispossessed refugees.

Third, the argument assumes that Israel is a legitimate state and, therefore, that any exceptional application of the principle of self-determination to the whole of historic Palestine would violate the right of self-determination possessed by standard beneficiaries. On what grounds could Israel's legitimacy be questioned? From its inception, Israel has satisfied the minimal conditions necessary for the existence of a state, specifically, a permanent population, control over a territory in which that population resides, and sovereign government agencies exercising their powers on behalf of that population. Moreover, the facts that Israel is a democracy, is recognized by a large number of countries, and is a member of the United Nations are unquestionably strong reasons for concluding that it has acquired the status of a legitimate state. But, are these considerations enough to settle the issue of legitimacy? It is important to understand that a state's legitimacy concerns sovereign right and entitlement to recognition, and this goes beyond the mere factual matter of existence. Legitimacy can be examined on three fronts; whether the state was legitimately established, whether the state is rightly constituted, that is, whether its basic laws and institutions conform to minimal demands of justice, and whether it is inclusive, that is, whether its existence derives from the popular consent established through a mechanism that includes participation by all the legitimate residents of the territory it governs. Israel's legitimacy can be challenged at each levels.

I have argued above that the establishment of a Jewish state in Palestine violated the principle of self-determination. For some, this is enough to undermine any claim to current legitimacy. Yet, the establishment of a great many states has been oblivious to rights of self-determination of indigenous populations. States are born to both cheers and tears. As time passes, the mode of establishment becomes increasingly irrelevant to a state's legitimacy as it gains recognition, is a party to international agreements, develops its institutions, and extends its protection to newly born generations which had nothing to do with its emergence. Thus, failure to be legitimately established does not automatically undermine current legitimacy. After nearly 60 years, and numerous successes both internationally and domestically, doubts about Israel's current legitimacy due to the injustices of its establishment may have been overridden by time.

A state's legitimacy also depends also on its character. The former South Africa was condemned as an illegitimate state on the grounds of its discriminatory system of apartheid, and it was subsequently subjected to international sanctions that precipitated its downfall. Israel prides itself on being both a democracy and a Jewish homeland. While its Declaration of Independence asserts that it is 'the natural right of the Jewish people to lead, as do all other nations, an independent existence in its sovereign State,' it also proclaims that Israel 'will uphold the full social and political equality of all its citizens, without distinction of religion, race, or sex.' Still, Israel remains a Jewish state, even though approximately one-fifth of its citizens are non-Jews. Its official symbols are Jewish religious symbols, and statutes governing land ownership and the Law of Return explicitly favor Jews over non-Jews. As pointed out above, a 1985 amendment to the 1958 Basic Law of the Knesset specified that no political list of candidates for the Knesset will be permitted if negates 'the existence of the state of Israel as the state of the Jewish people,' and in January 2007, the Knesset passed a law whereby denying the Jewish character of Israel is an 'unpatriotic' act that can lead to the loss of citizenship. These provisions come as close as can be to declaring in law the exclusively Jewish character of Israel. It is a state of the Jewish people, not of all its citizens, a selective democracy that threatens equal protection under the law and equality of opportunity for all citizens. Successive Israeli governments have discriminated against Arabs in areas of education, municipal funding, economic development, and marriage (Jiryis, 1976; Lustick, 1980; Cook, 2006; Yiftachel, 2006), while in the occupied territories, Israel's discrimination and abuses of human rights has been condemned by human rights organizations around the world. The irony which has accompanied Zionism throughout remains; to solve one case of prejudice against a cultural minority it has effectively generated another. Unless some means can be found of harmonizing its national character with equitable relations to the Arabs and, the character of its symbols, laws, institutions, and policies will keep the question of Israel's legitimacy alive. More poignantly, if legitimacy precludes a state's basic institutions and laws from *de jure* discrimination, then the Jewish state—like any state whose institutions systematically discriminate in favor of one religious, ethnic, or national constituency to the detriment of others under its rule—is illegitimate.

Finally, a state's legitimacy also depends on whether it is exclusionary or not, that is, whether its continued claim to sovereignty is derived from the ongoing consent of the legitimate residents of the territory in which it is constituted. The state of Israel fails to meet this condition. The Palestinians who fled or were driven from their homes in 1947–49 did not lose their residency rights by force, nor have they lost them through international law, nor have they voluntarily abandoned their rights through subsequent political agreements. General Assembly Resolution 273 under which Israel was admitted to the United Nations on May 11, 1949, made its membership conditional on a commitment to respect 'unreservedly' U.N. resolutions pertaining to the Arab–Israeli conflict, including Resolutions 181 and 194. The latter concerned the rights of Palestinian refugees to return to their homes, a right that they still retain (as Halwani argues in Chapter 2). Had this resolution been observed, the balance between Jews and Arabs within Israel would likely be so different that the exclusively Jewish character of the state could not have been achieved on the basis of popular consent of the citizenry.

Since these refugees remain legitimate residents, then the state of Israel is exclusionary.

Note the argument. Israel is currently not a legitimate state. The reason is not because its establishment violated the principle of self-determination, nor because Israel is an ethnocracy (Yiftachel, 2006). Instead, its current illegitimacy is based on its continued refusal to allow exercise of the right of self-determination belonging to the legitimate residents of the territory it governs. To deny this conclusion is to deny either that the principle of self-determination places a constraint on state legitimacy or that Palestinians are legitimate residents of region under dispute. The first option is to jettison one of the fundamental tenets of modern political thought, while the second is simply incredulous given that Palestinians constitute half the population of present-day Palestine and that a good many Palestinians on the outside have a claim to being legitimate residents of this area as well.

Israel might become legitimate if it ceases discriminatory practices and gains recognition from the Palestinian population in the wake of a negotiated settlement. For these reasons, and because sovereignty throughout the entire territory of historic Palestine is contested by the parties to the Israeli-Palestinian conflict, then Palestine is both an unsettled and troubled region calling for an exceptional application of the principle of self-determination.[41] This is not to accord a right to Palestinian Arabs that Israeli Jews lack; the principle does not grant the Palestinian people as such a right of self-determination any more than it grants to Jews sovereignty over Palestine *qua* Jews. While both rights can be defended on the national interpretation of the principle, the regional interpretation defended above confers the right of self-determination upon the totality of legitimate residents, however else they might be characterized. To be sure, a full exercise of this right does not rule out recognition of either an Arab or a Jewish state, for though a single regional state might satisfy the requirements of self-determination, the vast majority of 'the people immediately concerned' might prefer a solution in terms of distinct nation-states. But that itself would be a result of applying the principle of self-determination interpreted regionally.

The normative discussion must not be stalemated by the fact that the fundamental principle for resolving disputes over sovereignty leaves us with options, otherwise we open the door to political chaos, violence, and the temporary rule by the strongest. If a reasonable compromise that respects the rights of both Arab and Jewish residents cannot be achieved, then radicalism on both sides is likely to intensify, with sobering consequences for everyone involved. Over 65 years ago, Alfred North Whitehead warned that the ideal visions of zealots and one-sided bargains in the dispute over Palestine 'spell disaster for the future' (Whitehead, 1939), and his predictions have been amply confirmed. If a just and lasting peace in the Middle East is to be achieved before another 65 years elapse, then Palestinian Arabs, like Israeli Jews, must be permitted to meaningfully participate in choosing the political institutions they are to be governed by in Palestine, whether in an independent state of their own or as part of a larger state. Short of that, war and atrocity, beyond what we have already seen, will become increasingly familiar—a prospect that the entire world should shudder to contemplate.

Notes

1. This argument was made in a report by the Executive Committee of the Arab Palestine Congress presented to Winston Churchill on March 28, 1921.
2. Porath (1974, p. 44) writes that Wadi al-Bustani was among the first Palestinian Arabs to publicize the apparent incompatibility of the Mandate with Article 22. In 1948, the Palestinians' Arab Higher Committee cited this article in justifying entrance of Arab states into Palestinian territory. For contrasting interpretations of the article, see Cattan (1976, pp. 65–8) and N. Feinberg (1970, pp. 41–4).
3. See Antonious (1965, p. 264). There is debate about what was promised to Arabs in the Hussein-McMahon letters. Two days after the agreement, McMahon wrote that the only areas excluded from Arab independence were 'portions on the Northern Coast of Syria' (Porath, 1974, p. 322). However, in a 1937 letter by MacMahon to the *Times*, he claimed that Palestine 'was not or was not intended to be included in the territories in which the independence of the Arabs was guaranteed in my pledge' and that this was understood by Sheriff Hussein (Stone, 1981, pp. 146–7). This interpretation does not agree with Lord Curzon's view, nor with the description of Hussein's views by Lloyd-George who wrote that MacMahon himself was then (in 1915) 'very reluctant' to discuss boundaries despite the insistence of Hussein to include all the area along the eastern Mediterranean coast up to Mersina, an area which incorporates Palestine even though it was not mentioned by name (Lloyd-George, 1939, pp. 660–2). See also the discussions in Antonious (1965, chap. 9) and Smith (1996, pp. 43–9, 56–9). On the interpretation of the agreement as a treaty, see Porath (1974, p. 46).
4. An individual's right to political participation is mentioned in Article 21 (1) of the *Universal Declaration of Human Rights* (1948), and it is noteworthy that item (3) of this article is the principle of popular sovereignty. Article 25 of the *Covenant on Civil and Political Rights* (1966) is the closest that international law comes to granting an individual a right of self-governance. De George (1990) argues that any right of collective self-determination is at

best derived from the moral right of individuals to be autonomous, namely, when individuals autonomously decide to act collectively.

5. See Ofuatey-Kodjoe (1977, pp. 156–9) and Copp (1997, pp. 288–91). Copp adds that the group must have a 'stable and widespread desire among its members that it constitute a state' (1997, p. 293). This is more controversial. Not only might there be significant differences within a group with no clear majority for a single state, but majority preference can fluctuate over time, making it dubious as a necessary condition for a group's right to be self-determining.
6. Margalit and Raz describe national groups as 'self-encompassing groups' whose members self-consciously share a cultural identity vital in determining the self-identity of each (Margalit & Raz, 1990). Ernst Renan also mentioned that a group must feel itself to be distinct, and that there must be a desire on the part of its members to live together and interrelate within the framework of their common culture (cited in Dahbour & Ishay, 1995, p. 153). Yael Tamir writes that by belonging to a nation, an individual is consciousness of his or her cultural identity and is able to recognize other individuals as sharing in that identity (Tamir, 1991, pp. 573–4). It is this self-consciousness, she insists, that distinguishes a 'nation' from a 'people.' Copp argues for another objective characteristic, namely, that a group is a nation only if it 'has' a territory within which it could constitute a state (1997, p. 289). There is some doubt about what it is for a group to 'have' a territory, but the existence of refugee populations raises a problem if this characteristic is proposed as a necessary condition.
7. This point is made by several writers, for example, Buchanan (1991, pp. 22–80, 151–62) and Gellner (1983), and see also Tamir (1993, p. 158) and Miller (1995, pp. 108–10) which are otherwise supportive of a nationalist principle.
8. Arguments for the regional interpretation of self-determination within international law can be found in both Ofuatey-Kodjoe (1977, chap. VII) and Crawford (1979, pp. 84–106). There is no doubt, however, that Wilson's own language, for example, his reference to 'peoples' and his employment of 'national aspirations,' did lend itself to a nationalistic interpretation. Cobban (1945, pp. 19–22) argues that Wilson applied a criterion of nationality in promoting self-determination, an interpretation which he underscores by citing Wilson's own Secretary of State, Robert Lansing. The latter's reception of Wilson's principle was anything but sanguine: 'The more I think about the President's declaration as to the right of "self-determination," the more convinced I am of the danger of putting such ideas into the minds of certain races. It is bound to be the basis of impossible demands on the Peace Congress and create trouble in many lands. What effect will it have on the Irish, the Indians, the Egyptians, and the nationalists among the Boers?... How can it be harmonized with Zionism, to which the President is practically committed? The phrase is simply loaded with dynamite. It will raise hopes that can never be realized. It will, I fear, cost thousands of lives. In the end it is bound to be discredited, to be called the dream of an idealist who failed to realize the danger until too late to check those who attempt to put the principle in force. What a calamity that the phrase was ever uttered! What misery it will cause!' (Lansing, 1921, pp. 97–8). Curiously, while the

reference to 'races' suggests a national interpretation, the passage—which Cobban did not cite in full—can also be read as though Lansing thought that Wilson's 'idealistic' principle was oblivious to national demands for autonomy, especially given Lansing's contrast between Zionism, an exclusively nationalistic movement, and what he took Wilson to be calling for. In a conversation with the American Supreme Court Justice Brandeis, Balfour was reported to have had great difficulty in seeing how President Wilson could possibly reconcile his adherence to Zionism with any doctrine of self-determination and he asked the Justice how he thinks the President will do it (Khalidi, 1971, pp. 197–8). See also Christison (1999, chap. 2), which argues that Zionism and Wilson's principle of self-determination could not be reconciled.

9. Wilson had spoken of self-determination in his own scholarly writings years before. In a 1901 paper, for instance, he spoke of the American Revolution as having 'struck a blow for all the world' for self-determined government (Notter, 1965, p. 118, 69, 100, pp. 110–1).
10. The possibility of dissolution arises when there are rival claims among subgroups of the population. Muhammad Ali Khalidi provides an interesting format for resolving the conflict in terms of what he calls a smallest region principle according to which a population of a region R1 has the right to self-determination if (i) a substantial majority of R1 desires self-determination and (ii) there is no smaller subregion R2 within R1 whose substantial majority desires to exercise self-determination independently of the rest of R1 (M. A. Khalidi, 1997, p. 79).
11. Seen in this way, the right of self-determination in endangered regions is similar to Locke's doctrine of the right to revolt, itself an offshoot of the theory of popular sovereignty, viz., that the legitimacy of government is based on the consent of the governed. Revolt can take the form of overthrowing a tyrannical or negligent government, or seceding from a larger political union. In both cases, the rationale is protection of individual rights from the intrusion of, or volition by, other individuals, institutions and, especially, governments. Buchanan (1997a, pp. 310–1), also lists 'past unredressed unjust seizure of territory,' and 'discriminatory redistribution' as grounds for secession. He calls this the 'remedial' or 'grievance' theory of self-determination (pp. 317–8). Norman (1998) also advocates a just cause theory of secession. Moore (2001, pp. 146–7) is well aware that this 'just case' justification of secession places the latter with a general framework of human rights, but her objections to this approach in favor of a nationalistic reading of self-determination are weak (pp. 147–53). The preferred mechanisms for initiating the exercise of self-determination by exceptional beneficiaries are referenda, specifically, plebiscites (see Cobban, 1945; Johnson, 1967; Umozurike, 1972; Farley, 1986).
12. Articles 18–20 of the Universal Declaration of Human Rights, and Articles 18, 19, 21, 22, and 27 of the Covenant on Civil and Political Rights are the closest that International Law comes to acknowledging an individual's rights to cultural participation. See Lichtenberg (1997) which discusses the attempt to base national self-determination on individual rights.
13. David Copp has argued that democratic philosophy grants self-determination to the entire population of a region, not to a preferred subclass

as the doctrine of national self-determination would have it (Copp, 1997, pp. 290–7). The ideals of democracy require that all individuals have similar rights, privileges, and responsibilities, including the rights and duties that go with of political participation in any society they inhabit. In short, a democratic society is one guided by a fundamental principle of equality, and it is precisely this principle that is endangered when a national state governs a culturally diverse population.

14. Amendment 9 of the Basic Law of the Knesset, passed in July 1985, prohibits a candidate's list from participating in elections if it includes 'negation of the existence of the State of Israel as the state of the Jewish people.' http://www.jewishvirtuallibrary.org/jsource/Politics/Basic_Law_Knesset.html (date of access: January 18, 2007). Emil Fackenheim writes that the Law of Return is next in importance to the Jewish essence of Israel as the Return itself (1988, p. 14). Michael Rice, on the other hand, finds the law to be 'a nakedly racialist concept' since it allows any Jew, from the Hungarian Banker to the Yemenite farmer, a right to immigrate to and become a citizen while denying the same to Palestinian indigenes to whom it stands as 'a most cruel affront' (Rice, 1994, pp. 41–2). See the brief, but interesting defense of the law in Margalit and Halbertal (1994, pp. 509–10).
15. Chances for interstate belligerency are raised when a given cultural minority within a state has strong cultural and political links to powerful communities on the outside. This was an important factor in Nazi propaganda towards expanding Germany, and is relevant to understanding the conflict among Palestinians and Israelis, since both parties have strong links to external communities, which give it the international dimension it has.
16. I found this passage from Joyce's novel in Beiner (1999, p. 1).
17. At the Paris Peace Conference in 1919, the World Zionist Organization presented a map of Palestine that incorporated southern Lebanon, the Golan Heights, and the east bank of the Jordan River (Pappe, 2006a, p. 288). Lloyd-George (1939, pp. 721–73) relates some of the controversies concerning the borders of Palestine that occurred during the years 1917–21.
18. See Khalidi 1971, p. 841.
19. This aspect of the Balfour Declaration was not accidental, as argued in Jeffries (1971). The role of the Zionist leadership in drafting the document is discussed in both Jeffries (1971) and Manuel (1971).
20. The King-Crane recommendations are reported is reprinted in Khalidi (1971, pp. 213–8). Zionists are fond of citing a January 3, 1919 agreement between the Emir Feisal of Mecca, a leader of the Arab resistance in 1915–18, and Chaim Weizmann. It called for Jewish immigration into Palestine provided that the rights of Arab farmers be protected and 'no religious test shall ever be required for the exercise of civil or political rights' (Stone, 1981, pp. 147–8). However, Feisal added that the agreement shall be void unless the Arabs achieve independence as promised by the British, and in a subsequent letter to Felix Frankfurter, an American Zionist, Feisal made it clear that Arabs would not accept a Jewish state as such but only a possible Jewish province in a larger Arab state (Khouri, 1976, p. 12). There was neither popular representation of nor support by Palestinian Arabs in the making of this agreement, as the results of the King-Crane Commission pointed out (see Hocking, 1945, reprinted in Khalidi, 1971, p. 502). To the contrary,

there was outright opposition (Muslih, 1988, chap. 5). In 1925, shortly after the Balfour Declaration had been incorporated into the terms of the 1922 Mandate for Palestine, the international lawyer, Quincey Wright, reported that Palestinian Arabs viewed the Declaration as a political decision constituting 'a gross violation of the principle of self-determination proclaimed by the Allies' (Quigley, 1990, p. 18).

21. In August 1922, the high commissioner of Palestine, Sir Herbert Louis Samuel, proposed establishment of a legislative council composed of 23 members: the high commissioner, ten appointed British members, and 12 elected members—ten Palestinians (eight Muslims and two Christians) and two Jews. The council would not have legislative authority over such central issues as Jewish immigration and land purchases. Palestinian leaders argued that participation in the council would be tantamount to acceptance of the British mandate and Balfour policy, which they opposed. They considered unfair the allocation of only 43 percent of the seats to Palestinians, who constituted 88 percent of the population, and they objected to the limitations placed on the power of the council. A campaign against the proposed council by the Palestine Arab Executive and the Supreme Muslim Council was a potent factor in the Palestinian boycott of the council elections in February 1923. The poor election turnout caused the high commissioner to shelve the proposal. The idea was revived repeatedly from 1923 until 1936. It was discussed, for example, in 1928 when a new high commissioner, Sir John Chancellor, took over, but it was derailed by the disturbances of 1929, only to reemerge as a proposal in the Passfield White Papers of 1930. Although the new proposal was similar to the 1922 proposal, the Palestinians this time did not oppose it, but the Jews rejected their minority role in the council. Intermittent discussions continued until 1935, but there was opposition from both sides to British suggestions. This opposition prompted the British government to once again suspend its implementation, and the concept finally died with the start of the Arab Revolt of 1936–39. See http://www.answers.com/topic/legislative-council-palestine.
22. Ben-Gurion echoed this argument: 'The conscience of humanity ought to weigh this: where is the balance of justice, where is the greater need, where is the greater peril, where is the lesser evil and where is the lesser injustice?' (Jewish Agency for Palestine, 1947, p. 325). In 1937, Jabotinsky made the same point in contrasting Arab preference with Jewish need: 'it is like the claims of appetite versus the claims of starvation' (Hertzberg, 1977, p. 562).
23. A related argument was anchored on the Lockean premise that the land belongs to those who develop it. It was popularized by Labor Zionists like A. D. Gordon (Taylor, 1974, p. 93) and Ben-Gurion (Gorny, 1987, p. 210), but also impressed the more conciliatory. For instance, Buber wrote, 'Ask the soil what the Arabs have done for her in 1300 years and what we have done for her in 50. Would her answer not be weighty testimony in a just discussion as to whom this land belongs?' (Shimoni, 1995, p. 348), and Hannah Arendt felt this argument was 'better and more convincing' than considerations of the Jews' 'desperate situation in Europe' (1978, p. 173).
24. There is evidence that a large segment of the Eastern European Jews are descended from the Khazars, a central Asian people who adopted Judaism as their religion and fled westward to escape the Mongol invasions (see the

sources cited in Quigley, 2005, pp. 70–1, p. 265). Wexler (1996) argues that Sephardic Jews descend from converts to Judaism in Asia, north Africa and the Iberian Peninsula. Thus, any constancy of historical presence or of right to 'return' belongs, at best, to a cultural unit, not to an ethnic community united by historical ancestry.

25. This point was made in the 1946 Anglo-American Committee's report (Esco Foundation, 1947, p. 1225). The American philosopher William Ernest Hocking wrote that the Zionist territorial demands were 'like asking for a microscopic section across one wrist' (1945, p. 222).
26. See the Jewish Agency for Palestine (1947, p. 110). Margalit (1997, p. 85) cites a similar consideration of Sir Isaiah Berlin, who justified Zionism because 'it would provide a home for a nation that has lost the feeling of being at home.'
27. The figure of 770,000 is given by Flapan (1987, p. 216), Morris sets it from anywhere between 600,000 and 760,000 (1987, p. 298), and Khalidi at 727,000 to 758,300 (1992, p. 582). For many years, defenders of Israel propagated the notion that the Arab refugees left their homes at the behest of Arab authorities, for example, Abba Eban in a 1958 speech (Laqueur, 1976, pp. 151–64). This myth has since been exposed in several sources, for example, Childers (1961), Khalidi (1971) (Introduction), Flapan (1987), Morris (1987), and Finkelstein (1995).
28. Israel countered that Arab countries had waged war in defiance of the international community and that they could absorb Arab refugees just as the Israel was now accepting Jewish refugees not only from Europe, but also from the Middle East and north Africa (numbering 335,000 from 1949 to 1952). The issue of 'boundaries' was not fully settled in any case. While officially accepting the principle of partition, Ben Gurion's diaries indicated another vision: 'Take the American Declaration of Independence, for instance... It contains no mention of the territorial limits. We are not obliged to state the limits of our State' (W. Khalidi, 1997, p. 17).
29. Chaim Weizmann said in 1944, after his meeting with President Roosevelt: 'I maintained the thesis that we could not rest our case on the consent of the Arabs; as long as their consent was asked, they would naturally refuse it' (Weizmann, 1966, p. 395). It is ironic that UNSCOP acknowledged that the League of Nations Mandate had violated the Palestinian Arabs right of self-determination and that the creation of a Jewish National Home in Palestine 'ran counter' to the principle of self-determination. See Quigley (2005, p. 33) who cites the *1947 Report on Palestine, Report to the General Assembly by the United Nations Special Committee on Palestine*, with a foreword by Senator Robert F. Wagner (pp. 115–6).
30. Since the 1967 War, numerous resolutions have used the language of 'self-determination: for example, G. A. Resolutions 2535 B of Dec. 10, 1969; 2649 of Nov. 30, 1970; 2672 C of Dec. 8, 1971; 2792 D of Dec. 6, 1971; 3210 of Oct. 14, 1974; 3236 of Nov. 22, 1974; 3376 of 1975; 34/65 of Nov. 1979; and more recently, UN-GA 52/114. A more complete list of resolutions on the Palestinian/Israeli conflict can be found in a Wikipedia entry on UN Resolutions Concerning Israel at en.wikipedia.org/wiki/List_of_the_UN_resolutions_concerning_Israel (date of access: January 23, 2007).

31. Information on these and other aspects of the Israeli occupation can be found at several websites, including those of the Israeli human rights organization B'tselem (http://www.btselem.org), the Palestine Monitor (http://www.palestinemonitor.org), and the Electronic Intifada (http:// electronicintifada.net).
32. A number of UN Security Council Resolutions which have condemned Israel's settlement program as contrary to Article 49 of the fourth Geneva Convention. Concurring discussions can be found in Mallison and Mallison (1986), Roberts (1990), and Quigley (2005). Israelis have contested these judgments (e.g., Stone 1981, pp. 177–81), but they stand alone on this matter. Eugene Rostow cites Stone in a letter to *The American Journal of International Law 84* (1990, pp. 717–20), in defending the legality of Israeli settlements. Robert's response to Rostow is gentle, but, for the most part, decisive (Roberts, 1990, pp. 720–2). For a more recent study, see Al-Rayyes (2000, pp. 85–92).
33. John Mearsheimer, 'The Impossible Partition,' *The New York Times*, January 11, 2001. See also the description of the Camp David talks by Clayton Swisher who concluded: 'Because of what was accepted as Camp David orthodoxy, better stated as the untruths of Camp David, the ideological advice provided by Bush's advisers filled the new president's intellectual vacuum, laying the groundwork for a destructive American Middle East policy that gives blanket endorsement to Sharon's unilaterialism and refusal to negotiate' (2004, p. 405).
34. These figures, as well as details about Israel's control over Gaza, are available from B'tselem website http://www.btselem.org/english. See also the sources cited in Abunimah (2006, pp. 84–6, 203–4) and 'Israel's invisible hand in Gaza' Alex Johnston, BBC News, January 17, 2007, http://news.bbc.co.uk/2/hi/middle_east/6270331.stm (date of access: January 20, 2007).
35. Upon hearing of the Knesset's decision, Hanna Nasser, mayor of Bethlehem, stated: 'This is state theft, pure and simple... When the Israel started building this wall, they stopped letting people use this land.' *The New York Times*, January 26, 2005. Effects of the wall on Palestinians are also documented in a report funded by the British Government ('Israeli separation barrier is cutting off Palestinians from their livelihood,' *The Independent*, January 27, 2007, http://news.independent.co.uk/world/middle_east/article2177982.ece (date of access: January 28, 2007).
36. The Court opined, 'The construction of the wall being built by Israel, the occupying Power, in the Occupied Palestinian Territory, including in and around East Jerusalem, and its associated régime, are contrary to international law,' and that 'all States parties to the Fourth Geneva Convention... have in addition the obligation, while respecting the United Nations Charter and international law, to ensure compliance by Israel with international humanitarian law as embodied in that Convention.' The Court also cited Article 2, paragraph 4 of the UN Charter, the Hague Regulation of 1907, and General Assembly Resolution 2625 (XXV) in which it is emphasized that 'no territorial acquisition resulting from threat or use of force shall be recognized as legal.' That resolution also stated that States have an obligation to promote the realization of the right of self-determination in conformity with provisions of the UN Charter. The Court stated 'international law in regard to non-self-governing territories, as enshrined in the

Charter of the UN, made the principle of self-determination applicable to all [such territories]' and that the right of peoples to self-determination is today a right *erga omnes*. The full text of the Court's ruling is available at http://www.icj-cij.org (date of access: September 7, 2006).

37. See, for example, books by Reinhart (2002), Davis (2004), Qumsiyeh (2004), and Carter (2006) and articles by Michael Ben Yair, 'The War's Seventh Day,' *Ha'aretz*, March 3, 2002; Shulamit Aloni, 'Indeed, there is Apartheid in Israel,' *Ynet*. http://www.ynet.co.il/articles/0,7340,L-3346283,00.html (date of access: February 27, 2007); Alan Johnston, 'UN envoy hits Israel 'apartheid,' BBC News, February 24, 2007, http://news.bbc.co.uk/go/pr/fr/-/2/hi/middle_east/6390755.stm (date of access: February 27, 2007); Anna Baltzer, 'From Sharpsville to Nablus: Tragedies of Ethnic Apartheid,' March 21, 2007, http://www.AnnaIntheMiddleEast.com (date of access: March 23, 2007); and Richard Waddington, 'UN rights envoy likens Israeli actions to apartheid,' Reuters, March 22, 2007 (date of access: March 23, 2007).
38. Pape's evidence goes against the suggestion in Halberstam (1994) that self-determination 'was never truly the issue' in the Arab–Israeli conflict, though territory is. Halberstam's mention of 'territory' is difficult to understand what this could mean apart from a dispute about who has the right to govern a territory. Her suggestions go against the three-decade-long international consensus that a two-state solution within mandated Palestine is the only way to end the Israeli–Palestinian conflict. Most of the international community accepts the claim that the Palestinians have a right to self-determination. In December 2003, for instance, the General Assembly passed a resolution 'affirming the rights of all states in the region to live in peace and within secure and international recognized borders,' and 'the right of the Palestinian people to self-determination, including the right their independent state of Palestine.' This passed by a vote of 169 for and 5 against the United States, Israel, Marshall Islands, Micronisia, Palau. A January 2004 resolution of the General Assembly called for self-determination for Palestinians. Both resolutions call for a withdrawal of Israeli forces from 'the Palestinian territory' (Finkelstein, 2005, pp. 293–4).
39. Who are the legitimate residents of the occupied territories? Certainly, the indigenous Palestinians qualify, but what about the Israeli inhabitants of the settlements? The problem is that these people came to populate the region only against the will of the established residents and in violation of international law, specifically, the Fourth Geneva Convention which prohibits an occupying power from relocating its own civilians into occupied territory. Hence, the settlers currently reside in the occupied territories illegally according to international law, and this discredits any claim of legitimate residency they might raise. If the political *status quo* endures, however, then with a sufficient lapse of time, their descendents, who had no choice about where they were born and raised, might acquire the status of legitimate residents of those territories. The settlers are not left out of the equation in any case, for they are currently legitimate residents of Israel and, hence, of any larger territory that might include present day Israel within a comprehensive political solution.

40. Several observers, for example, Cattan (1976), Mallison and Mallison (1986), Quigley (1990), Roberts (1990), and Boyle (2003), have argued that the *status quo* cannot be justified by any other aspects of international justice or law.
41. Even this observation does not settle the matter, for one might raise the question of an exceptional application of the principle of self-determination throughout a much broader territory. Much depends on what counts as an 'endangered' region (see Section 4 of this chapter), and while there is no clear criterion for settling this sticky normative question, it has to be remembered that the division of the Middle East into its current states was largely the result of foreign intervention. If we broaden our domain of concern from historic Palestine to surrounding regions, we cannot neglect the interests of a much larger group of people who may very well decide that their safety and well-being require a more comprehensive unified political arrangement throughout the Fertile Crescent and Arabian Peninsula—the region in which that Sheriff Hussein of Mecca sought self-determination in 1915. Indeed, population numbers, historical association, and the current economic, political, and military threats to the Middle Eastern peoples by aggressive Western powers lend force to arguments that the legitimate interests of Arabs require a measure of political and geographical unity throughout their traditional domain. Plainly, at this point in time, there is nothing in the principle of self-determination itself—as articulated above and as set forth in the relevant international documents—that restricts a potential exceptional application to historic Palestine, much less to the occupied territories alone.

2
The Right of Return

Raja Halwani

The Palestinian refugees are those Palestinians (now including their descendents) who in and around 1948 fled or were expelled from their homes and villages in pre-Israel Palestine, and which became part of Israel's territory. The right of return entails the option for these refugees to permanently return to the sites of their original lands and villages. It is one of the most contentious aspects of the Israeli–Palestinian conflict and one of its defining aspects. Indeed, there can be no genuine peace in the Middle East if left unresolved. This chapter achieves three connected tasks: (i) identifying the *nature* of the right of return; (ii) offering an argument for the *existence* of this right for both the first wave of Palestinian refugees and for their descendents; and (iii) showing that the right of return should be *implemented*.

The arguments of this chapter focus on the Palestinians and need not apply to other refugees. For instance, even though Section 3.3 discusses whether Jews also have a right of return to historic Palestine, it would stretch the term 'refugee' to consider the current Diaspora Jews to be refugees. Moreover, although the arguments have significant relevance to refugees rendered as such by the direct actions of other human beings, they would be difficult to apply to refugees who are so due to natural disasters, indirect human actions, or a combination of both (e.g., some forms of economic hardships).

The arguments do apply to all types of Palestinian refugees who fled or were expelled between 1947 and 1949, in the early 1950s, and after the 1967 war. Most reside in Lebanon, Jordan, Syria, the West Bank and the Gaza Strip, and Israel ('present absentees' under Israeli law), but some also in the rest of the world. This chapter, however, focuses on the refugees of the period from 1947 to the early 1950s, including those same people rendered refugees again during the 1967 war. I exclude the 1967 refugees because they are from villages in the West Bank and the Gaza Strip, two areas that are supposed to be part of a future Palestinian state. Hence, their return to these areas should not pose special difficulties (similarly for the nearly 100,000 Syrian refugees and their descendents driven out by Israel from the Golan Heights during the 1967 war).

1. Background

1.1. Numbers

There are about 3.7 million Palestinian refugees registered with the United Nations Relief and Works Agency (UNRWA). Over 1.2 million of them live in refugee camps in the West Bank, the Gaza Strip, Jordan, Lebanon, and Syria (Abunimah & Ibish, 2001, p. 6; see Map D).[1] However, the total number of refugees, including those not registered with UNRWA, is about 5 million (Abu Sitta, 2001a, p. 14).[2] The severity of the conditions of their lives varies depending on the host country and on other factors. Most Palestinian refugees became refugees between 1947 and 1949, the years centered around the Arab–Israeli war of 1948.[3] A number of potential solutions to the refugee problem have existed since the early 1950s. None succeeded.[4]

1.2. History

Between 1947 and 1949 (and, in smaller doses, in the early 1950s), about 800 000 Palestinians left their homes and villages for Lebanon, Syria, Jordan, and what are today the West Bank and the Gaza Strip (and to other Arab countries, such as Egypt, Libya, and Iraq) because of war. Some were directly attacked or expelled. Others were intimidated into leaving by fear, propaganda, whispering campaigns, and news of massacres by the Jewish militias who were fighting to bring Israel into existence.[5] Many Palestinians fled prior to Arab states attacking the newly formed state of Israel in May 1948. The Jewish militias' campaigns against the Palestinians began soon after the United Nations' November 1947 approval to partition historic Palestine into a Jewish state and an Arab state. Indeed, between November 1947 and May 1948, Jewish forces controlled over 200 towns and villages and expelled their inhabitants, who made up over 50 percent of the Palestinian refugees, in an attempt to take control not only of the territory designated by the United Nations as a Jewish state, rendering it as demographically Jewish as possible, but also of territories meant to be part of the Palestinian state, including the cities of Jaffa and Acre (Abu Sitta, 2001a, pp. 6–7;

Pappe, 2006a, chap. 5; see also Notes 3 and 32, and Map C). In the early 1950s, Israel continued the campaign of cleansing its area of control of Palestinians by expelling and evacuating people from a number of remaining Palestinian villages and Bedouin encampments (Morris, 1994, chap. 10; Morris, 1999, chap. 6; Pappe, 2006a, chap. 8). The refugees of 1947–49 and those of the early 1950s make up the first wave of Palestinian refugees.

1.3. Meaning of 'return'

'Return,' in the phrase 'right of return,' refers to the return of the refugees to the sites of their homes, villages, and lands in historic, pre-Israel Palestine from which they fled or were expelled. Excepting some of the 1967 refugees, the return is not meant to be a return to some future Palestinian state that might exist next to Israel. In this sense, implementing a two-state solution and having the Palestinian refugees return to a future Palestinian state would not be an implementation of the right of return, although it might solve the refugee problem. The right of return entails the option for refugees to come back, not close to Israel, but to the original homes and lands in Israel. This is, of course, why the Palestinian refugees' return is a contentious issue.

However, the term should not be narrowly understood to mean a return to the actual and original houses that existed prior to 1947. Israel declared some as vacant and allowed Jewish citizens to move into them, but most of these houses no longer exist as they were demolished by Israel. Thus, the return should be understood to mean a return to the village sites. For a less contentious demonstration of this nuance, suppose a hurricane destroyed my house. If I have a right to return, it would be wrong to say, 'Your house was destroyed and so your right of return is void.' A more reasonable claim is that I do have the right to return, but, because my house was destroyed, I will have to rebuild it. So the notion of 'return' should be understood to mean a return to the village sites and to the lands containing and surrounding them (more on this below). John Quigley puts it well: 'a right of return is not defeated by the fact that the area from which a person was displaced has changed in character. Reasonable accommodation must be made between the returnees and the current inhabitants' (1999, p. 161).

1.4. Israel's law of return

Israel has its own law regarding the Jews' return to Israel. On July 5, 1950, the Israeli Knesset (parliament) unanimously passed the Law of Return, a law basically allowing any Jewish person to become an Israeli citizen upon entry into Israel.[6] One possible justification for this law is that because Israel is the Jewish ancestral and historical homeland, and because Jews have lived in exile since ancient times, they have the right to return to Israel from wherever they are. As Shlomo Avineri puts it, 'It was because of [the Jews' link to the Land of Israel] that Jews were considered by others – and considered themselves – not only a minority, but a minority *in exile*' (1981, p. 3; emphasis is in original). In a sense, this justification claims that the Jews living in the Diaspora have always been refugees. Now that their country—Israel—has been reborn, they have a right to return to it. I mention the Law of Return at this juncture because we will need it for a discussion of further issues, such as whether it can be truly justified (Section 3), the statute of limitations (Section 2.4), and the one-state solution.

1.5. Palestinian and Israeli political positions

Historically, Palestinian political representatives, such as the Palestine Liberation Organization, have insisted on the existence and implementation of the right of return. Recently, however, there has been some wavering. In his op-ed piece in *The New York Times* (February 3, 2002), Yasser Arafat relied on the distinction between the existence of the right of return and its implementation, claiming, 'We understand Israel's demographic concerns and understand that the right of return of Palestinian refugees... must be implemented in a way that takes into account such concerns.' Although Mahmoud Abbas, the current president of the Palestinian Authority, announced on January 3, 2005, that the Palestinian refugees will be able to return one day ('Abbas Vows Refugees Will Be Able to Return,' *The Daily Star*, January 4, 2005), he changed his mind after becoming president, claiming that the right of return should be considered 'realistically,' meaning that it cannot be fully implemented (Amos Harel, 'Abbas to Announce New Stance on Right of Return,' *Ha'aretz*, March 14, 2005). Even Hamas (the Islamic Resistance Movement)—currently (2007) heading and constituting the Government—seems to be softening its position on all sorts of issues, including the right of return, due to international pressure. In a recent article by its leader-in-exile Khaled Mish'al, he merely claims that the right of return should be 'acknowledged' ('Our Unity Can Now Pave the Way for Peace and Justice,' *The Guardian*, February 13, 2007).

The Geneva Accords—an unofficial treaty agreed on by Yossi Beilin (Israeli leftist, former minister, and member of the Knesset) and Yasser Abd Rabbo (former minister in the Palestinian Authority), and signed in Geneva in November 2003—seem to declare the right of return, in effect, void.[7] Beilin stated, 'No Palestinian will enter Israel under a "right of return." There will be nothing like this. This does not exist in any document. There will be no right of return... there is no right of return in this agreement and there will be none' (Mazal Mualem, 'Beilin: No Right of Return in Geneva Accord,' *Ha'aretz*, October 14, 2003).

The Ayalon-Nusseibeh agreement ('The People's Voice')—jointly launched in June 2003 by Ami Ayalon (former chief of the Shin Beth internal security services of Israel) and Sari Nusseibeh (Palestinian intellectual and head of Al-Quds University)—straightforwardly annuls the right of return, by stipulating that the 3.7 million registered Palestinian refugees could return only to a future Palestinian state, not to their original villages inside Israel.[8] Other recent agreements, such as the Oslo Accords of 1993 and the more recent U.S.-backed Road Map, relegate the right of return to final status issues. This is a mistake since the right of return is one of the defining features of the conflict (Al-Qasem, 1999, pp. 142–5).

The official Israeli position has been a refusal to acknowledge the right of return, with occasional willingness to allow a small number of refugees to return on humanitarian and family reunion grounds. In 1961, for example, David Ben-Gurion, Israel's first prime minister, stated, 'Israel categorically rejects the insidious proposal for freedom of choice for the refugees, for she is convinced that this proposal is designed and calculated only to destroy Israel. There is only one practical and fair solution... to resettle them among their own people in countries having plenty of good land and water and which are in need of additional manpower' (quoted in Arzt, 1997, pp. 133–4). More recently, Ehud Barak, another Labor Israeli prime minister, stated, 'We cannot allow even one refugee back on the basis of the "right of return." And we cannot accept historical responsibility for the creation of the problem' (Morris, 2002a, p. 44). Barak was willing to allow some refugees to return on the basis of family re-unification programs. Although humanitarian as a gesture, its grounds is not the refugees' right to return, but the refugees' suffering.[9] In 2001, the Knesset passed a law barring Israeli negotiators from discussing the right of return (Pappe, 2006a, p. 244).

1.6. Legality

A strong legal case can be made for the right of return. The United Nations mediator for Palestine, Count Folke Bernadotte, recommended in his Progress Report of September 16, 1948 that 'the right of the Arab refugees to return to their homes in Jewish controlled territory at the earliest possible date should be affirmed by the United Nations' (quoted in Abunimah & Ibish, 2001, p. 23). This specific recommendation by Bernadotte partly stems from one of his 'seven basic premises' ('Right of Repatriation') also stated in his Progress Report: 'The right of innocent people, uprooted from their homes by the present terror and ravages of war, to return to their homes, should be affirmed and made effective, with assurance of adequate compensation for the property of those who may choose not to return' (quoted in Mallison & Mallison, 1980, p. 127). Bernadotte is not recommending the *creation* of such a right but affirming its existence and implementation (Mallison & Mallison, 1980, p. 128). Tragically, the Jewish terrorist group, the Stern Gang, assassinated Bernadotte the very next day after he submitted his Progress Report.

Shortly after the end of the major hostilities in 1948, the United Nations General Assembly, partly relying on Bernadotte's recommendations, issued Resolution 194 (December 11, 1948). The General Assembly:

> Resolves that the refugees wishing to return to their homes and live at peace with their neighbors should be permitted to do so at the earliest practicable date, and that compensation should be paid for the property of those choosing not to return and for the loss of or damage to property which, under principles of international law or in equity, should be made good by the governments or authorities responsible. (quoted in Mallison & Mallison, 1980, pp. 128–9)

The resolution makes clear that the refugees can choose whether to return to their homes 'within the *de facto* boundaries of the State of Israel,' and that the refugees are entitled to compensation whether they choose to return or not (Mallison & Mallison, 1980, p. 129). This resolution has been reaffirmed by the General Assembly almost yearly (Tadmor, 1994, p. 413). Very recently, the United Nations Committee on the Elimination of Racial Discrimination called on Israel to allow the Palestinian refugees to return (Yoav Stern, 'UN Committee: Israel Should Let Palestinians Return to their Land,' *Ha'aretz*, March 11, 2007). It is not clear, however, what exactly is the legal standing of such a measure.

Other aspects of international law support the Palestinian refugees' right of return, though they do not address the Palestinian refugees, or refugees in general, as such. Article 13 of the Universal Declaration of Human Rights states that 'Everyone has the right to leave any country, including his own, and to return to his country' (quoted in Abunimah & Ibish, 2001, p. 21), implying that people who are forced to flee their country due to war, for example, would have the right to return as soon as hostilities end. Abunimah and Ibish add, 'It is generally recognized that, when sovereignty or political control over an area changes hands'—as happened in Palestine in 1948—'there is a concurrent transfer of responsibility for the population of that territory. Therefore, it cannot be argued that Palestinians... no longer had any rights with regard to the country in which they had lived simply because of a change in the nature of the state or government in that territory' (2001, p. 21).[10]

So there is a strong presumption for a *legal* right of return for Palestinian refugees. However, although such a legal right's existence is crucial, this chapter focuses on the moral right of return, whereby 'morality' refers to the most comprehensive, basic, and overriding normative relations between people. Moral considerations are, theoretically speaking, what we resort to in order to justify legal norms or, in some cases, to argue against them. After all, legal rights are sometimes themselves immoral, as when slavery used to be legal in many countries. Moreover, there are moral rights that are not enshrined by law and perhaps should not be, such as the right to gratitude from a beneficiary and the right to one's own opinion on trivial matters (Almond, 1991, p. 261). Thus, a moral right of return would be more basic and would justify the legal right.

2. The nature of the right of return

Showing that the right of return is a moral right requires delineating its nature and showing its existence.[11] After achieving both tasks, I show why it is a moral right. This section, which assumes the existence of the right of return, identifies its nature, and distinguishes it from other, closely related, rights.

Rights are tricky concepts. As one philosopher puts it, 'talk of rights, although perfectly legitimate, is horrendously *ambiguous*. The simple fact of the matter is that people mean a large number of things when they talk about rights' (Kagan, 1998, p. 170; emphasis is in original). But other difficulties have to do with the nature of rights, what purposes they serve, how many rights exist and what their types are, and the justification of rights. Some philosophers have also denied the existence of natural rights (MacIntyre, 1984) while others have tried to prove that such denials are incoherent (Gewirth, 1978).

Despite the philosophical difficulties besetting the discourse of rights, philosophers generally agree about their importance. As Ronald Dworkin famously put it, 'Individual rights are political trumps held by individuals' (1977, p. xi). The trump metaphor refers to the crucial moral purpose that rights serve: curbing the unbridled pursuit of social and collective goals when they come at the expense of individuals' goals. Moreover, rights impose limits on what individuals may do to one another. Rights, then, are constraints on our behavior; they delineate areas into which we may not enter in pursuit of collective and individual goals. Moreover, although few philosophers consider rights to be absolute—only rights against torture, slavery, and genocide are serious candidates for being absolute rights (Sumner, 2000, p. 293)—most agree that to justifiably override a right, the good to be promoted has to be quite high; otherwise, rights would be pointless and worthless. However, there does not seem to be a principled way of deciding on how high the good must be to override a right (Thomson, 1990, chap. 6).

Assuming that the right of return exists, I identify its nature by explaining how it fits the profile of rights: their aspects, structure, and classification.

There are four important aspects to asserting a right. The right has to (i) entail a constraint on the behavior of others, (ii) be waivable, (iii) embody an option, and (iv) be enforceable (Kagan, 1998, pp. 172–5). Consider the following illustrations. (i) Having the right to not be harmed imposes a constraint on the behavior of others to not do me harm, a constraint that can be overridden, as when I unjustifiably aggress against someone. (ii) If I have the right to exclusive use of my house, I can waive this right by, for example, allowing others to use it. (iii) If I have the right to use my house, I have the option to not use it; having a right to do something does not mean that I must do that thing, only that I may do it, that no one has a duty against me that I refrain from doing it. Note how (ii) and (iii) are different: if I choose to not use my house now this does not mean that I have waived my right to use it. (iv) If I have a right to use a piece of property, I or others acting on my behalf may prevent others from using that property, even by force (this has limits: I cannot, for example, prevent you from using my land if your very life depends on you using it).

The right of return of Palestinian refugees fits these four aspects. (i) It constrains the behavior of others, prohibiting their interference with the implementation and exercise of the right. (ii) It is waivable because a refugee can give up his right to return. (iii) It contains an option since a refugee may decide to not exercise his right to return today, or next week, or this year. (iv) It is enforceable as the refugees or others acting on their behalf may use severe measures—within moral limits—to exercise the right, such as sanctions, boycotts, and diplomatic or political pressure.

Let us now consider, starting with a simple example, the structure of rights. If I promise to help Lisa move on (this coming) Sunday, Lisa has a right (against me) that I do so. Note three initial elements of this right. First, Lisa is the *subject* (possessor, bearer, holder) of the right. Second, I am the *respondent* (object) of the right, the person against whom the right is possessed, borne, or held. Not all rights have only one respondent; some have many: my right to not be killed has everyone else as its respondent. Third, helping Lisa to move is the content of the right, what the right is to. To these three features some philosophers add the nature of a right, its justificatory grounds, and its strength. I return to these below, discussing strength in some detail.

Regarding the right of return, since it is an individual right, there are as many subjects of it as there are individual refugees: each Palestinian refugee has a right to return and he or she is the subject of this right. This is no more controversial than that there are as many subjects of the right to not be killed as there are people that have this right. Second, the respondent of the right is everyone else (more on this below). Third, the content of the right is the one identified above, namely, to return to the sites of the original homes and lands that the Palestinian refugees inhabited.

But rights are a bit more complicated than so far indicated. Adapting Wesley Newcomb Hohfeld's distinctions among legal rights to rights in general (1964), we get a four-way classification of rights: claims, privileges (liberties), powers, and immunities. Go back to the Lisa example. Because I promised Lisa I would help her move on Sunday, Lisa has a claim against me that I do so. Because claims generate corresponding duties, I, and no one else, have a duty to help Lisa move on Sunday. Compare this to my right to not to be harmed, which generates duties on everyone else to refrain from doing so, not just on one other person. With the right of return, it would need to be the case, if the right of return is a claim, that everyone else other than each Palestinian refugee in question has a duty to allow and to not prevent the refugee's return.

Consider next liberties or privileges. If I rightfully own a house, I have a liberty right with its respect: I can do with it as I please. That is, no one has a claim against me that I treat the house in certain ways (unless not doing so would harm others or violate more stringent rights they have). The subject of this right is myself, its content is to do with it as I please, and its respondents are everyone else: they have a duty to not interfere with my use of it.

With the right of return, everyone else has a duty to not prevent the refugees' return, thus making this right both a claim and a liberty right. This is not surprising. Typically, claim rights are exemplified by contractual rights and by 'rights to security of the person (held against everyone in general),' while liberty rights are 'exemplified primarily by property rights and by rights to various freedoms (of thought, belief, conscience, expression, etc.)' (Sumner, 2000, p. 290). As I argue below, the right of return is a form of both a 'security' right and a right to freedom. Thus, it is both a claim right and a liberty right. More generally, liberty rights tend to also be claim rights: my liberty right to express my opinions freely is also a claim right that others not interfere with this expression.

Consider next power rights. If Lisa chooses, she can release me from my promise to help her move on Sunday; she can (has the power to) do so. But suppose she does not waive her claim. Because I promised to help her, I am morally constrained by my promise in what I can and cannot do on that Sunday. I cannot, for example, spend Sunday lying in my hammock drinking beer. Regarding the right of return, each Palestinian refugee has the power to waive his or her right of return. And each refugee has the power to curb what others can do with respect to his or her return: others may not morally prevent the refugee from returning. So the right of return is also a power right.

Now consider my house again. Because I own it, I have an immunity right with respect to it. So others cannot prevent me from enjoying it; they lack the power to do so. In the Lisa example, because I promised to help her move, she has an immunity right against me: I do not have the power to release myself from my promise. The right of return is also an immunity right: others do not have the moral ability to step in and tinker with the claims that the Palestinian refugees have.

So, assuming its existence, the right of return is a *cluster* right, consisting of a claim right, a liberty right, a power right, and an immunity right. Again, this is not surprising. Many of our 'ordinary' rights, such as property rights, are cluster rights, though not all are, such as the rights to not be harmed and to not be killed (they are not liberty rights).

We need to make one more distinction between restitution and non-restitution rights. The former are compensatory in nature and are derived from the violation of other rights.[12] For example, my right to the use and enjoyment of a book I own is derived simply from my ownership of the book; it is not a restitution right. However, if someone culpably damages or loses the book, I have the right to be compensated for it, either by giving me another copy of the book or an appropriate amount of money. Restitution rights are crucial, for, as one philosopher puts it, 'remedial justice lies at the core of the logic of rights' (Campbell, 2006, p. 89).

The discussion so far is subject to an important restriction, namely, the applicability of the 'everything else being equal' clause, a clause having to do with the strength of rights. For example, on my way to Lisa's house to help her move, an anvil falls from somewhere and crushes my foot. This seems to justifiably override Lisa's claim against me that I help her move. 'Everything else being equal' means that my foot—or any other bodily part—is not crushed by an anvil—or any other object. It, indeed, assumes that many other such events do not occur. But generally speaking, which rights are permissibly outweighed, by what considerations, and under which circumstances is a matter that is difficult, perhaps impossible, to settle in a principled manner. That rights can be infringed or overridden is obvious; but when, how, and under what circumstances is a question much more difficult to answer.

So if the right of return exists, it is a cluster right constituted by the four types of rights previously discussed. In Section 4, I consider whether it should be implemented or whether it may be overridden.

So far, I have discussed the formal nature of the right of return and how it fits the profile of rights. We need to discuss its nature more substantively, seeing how it is an individual right, and distinguishing it from other, closely related rights that the Palestinian refugees also have.

In the literature on the right of return, one often finds the idea that it is an individual right, possessed by each and every Palestinian refugee. Thus, it is not merely a collective right, possessed by the Palestinian refugees as a group [this also seems to be the case, legally speaking (Quigley, 1999, p. 158)]. But does 'individual' refer to units of families or, literally, to each refugee? In addition to its theoretical importance, this issue is also practically important: depending on whether we speak of families or individuals, the number of returnees would be different, which means that the needed accommodation would also be different.

Excepting cases where an authority, such as a legal guardian, must make decisions on behalf of another, such as a child, an infant, and a mentally challenged person, we should take 'individual' to refer to individuals literally, because the right of return is a life-affecting choice such that the decision to exercise it should reside in a single, competent person (perhaps this is one rationale for the choice component in the UNGA Resolution 194). Of course, in some cases, a whole family might wish to return. But here, at least ideally, the family would jointly decide on this issue.

But why believe that the right of return is an individual and not merely a collective right? After all, if the Palestinians were expelled or driven to flee as a people, why not think of the refugees as having the right of return as a people? Because the decision to return to one's original home or village or country is a central, life-affecting decision, and given the depth and span of the I-P conflict, it is morally important that each individual be able to make this decision for him or herself. Even if the nascent Israeli army in 1947 and 1948 desired to get rid of the Palestinians as a people, this would not affect the claim that the choice as to whether to return or not is an individual one. Consider a hurricane that devastates an entire community. Though the people as a community were forced to flee, it is inappropriate to say to them, 'You must, all of you, return to your land.' Barring considerations that override giving each member of the community the choice to return, each member of the community should make this decision for him or herself, precisely because this is a central, life-affecting decision.[13]

The right of return also entails a choice on its possessor's behalf to either exercise or not exercise the right (captured by 'wishing' in UNGA Resolution 194). That is, implementing the right of return does not mean that each and every refugee will or must return. Re-emphasizing this point is important because a typical objection to the implementation of the right assumes that millions of refugees return to Israel. But this is false. Because the right of return entails a choice, not every Palestinian refugee need return. Indeed, it might be that not many would.[14]

To distinguish the right of return from other rights that Palestinian refugees have, keep in mind two points. First, in most cases, the homes and villages of the Palestinian refugees were either razed to the ground by the Israeli army (and had Jewish settlements built next them—these were rarely built on razed Palestinian ones) or became inhabited by Jewish immigrants (this was mostly the case with respect to Palestinian homes in urban centers, such as West Jerusalem and Haifa). A few houses, however, remain standing in a few village sites.[15]

Second, the causes for the Palestinians' flight were almost all due to direct or indirect actions by Jewish troops (which, after May 15, 1948, became the Israeli army), such as outright expulsion of Palestinians from their towns, attacks on towns and shelling them to scare the inhabitants to leave, and the Palestinians' fear of being attacked. However, fear played a greater role later in the Palestinian exodus. Earlier, Palestinians rarely left simply out of fear of an impending attack.[16] Thus, it is difficult to accuse those Palestinians who fled later of doing so out of unjustified or unreasonable fear, because, first, they were aware of why other

Palestinians fled in the early stages of the war, and, second, because they were now fully aware that a Jewish state was being brought into existence. Hence, they were justified in believing that what the nascent Israeli army and Israeli political leadership wanted was a state as demographically Jewish as possible. All this underscores the fact that, contrary to what many of Israel's apologists claim, the Palestinian refugees did not leave voluntarily; they left because they were coerced to leave.[17]

The right of return should not be confused with other rights that Palestinians have that were overridden in numerous ways during their flight (the issue is not whether these rights were permissibly or impermissibly overridden, but that they are different from that of the right of return). First, given our rights against bodily invasion, those Palestinians who were forcibly and directly expelled from their villages and towns had this right overridden, since direct expulsion requires the use of the bodies of those being expelled against the latter's wishes. Jewish troops also used Palestinians' bodies without their consent even in cases in which Palestinians fled out of fear and without direct expulsion, as long as these Palestinians fled due to the justified belief that they had no other viable options.[18] In times of war, especially when two ethnic groups vie for the same territory—the conditions prevalent from 1947 to 1948—noncombatants are often justified in believing that their lives are at stake during impending attacks. Thus, Palestinian noncombatants were justified in believing that their lives were at stake. By forcing them to leave, the Jewish troops did override the Palestinians' rights against bodily invasion.

Second, the right of return should not be confused with rights against harm. One harm that many Palestinian refugees suffered was direct bodily harm, including death, on their way to their final territorial destination: many suffered hunger, dehydration, injuries from having to walk such long distances under difficult circumstances, injuries from being fired on by Jewish troops, and being killed in massacres (Morris, 1987; Pappe, 2006a). Another harm that many Palestinian refugees suffered was having their lives impaired because of expulsion. A third harm is suffering distress due to forcible relocation, to having to do this under mostly harsh conditions, and to having to live in camps under also quite difficult conditions.[19]

Third, Palestinians' property rights were overridden. The Israelis took or razed most Palestinian homes. Gradually, and through various departments and agencies, Israel seized and confiscated the lands and homes of all the refugees. Some Jews moved into some Palestinian homes and others utilized the latter's lands and farms (Fischbach, 2003, chap. 1;

Pappe, 2006a, chaps. 9, 10). These were infringements of property rights.[20]

The right of return is not the same as other potential restitution rights that may arise from the infringement of the above rights. That is, if the above-mentioned overridden rights call for restitution, the restitution is not that of return.[21] For example, the distress the Palestinians underwent due to expulsion is harm irreparable by a restoration of the *status quo ante* (reestablishing the original state of affairs). Nothing, short of going back in time, can reverse the experienced distress. Thus, the reparation called for is of a different type, such as financial compensation. Similarly for bodily harm (including death) and bodily trespass. Restitution for infringements of property rights is trickier. In some cases, full restitution is possible: when the houses still stand and are uninhabited, their Palestinian refugee owners can return to them. In those cases in which the houses are still standing but inhabited by people other than the original Palestinian owners, only partial restitution can be possible: the original owners can have their property restored back to them, but they might have to lease it to the current inhabitants.[22] In those cases in which the property is destroyed, only a different type of restitution, such as financial, is possible.

When it comes to the right of return, restitution is, in general, possible: allow the refugees to return to their lands and to live there. This will obviously encounter practical and moral difficulties, for much hinges on who currently inhabits the areas to which the refugees are to return. I address these issues below. The point now is that the right of return is a different kind of reparation from that required by the infringement of other rights: anchored in the notion of returning to one's home, village, and land, the reparation it requires is restoring the *status quo ante*.[23]

3. The existence of the right of return

The Palestinian refugees from 1947 to the 1950s can be divided into two groups. The first comprises the refugees from the early years of Israel's existence (roughly, from 1947 to the early 1950s). The second comprises their descendents. In two stages, I argue that the refugees in each group have the right of return.

3.1. The existence of the right for the first group of refugees

We need first to state and defend two theses and one principle—in themselves neutral and independent of the right of return—crucial to the argument. The first thesis, the 'Right to Continued Residency Thesis' ('CRT' for short), is as follows:

> Individuals have non-absolute claims (rights) against other people that they not be prevented from continuing to reside in their lands and homes when their residency in these lands and homes is justified by legal facts, historical facts, or facts pertaining to having a sense of belonging.

For brevity, I sometimes abbreviate 'justified by legal facts, historical facts, or facts pertaining to having a sense of belonging' to 'legitimate residence.'

CRT requires explanation. First, like most rights, the right to continued residency is not absolute. It can be permissibly overridden, as when, for example, a family's home needs to be demolished to make room for a badly needed highway. Second, CRT should not be confused with a similar thesis to which it is equivalent but that omits the clause, 'when their residency in these lands and homes is justified by legal facts, historical facts, or facts pertaining to having a sense of belonging.' This latter thesis is less defensible than CRT because individuals might not have claims against others to not be prevented from continued residence in their homes and lands if their residence is not legitimate (although it may nonetheless be overall wrong to prevent them from continuing to reside). This other thesis might be true, but it is more contentious than CRT, and, in any case, we do not need it.

Third, the claim in CRT is against other people. It is not, for example, against forces of nature like hurricanes. Barring the possibility that the victims of such disasters cannot return and rebuild their homes, it is only decent that they may do so. But whether they have a right to do so is another question. They might have a right to return and rebuild. But if they do, it is not because CRT entails it. Similarly, consider a case in which harsh economic conditions force people to immigrate to another country. The people were, in a sense, coerced into leaving. If they have a right to return, this would be, again, not because CRT entails it, for CRT asserts a claim that people have against other people, not against nature or general economic and social conditions.[24]

Fourth, 'residency is justified' by legal facts' includes three related conditions. 'Legal facts' means what it usually does, that the laws of the governing bodies by which the individuals in question abide permit their residence. This includes, but is not confined to, the ownership and leasing of property. However, the laws themselves must be morally legitimate. Suppose, for example, one country occupies another and settles members of its people in houses and lands belonging to the occupied country. The occupying country then devises laws proclaiming the settlers' residence in these houses and lands to be legal. Although their residence is legal under the laws of the occupying country, the settlers do not have a moral right to live in these houses and lands, for the laws themselves must be morally permissible or justified.

In addition to legally defined residence, part of what justifies one's residence in a place is a historical relationship to the area, to the effect that the residents in question, and their ancestors, have resided in the land for several generations. It is not clear exactly how length of stay justifies one's residence, though continued residence without rival claims by others to the land certainly helps. Nor is it clear how long one must remain in order for one's residence to be justified. But we do think that history is an important part of it; that, somehow, living on a land and in a home for a long time gives the residents some title to be there.

The third condition is 'having a sense of belonging.' This is a sense of familiarity, of making a life for oneself where one is, of being-at-home, usually (but not invariably) because one has resided in the place for a long time. Thus, this sense must be rooted in objective facts, such as an actual physical residence in the land, fuzzy cases not withstanding. 'Sense of belonging' does not entail that the residents in question are all leading happy and fulfilled lives, for one can belong but be quite miserable for a number of reasons. The idea is simply that of being rooted in familiar surroundings.

Legality, history, and a sense of belonging are contingently connected. For example, living in a place for a long time and being attached to that place are connected to the idea that one is entitled to some legal recognition of these facts (like common law marriage). A person often feels a sense of belonging or attachment to a place precisely because his ancestors have resided in the place for a long time. And vice versa, residing in a place for a long time allows a person to develop a sense of attachment to the place. These three are the minimum number of conditions that go into CRT. They are all we need to defend it.[25]

Each of legality, history, and belonging is sufficient for possessing the rights asserted by CRT. None is necessary, not even legality, since CRT would be true even in societies, actual or hypothetical, that have no legal conceptions regarding residency rights. In such societies, one's residency in a place for a long time is sufficient to accord one a right not to be prevented from continued residency. So is belonging, as long as it is understood objectively, as I mentioned above.

Finally, CRT does not refer to specific national, ethnic, racial, or state aspects. This is as it should be, because it is not true that my right against being prevented from continued residency disappears where I to suddenly find myself in the midst of an ethnic group that was not there yesterday, or where I to find myself suddenly residing in a different country (a coup occurred during the night whose leaders make their first political action the annexation of the country to a bigger one). The right CRT asserts might, fully or partly, ground other rights (if these are genuine rights), such as the right to live in a community and the right to national self-determination.[26] In any case, it is more basic than these.

CRT is intuitively plausible. It coheres with our intuitions regarding people's ability to maintain their legitimate residences without having to worry about if, when, and how they might not be able to continue to live as and where they do. Indeed, the right in CRT is a basic right. One of the most frightening aspects to Thomas Hobbes's state of nature is the ability for anyone strong enough to take control of where I live. Much like the need for rights against harm and bodily trespass, we need to constrain others' behavior regarding our legitimate places of residence, for otherwise we would have no security. A society in which people retain their legitimate residency by depending on the sympathy of others is a society in which people cannot claim or demand that such retention be maintained.[27] How they lead their lives depends on the mercy of others, making it difficult and pointless for them to plan their lives. Thus, the need to be protected in maintaining our legitimate residencies is basic; without it, we are virtually unable to plan and chart our lives under our own lights. Thus, like the right against harm, being able to maintain one's legitimate residency is also a crucial right.

There are two dominant conceptions of rights: as protected interests and as protected choices. 'Central to [the former] conception is the idea of the right-holder as the beneficiary of a set of duties imposed on others, or as the one whose interest provides the justification for imposing such duties... Central to [the latter] conception is the idea of the right-holder having the freedom to choose among a set of options, and of this freedom being protected by a set of duties imposed on others' (Sumner, 1987, pp. 45–6). It is not easy to derive specific rights from these two general conceptions. However, the right in CRT can be plausibly derived from either, and so supports the intuition that CRT is, indeed, true.

On the first conception of rights, the right in CRT would have to be a right necessary to protect individual interests. If the argument presented so far about the importance of maintaining our legitimate residence to our security and well-being is sound, the right in CRT would be a right on this first conception. For our ability to maintain our legitimate residence is an important and basic interest. In contrast, someone who, say, claims that it is in his interest to be continuously supplied with tubs of ice cream would convince barely any one. But because our ability to maintain legitimate residence is crucial to our plans and so is a crucial interest of ours, we can claim it as a right.

On the conception of rights as protected choices, we achieve the same result. Again, and as I have argued, the ability to maintain legitimate residence is crucial for planning our lives and leading them accordingly. Without the minimal security afforded by a protection against others from interfering in my residency, it is difficult to see how I can have much freedom to choose among a set of options. Because my ability to choose must rest on some foundations, such as rights against bodily trespass, harm, and evictions, my choices would be hollow without secure foundations. To make genuine choices and act on our decisions, our lives require firm and stable foundations, one of which is that we are not hostage to being prevented at any moment from using our houses.

So it seems that CRT is true.

The second thesis is the corollary of CRT. Blandly calling it the 'Restitution Thesis' ('RT' for short), it states:

> If the right asserted in CRT is violated, then the individual whose right has been violated is owed restitution.

RT does not state, 'If the right asserted in CRT is justifiably overridden or infringed, then . . . ' in order to avoid the controversial claim that the individuals whose rights have been justifiably overridden are still owed restitution. Possibly true, this is nonetheless a claim we do not need. Note that RT does not deny that people can be owed restitution even if none of their rights has been violated or if they have been permissibly overridden. RT simply states that the violation of rights is sufficient, though it may not be necessary, for restitution.

Before we begin the argument for the right of return's existence, we need the Principle of the Closest Possible Restitution (PCPR). It states:

> If X is owed restitution, then the restitution should take the form of the (non-numerically identical) *status quo ante*.

According to PCPR, the restitution should take the form of restoring the original way things were. If this is not possible, owing to, say, morally prohibitive costs, the restitution closest to the *status quo ante* is required. PCPR contains a familiar idea and reflects our moral intuitions. It is a principle of justice, namely, that, if one's rights have been violated, then, one is entitled to having certain states of affairs restored to their *status quo ante*; failing that, one is entitled to the state of affairs closest to that of the *status quo ante*.[28] Note that 'restitution' does not necessarily refer to financial compensation, but to the restoration of whatever type of object or state of affairs lost in the violation of the right in question.

Usually restoring the original state of affairs is impossible. If you kill my aunt, she cannot be restored. But, as long as we do not understand PCPR (as we should not) to mean a return to the state of affairs exactly identical with the original, some cases are feasible. Suppose I lend a chemist friend of mine a copy of my favorite Danielle Steel novel. Out of sheer negligence he accidentally spills sulfuric acid on it and thus destroys it. I am then entitled to reparations from him. Typically, he would buy me a new copy of the novel. Even though the new copy is not identical with the one destroyed, the replacement satisfies the idea of a return to the *status quo ante*.

But suppose that the copy I lent him either (i) contained the author's non-personalized signature, (ii) was signed specifically to me, or (iii) the copy, also signed to me, contained my margin notes and my underlining of crucial passages. PCPR states that depending on how possible it is to restore an object identical (though not numerically) with the original, I am entitled to a form of restitution as close as possible to the original. Depending on the variations of the book example, the ability of my friend to restore the original state of affairs varies. If (i) is the case, he can simply buy me another copy of the book. If (ii), he can buy a new copy of the book, locate the author, and get another personalized signature (though this might be avoided, under PCPR, as being morally prohibitive). If (iii), he would be unable to restore the original state of affairs, for no substitute for the copy is available. He would then need to compensate me with something of comparable value.[29]

Consider an example closer to this chapter's topic. Suppose I was expelled from my home or prevented from returning to it for no good reason. If my home is neither destroyed nor inhabited by others, I would be entitled to restitution in the form of being allowed to return. Suppose now that my home is destroyed. I do not lose my restitution right to rebuild it. Preventing my return would be unjust and returning to the site of my home would not deprive others of a comparatively more important moral good or right. That I be allowed to return and rebuild is not simply a matter of moral decency, but a right of restitution, specifically, a privilege or a liberty. I have the liberty to return and build, and I have a claim against others that they not prevent me from doing so. It is, in short, my right to do so.

Note that PCPR has a built-in flexibility allowing it to adapt to the nature of the rights violation at hand. In the book example, my ownership rights to a specific object were violated, and so the owed restitution is a book as similar as possible to the one lost. In the home example, the type of right violated was my ability to continue to inhabit a home and a piece of land, and so the owed restitution is a choice to return to the home and the land. The 'form' in PCPR, then, refers to the object lost in the type of right violated.

We are now in a position to state, explain, and defend the argument for the existence of the right of return for the first group of refugees. It goes as follows:

1. The Palestinians who were rendered refugees had rights to continued residency in their homes and lands (follows from CRT and historical and legal facts).
2. In being rendered refugees, these rights to continued residency were violated (follows from historical facts and moral norms).
3. These Palestinian refugees are owed restitution (follows from 2 and RT).
4. Their restitution takes the form of returning to their homes and lands (follows from PCPR).
5. Therefore, the Palestinian refugees have the right of return (follows from 3 and 4).

Each of these premises requires defense.

The first premise is the easiest to defend. Under the laws current in Palestine in 1948, and prior to the establishment of Israel, the Palestinians' residency was legal. Neither the laws of the Ottoman Empire nor those of the British Mandate declared their residency illegal. Even the Balfour Declaration of 1917 (whose legality is questionable) promising the Jews a homeland in Palestine implicitly recognized the right of the Palestinians to continue residing in Palestine. Before Israel controlled the land, the Palestinians resided in their homes and lands for quite a long time, and, as a group, never expressed a desire to migrate.[30] They certainly had a sense of belonging to and being rooted in their lands and homes. Indeed, almost all Palestinian refugees, whether they wish to return or not, express this attachment. Although some of the claims can be attributed to political bravado or as the effect of more than 50 years of conflict, no one can seriously deny the Palestinians' attachment to their land. Like any other people, it is expected they have such a relationship; the surprise would be if they did not.

To defend the second premise—that the Palestinians' rights to continued residency have been violated—we need to show that rendering Palestinians as refugees was morally unjustified.

The historical record does show that the majority of the Palestinians were forcibly removed, under any understanding of 'forcibly.' Moreover, the Palestinians were coerced to leave not by some overwhelming force of nature, but by the direct actions of human beings, specifically, the actions of and by Jewish troops.[31] Plan D (Dalet), a military plan produced in March of 1948 (thus prior to the official establishment of Israel in May 1948) by the Haganah (the main Jewish militia at the time), aimed at conquering and occupying or leveling Palestinian villages. Its goal seems to have been the ethnic cleansing of the Palestinians, though there is controversy about its aims and purposes, about how widely adopted it was, and at what level of Jewish officialdom in Palestine it was adopted.[32]

At this juncture, it is important to address a common and popular idea believed by many of Israel's apologists, namely, that the Palestinian refugees left 'voluntarily,' the reasoning being that if the Palestinians left of their own will, then they gave up their rights to residency in Palestine.[33] However, much depends on how we understand 'voluntary' in this argument. When every morning I voluntarily leave my house to go to work, do I waive my right to continued residency in my house? Clearly, no. Otherwise, our rights to continued residency would be utterly pointless. So if the Palestinians left voluntarily to seek safety from war, they did not waive their rights to continued residency in Palestine. It is disingenuous to reason that the choice to leave or stay was ultimately up to the Palestinians, and—since they chose to leave—they waived their rights. Such a line of thinking would result in classifying many cases of genuinely involuntary actions as voluntary, such as giving my wallet to the mugger who holds a gun to my head, since the decision to do so was up to me.

Only one meaning of 'voluntary' entails the Palestinians' giving up their residency rights: that they willingly and at their own initiative left their homes, lands, and villages to whomever might take them (as some form of a gift). It is as if the Palestinians had said, 'Oh, they want our lands and homes to create a Jewish state? Why didn't they just ask? Of course they can have them. We'll just take our things and move to these fellow neighboring Arab countries.'[34] However, neither the historical record nor common sense bears this attitude out.

So in whatever way the Palestinians left is mostly irrelevant. Whether Jewish troops expelled them, shelled them, scared them into flight, or massacred them, or whether they left because they were heeding Arab calls to do so, become factors that are less and less important as far as the rights asserted in CRT are concerned. The pertinent historical fact is that Israel refused to allow the refugees to return to their homes and lands, deciding this in June 1948 and reaffirming it in August of the same year (Takkenberg, 1998, p. 16). That is, even if Israel did not forcibly remove the Palestinians, the fact that it consistently and actively prevented them from returning would constitute a clear infringement or overriding of the Palestinians' rights asserted in CRT.

But, returning to the premise at hand, would it constitute a violation of these rights? To answer this question, we need to consider why some argue this infringement is justified, meaning that it must somehow be morally necessary, or, at least, highly important. First, it might be a military necessity to more or less empty the land of the Palestinians. But this is not convincing as a justification of infringing the rights to residency. The very distinction we make between combatants and noncombatants and the very rules of war (*jus in bello*) that exist indicate that we do not think that typically noncombatants pose a military risk. If we did, we would think that any treatment of noncombatants, short of unnecessary torture and cruelty, would be permissible. What then needs to be shown is that in the specific case of the Israeli–Palestinian conflict, the Palestinian noncombatants of 1947–50 did indeed pose such a risk. This, however, is difficult to do, since they do not stand out as being a threatening civilian population. Indeed, according to the historian Ilan Pappe, they were averse to warring with the Jewish troops (2006a, p. 51). The burden of proof falls on those who think otherwise. At best, perhaps such measures were militarily necessary but only as temporary actions, until calm and security returned. If so, the most we can conclude is that the infringement of the Palestinians' rights was justified only as a temporary measure (and not all of the infringements, such as razing their homes and confiscating them, would be justified). More important, it would not justify continuously blocking the return of the refugees, which converts a justified infringement into a violation.

The second possible reason why it was morally necessary to depopulate the Palestinians is to enable the creation of a more or less fully exclusive Jewish state (perhaps the risk the noncombatants posed was impeding the development of a more or less exclusive Jewish state).

However, it is not clear why this would count as a moral reason. On the assumption that the Jews constitute a national people, it is generally morally impermissible for nations to create states in territories rightfully inhabited by others at their expense. Even if nations have a moral right to self-determination, and even if the Jews of Palestine (and of the world) self-determined that they want a state more or less cleansed of Palestinians, this would not show the moral permissibility of depopulating and preventing them from returning. As Jean Hampton puts it, 'even assuming that a nation has the right to be a state, such a right cannot be sufficiently powerful to trump *all* other rights held by outsiders' (1997, p. 235; emphasis is in original, see also Chapter 1 in this book). If the Palestinians are outsiders—they are not part of the Jewish nation—Hampton's claim applies. If they are 'insiders'—they are inhabitants of the land on which Israel was created—Hampton's claim applies even better, insofar as we think our obligations to 'insiders' are stronger than those to 'outsiders.' Again, the burden of proof falls on those who believe that it was morally necessary to expel the Palestinians. (I return to some of these points below.)

One might argue, however, that irrespective of issues of national self-determination, the creation of a Jewish state is a good so great it surpasses respecting the residency rights of the Palestinians, especially in light of the Holocaust occurring just before Israel's creation. But this is not a convincing justification for ridding the land of its Palestinian population. Granted that the Jews, because of the Holocaust and anti-Semitism, needed a new state to safeguard their interests and well-being (a claim by no means obviously true), it does not follow that this must be at the expense of the Palestinians, who had nothing to do with the Holocaust or anti-Semitism. Their hostility towards the Jews then was not directed at them as Jews, but as potential usurpers of their land and hence their lives, and the Palestinians had ample reason for such fear. Thus, it is not a simple step from the claim that the Jews needed a new state to the claim that this justified the infringement of the Palestinians' residency rights to their lands and homes. To do so, one must argue that the Jews must have a more or less exclusively Jewish state for them to survive, that the state must be in historic Palestine, and that the state must be free of as many non-Jewish Palestinians as possible, despite the Palestinians' rightful residence. This is a task impossible to fulfill.

Because these two possible reasons do not justify depopulating the Palestinians, the infringement of Palestinian rights asserted in CRT was impermissible; it was a violation of these rights. Thus, the second premise in the above argument is true.

The third premise states that the Palestinian refugees are owed restitution. This follows from the fact that their rights asserted in CRT have been violated in conjunction with the Restitution Thesis. Note that the word 'owed' in this premise entails that it is a matter of rights that the refugees be given restitution, not merely humanitarian support.

The fourth premise is also true: since the Palestinians' rights to continued residency in their lands were violated, since they are owed restitution, then, according to PCPR, the closest possible compensation is to allow the refugees to return to the sites of their villages and lands and to rebuild their homes. Note that the fourth premise—that the restitution takes the form of return—is crucial: coupled with the third, it renders the Palestinian refugees' ability to return a matter of rights.

Given that the Palestinians' rights asserted in CRT were violated, given their entitlement to restitution, and given PCPR, they have the right to return to their homes and lands.

Before moving to the argument for the existence of the right of return for the descendents of the first wave of refugees, we need to address one worry: if those Jewish officials and others who played a major causal role in getting the Palestinians to leave their homes and lands between 1948 and the early 1950s [all identified and named in Pappe (2006a)] no longer exist, who, in Israel, has the duty corresponding to the refugees' right to return? If the right of return is a claim-right (in addition to being a privilege-, liberty-, and immunity-right), then someone or some party must bear the corresponding duty. Who would this be?

Since the right of return is a restitution right, the right to allow the refugees, if they choose, to return to the sites of their homes and villages, the party that has the corresponding duty would not only be a handful of Jewish officials from the 1940s, who may or may not currently exist, but Israel. The people of Israel, represented by their democratically elected representatives, are of course the most relevant party, for it is they who have the actual say, given their sovereignty and control over the land, on whether to allow the refugees to return. Because Israel has continuously blocked the implementation of the right of return, it has inherited the role of being the main party that bears the duty corresponding to the right of return.

3.2. The existence of the right of return for the refugees' descendents

Does the argument apply to the Palestinian refugees' descendents? Has their claim to not be prevented from continued residence in their homes and lands been violated? The issue here is whether the residency clause in CRT applies not only to those who lived in Palestine but also to their descendents who rarely, if ever, have been to this land.

Note that CRT is not a thesis only about property rights, such that without the appropriate legal mechanisms in place, one's family cannot inherit one's property. Indeed, most property laws require that one's property, in the absence of a will, revert to one's next of kin when one dies. If Israel's appropriation of Palestinian refugee lands in Israel were itself illegal, then even if CRT were simply about property, we cannot easily dismiss the claim that the descendents of the original refugees, were the latter to now be dead (and many are not), are not entitled to the property.[35]

Still, CRT concerns more than property rights, asserting rights that stem from historical connections to the land and from an objective sense of belonging to the land. The descendents of the first wave of refugees are not merely connected to the latter by the causal mechanisms of biological birth, but also as members of the same people, the Palestinians, belonging to generally the same culture, history, identity, and politics. More importantly, however, is that the descendents are connected to the first wave of refugees by family ties. This means that the children and grandchildren, and in some cases, the great grandchildren of the original refugees form families not in a mere biological sense, but also in the normative sense in which we understand the notion of 'family,' whereby emotional, cultural, historical, and other such ties are established, maintained, and passed on (this is not an ironclad law about families, but a true, general characterization).

Moreover, the Palestinian refugee problem is not old. The current descendents of the first wave are not remote in time from the events that, less than 60 years ago, led to the dispossession of their parents and grandparents. Thus, the claim that the descendents have a historical connection to Palestine is not an inflated, overly subjective, or false claim. This closeness in time establishes that the descendents have a historical connection to the lands and homes of their parents and grandparents in Palestine. The role of remoteness in time has to do with how such connections establish, or are connected to, claims or rights. I may be correct in claiming, for example, that I have a historical connection to Saudi Arabia by virtue of the fact that it is where my forefathers originated hundreds of years ago. But this claim does not, due to the remoteness of my ancestry, ground any rights or claims I have to reside there. The descendents of the original refugees, however, are not remote in time from the events of 1948. Given the temporal closeness, given their familial connections to the original refugees, and given the applicability of the rights in CRT to the original refugees, their descendents also have these rights. In short, historical facts justify the descendents of the original refugees' possession of residency rights to their ancestors' original homes and lands.

The third component of legitimacy, a sense of belonging, also justifies the descendents' possession of the right to residency, but in a weaker way. Although almost all the refugees, including the descendents, claim a sense of belonging to Palestine, some of it is due to political bravado on their part, to a desire to assert their attachment to the land in the face of adamant Israeli refusal to acknowledge their demands, its role in causing historical injustices, and its responsibility for this role (and in the face of bad treatment at the hands of the Arab governments that host some of the refugees). Sense of belonging cannot also as strongly justify the descendents' possession of the rights to residency as can historical connections because it is difficult to see how one can have a full-blown sense of belonging to a home, village, or land when one has never seen or inhabited that home or village.[36]

Nonetheless, the descendents do have a genuine sense of belonging. It has two sources. The first is negative: the experience of being a refugee, of statelessness, of not belonging to where one is. Indeed, even refugees who live in the West Bank and Gaza, which are Palestinian lands, often experience alienation because they are sometimes regarded by their fellow Palestinians as not from these two areas. Such experiences of not belonging fuel the sense that they can only belong to where they originally came from. The second source is the positive connection they feel they have to their original homes and lands, especially given the political, familial, historical, and educational contexts. Those aspects of the sense of belonging due to political bravado notwithstanding, they have a genuine sense of belonging. It is expected, appropriate, and, most importantly, rooted in a historical connection to the lands and villages by familial ties.

To sum up, the descendents of the original refugees have the residency rights asserted in CRT, with much of its justification found in their strong historical connection to the lands, homes, and villages of their parents and grandparents. If this is correct, their rights to residency have also been violated. Their right of return would then be generated by the same argument that showed the existence of the right of return for the original refugees. Although the descendents were not expelled or forcibly removed or made to leave by the Jewish troops in 1948 and the early 1950s, the argument for the existence of the right of return for the first wave of refugees does not hinge on these facts but on the fact that they are prevented from returning. It is this that violates the descendents' residency rights, thus grounding, by the above argument for the right of return for the original refugees, the right of return for their descendents.

Moreover, just as Israel bears the primary duty corresponding to the original refugees' right of return, it also bears the same duty corresponding to the descendents' right of return, since it is the party ultimately responsible for preventing their return.

But, one might wonder, since the majority of the descendents of the refugees and, indeed, some of the original refugees, have lived their lives in Arab countries (most relevant here would be Jordan, Syria, and Lebanon) or on Palestinian land (the West Bank and Gaza), and given the existing cultural, historical, geographical, and political affinities among the Palestinians, the Jordanians, the Syrians, and the Lebanese, do the Jordanians, the Syrians, the Lebanese, and the (non-refugee) Palestinians not have duties to settle the refugees, or at least some of them, in, respectively, Jordan, Syria, Lebanon, and (the future) Palestine?[37] Why should Israel bear the primary duty to allow the return of the refugees?

The above Arab peoples do have duties towards the refugees, but these duties are 'non-primary.' Insofar as the Palestinian refugees have a right of return, then, given the logic of the right, the refugees have a choice as to whether to return to Israel. That is, the content of the right is the option of returning to the villages and lands in Israel. Because some refugees might opt not to return and would choose to reside elsewhere, these cases require countries other than Israel to settle the refugees. Which countries have this corresponding obligation, and how they are to divide the refugees between them, are open questions, though Jordan, Syria, Lebanon, and the (non-refugee) Palestinians, in virtue of their cultural, historical, and political ties to the refugees, are obvious candidates. Now if the argument that the right of return exists is sound, these refugee claims against other countries are 'non-primary' because the right is a claim against Israel, first and foremost: Israel is the state with sovereignty over the sites of the refugees' villages. So the 'non-primary' duties or obligations held by countries other than Israel are derivative from the right of return, not established independently of it (though there might be such claims that stem from our moral obligations to each other as human beings).[38]

Having argued that the right of return exists for the first wave of refugees and their descendents, we can now see that it is a moral right. At its core, it is the right of the Palestinian refugees to be allowed to return to the sites of their homes, villages, and lands and to carry out their lives there as they see fit (within moral bounds). Because the right of return is about some human beings'—the Palestinian refugees'—ability to chart their lives as they choose, it is a basic, fundamental right, and so is a moral right. The reasoning is not that because the rights to residency asserted in CRT are basic rights and therefore restitution rights stemming from their violation are also basic, moral, rights; this is fallacious reasoning.[39] Rather, the right of return is a basic right because of the nature of the restitution involved, namely, being able to decide what to do with one's life by being allowed to reside in a particular geographical area. No doubt, the Palestinian refugees can be given the ability to chart their own lives by giving them options exclusive of returning to Israel. Of course, this would not deny that the right of return is a basic, and so moral, right. At best, it would show that the right of return is not one of the most basic rights that the Palestinian refugees, in virtue of being human beings, in general have, such as rights to freedom, security, life, and to live somewhere. But it would still be a basic right to Palestinian refugees: because of their strong historical, cultural, political, and familial connections to Palestine, denying them this right is tantamount to denying them the ability to chart their lives as individuals belonging to a particular people stemming from a particular way of life.

We can also see how the right of return is both a freedom and a security right. It is a freedom right because it provides the refugees with the ability to chart their lives as they see fit. It is a security right because of the kind of freedom right that it is: without it, people cannot be secure in their lives. Without the ability to plan my own life, there would be very little security in it; everything basic and important that I desire to do or achieve would be hostage to the dictates of others.

3.3. Replies to possible objections

There are three important objections against the existence of the right of return. First, due to the statute of limitations, the right has 'expired.' Second, because the right is impossible to implement, it does not exist. Third, there are considerations that render the refugees to have lost the right. I will take these up in turn.

It is reasonable to ask whether there is a statute of limitations of sorts that applies to the Palestinian refugees, especially in light of the fact that the refugees are now in their second, third, and even fourth generations. If the right of return has somehow expired, then, obviously, it no longer exists.

Usually, the concept of the statute of limitations is a legal one. It would be instructive, then, to briefly review some salient aspects of international law that apply or might apply to the Palestinian refugees. Article 13 (2) of the Universal Declaration of Human Rights (1948) states, 'Everyone has the right to leave any country, including his own, and to return to his country.' If we accept that the country of the refugees is Palestine (a notion rejected by some Israeli scholars, on the grounds that there was no country of Palestine in 1948 and since), Article 13 then seems to claim that the refugees would have the right to return to their country. The crucial point is that the article does not mention any statute of limitations on returning, though whether this is intentional is unclear.

The United Nations International Covenant on Civil and Political Rights (December 16, 1966; entered into force March 23, 1976) is also relevant. Article 12 (4) states, 'No one shall be arbitrarily deprived of the right to enter his own country.' No statute of limitations is mentioned. Indeed, Article 12 (3) states, 'The above-mentioned rights [freedom of movement and residency within one's state, and the freedom to leave any country] shall not be subject to any restrictions except those which are provided by law, are necessary to protect national security, public order, public health or morals or the rights and freedoms of others, and are consistent with the other rights recognized in the present Covenant.' Again, no statute of limitations is mentioned. Moreover, and even though Article 12 (3) occurs before Article 12 (4), it is hard to see why the provisions in (3) would not apply to (4). Although one can, in connection with the Palestinian refugees, quibble about the relevance of certain clauses to them, such as the notions of country and (Israel's) national security, the fact is that no statute of limitations is mentioned.

The United Nations Convention Relating to the Status of Refugees (1950, entered into force in 1954) is also relevant. Applying the Convention to the Palestinian refugees,[40] it does not mention a statute of limitations regarding a time by which refugees' claims to return to their original countries expires. But again, as with the Universal Declaration of Human Rights, this might not have been intentional.

Perhaps the most relevant aspect of international law is United Nations General Assembly Resolution 194 (see Section 1). Again, this Resolution does not mention any statute of limitations. Indeed, that it has been continuously affirmed indicates that the General Assembly does not intend, for the near future, to impose a statute of limitations on the return of the Palestinian refugees.

We can cautiously conclude that international law is silent on the issue of the statute of limitations when it comes to refugees. Indeed, according to Quigley, the 'answer given by the law . . . is that the right [of return] continues until such a time as a displaced individual voluntarily abandons the attachment to the home area' (1999, pp. 161–2). Quigley gives as an example a refugee who decides to reside permanently, and who is naturalized, in another state (1999, p. 162). This, however, takes us into issues of the voluntary giving up on one's right of return, issues I discuss in my reply to the third objection.

But even if legally there is no limitation on the right of return, can a case not be made for a moral statute of limitations? For, surely, with the passage of time people's claims to return to their original places of residence diminish in force. Humanity's history is riddled with cases of displaced peoples, and it is obvious that there is little moral force to demands to return to one's country after hundreds of years have elapsed.[41] However, although it is true that as time goes by demands to return diminish in moral force, it is unclear how long it takes for claims to return fully expire. Moreover, given that the Palestinian refugees were rendered refugees only less than 60 years ago, it is safe to assume that their claims to return have not expired. This conclusion is strengthened by the fact that the majority of refugees are easily locatable and that most of their properties are documented (Fischbach, 2003).

Moreover, Israel, specifically, is not in a strong position to apply the statute of limitations to Palestinian refugees, because of its own Law of Return—passed in the Israeli Knesset unanimously on July 5, 1950—that allows any Jewish person to become an Israeli citizen upon entry into Israel. This law expresses the idea that the Jewish people have claims to the land of Palestine based on historic and religious connections. So if any Jew has the right to settle in Israel, even if he and his ancestors have not been to, let alone resided in, the area for hundreds and even thousands of years, it is difficult to see why Palestinian refugees, who also have claims to the land, should not be allowed to return, no matter the length of the elapsed time. However, because the Law of Return might be justified on grounds other than historical claims to the land, we should not make much of this point (see Section 4).

So while international law is, at worst, silent on and, at best, very permissive of the issue of the statute of limitations, morally speaking, the right of return has not expired due to the short length of time since 1948, to the fact that most refugees can be located, and to the existence of documentation of their property.

Let us now turn to the second objection. If the refugees have the right of return, it follows that it is permissible that they return. However, if—for some reason—they cannot return, then, logically, it cannot be that it is permissible that they return, for permissibility depends on ability. If the refugees were not able to return, then it would not make sense to say that it is permissible that they do so. Hence, they would have no right of return, for the existence of the right logically depends on the embodiment of an option, one fork of which is permissibility.

The crucial premise in this objection is that the refugees cannot return, which may be supported by two reasons: first, there is no room for the refugees; second, even though there is room, their houses have either been demolished or are being lived in by Jewish Israelis (or others), and their lands are being cultivated and are owned by Jewish Israelis (or others).

One Palestinian scholar, Salman Abu Sitta, has written, and continues to write, on this topic. His conclusions are highly important, and I know of no research that has refuted them. A summary of the relevant aspects of his work is important to address the second objection.

Abu Sitta argues that the majority of Israeli Jews (67 percent to about 3 million) is concentrated in one area that makes up eight percent of Israel's territory. This is basically the central coastal plain, containing Tel Aviv, and is the same area that the Jews lived in prior to the creation of Israel in 1948 and that was acquired during the British Mandate.[42] A second area, comprising six percent of Israel, contains about 10 percent of the country's Jewish population. This second area is the land that encircles Lydda and Ramleh (1508 square kilometers), having a mixed population of Palestinian Israelis (90 000) and Jewish Israelis (440 000). 'Thus, 77 percent of Jews live in 15 percent of Israel's area' (Abu Sitta, 2001b, p. 303). The third area comprises two large chunks of land, one in the north (roughly, the areas around Acre, Safad, Tiberias, Nazareth, and Baysan) and one in the south (roughly, the area around al-Majdal and the Negev desert): 'This is the land and heritage of about 5 million refugees who were expelled from their homes in 1948 and their descendents' (Abu Sitta, 2001b, p. 303). There are Israeli Jews who live in this third area (about 1 million), but they mostly (80%) live in 'cities that were originally Palestinian and are now mixed, or in a number of small new "development towns"' (Abu Sitta, 2001b, p. 303). If all this is correct, and if 'no room' means 'no geographical space large enough to accommodate the refugees,' the argument that there is no room for the refugees fails (keep in mind also Israel's Law of Return and its continuous encouragement of world Jewry to immigrate to Israel). Not only is there room for the refugees, it is roughly the same areas where the majority of them resided (see Map H).[43]

Moreover, the above discussion assumes that if the right of return were to be implemented, all, or almost all, the refugees would return.

This is, however, an assumption, and as far as the 'no room' argument is concerned, its plausibility only gets weaker the fewer the refugees who would actually return.

The second reason why the Palestinian refugees cannot return is that their homes and villages no longer exist; there is nothing to return to. However, it is worth quoting Abu Sitta at some length regarding this issue:

> Another Israeli claim is that all village traces are lost and have been built over by housing for new immigrants . . . The striking result is that the sites of the absolute majority of such villages [the 530 towns and villages depopulated in 1948] are still vacant. All village sites, except one each in the subdistricts of Safad, Acre, Tiberias and Nazareth, are vacant. Naturally, the area most affected is the coastal strip, especially in the Tel Aviv suburbs. There, a dozen village sites have been built over as a result of the expansion of the city. The displaced refugees from these built-over areas now number 110,000, or only 3 percent of all registered refugees . . . A number of village sites west of Jerusalem, and north and south of Tel Aviv, have been built over. However, well over 90 percent of the refugees could return to empty sites . . . The accommodation of the returning refugees from the affected villages [by Israeli construction] is fairly simple, at least from an operational point of view: they could retain the property rights and grant a forty-nine year lease to existing occupants, most of which are institutions. Meanwhile, they could rent or build housing for themselves in the vicinity. (2001b, p. 304)

So while most of the houses in the abandoned villages have been demolished, the sites themselves remain vacant. If the majority of the refugees can return to these sites, they would fulfill what it means to have the right of return: the return to one's land and village area.

Walid Khalidi's *All That Remains* (1992), corroborates the findings of Abu Sitta, especially as far as the issue of empty village sites is concerned. Of the 418 villages documented in Khalidi's book, 79 of their sites were fully built upon, partly built upon, or partly inhabited by Jewish Israelis (in those cases where some of the original houses are still standing). In the last type of case, in about six villages, Israeli Jews inhabited only one house on each village site. This is approximately 19 percent of the total. A number of the empty village sites are used as grazing grounds or are partly cultivated by nearby Jewish settlements.[44] Thus, the majority of the village sites are empty. In principle, then, the majority of the refugees can return to them.

But this leaves us with a crucial issue. If the right of return is the right to return to one's home, then how can it be fulfilled if the homes no longer exist? How can it be fulfilled if residents live in some of the homes (in some of the village sites and in many urban places as is the case with most Palestinian homes in West Jerusalem and other cities)? This is the claim that the right of return does not exist because there is nothing to which to return. It often underlies claims by Israeli and, indeed, some Palestinian officials to the effect that there is not much difference between the refugees returning to inside Israel or returning just a few miles across the green line into a future Palestinian state. After all, if you have to rebuild, what difference does it make if you do so in the West Bank?

However, based on PCPR, the refugees are entitled to the closest possible restitution. In this case, 'closest' means the option to continue their lives in the areas where their original houses used to exist. Hence, even if the refugees' original houses were destroyed, the right of return entails the option to be restituted in the closest possible way to what is lost. Of course, some of the village sites (as opposed to the lands around the sites) are now cultivated or used as grazing fields by nearby Jewish settlements, so an accommodation would need to be reached for both people to live off the land. The cases in which the homes of the refugees still stand but are inhabited by Israeli Jews (or others, as the case may be) are more complex, for it may be impermissible that the newer inhabitants be evicted from their homes, if CRT applies to them. Briefly, however, closest restitution to the refugees would entitle the refugees to build next to their original homes if they so choose and if feasible, to retain property ownership of the houses (if they originally owned them) and lease them to the current occupants, and so on.

The above sketch of the return of the refugees is programmatic yet shows that there are no in-principle, theoretical obstacles to the return of the refugees. The actual mapping out of the return and the details of how it will work are basically non-philosophical issues and so require separate treatment.

The third objection against the existence of the right of return has to do with how this right can be rendered non-existent. This can happen in at least three ways (ways by which rights in general can become non-existent): The refugees could waive their right of return; they could forfeit it; or a higher authority, especially a government, could render it void.[45]

One can usually waive one's right to X by consenting to let someone else have X, or by declaring that one no longer wants X. Have the Palestinian refugees waived their right of return in such ways?

One pervasive argument offered by many who deny the existence of the right of return asserts that the Palestinians who fled their homes did so at the behest of certain Arab governments. In so doing, they left voluntarily and thus have relinquished their right of return. I have argued above that the only sense of 'voluntary' this argument needs to succeed is corroborated neither by history nor by common sense.

One other argument that, if sound, would entail that the Palestinian refugees have waived their right of return is that of 'population exchange.' Roughly, the reasoning claims that since there were Jewish refugees from other Arab countries who went to Israel, and since there were Palestinian refugees from Palestine who went to different Arab countries, this is tantamount to an exchange of populations. Through this exchange, the Palestinian refugees have (implicitly?) waived their right of return (Karmi, 1999b, pp. 206–10; Abu Shakrah, 2001).

Setting aside the issue of the circumstances under which Jewish Arabs left their original countries, the fact is that even though there are Palestinian refugees, there are no longer Jewish refugees from Arab countries in Israel, mainly because they have settled in Israel and have, for the most part, willingly become Israeli citizens. (This does not mean that they are not entitled to compensation for property left behind; they are.) But the Palestinian refugees have not been given citizenship in some countries (such as Lebanon and Syria), they have not given up on their right of return, and they have not considered themselves part of an exchange of populations. Thus, even if both Israel and the Arab countries hosting the refugees have undertaken an agreement to exchange the two refugee populations (something which did not happen), this would not negate the Palestinian refugees' right of return.[46]

Given that the Palestinian refugees have, if anything, been insisting on their right of return,[47] and given that the above two arguments are unconvincing, it seems that the refugees have not waived their right to return.

Have the Palestinian refugees forfeited their right to return? Generally, one way to do so is to just 'let it lie': 'If the prize in the lottery is the privilege of dining on an evening of my choice with the Vice-President, I may simply make no choice, I may forfeit the privilege, and without fault' (Thomson, 1990, p. 361). But Palestinian refugees have not forfeited their right to return by letting it lie. Most of them, as I mentioned, have been insisting on it. Perhaps for some subclass of Palestinian refugees—those who reside in places where they are happy to be and who have no intention of living somewhere else, let alone returning to Israel/Palestine—it may be true of some of them that they have forfeited their right to return by letting it lie ('true of some of them' because the characterization of this subclass might not be sufficient for all its members to have forfeited their right to return by letting it lie; one may have no intention of relocating from one's residence and yet insist on the right—the ability, the option—to being allowed to return). What it means to forfeit a right by letting it lie is not obvious, especially with respect to the right of return. Nonetheless, most Palestinian refugees have not forfeited their right by letting it lie. If anything, they have been demanding it.

One other way to forfeit a right is by aggressing against someone. If I attack Tom, and the only way for Tom to defend himself is by harming me, I forfeit my right against being harmed by Tom (and arguably by those who can interfere to defend Tom). Tom cannot defend himself by harming me in any way he chooses. If I attack him with the aim of pinching his arm, he cannot defend himself by killing me if he has other options (indeed, he may not kill me even if that is the only way he can prevent me from pinching him). So how does this translate to the Palestinian refugees? One can argue that since they were, and continue to be, aggressors, they forfeit their right to return.

There is no denying the fact that a number of refugee Palestinian men (and a few women) engaged and continue to engage in military operations against Israel, mostly from Lebanon (very roughly from 1970 to 1982) and Jordan (very roughly, during the 1960s), with some plausibly described as terrorist. Moreover, shortly before the borders with Jordan were controlled more efficiently (during the early 1950s), a number of refugees tried to enter their lands through the armistice lines ('green lines') with Jordan.[48] Initially, almost all these 'infiltrator' refugees went back to try to retrieve personal property or to harvest their crops. Israel's policy against them was extremely harsh, and subsequent 'infiltrators' were bent on exacting revenge by killing Israeli civilians. Today, barely any refugees from the three neighboring Arab states engage in such military operations against Israel; the ones who do come from refugee camps inside of the West Bank (and their numbers have been diminishing since Israel started constructing its wall), and very few from the Gaza Strip, since the Strip is effectively sealed.

The question, however, is what this would show. First, it would not show that all, most, or even many refugees were and are aggressors. Second and more important, assuming that most refugees are aggressors, we must ask whether their aggression entails their forfeiture of the right of return.[49] Given the history and the politics of the Israeli–Palestinian conflict, their aggression is an attempt to address and redress past grievances. The general aim of the aggression on the part of the Palestinians, refugees or non-refugees, is not to annihilate the Jews, as some contend, but to restore a just situation in the region.[50] Although this entails the aggressors' forfeiture of some rights, perhaps even the right of return of the individual aggressors,[51] it does not entail the forfeiture of the right of return in general or for the other, non-aggressing refugees. The most we can say is that given the level of hostility between the two parties, the right of return should be implemented only as part of a comprehensive, just agreement, since there is general resentment between the two populations.

But perhaps the issue that underlies the aggression worry is not that the Palestinian refugees are aggressors, for obviously the overwhelming majority are not, but that many of them would aggress were they able to, given the hostility between the two main parties. But, of course, it is debatable whether an intention to aggress is sufficient for forfeiting rights. Moreover, if the refugees have such intentions, it is because they are denied their rights. That is, remove the causes of their hostility and you remove these intentions. So we cannot use such intentions to deny the refugees rights when those very intentions are caused by the denial of these rights.

This leaves us with the possibility that a higher authority, especially a government, can make one cease to have rights. Have any governments proclaimed that the Palestinian refugees have no right of return? No Arab government has claimed this, nor has the Palestine Liberation Organization, nor the Palestinian Authority, although it is unclear whether the last endorses certain peace proposals (e.g., the Geneva Accords) that annul the right of return. The United Nations also has not made such a proclamation. The only government that has done so is Israel.[52] But under what conditions can a government make one cease to have a right? Two plausible conditions are that 'the lawmaker is legitimately the lawmaker of the society, and the lawmaker acts [morally] permissibly in depriving of the legal privilege' (Thomson, 1990, p. 356). The first of these two conditions renders void the declarations of the Israeli government, for Israeli politicians are not the legitimate lawmakers of the Palestinian refugees (this also applies to Arab governments and any other non-Palestinian representative lawmakers and governments).

However, even if the Palestine Liberation Organization or the Palestinian Authority has actually annulled the right of return, this would not render the refugees lacking the right. For even if a government legitimately represents its people, it can only make the people, individually or collectively, lose a right if it acts morally permissibly in doing so, according to the second condition. And this issue cannot be settled until we decide whether there could be compelling moral reasons for doing so. So far we have seen that there are not.

So the objections against the right of return's existence fail. Given the positive argument for its existence, I conclude that the right of return for the Palestinian refugees does indeed exist.

But suppose someone now exclaims, 'So you have established the right of return's existence. Big deal. We all have all sorts of rights. The important issue is when and under what conditions we can exercise those rights, and when and under what conditions they can be overridden. Showing that the right of return exists does not show that it should be implemented, which is the really important issue.'

This reasoning is partly correct: issues surrounding the implementation of rights and the permissible overriding of these rights are very important. But showing that rights exist is also very important, because, as stated earlier, rights are constraints on people's behavior towards each other. Showing that a right exists shows that people may not behave in just any way they desire towards those who have that right. For, first, right-holders are able to morally demand (as opposed to merely request) that others—those against whom the rights are held—act or refrain from acting in particular ways towards them. The Palestinians' right of return is one they have primarily against Israel and secondarily against the international community; it is a right on the basis of which they can demand to be given the option of returning.

Second, especially in the case of important and basic rights, high amounts of goods are needed to permissibly override these rights. Since the right of return is a basic and important right, not just any justification for its non-implementation will suffice. The justification must show that there are extremely important goods (possibly also including other, competing rights) whose existence is at stake, goods that would not be obtained or that would be lost were the right of return to be implemented.

4. The implementation of the right of return

Granted that the right of return exists and that it is a moral right, should it be implemented? Or are there considerations that justify overriding it? If there are moral goods that can obtain only by overriding the right, are they important enough to justify this? There are a number of different such goods; in discussing them, I conclude that none is strong enough to justify overriding the right of return. To re-emphasize, the moral goods need to be quite strong to justifiably override the right of return; if minor goods can do the job, rights would be pointless. Because the right of return is no trivial right, these moral goods do indeed need to be quite strong.

4.1. Rights-based goods

Some of these moral goods are rights-based and some are consequences-based. I start with the former, discussing two arguments on which they rely.

The first argument—a variation of the 'no room' argument discussed above—states that if Jews possess a comparable right of return to historic Palestine, the two groups' rights would clash, resulting in a philosophical stalemate such that only one group's right of return can be implemented. Since Jews already inhabit Israel, and since Palestinians can settle in Arab countries, the latter's right of return should be the one to not be implemented.

This argument is not convincing. First, there is no good reason to believe that Jews have a comparable right of return. Second, the two groups' rights need not clash.

How might a right of return for Jews to historic Palestine be justified? One way is to consider Diaspora Jews as refugees. Shlomo Avineri writes, 'It was because of [the Jews' link to the Land of Israel] that Jews were considered by others – and considered themselves – not only a minority, but a minority *in exile*' 1981, p. 3; emphasis in original). But assuming that Jews outside Israel are refugees, this is not sufficient to ground a right for their return, for it has been about 2000 years since the destruction of the Second Temple and the eventual dispersal of the Jews from Palestine in the second century. No matter how generous we are in stretching a moral equivalent of a legal statute of limitations, it would probably not extend to 2000 years. Thus, given the length of elapsed time, any right of return of the Jews has 'expired.'

Perhaps a more convincing way to ground a right of return for Jews is to think of 'minority in exile' as meaning not 'refugee' but 'being out of place.' Avishai Margalit and Moshe Halbertal (1994) argue for the existence of an individual's right to culture, a right from which we might derive a Jewish right of return (the authors do not use the right to culture to ground such a right). Margalit and Halbertal argue that the right to culture is the right to three things: (i) the ability to 'maintain a comprehensive way of life within the larger society without interference, and with only the limitation of the harm principle' (p. 498); (ii) 'the recognition of the community's way of life by the general society' (p. 498); and (iii) 'the support for the way of life by the state's institutions so that the culture can flourish' (p. 499). Margalit and Halbertal justify the right to culture on an individual's interest in belonging not just to any culture, but to his or her specific culture: 'In our view, which links the right to culture with identity rather than freedom, every person has the right to her own culture and not merely to culture in general' (p. 506).

Assuming that Margalit and Halbertal are correct, would the right to culture ground a right of return for Jews to historic Palestine?[53] One argument might be as follows: if every Jew has a right to culture, and if Israel contains a thriving Jewish culture, every Jew would have the right to move to Israel to satisfy his right to culture.

The conclusion, however, does not follow. Whether 'Jewish culture' refers to a specific sub-group of Jewish culture (e.g., the ultra-Orthodox in Israel, one of the examples that Margalit and Halbertal give) or to monolithic Jewish culture, it does not follow from the fact that, say, an ultra-Orthodox Jew has a right to the culture of ultra-Orthodox Jews that he has the right to that culture *in Israel*. This follows only if the only ultra-Orthodox Jewish community left in existence is the one in Israel, something not in fact true. The same reasoning applies to a monolithic Jewish culture. Thus, the right of a Jewish person to a subculture or Jewish culture would ground his right of return to historic Palestine only if that subculture (or Jewish culture) exists only in historic Palestine (with no other overriding conditions). Since this does not characterize Jewish subcultures (excepting perhaps Sephardic Jews from Arab countries) or Jewish culture in general, such a right to culture would not ground a right of return for Jews.

Finally, because Jews are not merely a religious group (many are secular), religious connections to Israel will not justify their right of return. And even if Jewish identity were merely religious, it does not follow that they have a right to return to historic Palestine, just as it does not follow that Muslims have a right to return to Saudi Arabia or Christians to Palestine from the fact that these religions have their roots in those places.

It seems difficult, then, to show that there is a right of return for Jews to Palestine. As I have argued, historic links are too remote in time, cultural links too weak, and religious links not encompassing enough to ground this right. The only contender left is to understand Israel as a refuge for Jews: like all persons, Jews have a right to lead safe lives and free from harassment, but owing to anti-Semitism, they may deserve some priority. Since Israel is the Jewish state, it follows that Jews have a right to move to Israel to seek such lives. Thus, a right of return for Jews would be grounded on their right to security and well-being.

But this argument is also invalid. Supposedly, the right of return for Jews to Israel or historic Palestine is based on their right to lead secure and free lives. But it does not follow that they have a special right of return specifically to Israel. If, for example, Canada starts to persecute its Jewish population, it follows that Canadian Jews have the right that such persecution cease and that all necessary measures be put in place to prevent present and future persecution. Also, if such persecution does not cease, Canadian Jews have the right to leave Canada to a safer place. But it does not follow that they have a right to go to historic Palestine any more than it follows that they have a right to go to Sweden (under Israel's Law of Return, Canadian Jews would be allowed into Israel, but this law confers a legal right of return and so itself requires moral justification.)

Thus, even though it is good or desirable that Jews return there, they have no right of return to historic Palestine.

But suppose for the sake of philosophical inquiry that such a right does exist. What follows regarding the Palestinian refugees' right of return? Unless we assume an ensuing clash of rights, nothing, really. Both Jews and Palestinian refugees would have a right of return to historic Palestine, a situation containing no philosophical difficulties. Rights of return are not exclusive of each other. If each of X and Y has the right to return to a country, both can return. Practical difficulties, such as lack of enough water, can be addressed by importing water from other regions or building desalination plants. Thus, neither Jews nor Palestinian refugees have to give up their rights of return to accommodate the other.

Another potential right that might clash with the Palestinian refugees' right of return is that of Israeli–Jewish self-determination: Israeli Jews, as a people, have the right to national self-determination. If they determine that they do not want the Palestinian refugees to live among them,[54] we seem to have a clash of rights. On the one hand, the Israeli Jews have the right, stemming from the right to self-determination, to refuse the return of the Palestinian refugees. On the other, each individual refugee has the right to return. Could it be that the former right trumps the latter because it protects highly important moral goods?

Assuming that there is such a right, that it is properly justified and formulated, and that it should be construed along national lines,[55] it is, like any right, constrained by what we can permissibly do to others in exercising it (Margalit & Raz, 1990). When positioned against the Palestinian refugees' right of return, we need to ask what it is about Israeli Jews' right to national self-determination that would permissibly block the implementation of the right of return, for it does not follow from the mere assertion of the Israeli Jews' right to self-determination that it is permissible to infringe the refugees' right of return. That is, the right to national self-determination cannot, as such, permissibly block the implementation of the right of return. We need to inquire into the possible moral reasons underlying the right to national-self determination that block this implementation.

The possible answers to this question bring us to consequence-based moral considerations that could justify overriding the right of return.

4.2. Consequences-based goods

One possible moral reason is that Israeli Jews would be endangered were the refugees to return. The argument—specific to the conflict with the Palestinians—goes as follows: there is a tremendous amount of enmity between Israeli Jews and Palestinians. To allow the refugees to return is to implant a hostile population in the middle of another that happens to be its object of hostility. This endangers the lives of Israeli Jews. Since preserving human lives is a greater good than allowing refugees to return, the right of return can be permissibly overridden.

This argument, while common, is not convincing for two reasons. First, it does not inquire into the reasons for Palestinian anger (I focus on anger rather than hate because anger is the root of the issue; the hate, when it exists, stems from the anger), an issue in need of airing to ascertain whether the Palestinian refugees would indeed pose a threat to the Israeli Jews. Put simply, the Palestinian refugees are angry at Israel because they rightly see it as the main cause of their dispossession and as not only unwilling to take any responsibility for their dispossession, but as taking a misleading attitude towards them, presenting them as hate-filled and intent on destroying Israel. Such Israeli attitudes and postures justify Palestinian anger. If Israel were to acknowledge its role in the dispossession and offer a sincere apology, much of the anger would simply go away.[56] Imagine, then, if Israel were willing to give the refugees the option to return and to live in dignity with Israeli Jews. Not only would the anger go away, I bet it would also be probably replaced with trust, gratitude, and possibly affection.

This point is common in the philosophical literature: emotions are parasitic on beliefs; change the beliefs, and you, eventually at least, change the emotion. If I am angry with Steve because I think he insulted me, my anger would go away on discovering that he did not actually insult me. Now if my anger at Steve is due to a serious grievance, and if Steve continues to neglect my demand for an apology, justification, or even reparation, my anger is likely to grow, perhaps mutating into hatred. The same analysis seems to apply to groups of people, rather than just individuals.

Israel is not only guilty of being the main cause of the refugee problem but also of refusing to acknowledge its role in it and of perpetuating a miserable life for a large number of refugees, namely, those who live under its rule in the West Bank and the Gaza Strip. The conditions that the Palestinians have to go through at the hands of the Israeli army and authorities justifiably make the Palestinians angry. But this anger is not against Israeli Jews as such.[57] So when their oppression ends, and when the refugees are restituted, their anger and hostility will wither away.

The second way, however, in which the argument under discussion goes wrong is in confusing the general acceptance of implementing the right of return with how the right of return is to be implemented. To agree to implement the right is not necessarily to agree that right now the refugee population should move back to Israel. The implementation of the right requires careful study, such as mapping out the areas to which the refugees are to return, in what stages, how many are to return at each stage, and who are the first to return. More importantly, it must occur as part of an overall, just peace agreement that allows both people to trust each other (after all, it is not just the Palestinians who 'hate' the Israeli Jews; the hate is mutual). Otherwise, any implementation of the right of return would probably be disastrous.[58]

It is important to mention a variation of the above argument not specific to the contemporary I-P conflict, but having an older time-span: Palestinians are anti-Semites, and no peaceful resolution with Israel will reduce their danger to Israeli Jews, for, unlike what is premised in the first variation of this argument, the Palestinians' hatred has nothing to do with grievances and much to do with the usual age-old hatred of Jews.[59] As Benjamin Beit-Hallahmi puts it, 'Tying opposition to Israel or to Zionism to anti-Semitism has become a great excuse and a favorite rhetorical device for the defenders of Zionism. Everybody speaking out against Israel or Zionism is labeled anti-Semitic, and thus all criticism is effectively silenced and blocked' (1992, p. 173).

This argument attributes to the Palestinians anti-Semitism as the specific cause for their behavior towards Israeli Jews, in contrast to what the Palestinians explicitly declare this cause to be (legitimate grievances). Yet the historical evidence affirms the Palestinian claim. The Palestinians' enmity towards Israeli Jews started when Palestinians became aware that some Jews were planning to convert Palestine into a Jewish state and when some Jews bought lands in Palestine and evicted the Palestinian workers and farmers, hiring Jewish ones in their place.[60] Given this early history, given that prior to this time relations between Arabs and Jews during the Ottoman empire were generally amicable, and given what we know about what happened since Israel came into being, we need to choose between two explanations for the Palestinians' enmity, the first attributing it to genuine, or perceived, grievances against Zionist Jews, and the second attributing it to anti-Semitism. It seems that the better explanation is the first. After all, the Palestinians are not the only people who have developed anger due to dispossession and oppression; one might even call it human nature. At best, one can say that if some Palestinians are indeed anti-Semitic, this is because the intensity of the I-P conflict has bred much hatred.[61] Note also that quite a few Jews (Israeli and non-Israeli) offer their share of anti-Arab speeches, attitudes, and behavior.[62] If one were to claim that they are racists, one good reply would attribute such vehement behavior to the frustration of the conflict. But then why not apply the same explanation to the Palestinians?[63] In short, attributing anti-Semitism to the Palestinians neglects obvious historical and psychological facts and seems to be a way of absolving Israel from any causal and moral role in the conflict.

The major reason usually given as to why the Palestinian refugees should not be allowed to return is that the Jewish character of Israel would be eroded, that Israel would no longer be a Jewish state. Typically, this claim is understood in terms of numbers: the Palestinian refugees, given their higher birth rate, would soon outnumber the Jews.[64]

Note first that although there are quite a few philosophers who believe that preserving a national group is a moral good (either as good in itself or derivative from other goods, such as the good of the individuals comprising the national group), few think that this good can trump all other moral considerations (Kymlicka, 1989; Tamir, 1993; Dummett, 2001).[65] For example, Jean Hampton argues that the right to reside somewhere is stronger than the right to preserve the culture of a group, and that 'a nation cannot prohibit citizenship to non-nationals when substantial numbers of non-nationals have lived long, productive lives within the territory of the state and require citizenship in order to live on an equal basis with other nationals' (1997, p. 235). In other words, denying such citizenship would come at the cost of inequality, and no democratic state could morally accept this. Preserving a culture or a national identity is not such a strong moral consideration to trump all, or even most, others. Regarding Israel, a massive return of the Palestinian refugees means that in a short time the Palestinians would vastly outnumber the Israeli Jews, rendering the latter a minority. Thus, if we understand 'Jewish character' in terms of numbers, Israel's Jewish character would indeed be negatively affected.

But why is this a moral issue? Unless we assume that the Jewish minority will be ill treated, we cannot simply claim that maintaining a Jewish majority is a matter of important moral force. And we cannot assume that the Jewish minority will be ill-treated, for the return of the refugees, as such, says nothing about their behavior towards Jews, including the possible political arrangements that would be in place after their return. So we need a defense of the claim that maintaining a Jewish majority is a moral good strong enough to trump the implementation of the right of return. Indeed, given Hampton's argument, unless tied to important goods (e.g., preserving culture and identity) we have not the remotest reason to believe that maintaining a numerical majority has any moral standing.

With one exception, any non-numerical meaning of 'Jewish character' is morally pernicious, such as maintaining a form of discrimination in favor of the Jewish population of Israel. The exception is that 'Jewish character' means that the state of Israel has a distinctive Jewish culture to it. The idea here is that allowing the refugees' return would erode this distinctive cultural aspect. Since this is a moral good, it justifies overriding the right of return.

To address this argument, let us assume that there is such a thing as one Jewish cultural aspect to Israel—a tall order, since Jewish Israelis have different cultural backgrounds.[66] Is there a reason to think that the Jewish character of Israel understood in this sense would be eroded? Many countries, such as Canada, India, Lebanon, and Switzerland, have ethnic or religious majorities but whose minorities maintain their own cultural distinctiveness such that they rub off on the country as a whole. Moreover, Israel—like Canada—can see to it that it has both Jewish and Palestinian cultural aspects. For example, the state's school system, national symbols, languages, and, among others, political structure can reflect these two. Moreover—and suspending the assumption of having one unitary Jewish culture—Israel has a large number of Palestinian citizens and of Jews who came from Arab countries (mostly in the 1950s), both of whom have many cultural affinities with Palestinians.[67] The point is that having the Palestinian refugees return would not impose an alien culture on the Israeli one, since the latter is already diverse and contains cultural connections with Palestinian culture(s).

This conclusion would be true even if cultures have rights to not be 'submerged,' to use a term from Michael Dummett, who claims, 'The right is one possessed by groups united by race, religion, language or culture: such groups have a right not to be submerged' (2001, p. 14). He claims that this right is of limited applicability (p. 14) and that usually the culture of immigrants has only a 'faint, and usually beneficial' influence on the host culture, 'unless the number of immigrants is very large, or their culture powerfully dominant' (p. 15).

Not explicitly defining 'the right not to be submerged,' Dummett mainly gives examples: 'In Malaya the influx of Chinese, serving to promote commerce, and on a lesser scale of Indians to work the rubber plantations, came very close to reducing the Malays to a minority in their own land' (pp. 15–6). This example indicates that reducing a population to a minority in its own land is one form of cultural submersion to Dummett. But it is difficult to see why this reduction as such entails cultural submersion.[68] Minority cultures, after all, thrive in many countries. Perhaps what Dummett should have claimed is not so much that cultural submersion consists of reduction to minority status, but that it is confined to small and isolated circles and reservations, such as what happened to Native American and indigenous Australian cultures. Being reduced to minority status would be necessary, then, but not sufficient, for cultural submersion, since it is hard to see how a culture can be the majority culture and yet be submerged.

Dummett claims that a nation's right not to be submerged derives from some notion of identity: 'Each person's sense of who he is derives from many circumstances: his occupation, his ideals and beliefs, but also from the customs and language he shares with those about him... We each need to be able to feel at home somewhere; not just in some locality, but within the institutions and among the groups of those we are bound to by common endeavors and concerns' (pp. 17–8). So the right not to be submerged is a group right based on liberal principles: it ultimately derives from the individual's need to feel 'at home' (p. 18). Because some cultures are fragile when it comes to the cultural influence of others, 'it is an injustice that immigration should ever be allowed to swell to a size that threatens the indigenous population with being submerged' (p. 20). Adding that this is rare, one of the ways in which it can happen is 'when a government is determined to obliterate a minority, and sets about it...by systematically settling large numbers in its territory who do not share the culture of the original inhabitants. Examples from recent times are East Timor and Tibet' (p. 20).

Note that in connection to the Palestinian refugees (who Dummett nowhere mentions in his book), Dummett's argument is of tenuous applicability. First, it is an empirical question whether the return of the refugees would seriously threaten Jewish Israeli culture with submersion. There are, moreover, numerous ways with which to ensure that Jewish culture is not submerged were the refugees to return. Second, and in connection with the issue of rights, Dummett's discussion is about the more common type of case whereby the culture threatening submersion is one *that has no claims to live with, or side by side with, the threatened culture, claims based on prior injustices on the part of the latter culture.* This does not apply to the Palestinian refugees, for they do have such claims. This second point, moreover, shows that, at worst, Dummett-like arguments have no applicability to the Palestinian right of return, or that, at best, they need to explain how strong the right not to be submerged is in the face of such claims. Dummett does claim that the right not to be submerged is not absolute, on the basis that refugees and immigrants have rights against countries, especially wealthy ones, to be given refuge. But note that these rights are not based on (at least direct) injustices that the countries have committed against the refugees and immigrants, but are anchored in our obligations towards each other as human beings and as political groups (Dummett, 2001, especially Chapter 3).

In short, if the issue was Israeli Jews' ability to maintain their culture, there is no good reason why having a majority of Palestinians endangers this. More important, because the Palestinian refugees have a right to return, the mere existence of such risks to cultural submersion are not enough to override the implementation of the right. Even if the risks or dangers were clear, imminent, and high, this would not show that the right not to be submerged trumps the right of return, for the latter is a claim specifically against Israel, based on the particulars of the history of the I-P conflict, and not a general humanitarian claim. But given that there are ways to safeguard cultural preservation, these risks cannot justify the overriding of the right of return.

Note that the above considerations are sufficient to address arguments, based on the idea of preserving Jewish national identity, advanced by a number of supporters of Israel as a Jewish state. For example, Shlomo

Avineri argues that Israel and Zionism are necessary to preserve Jewish national identity: 'Being Jewish meant not only personal commitment to a set of beliefs or norms but also belonging to a Jewish public. One could not maintain one's Jewishness in isolation from other Jewish people' (1981, p. 218). The rise of nationalism in Europe meant that Jews either became fully assimilated or faced the dilemma of being Jewish and yet also belonging to another nationality (1981, pp. 8–10). Thus, the only way to maintain being Jewish is for the Jews, as a people, to live in their own state.

However, given that another people inhabited Palestine at the time of the creation of the state of Israel, the creation of a Jewish state needs to morally come to grips with this issue. The question is whether the Jews can preserve their identity in a state comprised of another people. Partition solutions (discussed in Chapter 4) fail since, briefly, they either entail a form of ethnic cleansing of the Palestinians in order to maintain a Jewish state or they have to accommodate a sizeable Palestinian population, in which case we are back to the very considerations offered above about how a Palestinian sizeable presence would not necessarily erode Jewish culture and identity. So the considerations offered above do, in principle at least, indicate that there is no reason why preserving Jewish identity cannot happen in a country shared with another people. The country would have to be structured in such a way that Jewish cultural and national preservation is one of its main interests and goals.[69]

One important argument against the implementation of the right of return does not specifically involve Palestinians or Arabs in general, but centers on the Jews, given their history. It basically states that given a history of anti-Semitism and the Holocaust, Jews need a state in order to preserve themselves, literally, and not just culturally or nationally, as a people. Denying the right of return to Palestinian refugees has nothing, as such, to do with the Palestinians in general or the refugees in particular, but with the Jews being able to be in one place where they can decide on their own destiny. Such a state shields them from being subjected to the political whims of others and enables them to preserve their very lives.

This is a powerful argument, rightly appealing to our sympathies towards the Jews and their need for their own state. But it must address some difficulties pertaining to balancing the Jews' need for a state against the Palestinian refugees' right of return.

First, how effective are nation-states in preserving their peoples? Twentieth-century history indicates that they are not that effective, that nation states have often been the source of, rather than solutions to, conflicts. As Hampton puts it, 'When people want to kill one another, rearranging political boundaries can make things no better and sometimes worse' (1997, p. 240). This difficulty is exacerbated when the nation-state is built in territories containing other ethnic or nationalistic minorities. Here is Hampton again: 'recent history would seem to show that even if a unicultural state sometimes protects cultural units in some parts of the world, it is one of the *worst* vehicles for the preservation of cultures in situations where substantial numbers of people who belong to other groups also reside in the same territory – and that includes most areas of our world today' (1997, p. 241; emphasis is in original). This fits the I-P conflict. Although the Palestinian refugees do not currently reside in Israel, they did do so in the territory that became Israel. The historical grievance of being forced to leave and not being allowed to return has dogged the I-P conflict from its beginning, and has turned it, in addition to the Israeli occupation of the rest of historic Palestine, into one of the most intractable current conflicts.

Second, if the Jews need a state for protection, how can this be effective in an age of technological weaponry? Perhaps prior to the development of weapons of massive destruction, people having their own state was a good way to preserve and protect themselves. But somehow the idea of amassing as many Jews as possible in one little piece of land does not sound very reassuring in an age of advanced technological weaponry. And Israel's nuclear arsenal – its open secret – helps little.[70] It means either destroying Israel in the process of a nuclear war, or destroying the areas around Israel (if Israel were to fire first). And what kind of prosperity would Israel have in such a wasteland?

Third, not all world Jewry resides in Israel. There are many Jews in North America, South America, Europe, and other places who are leading good, prosperous lives in relation to their fellow citizens.[71] Thus, Jews already preserve their culture and their ability to lead good lives outside Israel, and Israel is not needed for this task. Jews living in democratic states, where they are treated as full and equal citizens and where they participate in the political process, is one other way of preserving Jewish culture and Jewish lives. But can things not change? Can hostility not spring up and anti-Semitism again kick in? However, surely living in Israel is no guarantee either. And surely living in democratic countries means having procedures for handling such issues.

We must also remember that, as far as the I-P conflict is concerned, that first, Israel was not built on uninhabited land, and, no matter how strong the Jews' claim to the same land is, it cannot simply void the other inhabitants' claims. Second, the Palestinian refugees are not alien people knocking on Israel's door demanding entrance, but original inhabitants of the land forced to leave by the Zionists. They have, in short, rights against Israel. Thus, the argument based on the need of the Jewish people for a state on their own cannot be used with justification to infringe the Palestinian refugees' right to return. At best, it shows that the two people need to share the land.

No doubt, were the right of return to be implemented (even carefully and as part of an overall settlement), and were the majority of the refugees to return, there would be risks, given the conflict and the hostilities. But risks are not enough to permissibly infringe rights. If they are, they need to be quite high. As Ronald Dworkin puts it, 'Rights would be worthless – and the idea of a right incomprehensible – unless respecting rights meant taking some risk' (2003, p. 41). As I have argued, much of the hostility stems from the lack of respecting rights to begin with, and so we should not exaggerate the risks.

One final argument against implementing the right of return goes as follows: surely one great moral good is solving the I-P conflict; if not implementing the right of return helps solve this conflict, would this not be a very good reason for not implementing it? Indeed, if Palestinian insistence on, and Israeli rejection of, this right has stymied the ability to solve the I-P conflict, it seems that setting the right aside is the way to go.

Subjected to scrutiny, this seemingly plausible argument is actually incoherent, for the right of return can be set aside in one of two ways, either by forcing the refugees to set it aside or by them willingly doing so. The first option is not really a way to solve the I-P conflict at all, since, in effect, if it has to be imposed on the refugees, it would be a solution they reject. Yet if they reject it, and if accommodating the refugees is crucial to solving the conflict, this imposition will not work. The second option in effect calls for recognizing the right of return, for it asks the refugees to waive the right. But in order to do so, we need to recognize it first (we cannot ask X to waive a right if we think X has no such right). Once recognized, the refugees can exercise it by either returning or not returning. If we allow them both options, the argument under review really has come to nothing, since its whole point was to set the right of return aside. If we block the return option, we force the refugees to set the right aside, in effect going back to the forced way just discussed above, a way that will not solve the I-P conflict. So this argument is incoherent.

5. Conclusion

I have argued that the Palestinian refugees' right to return exists and that in the absence of a good reason not to, it should be implemented. The return of the Palestinian refugees is a matter of rights: it is Israel's obligation to acknowledge and facilitate the right and its exercise, not merely of moral decency on Israel's part to do so. Without the notion of rights, the Palestinian refugees cannot make demands specifically on Israel, and Israel would have no moral duty to accept them. Thus, allowing the refugees to return is a matter of justice.

It is worthwhile to mention two points. First, to claim that the right of return should be implemented is to claim also that the Palestinian refugees are legitimate residents of Israel. This point is normative; it does not mean that they actually reside in Israel, but that they ought to be able to do so. This is a point we shall need for Chapter 4.

Second, if the right of return is implemented, this does not mean that the task of morally repairing the wrongs done to the Palestinian refugees is complete. Restitution rights, and rights generally, do not exhaust the moral domain, and other things, such as apologies and acknowledgements of wrongs done, might be in order. Moreover, not all the wrongs can be fully repaired. The deaths and suffering of refugees are ills that nothing can fully rectify. As one philosopher puts it, 'In the cases of serious, violent, traumatic, or shattering harm... it is a simple and poignant fact that no wrong is ever undone' (Walker, 2006, p. 7). After the implementation of the right of return, and apologies and acknowledgements by Israel – but also by the Arab world, the United Nations, and other relevant countries, most notably the United States – needed for redressing their moral health, it is up to the refugees to forgive their wrong doers and pick up their lives.

Israel may never actually allow the refugees to return, and, given Israeli officials' political rhetoric since 1948, the chances that Israel would do so is almost nonexistent. If Israel were to continue in its refusal, it would be committing a grave injustice and moral wrong. Because of *realpolitik* considerations, it might be that the feasible options facing the concerned parties are not to insist on the right of return and to find ways to ease the suffering of the Palestinian refugees by settling them in countries other than Israel. Such options, however, are morally suspect, because the refugees' suffering can be eased in ways other than giving up on the right of return, and because these options are close to capitulation in the face of injustice. However, they also raise the issue whether it is instrumentally rational for the

Palestinians to insist on the right of return given *realpolitik* considerations: Would it not be bad for the Palestinian cause in general, such as achieving genuine statehood, if the Palestinians insist on the right of return?

It is difficult to clearly answer this question since it is hard to accurately predict what the future holds. However, two considerations indicate a negative answer. First, the history of the I-P conflict is riddled with Palestinians backing down on their demands, and this, it seems, has not gotten them very far. If history were a reliable guide, then, backing down on the right of return would not reap the Palestinians any substantive gains. Second, and connected to the first point, and as Muhammad Ali Khalidi recently pointed out, it might seem that backing down on the right of return is a rational strategy for the short term, but it might not be so for the long one.[72] It might be as rational for the Palestinians to insist on the right of return as not to insist on it, sit tight, and wait for political facts to change.

If the right of return is implemented and a sizeable number of Palestinian refugees return to their homes and live in Israel with Jewish and Palestinian Israelis, this ought not to be, as some writers often make it sound, a bad option that we are somehow forced into.[73] Rather, it ought to be celebrated: Israel, with its Jewish and Palestinian people, can become a beacon to the world, showing how two populations with a history of enmity can bury the hatchet and live together in a true democracy.

Notes

1. The UNRWA-run camps (described by Genet as 'the discarded refuse of "settled" nations' [1986, p. 15]) are dispersed in the West Bank, the Gaza Strip, Lebanon, Syria, and Jordan. For data and profiles on these camps, see http://www.un.org/unrwa/refugees/.
2. UNRWA, established by the United Nations General Assembly Resolution 302 (IV) on December 8, 1949, began its work in May 1950. UNRWA defines 'Palestinian refugees' as 'those persons whose normal place of residence was Palestine between June 1946 and May 1948, who lost both their homes and means of livelihood as a result of the 1948 Arab-Israeli conflict.' The definition also 'covers the descendents of persons who became refugees in 1948.' It does not cover those refugees who left after May 1948 (http://www.un.org/unrwa/refugees/wheredo.html; date of access: June 6, 2004).
3. For some historical accounts, see Aruri (2001), Flapan (1987), Talhami (2003), Hirst (2003), Masalha (1992, 1997, and 2003), Morris (1987, 1994, and 1999), Palumbo (1987), Pappe (1992, 1999, and 2006a), Rogan and Shlaim (2001), Said and Hitchens (1988), Said (1992), and Segev (1986). For

a detailed account of the villages depopulated in 1948, see W. Khalidi (1992) and Map C. Other important treatments of the refugee issue are Abunimah and Ibish (2001), Abu Sitta (2001b), Arzt (1997), and Zureik (1996). A good resource on the background to the 1948 conflict is W. Khalidi (1987). For an introductory yet detailed treatment of the Arab–Israeli conflict, see Smith (2001). For analyses of recent events in the I-P conflict, see Bennis (2002), Carey (2001), Hunter (1991), Kimmerling (2003), Reinhart (2002, 2006), Said (2000) and Usher (1995).

4. On such plans, see Zureik (1996).
5. As Michael Fischbach puts it, 'It appears that it was a combination of fear of battle, fear of atrocities, and deliberate expulsion that explains why some 726,000 members of an overwhelmingly settled, rural population attached to its fields and homes would abandon them' (2003, p. 1).
6. For a full statement of the law, see Kushner and Solomon (2003, p. 279).
7. See Burrows (2004, date of access: January 3, 2004). For the text of the Geneva Accord, see http://informationclearinghouse.info/article5019.htm.
8. For the text of 'The People's Voice,' see http://www.mifkad.org.il/eng/default.asp.
9. Likud prime ministers are as hostile to the right of return. Speaking on June 8, 2003 to a convention of the Likud Party, Ariel Sharon said, 'I will never let any Palestinian refugees enter Israel – never... I clarified in the past and repeated in Aqaba that the solution for the Palestinian refugees will not be found within Israeli territory' (Agence France Presse, June 9, 2003).
10. The essays by Abunimah and Ibish (2001) and by Al-Qasem (1999) are useful on other aspects of international law. The former offers comparisons between the treatment of Kosovo and Palestinian refugees under international law and by officials of influential countries, such as the United States. Quigley (1999) offers other historical comparisons. The essays by Mallison and Mallison (1980) and Quigley (1999) discuss the United Nations' General Assembly and Security Council's treatment of the right of return. Arzt (1997, chap. 3), Quigley (1999), and Tadmor (1994) explain the Israeli claim that international law does not sanction the Palestinian refugees' right of return. The essays by Abunimah and Ibish (2001), Mallison and Mallison (1980), and Quigley (1999) contain responses to these arguments. Takkenberg (1998) offers a more or less comprehensive account of the refugees' status under international law. See also Akram (2001) and W. Said (2001).
11. I heed Judith Jarvis Thomson's advice that, 'It is plain enough that our rights have different sources... The student of the theory of rights does better, I think, not to begin by asking whether the one [right] is moral (or legal/moral) and the other [right] legal, but rather just to ask what those sources are' (Thomson, 1990, p. 76).
12. Whether people have restitution rights when their other rights are justifiably overridden or infringed, rather than violated, is controversial. Montague (1984) argues that they do not, while Thomson (1986, chap. 5) argues that they do. To make my argument as strong as possible, I merely rely on the claim that people have rights of restitution when their rights are violated (unjustifiably overridden).

13. Thus, insofar as the notion of a collective right makes room for individual choices regarding the right in question, the right of return is also a collective right.
14. Other than allowing the return, the individual refugees' decisions to return are dependent on other factors, including the kind of political arrangement under which they will live in Israel, the kind of life they currently lead, and the community in which they will live were they to return.
15. Almost all the depopulated villages are currently unmarked by the Israeli authorities; they have no official designations that they existed (Benvenisti, 2000; Pappe, 2006a, chap. 10). On the depopulated villages, see W. Khalidi (1992).
16. For example, Benny Morris, an Israeli historian, states, 'Undoubtedly, as was perceived by IDF intelligence during June, the most important single factor in the exodus of April–June [1948] from both the cities and from the villages, was the Haganah/dissident military attack on each site. This is demonstrated clearly by the fact that each exodus occurred during and in the immediate wake of each military assault. No town was abandoned by the bulk of its population *before* Jewish attack' (1987, pp. 130–31; emphasis is in original).
17. One might argue that in those cases in which Palestinians left out of fear, rather than direct attack or expulsion, they did leave voluntarily. But since the Palestinians' fear was justified and they reasonably believed that their lives were in danger, their flight was involuntary. Also, as I argue below, even if they did leave voluntarily, this is irrelevant to their having the right to return.
18. For example, Jewish troops sometimes used loudspeakers to frighten the Palestinians into leaving (Morris, 1987, pp. 52, 109; Finkelstein, 1995, pp. 65–6).
19. The examples reflect the catalogue of rights given in Thomson (1990, Part II).
20. For a comprehensive treatment of Palestinian refugee property claims, see Fischbach (2003). For a briefer treatment, see Karmi (1999b) and Kubursi (2001).
21. I qualify this sentence with 'if' because I have not shown that these rights were violated, and because whether mere overriding a claim calls for compensation is controversial (see Note 12).
22. I plausibly assume that in such cases it may be immoral to relocate the current inhabitants; the assumption is probably false as a general principle.
23. Insofar as much of the hardships suffered by the refugees are due to their treatment by their host Arab states, these states should shoulder some compensation for this hardship. But this is only in regards to compensating the refugees for hardships as refugees. The compensation owed them, if it is owed them, for the infringement of their other rights, including a needed, sincere apology and an even more needed acknowledgement of responsibility, falls on Israel. Moreover, the distinction between compensation owed to the first generation Palestinian refugees and that owed to later generations yields a complicated picture. On such complications in general, see Thompson (2001) and Sher (1980) (neither mentions the Palestinians).
24. 'Prevented' in CRT is an inadequate term, for it might apply to the indirect actions of others. I cannot find a better word to restrict the idea only to direct actions, but that is how I intend 'prevented' to be understood.

25. In her catalogue of rights, Thomson (1990) does not recognize rights similar to that in CRT. However, because the importance of this right goes beyond the importance of those found in Thomson's catalogue, I suspect it should be added to it.
26. Muhammad Ali Khalidi (1997) convincingly argues that a right to territoriality is necessary for a plausible formulation of the right to national self-determination.
27. J. Feinberg (1970) argues that even virtuous societies lacking in rights would lack something morally crucial, since rights enable people to make claims on one another.
28. RT does not entail PCPR; 'X owes Y restitution' does not entail 'X owes Y the closest possible restitution.'
29. In some cases, no remotely similar object can be a closest restitution. The set of coffee cups bequeathed to me by my grandmother is irreplaceable—not even a new set of coffee cups would be closest restitution in this case.
30. Indeed, so long, that their history might be traced back to ancient times (see Bowersock, 1988; Whitelam, 1996). The only attempt of which I know that claims that Palestinians did not live in Palestine for any long time is by Joan Peters (1984). However, it lacks serious scholarship: the theses are false and the research is flawed (Finkelstein, 1995, chap. 2). Regarding connections between the contemporary state of Israel and ancient, Biblical Israel, see Silberman (1989, chaps. 5, 6, 7, 12, 13) and Sturgis (2003) for discussion of archaeology's failure to substantiate some important Biblical claims.
31. See references in Note 3.
32. On Plan D, see, for example, W. Khalidi (1988), Morris (1987, especially chaps. 2, 3), Pappe (2006a, especially chaps. 4, 5), and Shlaim (2000, chap. 1). Morris (1987, p. 63) denies that senior Haganah generals viewed Plan D as a blanket expulsion policy (but in an interview with Ari Shavit about the revised edition of his book, Morris admits that there was some sort of expulsion policy initiated by Ben Gurion [Ari Shavit, 'Survival of the Fittest,' *Ha'aretz*, January 9, 2004]). Finkelstein (1995, chap. 3) argues that they did, given the evidence. Masalha (1992, chap. 5) also contests Morris' view. Pappe (2006a) argues that Plan D was a master plan for the ethnic cleansing of the Palestinians. See also Masalha (1992, 1997) for how the idea of 'transferring' the Palestinians played out in Zionist thought from 1882 and on.
33. See references in Note 3. See also Masalha (2001). Morris mentions a few calls by the Arab Liberation Army for some inhabitants to leave their villages, but these were done from military necessity and Morris himself downplays their importance (1987, p. 294). In his interview with Ari Shavit, Morris claims that there were more Arab calls for the refugees to leave than he documented in his 1987 book and thinks that this somewhat vindicates the claim that the refugees voluntarily left. But he is wrong, for the calls were made out of military necessity; the Palestinians were not being asked to empty the land for the benefit of the Jews (Ari Shavit, 'Survival of the Fittest,' *Ha'aretz*, January 9, 2004).
34. 'At their own initiative' is necessary, for 'willingly' and 'give *to* X' will not suffice. I can willingly give my wallet to the mugger, while still not doing so voluntarily.

35. Complicating the picture is that many of the refugees were not property owners, but renters, and one's next of kin do not 'inherit' one's house and land when one rents these.
36. Although some descendents have been able to visit the original sites of their villages and homes (but not return, rebuild, and live there), such visits do not ground in any robust way a strong sense of belonging.
37. Settling the refugees might require more than turning them into citizens of a state. This is reflected in international law, which distinguishes between being a refugee and being stateless (Takkenberg, 1998, chap. 5; Quigley, 1999, pp. 161–3). Jordan, for example, has granted most of its Palestinian refugees full citizenship, yet UNRWA and others still consider them refugees. The justification might be that granting refugees citizenship attends to their humanitarian and political status but not necessarily to other aspects, such as sense of belonging and right of return. In Jordan, the insistence on the refugees' right of return is reflected in Jordanian law (Talhami, 2003, pp. 77–85).
38. On how the passage of time complicates the justification of calls correcting past injustices by the descendents of the injustices' victims, see Waldron (1992). For replies, see Corlett (2002).
39. Sometimes the violation of a basic right can only be remedied by large sums of money, in which case the right to the restitution is not a basic right. Thus, violating a basic right does not entail a basic restitution right.
40. The Convention does not really apply to the Palestinian refugees for two reasons. First, its definition of 'refugee' focuses on the type of refugee who flees his country because of fear of persecution and who is either unable or unwilling to return to the country, a definition that does not apply to the Palestinian refugees (also, the 'unwillingness' phrase does not generally apply to the Palestinian refugees because of their more or less unique express desire to return). Second, Article 1.D. states, 'This Convention shall not apply to persons who are at present receiving from organs or agencies of the United Nations other than the United Nations High Commissioner for Refugees protection or assistance' (this clause was intentionally inserted in the Convention mainly at the behest of Arab states; see Takkenberg, 1998, chap. 3). Since the Palestinian refugees registered with the United Nations receive assistance from UNRWA, an organization separate from that of the United Nations High Commissioner for Refugees, the Convention does not apply to them, though it might apply to those Palestinian refugees not receiving assistance from UNRWA. In any case, despite the fact that this Convention does not apply to the Palestinian refugees, the United Nations, under UNRWA's auspices, still considers them so.
41. In October 2002, a number of Sephardic Jews from Turkey, Latin America, Hungary, and South Africa assembled in Barcelona, Spain, and demanded their right to return to Spain from which they were expelled in 1492—about 200,000 Jews were expelled, and their descendents now number around 4.5 million (Elizabeth Nash, 'Sephardic Jews Call for Right of Return to Spain,' *The Independent*, October 20, 2002). If granted, such a right would set a precedent for how far back in time people can press such claims.
42. Abu Sitta calls this area 'Area A'; indeed, he divides Israel into three areas, areas A, B, and C, 'to the ostensible horror of Israelis,' as Joseph Massad

jokingly puts it, in reference to Israel's division of the West Bank under the Oslo Accords into areas A, B, and C (2001, p. 115).

43. Although this summary cannot do justice to the complexity of his analysis, Abu Sitta also plausibly addresses issues that would have to be part of any serious and practical discussion of implementing the right of return, such as water resources, agriculture, and economy, and the very logistics of the return of the refugees. His work is also replete with maps and statistics. See Abu Sitta (1999, 2001a,b,c).
44. Note four things. First, Khalidi's and Abu Sitta's works rely on different sources, so relying on the former to corroborate the latter's findings is no futile exercise (Abu Sitta relies mainly on the Israel Statistical Abstract, whereas Khalidi and his team of researches rely on the *Palestine Index Gazetteer* and on site visits). Second, Khalidi's book lists only the villages, not the urban centers. Third, my number of the inhabited or built upon village sites is slightly higher than Abu Sitta's (I included village sites that contain only one house inhabited by Jewish Israelis so as to make the strongest possible case). Fourth, I included in the category of empty sites those that are currently (or at least in 1992, the date of the publication of Khalidi's book) used as closed military zones, grazing pastures, cultivated agricultural lands or fisheries for nearby settlements, archeological sites, tourist sites, forest preserves, recreational areas, and other such non-residential purposes. My reason is that changing such current usage in the event of the return of the refugees (or some of them) would not present as serious moral issues as having to possibly relocate current Israeli inhabitants.
45. I rely on Thomson (1990, chap. 14).
46. On the argument of the 'exchange of populations,' see Abunimah and Ibish (2001), Abu Shakrah (2001), Pappe (2006a, p. 213). A systematic and scholarly study is very much needed on the immigration of Arab Jews to Israel. For how some Iraqi Jews left Iraq, see Hirst (2003, pp. 281–90). On Moroccan Jewish immigration to Israel, see Black and Morris (1991, pp. 174–82).
47. They have been insisting on it since 1949. Refugees in the West Bank, Gaza, Lebanon, Syria, and Jordan have held rallies and conferences demanding recognition and implementation of the right of return. One recent protest was against the Geneva Accords and was held in Gaza City on December 1, 2003. There are conferences on the topic held almost annually. A recent poll among the refugees in the Gaza Strip shows that 96 percent of them insist on the right of return (*Xinhua*, 'Most Gaza Refugees Reject Abandoning Right of Return,' June 22, 2005).
48. This was prior to the 1967 war. A number of these refugees lived in tents and makeshift homes just outside the green line, and many of them could see their villages with their naked eyes. See Shlaim (2000, chap. 2), Morris (1999, chap. 6), and Hirst (2003, pp. 303–10).
49. The Palestinians understand it in the opposite way. The justification for the aggression is, and always has been, that it is needed to restore justice and to attain nationalist aspirations. I mention this in a note since one might plausibly argue that an aggressor's intentions are irrelevant to whether he forfeits certain rights in aggressing.

50. There are some factions of some extremist Palestinian groups that desire to be rid of Israel as a state. However, these, first, do not characterize these two movements in general, let alone the rest of the Palestinian population (see Seumas Milne, 'Too Late for Two States? Part I,' *The Guardian*, January 24, 2004). Second, their desire to eliminate Israel as a state is not the same as desiring to annihilate Israeli Jews, as some are quick to mistakenly infer. The former is compatible with a state in which both people live. As Brian Klug puts it, 'the alternatives are not black and white: either preserving the *status quo* or annihilation. There are a variety of constitutional arrangements in between. For example, Israel could continue to exist as a sovereign state but cease to define itself, in its basic laws and state institutions, as specifically Jewish. Or there is the so-called one-state solution: a binational homeland for Palestinians and Jews' (2004, p. 26).
51. 'Perhaps' because there could be other rights that they forfeit than their right of return. The United Nations' Convention Relating to the Status of Refugees, Article F states, 'The provisions of this Convention shall not apply to any person with respect to whom there are serious reasons for considering that (a) he has committed a crime against peace, a war crime, or a crime against humanity... (b) he has committed a serious non-political crime outside the country of refuge prior to his admission to that country as a refuge; (c) he has been guilty of acts contrary to the purposes and principles of the United Nations.' Granted that this Convention does not apply to the Palestinian refugees, one can still raise the issue whether Article F applies in spirit to some Palestinian refugees, namely, those who satisfy clauses F(a) through F(c).
52. The United States has an ambiguous record. But in April 2004, George W. Bush publicly declared his support for the Israeli position against the return of the Palestinian refugees to Israel.
53. To Margalit and Halbertal Israel's Law of Return is not justified because of the right to culture, but because 'the history of the persecution of the Jews necessitates a Jewish state that serves as a refuge' (p. 509)—the same as Theodore Herzl's (1970) justification (see also Pogrebin [2003, pp. 287–8] for a similar justification). About the Palestinian refugees' right of return, they state, 'We also believe that the Palestinians' history of expulsion necessitates a Law of Return in a Palestinian state for all the Palestinians in their diaspora' (pp. 509–10). To the authors, despite mentioning expulsions, the Palestinian refugees' right of return is not to their original villages in present day Israel.
54. According to some polls, the majority of Jews in Israel adamantly reject any state of affairs that would make them lose their status as a numerical majority (see Yulie Khromchenco, '64% of Israeli Jews Support Encouraging Arabs to Leave,' *Haaretz*, June 21, 2004).
55. See Kapitan's Chapter 1 in this book; Margalit and Raz (1990), Muhammad Ali Khalidi (1997), and Tamir (1993).
56. On this, see R. Khalidi (1999). Compare also Bill Clinton's apology, on March 25, 1998, to Rwandans for the West's failure to stop the 1994 genocide. The apology was welcomed, despite Clinton's controversial claim that he had not fully appreciated the depth and speed of the massacres (Nonna

Gorilovskaya, 'Never Again?' *MotherJones.com,* 5 April 2004 [date of access: November 2, 2004]). On the moral importance of apologies, see Gill (2002).

57. A number of Israeli journalists, most notably Amira Hass, Gideon Levy, and Danny Rubenstein, have written eloquently and movingly about the conditions of Palestinians under occupation (their writings can be accessed on the *Ha'aretz* Web site). Indeed, not a day goes by, ceasefire or no ceasefire, without Israel killing, injuring, arresting, or detaining a Palestinian, or without imposing a curfew, demolishing a home, or raiding a family's house (see Carey, 2001; Hass, 1999, 2003; Pearlman, 2003; Reporters Without Borders, 2002).
58. The mutual hate and anger has, of course, many exceptions. There are numerous stories of Palestinians and Jews, Israeli and non-Israeli, who have developed close, trusting, and caring relationships. A number of Israeli Jews volunteer in the West Bank and Gaza to shield Palestinians from settler attacks while they are harvesting their crops, to help Palestinians rebuild their homes after they have been demolished by the Israeli army, and, among other things, to help facilitate speedy movements across Israeli checkpoints for Palestinians. Palestinian attitudes, moreover, towards these Israelis express nothing short of gratitude, goodwill, trust, and friendship.
59. This argument is widespread among Israel's political defenders (see, e.g., Kollatt, 1971, pp. 75–6).
60. Hirst (2003), especially chapters 1 through 3; R. Khalidi (1988); Morris (1999, chaps. 1 through 5); Smith (2001, chaps. 4, 5). The Shaw Report of 1930, for example, whose results were confirmed by the Hope-Simpson Inquiry later in the same year, 'identified Zionist immigration and land practices as the reasons for the 1929 [Arab] riots' (Smith, 2001, p. 130). Palestinians also rejected all recommendations for partitioning Palestine.
61. Writing in *Ha'aretz,* Eliahu Salpeter states, 'Constant emphasis on the "perpetual presence" of anti-Semitism achieves the opposite results. It is both despairing and may also weaken the hand of those combating anti-Semitism. The fact that Islam... disseminates images borrowed from Christian-European anti-Semitism does not contradict the vast differences that still exist between the two forms of anti-Semitism. Christian anti-Semitism grew out of religious grounds and later adopted political and racist attributes and objectives. The other anti-Semitism, contemporary Muslim, was born out of political reasons and is now taking on racist attributes. Associating contemporary Muslim anti-Semitism with classic Western anti-Semitism is very convenient for extremists, both European and Israeli' ('The Jewish World/"Israel Is Bad for the Jews," ' November 6, 2003). See also Brian Klug (2004).
62. Suzanne Goldberg writes, 'I have lost count of the times I have heard Israelis describe Palestinians as animals, savage beasts intent on inflicting terror. Only Israelis rarely use the word Palestinian – their neighbors are much more commonly described as Arabs, part of that collection of more than 20 countries most have never seen' (' "It's Gone Beyond Hostility," ' *The Guardian,* August 12, 2002). Goldberg also describes Palestinians' general inability to see the humanity of Israelis.

63. All this assumes that if the Palestinians are anti-Semites, the right of return should not be implemented. But this is invalid reasoning; all that follows is that the refugees would pose a serious risk to the Israeli Jews. Whether risks are enough to justify the infringement of the right of return, however, depends on the risk. Moreover, risks due to anti-Semitism can be dealt with in ways other than keeping people away, such as education and the rule of law.
64. Maintaining a Jewish majority has been, and continues to be, something of an obsession on the part of many Israeli officials, academics, and others. Ehud Olmert, the current (2007) Israeli Prime Minister, stated that the main reason behind Sharon's unilateral disengagement plan from Gaza is demographic (Jonathan Freedland, 'A Gift of Dust and Bones,' *The Guardian*, June 2, 2004). On Israel's demographic policies towards its Palestinian citizens, see Cook (2006).
65. Michael Walzer (1983) might be one of these few. His claims that there is no universal theory of justice, and that each society is just if it distributes goods in accordance with its values, might entail any lack of constraints on the behavior of individual communities. However, Walzer acknowledges certain obligations that communities have towards strangers in accordance with the (severely restricted) principle of mutual aid (1983, pp. 35–48). Regarding refugees, Walzer states, 'So long as the number of victims is small, mutual aid will generate similar practical results; and when the number increases, and we are forced to choose among the victims, we will look, rightfully, for some more direct connection with our own way of life' (1983, p. 49). Assuming that Israeli and Palestinian 'ways of life' are different, given the large number of Palestinian refugees, and given the hostility between the two peoples, Walzer's claim would rule out allowing any Palestinian refugees into Israel (he does not discuss the Palestinian refugees specifically). However, Walzer also claims: 'Toward some refugees, we may well have some obligations of the same sort that we have toward fellow nationals. This is *obviously* the case with regard to *any* group of people whom *we have helped turn into refugees*' (1983, 49; my emphasis). This implies that Israel has obligations towards Palestinian refugees since Israel clearly 'helped' to make them refugees. Walzer neither recognizes nor comments on the tension between these two claims.
66. On Israeli culture, see Segev (2001) and Beit-Hallahmi (1992). On the argument about preserving Israel's Jewish character, see Abunimah and Ibish (2001) and Abu Sitta (2001a,b).
67. See Shohat in Kushner and Solomon (2003).
68. Dummett states, 'The danger of submergence occurs only when the immigrants arrive in a short time in such large numbers that they see no need to assimilate' (p. 52). So it is not just numbers at issue, but the time span during which immigrants arrive and their felt need to assimilate. But if they feel no need to assimilate, and if they maintain their own separate culture, it is difficult to see where the danger is.
69. Incidentally, a few thinkers sympathetic to Zionism, such as Martin Buber and Judah Magnes, favored a bi-national state. On the different strands in Zionism and the differences between them regarding Jewish claims to Palestine, see Shimoni (1995, chap. 8).

70. See Cohen (1998).
71. That is, barring recent waves of anti-Semitism in Europe, the nature and causes of which are subject to debate (see Butler, 2003; Judt, 2003a; Klug, 2004).
72. 'The Light of Reason and the Right of Return.' Presentation at the Central American Philosophical Association, Chicago, April 24, 2004.
73. See, for example, Yehiam Prior, 'Israel Can Still Be Saved,' *Ha'aretz*, August 15, 2003; 'Middle East Math,' *New York Times*, September 12, 2003; and Israel Harel, 'Being Driven Out by Demography,' *Ha'aretz*, December 11, 2003.

3
Terrorism

Tomis Kapitan

1. Introduction

Terrorism, as a form of politically motivated violence, is as ancient as organized warfare itself, emerging as soon as one society, pitted against another in the quest for land, resources, or domination, was moved by a desire for vengeance or found advantages in military operations against noncombatants or other 'soft' targets. It is sanctioned and glorified in holy scriptures and has been part of the genesis of states and the expansion of empires from the inception of recorded history. The United States itself emerged through the systematic ethnic cleansing of native Americans, a nearly 300-year campaign that featured the destruction of homes and crops, the theft of land, forced expulsions, massacres, and tears.[1]

While terrorist violence has been employed by both sides in the conflict over Palestine for over 80 years, the prevalence of the rhetoric of 'terror' to describe Arab violence against Israeli and Western targets is a more recent phenomenon. For more than three decades, this rhetoric has fostered the popular perception that Arab terrorism is the central problem in the Middle East crisis, and that once solved, progress can be made on other issues. Nothing could be more illusory. The Western obsession with Arab terrorism not only overlooks the fact that terrorist activity between Arabs and Jews has been reciprocal, but, more generally, that attempts to remove an effect without touching its causes are utterly futile. Terrorism between Palestinian Arabs and Israeli Jews is the product of deep divisions, entrenched strategies, and fundamental grievances and will not disappear so long as both sides cling to their present political ambitions and convictions. No informed discussion of its normative status can ignore its historical and political context. At the same time, terrorism is also the most tragic and sensational aspect of a bitter struggle for control of territory, and any serious attempt to grasp and assess the goals, methods, and passions of either party must recognize its centrality in giving the conflict the particular contours it has.

The object of this chapter is to investigate the role of both terrorism and the rhetoric of 'terror' in creating, sustaining, and resolving the Israeli–Palestinian conflict. Four questions are paramount:

- What exactly is terrorism?
- How has terrorism shaped the Israeli–Palestinian conflict?
- Does the rhetoric of 'terror' help or hinder efforts to understand political violence among Israelis and Palestinians?
- Can any terrorist actions or campaigns of terrorism in the Israeli–Palestinian conflict be morally justified?

2. What is terrorism?

The current 'war on terror' has increased the attention given to the very concept of terrorism, to what it means to wage war on terrorism, and to whether 'war' is the appropriate response to terrorist violence. Virtually, all discussions of these matters take for granted that terrorism is a problem, and much of the normative debate concerns how it might best be resolved. Obviously, no advance can be made on this front without first delineating the subject matter. Yet, there is considerable disagreement on the very meaning of the term 'terrorism.' It is sometimes used so broadly as to become synonymous with 'coercion' or 'coercive intimidation,' hence, no different from 'violence' (Wilkinson, 1986, p. 51; Primoratz, 2004a, p. 16). Often, an explicit definition is not even attempted, and even a cursory glance at the relevant literature reveals that there is no single universally accepted definition of the term—even the various agencies of the U.S. Government are not united.[2]

While lack of unanimity on a definition need not be a problem for rhetorical purposes, policy-making, legislation, and scholarship about terrorism require a definition in order to identify the phenomenon, justify ascriptions, and motivate moral judgments. In order to understand both the purposes and the effects of the contemporary rhetoric of 'terror,' and to set the stage for the investigation of the moral issues noted above, it is important to establish a meaning that is both suitably clear and unbiased, permits consistent ascriptions, and reflects common usage. Otherwise, how can we determine which actions and agents are 'terrorist' and which are not? How else can we fashion policies and statutes to deal with what some regard as a fundamental challenge to world peace? How else could proponents of a war on terrorism identify the enemy and justify their actions?

Most writers on the topic agree that terrorism is (i) a deliberate use or threat of violence, (ii) politically motivated, and (iii) directed against non-military personnel, that is, against civilians or noncombatants. Taking these as the only essential features of terrorism, perhaps the simplest and more accurate reportive definition is this:

> *Terrorism* is deliberate, politically motivated violence, or the threat of such, directed against civilians.[3]

Several terminological points must be addressed to clarify what I will henceforth refer to as this *standard definition* of 'terrorism.' First, where 'violence' refers to any coercive action or policy that causes physical harm, then violence is politically motivated if caused by desires to achieve certain political goals, where such desires are those of the agent or those of others whose actions have moved the agent to react. This allows that action born out of frustration over a political situation, brought about others pursuing their political agendas, is politically motivated even if the agent does not act from a plan in which terrorism is a means to a definite political goal. By a 'political goal' is meant any end concerned with establishing, maintaining, altering, or ending control or authority over regions, persons, or organizations.

Second, the term 'civilian' is ambiguous. In the widest sense, 'civilian' designates any person who is not a member of a state's military organizations, and in this sense the notion of civilian is different from that of noncombatant, a concept also used to define 'terrorism.' In a narrower sense, 'civilian' applies to all and only noncombatants, where a combatant is a member of any organization that uses force or the threat of force in order to establish or sustain a particular political order, or any individual who employs arms for such purposes. For simplicity's sake, I will use 'civilian' in this narrower sense, hence allowing it to be freely interchanged with 'noncombatant.'[4]

Third, the occurrence of 'deliberate' implies that the perpetrator is intentionally using or threatening violence to achieve political objectives and is identifying the victims as civilians. Some insist that the perpetrator must also view the victims as 'innocent' (thus, Primoratz, 2004a, p. 240), but this requirement would make terrorism much rarer than usually supposed.

Those who act from outrage over perceived injustices perpetrated by a certain state may view its adult civilians not as 'innocents' but as parties to the aggression—say, in virtue of paying taxes, supporting or benefiting from its policies, or, simply, being members of that political body—and thereby, deserving of their fate (see Section 9 below).

Fourth, while the combination of 'deliberate' with the phrase 'directed against' suggests that actual or threatened violence is intentional, harm to civilians might be incidental to the main aim of a terrorist action, say, to destroy property, to gain attention, or to provoke a government's response. For example, if the attacks on the World Trade Center towers were aimed solely at provoking an American military action, then, while harm to civilians was foreseen and deliberate, it might not have been viewed as essential to the action plan intended, and so, was not itself intentional. What was intentional was destroying those buildings in order to engage the U.S. militarily in the Middle East, not killing civilians. Even if one insists that intentional harm to civilians is essential to terrorism, it need not be the primary objective. Some distinguish the primary targets of terrorism, viz., those whom the perpetrators wish to move in some way, typically, governments, from the secondary targets, namely, the civilians, harm to whom is viewed as a means of moving the primary targets (Wellman, 1979; Primoratz, 2004a). Not all terrorism exhibits this duality; an act of vengeance caused by politically induced grievances might involve no distinction between primary and secondary targets, yet would still qualify as terrorism on the standard definition.

Fifth, it might be thought that etymology demands that terrorism involve the creation of terror, fear, and alarm. While several writers speak of such psychological effects as essential to terrorism, the use of 'deliberate' in the definiens of the standard definition once again requires care. Fear and alarm are typically the byproducts of actions that deliberately expose civilians to violence, and certainly many instances of terrorism have had such effects, especially since they are unexpected and unpredictable. But if the perpetrator's aim is simply to cause outrage and thereby provoke a response in order to achieve political objectives, then fear and alarm may very well be unintended and inessential. In this way, also, terrorists might carefully choose their secondary targets, making it erroneous to require that an act of terrorism be 'random,' 'indiscriminate,' or 'irrational.'[5]

Sixth, the standard definition does not imply that terrorism is unjustifiable. It might seem to have that implication given the use of 'deliberate' and 'civilians,' but a separate argument is needed to establish that a given act of violence directed against such persons is morally unjustifiable. Definitions that explicitly make terrorism illegitimate through such adjectives as 'unlawful,' 'random,' 'indiscriminate,' and so on make it much more contentious to classify a given action as a terrorist act. A definition that avoids this implication, by contrast, has the advantage that a moral assessment can be defended upon an examination of the case rather than being settled by arbitrary stipulation.

Seventh, the standard definition excludes no kind of person or organization—including a government or state—from being an agent of terrorism. There are several reasons to resist the stipulation that terrorism is practiced only by non-state agents or clandestine state agencies, never states (see Note 2). For one thing, there are no semantic grounds for restricting 'terrorism' to non-state agents, if we are to judge from the most recent editions of the *Oxford English Dictionary*, *Webster's Dictionary of the English Language*, the *Encyclopedia Britannica*, and the *Encyclopedia Americana*. Etymologically, 'terror' and, hence, 'terrorism' imply nothing about the identity of the agent. For another, 'terrorism' has been, and still is, applied to certain violent actions by states.[6] Moreover, the restriction to non-state actors is disingenuous. The term 'terrorism' has acquired a pejorative connotation, and for better or worse, it has become the term of art in labeling illegitimate methods of political violence. Exempting states from being agents of terrorism yields an unfair rhetorical advantage to established governments, especially since the weaponry and organization that modern states have brought to bear in pursuing their ends through violence against civilians consistently dwarfs any amount of harm achieved by non-state actors engaged in terrorist activity.[7] That states can commit criminal acts of warfare has long been recognized, as shown by the emergence of international agreements like the Hague Conventions of the late nineteenth and early twentieth centuries, the Geneva Conventions of 1949, and ongoing discussions in the UN. Insofar as the moral difficulties with terrorism concern *jus in bello*—not *jus ad bellum*—they have to do with nature of its victims, the methods employed, or the intentions with which it is done, not the identity of its agents.

Finally, there are different kinds of terrorism depending on motivations, modes, and mechanisms whereby harm is threatened or carried out. Terrorism is *strategic* if violence or coercive threat is part of a plan to achieve a political goal, but *reactive* or *retaliatory* (Khatchadourian, 1998) to the extent that it derives from an emotional response to politically induced grievances, for example, vengeance for confiscation of land or assassinations of leaders. Of course, since strategy and emotion can be jointly operative, and actions can have multiple agents, a given act might be both strategic and retaliatory. A further contrast concerns the causal route whereby harm is inflicted. An act of *direct* violence consists in assault or an immediate threat to do so, for example, killing or maiming someone or giving the orders to do so. However, violence can be committed by other means, say, by imprisoning people, depriving them of essentials, like clean water, food, or necessary medical supplies, or by damaging the institutional fabric of their society such as hospitals, schools, factories, and businesses, through legal and other authoritative mechanisms. States, in particular, accomplish such *structural* violence—to use John Galtung's term—when they systematically harm civilians by forcibly implementing or impeding certain institutions, laws, policies, and practices as a means to achieving political goals.

3. Strategic terrorism in establishing a Jewish state

The roots of terrorism in the Israeli–Palestinian conflict are not difficult to discern. Sheer demographics posed what was, and what continues to be, the central moral problem for Zionism, namely, that its seemingly noble—and to some, intensely spiritual—vision of a Jewish state with a decisive Jewish majority, could be fulfilled only at the expense of another people, the Arab inhabitants of Palestine. Despite the popular fiction that Palestine was 'a land without people' waiting for 'a people without a land,' the Zionist leadership was aware of an indigenous population, but argued that Jewish needs and rights to a homeland that Jews had been unjustly deprived of 1900 years earlier outweighed the claims of the Arabs. Faced with a demographic imbalance heavily favoring the Arabs, how was the Zionist vision to be achieved? Theodore Herzl's visionary book, *The Jewish State*, published in 1894, did not address the problem, but subsequently, he and other Zionist leaders came to favor a two-step program for demographic change: first, to promote massive Jewish immigration into Palestine, and second, to encourage the emigration of the Arabs into the neighboring countries.[8] The first step was partly achieved during the 1920s and 1930s when Great Britain opened the doors of Palestine to an influx of European Jews (see Chapter 1, Section 7).

The second step in the program of demographic change proved more daunting. Official Zionism advocated peaceful coexistence with the Arabs, insisting that there was ample room in Palestine for both peoples, that the Jews had no intention of dispossessing people of their property and that the Arabs stood to benefit by cooperation with the Jews. But the *maximalist* idea—that there is no room for two peoples sharing sovereignty in Palestine—predominated among Zionist leaders, such as

Chaim Weizmann, Israel's first president, David Ben-Gurion, Israel's first prime minister, and Vladimir Jabotinsky, the leader of the Revisionist movement within Zionism. In 1914, Moshe Shertok (Sharett), Israel's first foreign minister and second prime minister, insisted that 'if we cease to look upon the Land of Israel as ours alone and if we allow a partner into our estate—all content and meaning will be lost to our enterprise' (Morris, 1999, p. 91). With that end in view, the prospect of *transferring* the Arabs came to be seen as the 'obvious and most logical, solution to the Zionist's demographic problem' (Morris, 1999, pp. 140–1; Morris, 2001, p. 40; Smith, 2004, pp. 167–8).

In 1919, British authorities in Palestine, interviewed by the American King-Crane Commission (Chapter 1, Section 7), indicated that the Zionist project could never be achieved 'except by the force of arms' since the Arabs would resort to violence in order to stop a Jewish state from being established in their land (Khalidi, 1971, p. 216). One Palestinian, Pasha Dajani, summed up the Arab attitude in 1919: 'If the League of Nations will not listen to the appeal of the Arabs, this country will be come a river of blood' (Morris, 1999, p. 91). Men like Ben-Gurion understood this as well and began preparing the Jewish community for armed conflict and a forcible transfer of Arabs that would be easier in wartime (Pappe, 2006b, p. 9). The *Haganah* (Defense) was established in 1919 and fielded nearly 2000 men by 1921. Jabotinsky, one of its founders, stated that intentional demographic change was a necessary evil that was neither unprecedented nor a historical injustice (Brenner, 1984; Gorny, 1987, p. 270). In 1937, Ben-Gurion noted in his diary that,

> we must first of all cast off the weakness of thought and will and prejudice – that [says that] this transfer is impracticable.... Any doubt on our part about the necessity of this transfer, any doubt we cast about the possibility of its implementation, any hesitancy on our part about its justice may lose [us] an historical opportunity that may not recur. The transfer clause in my eyes is more important than all our demands for additional land. (Morris, 2001, pp. 42–3)

Speaking before the Jewish Agency in 1938, Ben-Gurion declared, 'I am for compulsory transfer; I don't see in it anything immoral.'[9]

Forcible removal of a population from their homes and lands for the sake of establishing a political order concerning which that population has no say constitutes violence against civilians; hence, one of the mechanisms of demographic change adopted by Zionist leaders was—and continues to be—terrorism. Attempts at transfer would expectedly evoke outrage, resistance, and similar terrorism by Arabs against Jews. Jabotinsky predicted this, but seeing no other alternative, he insisted that the tit-for-tat violence was something that the Jewish community had to endure. Since the end of Zionism is moral, he contended, so are the means necessary to achieve it, even if this requires an 'iron wall' of military might to prevail against Arab opposition. In a nutshell, this reasoning was the most simple and straightforward Zionist attempt to show that terrorism is not only rational, but morally justifiable.

Terrorism between Arabs and Jews germinated between the world wars, and it is idle to speculate on who initiated the violence or to describe one side as engaging in 'terrorism' and the other in 'retaliation.' In the broad perspective, the Zionists have been the aggressors in the territorial conflict, but, from the outset, both sides were quick to resort to the gun to settle differences. Rioting in Jerusalem in 1920 took the lives of five Jews and four Arabs, with scores injured, while in the Galilee, eight Jews were killed in battle, including Yosef Trumpeldor who acquired heroic status with his reported last words: 'It is good to die for our country' (Segev, 2000, pp. 124–5). In the following year, Jewish demonstrations in Jaffa provoked intercommunal violence that led to the deaths of 43 Jews and 14 Arabs, while subsequent fighting around Jewish settlements took the lives of another 47 Jews and 48 Arabs. Although a British fact-finding commission vindicated the Arab position, Ben-Gurion spoke of the carnage as 'the slaughter of 1921' and blamed Arab politicians for inciting the violence.[10]

Despite British–Arab negotiations during the 1920s to defuse the tense situation, Britain continued to allow Jewish immigration. In 1929, increased belligerence from some Zionist factions advocating a Jewish state spawned more violence in Jerusalem and surrounding towns. For the first time, native Palestinian Jews were targeted, including 64 civilians massacred in Hebron after local Arabs heard that the mosque of Omar was endangered and that Arabs had been killed in Jerusalem (Morris, 1999, p. 114; Hirst, 2003, p. 191). By the end of the fighting, a total of 133 Jews and 120 Arabs were killed (Smith, 2001, p. 130). Although another British commission faulted Zionist demonstrations, Weizmann was assured that Great Britain would continue to promote Jewish immigration and land settlement. Negotiations were suspended (Hirst, 2003, p. 195).

By the mid-1930s, as Jewish immigration accelerated and land sales to Jews increased, Arab tenant farmers were turned off the lands they had worked and lived on and were forced into cities under steadily deteriorating economic conditions. Their discontent was fertile ground for the revolutionary ideas of men like Sheikh Izzeddin Al-Qassam who called for an Islamic-based resistance to the Zionist invaders and their British protectors. Al-Qassam urged *jihad* (struggle) and exhorted his followers to 'die as martyrs' before he and some of his companions were killed by British forces in November 1935 (Hirst, 2003, p. 200). His example, together with rising unemployment and reports of Jewish efforts to stockpile weapons, led Palestinian Arabs to initiate a three-year campaign of attacks upon Jewish settlements and a revolt against the British forces.

The 1936–39 revolt featured a surge in the growth and development of terrorist tactics. The fighting that took place in this period reinforced the vision in both camps that armed struggle was inevitable and, among the Zionist leaders, that a separation between the two peoples was 'achievable only by way of transfer and expulsion' (Morris, 1999, p. 139). It also witnessed the first instances of indiscriminate bombing of civilians. Though the British allowed the Haganah to arm itself legally, Jewish underground groups were formed, notably, the *Irgun Zvai Leumi* in 1937. Its ideologue, Jabotinsky, urged 'retaliating' against Arabs who had targeted Jews and Jewish property and denied that there was a choice between pursuing 'bandits' and punishing a hostile population. Instead, the choice is between 'retaliating against the hostile population or not retaliating at all' (Schechtman, 1961, p. 485). Underground terrorism became increasingly sophisticated as the Irgun planted bombs in Arab marketplaces that killed 77 Arabs in three weeks in 1937 (Smith, 2001, p. 143), and in July 1938 massive marketplace bombs in Haifa, Jerusalem and Jaffa killed over 100 more Arabs, with the most devastating bomb taking the lives of 53 Arabs in Haifa (Segev, 2000, p. 386; Hirst, 2003, p. 225). Arabs responded by bombing Jewish civilians. In 1938 alone, 292 Jews were killed in Arab raids, while over 1600 Arabs were killed in British and Jewish attacks, including 486 that the British identified as civilians (Smith, 2001, p. 143). Greater force prevailed, and by 1939, British forces had crushed the Arab revolt, disarmed the Arab fighters, and exiled their leadership. Approximately 5000 Palestinian Arabs, 463 Jews, and 101 British were killed in the fighting during 1936–39 (Khalidi, 1971, pp. 846–9; Shaw, 1991, p. 185).

Despite defeat, the Arab recourse to arms succeeded in changing British policy. In 1939, Britain issued the MacDonald White Paper in which the government abandoned its intention of establishing a Jewish State and announced restrictions on further Jewish immigration and land sales. This reversal immediately brought the Jewish community in Palestine into direct conflict with the British authorities as well as

Palestinians, violence that was heightened after the World War II. In 1946 alone, Jewish terrorists killed 373 persons, 300 of whom were Palestinian civilians (Wagner, 2003, p. 122). The single most spectacular incident occurred when the Irgun bombed the British Headquarters in Jerusalem's King David Hotel, killing 91 people, the majority of them civilian workers, including 41 Arabs and 17 Jews (Clarke, 1981, p. 294). The mastermind of this attack, the Irgun leader Menachem Begin, subsequently rose to the top of Britain's most wanted list, yet his efforts were instrumental in causing Britain to refer the problem of Palestine to the United Nations and to announce its intention to terminate the Mandate by May 15, 1948.

Immediately after the passage of the United Nations partition plan in November 1947, fighting between Jews and Palestinians was renewed, with Jewish forces being more numerous, under a unified command, better trained, and better armed. Despite superior numbers, the Palestinian Arabs had no unified fighting force, but only loosely organized, ill-equipped, and rival groups waging localized battles (Hirst, 2003, pp. 258–9). Terrorism now occurred with greater frequency and on a larger scale than ever before. On the night of April 9, 1948, members of the Irgun and Lehi militias attacked the Palestinian village of Deir Yassin on the road between Tel Aviv and Jerusalem, killing scores of villagers and parading the survivors in Jerusalem while urging the Arab residents to flee.[11] Arabs retaliated with attacks upon Jewish soldiers and civilians, but Deir Yassin and similar massacres at Tantura and Dawaymeh precipitated a large-scale flight of Arab villagers and townspeople from their homes into what they felt would be safer areas (Morris, 1987, 2001). By the time the state of Israel was declared on May 14, 1948, over 300,000 Palestinians had fled from their homes and villages for fear of a similar fate, especially since the better armed and better organized Haganah had crushed the Palestinian resistance. In accordance with the Haganah's Plan D (*Dalet*), thousands more Arabs were forcibly expelled from their homes by Israeli forces after armies from five Arab countries entered the fray (Khalidi, 1988; Pappe, 2006a,b). Upon signing an armistice in 1949, Israel destroyed 531 Arab villages and emptied 11 urban neighborhoods of their Arab inhabitants (Pappe, 2006b, p. 7). Jerusalem was divided between the Israelis and Jordanians. No Palestinian Arab state was created, and the approximately 750,000 Arabs—more than half the Arab community in Palestine at the time—who had fled or been expelled from what is now Israel, became refugees in camps established in the West Bank, Gaza Strip, and the surrounding Arab countries.[12]

Here was strategic terrorism at its most effective; through violence, Zionists had taken a decisive step forward in solving the demographic problem and ensuring a Jewish majority in the newly formed Israel. Without removing a large portion of the Arab population, there would have been roughly equal numbers of Jews and Arabs living in the area designated by the Partition Plan for the Jewish state (Cohen, 1982, p. 273). After the war had ended, Menachem Begin wrote, 'Of the about 800,000 Arabs who lived on the present territory of the State of Israel, only some 165,000 are still there. The political and economic significance of this development can hardly be overestimated' (Begin, 1977, p. 164). For Chaim Weizmann, Israel's first president, the exodus of the Arabs was 'a miraculous clearing of the land: the miraculous simplification of Israel's task' (McDonald, 1952, p. 176). The conclusion is straightforward, yet shocking: without the use of strategic terrorism, it is unlikely that a Jewish state with a 'decisive Jewish majority' would ever have emerged in Palestine.

4. The deadly cycle of strategic terrorism

A miracle for one was a catastrophe (*al-nakbah*) for the other. With three-quarters of their homeland taken, and well over half their numbers in refugee camps, the Palestinians were initially too stunned and scattered to mount any serious attempt at reconquest, return, or reprisal. In the early 1950s, some refugees attempted to infiltrate across the ceasefire lines for social and economic reasons (Morris, 1993, p. 11, pp. 29–30) while the will to strike back led others to launch sporadic raids into what had become Israeli territory in the early 1950s. The Israeli Government responded to this predominately retaliatory terrorism with terrorism of its own, following a policy that Ben-Gurion had urged in 1948:

> Blowing up a house is not enough. What is necessary is cruel and strong reactions. We need precision in time, place, and casualties. If we know the family, strike mercilessly, women and children included. Otherwise the reaction is inefficient. At the place of action there is no need to distinguish between guilty and innocent. (Ashmore, 1997, p. 107)

In one incident, after a Jewish mother and her two children were killed by Palestinians in the town of Yahud in October 1953, Ben-Gurion sent in a military unit under the command of Ariel Sharon that unleashed an artillery barrage against the West Bank village of

Qibya. After being cleared of resistance, Israeli soldiers demolished 45 houses and the village mosque with explosives, killing 69 villagers (Morris, 1993, p. 246). All the victims were civilians, and three-quarters of them were women and children. A similar massacre occurred outside the village of Kafr Qassim in October 1956, when 47 villagers, including 15 women and 11 children, were shot dead by Israeli troops (Morris, 1993, p. 417; Hirst, 2003, pp. 312–3). These events exemplified a pattern that successive Israeli governments have followed to the present day.[13] Benny Morris estimates that in the period 1949–56, up to 250 Israelis were killed by Palestinian infiltrators, while as many as 5000 Palestinians were killed by Israel, the 'vast majority' of them being unarmed.[14]

Palestinian resistance became more organized after the establishment of *Al-Fatah* organization in 1959 under the leadership of Yassir Arafat. Its periodical, *Falastinuna,* declared in its September 1964 issue: 'Israel says, "I am here by the sword." We must complete the saying—"and only by the sword shall Israel be driven out"' (Hirst, 2003, p. 402). In the early 1960s, many restless refugees, dreaming of a return to their homeland, came to see armed violence by *fedayeen* (those who sacrifice themselves) as the ideal for Palestinians wishing to return to their homeland. Their resistance accelerated after Israel captured the remainder of Palestine during 1967 war, and Palestinians realized that they could not wait for Arab governments to solve their political problems. *Fatah* came to dominate the Palestine Liberation Organization (PLO) founded in 1964 and mounted many operations against the Israeli military in 1967–68, often from inside the occupied territories. Approximately 100 attacks were launched in 1967, a number that rose to about 2000 in 1970 (Pappe, 2004, p. 193). While *Fatah* had initially claimed that it would not target Israeli civilians, especially not women and children, this guideline was often ignored. One *Fatah* fighter, captured in 1968, told an Israeli court that he had been ordered to sabotage everything he could. Asked whether that meant the killing of children too, he replied, 'Yes, to destroy everything, because we haven't forgotten Deir Yassin' (Hirst, 2003, p. 431).

Despite some successes, PLO attacks against the Israeli military proved largely ineffective. After most of the PLO fighters were pushed out of the West Bank in 1968, some Palestinians resorted to more sensational terrorist tactics. These featured such events as rocket attacks against the Israeli town of Kiryat Shimona beginning in 1969, airplane hijackings by the Popular Front for the Liberation of Palestine (PFLP) in 1968–70, and, most spectacularly, taking Israeli athletes hostage during the 1972 Munich Olympics, culminating in the deaths of 11 Israelis and five fedayeen in the crossfire between the Palestinians and German police. In 1974, there were two highly publicized attempts to take Israeli hostages and exchange them for Palestinians held in Israeli prisons. These 'suicide' missions resulted in the deaths of 18 Israelis in Kiryat Shimona (eight of them children), 20 young Israelis in Ma'alot, and the Palestinian fedayeen.

Palestinian violence had its own strategic logic. In their minds, the Palestinians were victims of a massive injustice and, like all other peoples, possess rights of self-defense and self-determination in their traditional homeland. In an imperfect world, these rights cannot be won peacefully, and because attacks on Israel's military are largely ineffective, they must demonstrate that they can do enough damage by other means so that, eventually, their demands would be addressed and their rights secured. Terrorism, they felt, would also achieve three important intermediary steps in working towards this goal. First, by demonstrating an ability to strike against their enemies, a sense of unity and confidence would be heightened within their own community, thereby strengthening the Palestinian will to resist. Second, through violence against civilians, the Israeli sense of security would be undermined and Israeli leaders would be forced to consider the high price of continued occupation. In 1983, Mahmoud Abbas, years before he became the first prime minister of the Palestinian Authority, rivaled Ben-Gurion in articulating this steely strategy of violence:

> The human element is forever the most difficult problem...it constitutes the Achilles heel of the Zionist project...All military operations should target population centers to inflict the greatest magnitude of losses on the enemy by striking its most precious possession. This would erase what little sense of security remains from the hearts of settlers and plant doubt in their psyches about their future....We have only to know the joint that aches most. (Hroub, 2000, p. 248)

Third, through spectacular violence, the Palestinians could draw attention to their cause, neglected for over two decades by the world community. Here, they succeeded dramatically; probably some 500 million people witnessed the events in Munich on television, and as one Palestinian leader put it:

> The sacrifices made by the Munich heroes...didn't bring about the liberation of any of their comrades imprisoned in Israel...but they did obtain the operation's other two objectives; world opinion was

> forced to take note of the Palestinian drama, and the Palestinian people imposed their presence on an international gathering that had sought to exclude them.[15]

Though repelled by their tactics, thoughtful observers began to ask why the Palestinians had suddenly appeared on the world stage in so violent a manner. What are their grievances? What do they hope to achieve? Having grabbed the spotlight, by 1974, the PLO denounced the hijackings of radical Palestinian factions and expressed willingness to work towards a negotiated resolution of the conflict. It was rewarded with official recognition in many of the world's capitals and its leader, Arafat, addressed the UN General Assembly, declaring that he carried a 'freedom fighter's gun' in one hand, and warning not to let the 'olive branch' in his other fall to the ground. Despite the setbacks of the Lebanese civil war that began in 1975 and the Israeli invasion of Lebanon in 1982, the PLO emerged as a negotiating partner in the peace negotiations that began in 1991 and led to the signing of the Oslo Accords in 1993. Just as Menachem Begin had done 14 years earlier, Arafat underwent the miraculous metamorphosis from strategic terrorist to Nobel Peace Prize laureate.

Yet, the Palestinians paid a heavy price for availing themselves of this strategy. As the Israeli offensive against the PLO gained momentum, Palestinians were gradually transformed in the Western media from 'guerrillas' into 'terrorists' (see Section 8 below), and in some quarters, their cause became more difficult to defend. Some of the initial sympathy for Palestinians diminished, while those already favoring Zionism found new ammunition for their opposition to Palestinian aspirations for self-determination. Moreover, to undermine the diplomatic gains of the PLO, Israel began to eliminate moderate Palestinians capable of addressing a Western audience (Abou Iyad, 1981, p. 104; Hoffman, 2002; date of access: November 12, 2006) while exiling pro-PLO leaders from the occupied territories. Finally, as the Israeli military continued to pursue Ben-Gurion's policy of fighting terrorism with terrorism, Palestinian and other Arab civilians in Jordan, Syria, and Lebanon bore the brunt of attacks by the Israeli air force (Hirst, 2003, chap. 7, *passim*). Casualties in these air raids far exceeded those of the incursions that prompted them; after Munich, for example, between 200 and 500 people, mainly civilians, were killed by Israeli bombs (Hirst, 2003, p. 378).

In the years that followed, neither the Israeli government nor Palestinians militants have abandoned the pattern of countering one act of terrorist violence with another. Yet, the balance of terror has continued to be weighted against the Palestinians. From the emergence of the PLO in the mid-1960s through the 1980s, the total number of Israeli civilians who died at the hands of the Palestinians is estimated to be 436, whereas a conservative estimate of Palestinian civilians killed by Israelis in the period 1973–88 is well over 15,000, a ratio of approximately one to thirty (Khalidi, 1989, pp. 23–8). In 1978, after 38 Israelis were killed in crossfire during a bus hijacking in central Israel, Israeli forces invaded southern Lebanon, killing between 1500 and 2000 people and causing more than 100,000 villagers to flee northward into Beirut. This figure is dwarfed by the roughly 19,000 Lebanese and Palestinians killed during Israel's 1982 invasion of Lebanon, slightly more than 84 percent being civilians, not including the victims of the Sabra and Shatilla massacre (see Section 8 below).[16] From 1988 to 1997, 421 Israeli civilians were killed by Palestinians while at least 1385 Palestinians in the occupied territories were killed by Israeli security forces (all but 18 of these were civilians). In the period from 1998 to 2006, over 1000 Israelis lost their lives as against approximately 5000 Palestinians; in both cases, approximately three-quarters of the fatalities were civilians. In 2006 alone, B'tselem reported that 23 Israelis were killed by Palestinians, whereas 660 Palestinians were killed by Israeli security services, among which were 322 that had taken no part in hostile acts, including 141 children. Israeli abuses of human rights have included the use of children as human shields.[17]

5. Structural terrorism in the occupied territories

> [A] Jewish state in part [of Palestine] is not an end, but a beginning.... Establishing a [small] state... will serve as a very potent lever in our historical efforts to redeem the whole country.
>
> David Ben-Gurion in 1937 (Morris, 1999, p. 138)

During the 1967 war, the remainder of Palestine came under direct control of Israel. Since then, Israel has expanded and annexed East Jerusalem, with one of its first acts being to evict 5500 Arab inhabitants of the Jewish quarter from their homes (Hirst, 2003, p. 361). In the following years, Israel has established a ring of civilian settlements around East Jerusalem, occupied the Gaza Strip until the summer of 2005, and maintained control over the West Bank, arguing that its presence is necessary to ensure its security in the absence of an overall peace settlement. 'Security' has been largely a ruse, for successive Israeli governments have embarked upon a transformation of the landscape by progressively confiscating both public and private lands for the expansion of Jewish settlement throughout the area.

By 2006, at least 280 areas of Israeli settlement were spread throughout the West Bank, including East Jerusalem, with nearly 50 percent of the West Bank under direct control of the settlement network (see Map E). These settlements surround every major Palestinian population center, are often built on high ground, and are connected to each other and to Israel via a road network spanning almost 400 kilometers. They are situated to ensure Israeli authorities maximal surveillance and control over movement in the territories. Home to over 400,000 Jewish settlers, nearly half of whom surround East Jerusalem, the settlement blocs sit astride major West Bank aquifers from which Israel draws one-third of its water supply. While many of the settlers are ordinary Israelis taking advantage of the Government subsidized housing, others are armed zealots who openly advocate expulsion of the Palestinians and justify it in religious terms (see Friedman, 1992).[18] Many of the latter belong to militant organizations, such as the Gush Emunim, Kach, Kahane Chai, and Zo Artzenu, whose members have repeatedly engaged in terrorist actions against the resident Palestinians.[19]

The establishment and maintenance of the settlement system is a violation of the provisions of Article 49 of the Fourth Geneva Convention and numerous United Nations resolutions. The presence of settlements in the midst of a hostile population has only exacerbated tensions throughout the region and contributed to an ongoing cycle of violence. Thus, once established, the settlements had to be protected. To do this, Israel has subjected the Palestinian population to a vast institutional framework featuring land expropriation, destruction of property, regulation of movement, and a variety of restrictions affecting economic, educational, and cultural development. Loss of land, buildings, and orchards, restrictions on movement, and the stifling bureaucracy of permission and denial have inhibited the development of Palestinian institutions at each of these levels and impeded the Palestinians' ability to provide essential services to their own population. These Israeli measures constitute a subtle form of structural terrorism, for not only do they damage the institutional fabric of Palestinian society and well-being of its members, they are directly linked to the brutality of the on-going occupation and have increasingly taken their toll on the lives of Palestinian civilians.

Predictably, Palestinians protested the confiscation of land, settlement building, increased restrictions, and steady erosion of opportunity.

Throughout the 1970s and 1980s, they sought legal redress, demonstrated, went on strikes, their youth threw stones at Israeli soldiers and, occasionally, the more militant among them took up arms. Time and again, their efforts to bring about change were met by refusal as Israeli forces responded with more direct forms of violence, including house demolitions, destruction of trees, curfews, nightly raids, detention without trial, deportations, torture, shootings, and assassinations. This method of dealing with Palestinian protests accelerated during the first *Intifada* of 1987–93, when at least 1283 Palestinian civilians were killed by Israeli soldiers, including 120 Palestinians in undercover operations (Human Rights Watch, 1993, p. 1). Over 130,000 Palestinians were sent to hospitals with injuries, more land was confiscated, over 2500 houses demolished, and thousands of trees were uprooted. Of the Palestinians fatally shot, 271 were 16 years of age or younger, and this age group constituted almost 40 percent of the total number of Palestinians injured. Of medically treated injuries to Palestinian children under 15 years of age, 34 percent were caused by gunfire, 50 percent by beatings from soldiers, and almost 15 percent by tear gas.[20] These patterns were repeated throughout the second *Intifada* that broke out in September 2000, with much more deadly results. As many as 5000 Palestinians were killed by Israelis during the period from September 2000 through December 2006, and over 40,000 were hospitalized with injuries.[21] These *intifadas*, and the iron-fisted response with which they have been met, are unintelligible apart from the structural terrorism that accompanies Israel's colonization of captured territory (Roy, 2007, p. 251).

6. Suicide terrorism

> I am going to fight instead of the sleeping Arab armies who are watching Palestinian girls fighting alone; it is an intifada until victory.
> Ayat Akhras, age 18, shortly before killing herself and two Israelis in Jerusalem market on March 29, 2002.

Having endured the violence and humiliation of occupation since 1967, with little hope for an immediate end, Palestinian militants in the occupied territories have struck back with a more deadly form of terrorism. Drastically outclassed by superior Israeli arms, and motivated by both strategic reasons and desires for vengeance, they have chosen to hit whatever Israeli targets they could by the most effective means available. Since the 1970s, Palestinians who embarked upon attacks upon the Israeli military or Israeli civilians have known that there was little likelihood that they would return to tell about it, that, at best, they would be remembered as 'martyrs' for their homeland. In the past ten years, young Palestinians who have spent their entire lives under military occupation have resorted to a form of terrorism in which the chance of survival is reduced to zero—suicide bombings.

Suicide destruction of oneself along with one's enemies might astound those who have never known political oppression. Yet, the strategy is ancient. It existed in the Near East with the ancient Jewish Zealots and Sicarii—even before that if we can believe the story of Samson and the Philistines (*Judges* 17)—and in the eleventh and twentieth centuries with the Ismaili Assassins (Pape, 2005, pp. 11–2). In 1971, the historian Arnold Toynbee predicted that Palestinians would also resort to such measures:

> Today, the Palestinian faces the human stone wall, and it is no wonder if, after beating his head against it in vain, he seizes a stick of gelignite and blows up himself, the wall, and his unresponsive fellow human beings on the far side. What else is he, or anyone of us, to do? (Toynbee, 1971, p. 3)

Palestinians were not the first to use this technique. In the 1980s, the use of human beings as mobile bombs was employed by the Lebanese Shi'ite group Hezbollah in its battle against occupying forces from the United States, France, and Israel. It has since been used by liberation movements in Sri Lanka, Kashmir, Turkey, and Russia. In a detailed study of 18 suicide terrorism campaigns and 315 attacks from 1980 to 2003, Robert Pape concluded that desires for national self-determination and an end to military occupation were at the root of every instance of this form of terrorism (Pape, 2005, p. 79).

Suicide bombings emerged in the Israeli–Palestinian conflict in 1994. They first occurred after the PLO and Israeli Government signed the Oslo Accords of 1993 and continued sporadically during the 1990s despite the continuance of the unprecedented peace process between Israelis and Palestinians. The underlying reasons are not difficult to discern; the apparent progress towards peaceful relations masked developments on the ground which pointed in the exactly the opposite direction. As negotiations continued, Israeli consolidated its control over the territories, expanded the existing settlement network, and nearly doubled the number of settlers in the West Bank. The Palestinian economy suffered because of Israel's closure policy that limited movements of goods and people within and from the territories. Per capita GNP declined from

$2684 in 1992 to $1896 in 1999, and the Palestinian GDP declined 18 percent even though it increased in surrounding countries. Unemployment rates tripled and poverty increased; although over 100,000 Palestinians from the territories were regularly employed by Israel in 1992, that number had been cut in half by 1999. Besides uprooting some 80,000 olive and fruit trees to permit Israeli construction, the Israeli military also established various mechanisms of control to isolate Palestinian 'self-rule' pockets from each other by means of fencing, checkpoints, and other fortifications (see Map F).[22]

On February 25, 1994, a Jewish settler from Kiryat Arba, Baruch Goldstein, massacred 29 Palestinian worshippers at the Ibrahimiyya mosque in Hebron before losing his own life at the hands of outraged Palestinians. His suicidal terrorism was reported to be both retaliatory and strategic; while motivated to avenge the deaths of Jews at hands of Arabs, Goldstein also wanted to undermine the peace process that he and other Israeli settlers feared would lead to an Israeli withdrawal from the territories.[23] His action precipitated a wave of suicide bombings that took the lives of scores of Israeli civilians, carried out by Palestinian militias such as the *Harakat al-Muqawama al-Islamiyya* (Hamas). Founded in 1988, Hamas advocates *jihad* as the only means of liberation from the yoke of occupation. Initially, it confined its military action to what it regarded as legitimate military targets in the occupied territories, but after the Goldstein massacre and the failure of the Israeli Government to respond to its May 1994 offer of an 'armistice' in which civilians would be removed from the area of struggle (Hroub, 2000, p. 246), Hamas sent *istashaideen* (those who martyr themselves for an exalted purpose) on suicide missions against Israelis.

Like Jewish extremists, Hamas has offered a religious justification for the violent pursuit of its maximalist ends of an Islamic state throughout Palestine, though it has also appealed to the right of self-defense. It has argued that since the Zionists are intent on dispossessing the Palestinians of the remaining 22 percent of their homeland through an occupation that has generated a continuing stream of 'downright terrorism' (Alexander, 2002, p. 346), then, by all laws, human and divine, people have a right to defend themselves against those who employ violence to dispossess them of their homeland. Since appeals to justice and the world's conscience have been futile in stopping Israel's aggression, and since attacks against the Israeli military have been unable to abate Israel's expansionism, making Israel suffer by striking at civilian targets is the only mechanism Palestinians have left for self-defense. Hamas came to view the situation in Palestine in Jabotinskian terms, realizing that the choice is between 'retaliating against the hostile population or not retaliating at all,' and arguing that the effect of striking at 'the most vulnerable spot in the Zionist body' will be to exhaust Israel and weaken both its tourism and immigration programs. As with Goldstein, its terrorism has been retaliatory as well as strategic, for Hamas maintained that its specific operations are carried out to avenge massacres and assassinations (Hroub, 2000, pp. 245–51). Recovering from an assassination attempt by Israel in early June 2003, the Hamas political leader, Abdel Aziz Rantisi, said: 'Our people will teach the Israeli enemy tough lessons until the Israelis stop their terror and crimes' (*Chicago Tribune,* June 12, 2003). His assassination by an Israeli missile strike in April 2004 led to renewed terror against Israelis.[24]

Hamas, the Islamic Jihad, and Al-Fatah's Al-Aqsa Martyr's Brigades, have been at the forefront of armed resistance in the second intifada that began after Palestinians realized that the Oslo process had only reduced their own economic prospects while allowing Israel to consolidate its hold on the territories. Ariel Sharon's visit to the Jerusalem mosques on September 28, 2000, accompanied by 1000 Israeli police—the same sort of incident that sparked the violence of 1929 (Beinin, 2003, p. 22)—was the spark that set off a round of terrorism by both sides that eclipsed any previous level of violence seen during the previous 33 years of occupation. During the next two days, as Palestinians protested Sharon's visit, Israeli police and army killed 15 Palestinians, including four children, whereas one Israeli had been killed. By the end of the first three weeks, over 80 Palestinians and eight Israelis were dead, and an Israeli journalist reported in *Ma'ariv*, an Israeli newspaper, that the IDF had fired a million bullets in the occupied territories (September 6–13, 2002).

Strategic and retaliatory motivations were combined in this second intifada. If the leadership of the principal militant groups used terrorism as a strategy, their willing operatives have often been those who, out of outrage and despair, have sought vengeance against their oppressors (see El Sarraj, 2002, and the articles by Amira Hass, 'Driven by Vengeance and a Desire to Defend the Homeland,' *Ha'aretz*, July 17, 2002; Stephen Franklin, 'Jerusalem Bomber Identified,' *Chicago Tribune,* January 31, 2002; and Greg Myre, 'A Young Man Radicalized by His Months in Jail,' *The New York Times*, May 30, 2003). Young Palestinians, having lived under military occupation their entire lives, watching increasing numbers of their friends and relatives fall victim to Israeli soldiers, and finding little hope for improvement in their situation, began volunteering for suicide missions. As the violence swung into high gear, young women joined the ranks the martyrs, including Ayat Akhras, who heaped scorn upon 'sleeping Arab armies' in a farewell video. Before her, Wafa Idris, a volunteer medic at clashes between Palestinians and Israelis, killed herself and an Israeli. 'She is the first, but not the last,' said a middle-school teacher who knew her. 'You shouldn't think we don't love life and don't want to live. We do this only because it is the last thing we can do.' A student of psychology at the Islamic University in Gaza put it this way:

> Israelis play a major role in inducing the boys to choose a martyr's death. The arbitrary killing that we've experienced during the Intifada has caused every young person to say, 'If in any case I am destined to die, why shouldn't I die with dignity?' (*Ha'aretz*, July 17, 2002)

Suicide operations have not been confined to youth. On November 23, 2006, Fatma Omar An-Najar, a 64-year-old grandmother, blew herself up in a revenge suicide attack—the oldest of the 100 suicide bombers in the last six years—against Israeli forces sweeping the Jebaliya refugee camp. The Associated Press quoted her daughter as saying that the Israelis 'destroyed her house, they killed her grandson – my son. Another grandson is in a wheelchair with an amputated leg' ('Grandmother Blows Herself Up in Gaza,' aolnews.com, November 24, 2006).

Some in the Western media attempted to explain the outbreak of violence by citing religious hatred and a fanatical desire on the part of Palestinian militants to 'destroy Israel,' but more astute observers have cited the underlying causes as being the expansion of the settlement network—as claimed in the Mitchell Report of May 2001—and the failure of the Oslo peace process to end the Israeli occupation (Pape, 2005, p. 48). From 1994 to 2005, there were more than 120 Palestinian suicide attacks directed against Israeli targets in Israel or the occupied territories, yet during this time, Palestinians launched no terrorist attacks against Americans, Europeans, Christians, or Jews living outside Palestine. 'The pattern of the suicide attacks over the past decade suggests that the Palestinian terrorists are concentrating their fire against the state that is actually occupying the territory they view as their homeland' (Pape, 2005, p. 51).

Facing a greater proportion of armed Palestinians in this second intifada, Israel responded with more firepower than ever before, including the use of tanks, fighter jets, and attack helicopters. Prime Minister Sharon's directive to eliminate the 'terrorist infrastructure' involved the Israeli military more deeply in a war on civilians and, once again, attacks against children, a prominent feature of the first intifada, were renewed (see Note 20). 'The moment the IDF sends tanks into a densely-crowded refugee camp it puts all the inhabitants at risk' wrote the Israeli journalist, Gideon Levy. 'Thus, anyone who decides to send tanks into Jabalya is making a decision to kill civilians' ('Terrorism By Any Other Name,' *Ha'aretz*, March 9, 2003).

Sharon's government justified its response by claiming that Israel has a right to defend its citizens from physical harm, and the Palestinians pose a terrorist threat to all Israeli citizens. The only effective means of ending this threat, it argued, is through a massive military crackdown in the form of checkpoints, curfews, house-to-house searches, detentions, interrogations, house demolitions, and targeted killings. This line of reasoning has its Israeli dissenters, even from within the Israeli military (see the *Ha'aretz* supplement of September 14, 2001). In 2002, the Israeli Defense Minister Eliezar admitted at the end of the IDF offensive in late April 2002, that 'it is impossible to eradicate the terrorist infrastructure' and that 'military actions kindle the frustration, hatred and despair and are the incubators for the terror to come' (Zunes, 2003, p. 149). In a front page article in Israel's leading newspaper, *Yediot Achronot*, Israeli journalist Alex Fishman, commenting on the November 23, 2002 assassination of Mahmud Abu Hamoud, a Hamas leader, wrote that there had existed an agreement between Hamas and the Palestinian Authority that 'Hamas was to avoid in the near future' suicide bombings in Israel. Fishman wrote that 'Whoever decided upon the liquidation of Abu Hamoud knew in advance that the agreement with Hamas would be shattered. The subject was extensively discussed both by Israel's military echelon and its political one' ('A Dangerous Liquidation,' *Yediot Achronot*, November 25, 2001). As Fishman predicted, Hamas struck back less than a week later with suicide bombings in Jerusalem and Haifa that killed 25 Israelis. The effect of this cycle of violence heightened tensions and weakened the constituency in Israel and the U.S. favoring peace negotiations (Bleier, 2003; date of access: November 12, 2006).

Palestinian outrage over the Israeli assault led to widespread support of attacks against Israel. One 2002 poll found that the 65 percent of Palestinians in the occupied territories who favored suicide operations at the time cited as a main reason Israeli military incursions (Pape, 2005, p. 50). While the frequency of these suicide operations was something new, the violence conformed to the established pattern. For over three-quarters of a century, incident after incident in the Israeli–Palestinian conflict has shown that terrorism has succeeded in intensifying the propensity for violence on all sides, with ever more deadly results from the Israeli point of view. In the first *intifada*, there were 11 dead Palestinians for every dead Israeli, while during the second, the ratio was closer to four to one. One Palestinian, whose house was destroyed in Ramallah after Israeli soldiers blew up the building next door, reacted in this way: 'This just stirs up hatred. Now I want to blow myself up along with them [the Israelis]. Where can I go? The grave of the martyr is better for me' (*Chicago Tribune*, December 3, 2003).

Palestinian suicide terrorism is no different from similar suicide terrorist campaigns of the past 25 years. The underlying cause is not radical Islam, a hatred of Western values, or rabid anti-Semitism, as reported in numerous writings (e.g., Netanyahu, 1986, 2001; Dershowitz, 2003; Frum & Perle, 2003), but a combination of sentiments, ranging from the understandable desire to throw off the yoke of foreign military occupation to the more deadly emotions of despair, outrage, and vengance.[25]

7. The use and abuse of 'terrorism'

The depiction of terrorism and the venomous rhetoric of 'terror' cannot be ignored in any informed discussion of contemporary terrorism. Attempts to understand, evaluate, and craft a proper response to terrorism must come to grips with the fact that labeling someone a 'terrorist' is itself, more often than not, a political act in its own right. As a consequence, the words 'terror,' 'terrorism,' and 'terrorist' have become important weapons for molding thought and stimulating consent, weapons whose reach extends from the propaganda arsenals of government agencies and associated 'think tanks' through the popular media into political discussion, scholarly publications, classrooms, and, thereby, into the private thoughts of nearly everyone.

To appreciate the impact of this rhetoric, one must recognize two salient facts that underlie the political employment of the terms 'terrorist' and 'terrorism.' The first fact is that these words have acquired an intensely negative connotation in contemporary discourse. Terrorism is perceived as breaking the rules of legitimate political violence by refusing to respect the distinction between belligerents and civilians on the one hand, and, on the other, by using methods that should not be employed, for example, hijacking commercial airliners or killing hostages. As such, terrorism and its agents have come to be viewed as morally reprehensible.[26]

The second fact is that the terms are used as though they have an indexical, egocentric, or perspectival character, essentially dependent upon a speaker's point of view, much like the words 'stranger,' 'foreigner,' or 'enemy.' Obviously, no one is an enemy as such, but only an enemy to someone or other, so that when I use 'the enemy' I am inevitably talking about my enemy or our enemy. Similarly, when we hear people speaking of 'terrorism,' in actual practice they are talking about violence directed against 'themselves,' or, in first-person terms, against 'us.' No one has a monopoly here, and neither the American media nor the U.S. Government is unique in its speaker-oriented bias. Other countries, including Israel, Great Britain, Russia, India, and Egypt, routinely do the same, and so might any state in describing militant insurgents opposed to its policies, for example, the Nazis in describing resistance fighters in the Warsaw ghetto (Herman & O'Sullivan, 1989, p. 261). For this reason, the common observation that one man's terrorist is another's freedom fighter is not off the mark, especially since it allows that a person can be both.[27]

The two facts together explain why there is a manifest inconsistency in ascriptions of terrorism. Because of the negative connotation, no one wants to be accused of terrorism, and because of the indexical character, it is nearly incoherent to describe one's own actions, or those of your allies, as 'terrorist.' Thus, people who are labeled 'terrorist' are not all and only those who commit politically motivated violence against civilians; instead, the label is ascribed selectively to fit the perspective of the speaker and audience. To illustrate, it is unquestioned in the mainstream Western media that those who flew hijacked planes into the World Trade Center towers, or young Palestinians who have turned themselves into suicide bombers, are engaged in terrorist activity. But many actions that would qualify as terrorist under most definitions—certainly under the standard definition—are not described as such, nor are their perpetrators referred to as 'terrorists.' Some of these were committed by sub-national groups, for example,

- massacres of Bosnian civilians in the mid-1990s;
- assaults upon villagers by death squads in Guatemala, Nicaragua, and El Salvador during the 1980s;
- the massacre of over 2000 Palestinian civilians by the Israeli-supported members of Lebanese militias in the Sabra and Shatilla refugee camps in Beirut in 1982;
- attacks upon Palestinian civilians by Jewish settlers in the West Bank from the early 1980s to the present.

If we broaden our scope and examine some of the overt actions committed by states, then there are numerous examples that are not usually labeled as 'terrorist' though they qualify as such under those definitions that allow for state terrorism. These include,

- bombing by American and British forces in Iraq 2003–4 featuring the use of cluster bombs and phosphorus bombs;[28]
- the destruction of Grozny by Russian forces during the Chechnya war in 1999;
- the U.S. invasion of Panama in 1990;
- the U.S. bombing of Tripoli, Libya in April 1986;
- the Israeli aerial and land bombardment of Beirut in the summer of 1982;
- the Syrian army's attack on the city of Hama in the spring of 1982;
- the Iraqi and Iranian missile attacks on each other's cities in the mid-1980s;
- the Indonesian invasion and occupation of East Timor, 1975–98.[29]

These terrorist actions pale in comparison to more large-scale campaigns such as,

- the U.S. bombing of North Vietnam and Cambodia during the Vietnam war;
- the Allied bombing of German and Japanese cities near the end of WWII; for example, from March to August 1945, nearly 800,000 Japanese civilians were killed in U.S. air raids against Japan's 62 largest cities, and about 85,000 of these died on March 9, 1945 on the first day of the bombing in Tokyo,
- the Nazi mass murders of civilian populations during World War II.

If we consider the provisions of *jus in bello* as set forth in relevant Hague and Geneva Conventions as a part of international law, then governments have repeatedly used—in the words of the FBI definition—'force or violence' unlawfully 'to intimidate or coerce a government, [a] civilian population, or [a] segment thereof,' in order to achieve 'political or social objectives.'[30]

At the opposite extreme, some actions are routinely labeled 'terrorist' that do not qualify as terrorist under the standard definition nor under the definitions championed by U.S. governmental agencies. For example, the U.S. media is replete with references to 'terrorist' actions by

Lebanese and Palestinians against Israeli soldiers in occupied territory, targets that do not qualify as civilians or noncombatants under any acceptable definition. Apart from the State Department's unusually strict definition of 'noncombatant' (see Note 2), the same can be said for actions directed against the U.S. military, say, the bombing of the USS Cole in Yemen in October 2000, or the bombing of the U.S. Marine barracks in Beirut in October 1983.[31]

The inconsistencies are striking, perhaps understandable in light of the two mentioned facts about the contemporary rhetoric of 'terror,' yet, ultimately, unjustifiable. Unlike the term 'enemy,' nothing in the *semantics* of 'terrorism' warrants the egocentric usage. The standard English language dictionaries and encyclopedias indicate that the term depicts a mode of violence independently of identifying its agents. But even if we acknowledge that the term has evolved semantically to encompass a perspectival usage, that alone would afford no basis for moral claims about terrorism, for instance, that it is an unjust or immoral use of violence. Just as there is no automatic moral taint to being an enemy—many good people have been enemies to someone or other—so too, if a terrorist act is wrongful, it is not because it is politically motivated violence directed *at us*. If an action is morally wrong, it is because it possesses some universalizable morally relevant characteristic, say, that it is violence directed at civilians, or against innocent people, or that it uses improper means, or that it is politically motivated violence, or—from a pacifist perspective—that it is violence. For the purposes of making a moral claim, the egocentric character of the term 'terrorism' is irrelevant. Finally, it goes almost without saying that the mere negative connotation of a term is no grounds for moral opprobrium towards whatever or whomever it applies to. The terms 'enemy,' 'stranger,' 'foreigner' all harbor a degree of negativity, but they apply to everyone, saint and sinner alike. These subtleties of indexical usage and moral relevance are lost upon the general public, but not upon the numerous 'terrorism experts' whose job it is to denigrate those opposed to American, Israeli, and European policies in the Islamic world. As a consequence, the two features of the contemporary rhetoric of 'terror,' its pejorative overtones and its egocentric orientation, serve to distort the popular conception of who is and who is not carrying out wrongful actions in the world.

What's worse, the distortion is deliberate, not an innocent or accidental byproduct of linguistic usage. The rhetoric of 'terror' serves political ends as the labels 'terrorism' and 'terrorist' are used selectively by governments, their associated media, and propaganda agencies to describe those who forcefully oppose certain governmental policies. Because of their negative connotations, these labels automatically discredit any individuals or groups to whom they are affixed, placing them outside the norms of acceptable social and political behavior, and portraying them as 'evil' people that cannot be reasoned with. As a consequence, the rhetoric of 'terror' effectively dehumanizes any individuals or groups described as 'terrorist,' and thereby,

- erases any incentive an audience might have to understand the point of view of the 'terrorists' so that questions about the nature and origins of their grievances and the possible legitimacy of their demands will not even be raised;
- deflects attention away from one's own policies that might have contributed to the grievances of the 'terrorists';
- repudiates any calls to negotiate with 'terrorists';
- paves the way for the use of force and violence in dealing with 'terrorists,' specifically, by making it easier for a government to exploit the fears of its citizens and stifle any objections to the manner in which it responds to terrorist violence;
- obliterates the distinction between national liberation movements and fringe fanatics (whose recourse to violence is either unrelated to a legitimate grievance or a manifestly ineffective or disproportional response to an alleged offense).

The general strategy is nothing new; it is part and parcel of the war of ideas and language that accompanies overt hostilities. The term 'terrorism' is simply the current vogue for discrediting one's opponents and paving the way for violent action against them, before the risky business of inquiry into their complaints can even begin. If individuals and groups are portrayed as evil, irrational, barbaric, and beyond the pale of negotiation and compromise, then asking why they resort to terrorism is viewed as pointless, needlessly accommodating, or, at best, mere pathological curiosity.[32]

Rhetoric of this magnitude is bound to produce results in a context of political turmoil, especially among agitated people looking for solutions. The language of 'terror' fosters shortsighted belligerence among those oblivious to its propagandistic employment, while increasing the resentment of those who are so labeled. Far from contributing to a peaceful resolution of conflict, it prepares both types of person for more violence. Moreover, by so effectively erasing any incentive to understand the motives behind terrorist violence or to critically examine governmental policies, the rhetoric serves to silence meaningful political debate. Those normally inclined to ask 'why?' are fearful of being labeled 'soft' on terrorism, while the more militant use the 'terrorist' label to deface the distinction between critical examination and appeasement. Obviously, to point out the causes and objectives of particular terrorist actions is to imply nothing about their legitimacy—that is an independent matter—nor is it a capitulation to terrorist demands. To ignore these causes and objectives is to seriously undermine attempts to deal intelligently with terrorism, since it leaves untouched the factors motivating recourse to this type of violence.

More dramatically, for these reasons the rhetoric of 'terror' actually increases terrorism in at least four distinct ways. First, it magnifies the effect of terrorist actions by heightening the fear among the target population. If we demonize the terrorists, if we portray them as arbitrary irrational beings devoid of a moral sense and beyond all norms, we amplify the fear and alarm among civilians generated by terrorist incidents, regardless if this forms part of the political objectives of the perpetrators.

Second, those who succumb to the rhetoric contribute to the cycle of revenge and retaliation by endorsing violent actions of their own government, not only against those who commit terrorist actions, but also against those populations from whose ranks the terrorists emerge, for the simple reason that terrorists are frequently themselves civilians, living amid other civilians not so engaged. This policy, explicit in the thinking of Ben Gurion and Jabotinsky, was echoed in repeated remarks by U.S. President George W. Bush when he declared that we 'will make no distinction between terrorists and those who harbor them' ('A Nation Challenged,' *The New York Times*, October 8, 2001). The consequence has been an increase in politically motivated violence against civilian targets—'terrorism' under any other name—under the rubric of 'retaliation' or 'counter-terrorism.'[33]

Third, short of genocide, a violent response is likely to stiffen the resolve of those from whose ranks terrorists have emerged, leading them to regard their foes as people who cannot be reasoned with, as people who, because they avail themselves so readily of the rhetoric of 'terror,' know only the language of force. As long as they perceive themselves to be victims of intolerable injustices and view their oppressors as unwilling to arrive at an acceptable compromise, they are likely to answer violence with more violence. The latter can be either strategic, if directed against civilians to achieve some political objective, but, with the oppression unabated, it increasingly becomes the retaliatory violence of despair and revenge.

Fourth, and most insidiously, those who employ the rhetoric of 'terror' for their own political ends, are encouraging actions that they understand will generate or sustain further violence directed against civilians. Inasmuch as their verbal behavior is intended to secure political objectives through these means, then it is an instance of terrorism just as much as any direct order to carry out a bombing of civilian targets. In both cases, there is purposeful verbal action aimed at bringing about a particular result through violence against civilians. Here, as the rhetoric of 'terror' prepares public opinion to accept actions against civilians through a steady process of demonization, it has itself become a deadly weapon, with powerful psychological effects, designed to make it easier for governments to carry out their own terrorism. Thus, what is not often understood is that the rhetoric of 'terror' not only serves to increase the amount of terrorism in the world, it is one of the means whereby states carry out their terrorism. As such, the rhetoric is itself part of the problem of terrorism.

In his novel, 1984, George Orwell described *doublethink* as 'the power of holding two contradictory beliefs in one's mind simultaneously, and accepting both of them,' and he portrayed it as a device for destroying the capacity for independent critical thinking. Something like doublethink is occurring as the result of the rhetoric of terror. In condemning terrorism, well-meaning people think of it as something bad and to be eliminated at all costs, yet, in urging retaliation under the guise of 'counterterrorism,' they are insouciant about the massive destruction this might entail. In sanctioning the use of military force against terrorism, regardless of its impact upon civilian populations (see Note 33), people advocate the very thing they condemn—and this is closer to doublethink that we should ever wish to be.

My point is not to sweep the problem of politically motivated violence against civilians under the rug by denying the existence of this controversial mode of violence. It is all too real a problem. Rather, the point is that there is little hope of progress in solving this problem without examining the causes from which it springs, and the extent to which the rhetoric of 'terror' impedes rather than illuminates this examination is itself part of the problem.

8. The reign of 'terror' in the Israeli–Palestinian conflict

I have already observed that one price Palestinians paid for their recourse to terrorism was in terms of the violent reprisals by the Israeli military upon their communities. A second price has been their demonization in the mainstream Western press. In the late 1960s, Palestinian militants, working within groups like *Al-Fatah*, were described in the international press as 'guerrillas,' 'commandos,' and 'fedayeen.' It was not until after the September 1970 civil war in Jordan when the Palestinian resistance turned towards more desperate measures such as the highly publicized hostage takings in the early 1970s, that the Israeli designations of Palestinian fighters as 'murderers,' 'saboteurs,' and 'terrorists' became more commonplace. Too often, the Palestinians' complaints were lost in the sensationalism of the deed, and in the minds of many, disgust with the means outpaced sympathy with the plight of Palestinian refugees and trumped the patience needed to understand core grievances. As the 1970s wore on, and various leftwing groups in Europe and elsewhere made headlines with similar sorts of violence, the 'terrorists' came to be viewed as a new species of barbarians whose willingness to hijack airplanes, take hostages, and especially, carry their struggle into foreign lands, placed them outside the bounds of civilized behavior.

Israeli leaders realized that the rhetoric of 'terror' had now become a preeminent propaganda device, one that could be used not only to discredit their opponents, but also to obfuscate and to deflect attention away from their own controversial policies.[34] A prime example is a widely circulated book edited by Benjamin Netanyahu entitled, *Terrorism: How the West Can Win* published in 1986, featured in *Time* Magazine shortly thereafter, and often used as a text in courses in American universities during the late 1980s and 1990s. While the book offered the standard definition of 'terrorism,' the editor and the contributors used the 'doublethink' strategy by applying the term selectively and echoing the arguments of Ben-Gurion and Jabotinsky that the only way to combat terrorism is to 'to weaken and destroy the terrorist's ability to consistently launch attacks,' even at the 'risk of civilian casualties' (pp. 202–5). Very little was said about the possible causes of terrorist violence beyond vague allusions to Islam's confrontation with modernity (p. 82), or passages of this caliber from Netanyahu's own pen:

> The root cause of terrorism lies not in grievances but in a disposition toward unbridled violence. This can be traced to a worldview that asserts that certain ideological and religious goals justify, indeed demand, the shedding of all moral inhibitions. In this context, the observation that the root cause of terrorism is terrorists is more than a tautology. (p. 204)

The scholar can pass off comments like these as pure propaganda—if not a brand of psychological lunacy—but it is significant that Netanyahu's book reached a large audience, especially since its contributors included not only academics and journalists but important policymakers as well. Netanyahu himself went on to become the Israeli Prime Minister, and among the American contributors were the Secretary of State George Schultz, UN Ambassador Jeanne Kirkpatrick, and Senators Daniel Moynihan and Alan Cranston, each of whom voiced sentiments similar to those of Netanyahu. The upshot was that powerful people perpetuated the image of a terrorist as a carrier of 'oppression and enslavement,' having 'no moral sense,' 'a perfect nihilist' (pp. 29–30), and whose elimination is the only rational means for the West to 'win.'

Netanyahu's book—like numerous others, including Netanyahu (2001), Frum and Perle (2003), and Dershowitz (2003)—conceals an unspoken agenda (as pointed out by Beinin, 2003). By classifying Palestinian resistance to Israeli policies as 'terrorism,' and by portraying 'terrorists' as some sort of monsters unworthy of moral dialogue, the intent was to shift political focus away from the designs, policies, and actions of the Israeli Government in the occupied territories, for example, its land confiscations, settlement building, human rights abuses, and blatant violations of Security Council resolutions, towards the more sensational reactions by the Palestinians. Its strategy manifests this logic: *to commit a crime, demonize your victims*.[35]

The most devastating uses of 'terrorism' in the Israeli–Palestinian conflict have been to justify horrific actions against Palestinian refugees. In September 1982, for example, after the evacuation of PLO fighters from Beirut, Israeli officials contended that some '2000 terrorists' remained in the refugee camps Sabra and Shatilla in southern Beirut, a claim repeatedly echoed in the Israeli and American press. On September 15, the Israeli Defense Minister, Ariel Sharon, authorized entry of what were presumed to be members of various Lebanese militias into the camps that were then sealed off by Israeli tanks. The only resistance they encountered came from a few lightly armed boys. For the next 38 hours, aided by Israeli flares at night, the militiamen raped, tortured, mutilated, and massacred as many as 3000 civilians under the eye of IDF personnel (Kapeliouk, 1982, pp. 93–4; Hirst, 2003, pp. 553–60). An International Commission of Inquiry under the chairmanship of Sean MacBride found that Israeli authorities were involved in the massacre (Cattan, 2000, p. 180). Though Sharon was subsequently removed as Defence Minister because of 'indirect responsibility' for the massacre, four years later he was permitted to carry his chutzpah to remarkable heights in an op-ed piece entitled 'It's Past Time to Crush the Terrorist Monster' (*The New York Times*, September 20, 1986) in which he called upon Western countries and Israel to stage a coordinated 'war on terrorism' through pre-emptive strikes on 'terrorist bases' and sanctions against the state supporters of terrorism.[36]

As Prime Minister of Israel, 20 years after the events in Lebanon, Sharon was able to act on his ambitions once again, refusing to negotiate with the Palestinian leadership, intensifying settlement building in the West Bank, and adopting an iron fist approach to Palestinian resistance. After the on-going battles of the Al-Aqsa Intifada led to a rash of suicide bombings in Israel in March 2002, Sharon sent troops, tanks, and helicopter gunships into the Palestinian-controlled areas of the West Bank, vowing to destroy the Palestinian 'terrorist infrastructure.' The most brutal incident of the campaign occurred at the Jenin refugee camp, home to 14,000 residents and containing some 160 armed militants from the Islamic Jihad, Hamas, and Al Aqsa Martyr's Brigades groups. From April 4 to 13, the Israeli military besieged the camp, meeting fierce resistance at the outset. In the early morning hours of April 6, helicopters fired missiles into the camp, often striking civilian homes where no Palestinian fighters were present. The missile fire caught many sleeping civilians by surprise, and in the subsequent chaos, the army was able to move closer to the center the fighting had ended, resulting in a total leveling of Hawashin neighborhood down to the last house. According to Human Rights Watch the 'extensive, systematic, and deliberate leveling of the entire district was clearly disproportionate to any military objective that Israel aimed to achieve.'[37]

That the Israeli government could so easily succeed in convincing people that Israel was eliminating the 'terrorist infrastructure' of the Palestinians—rather than a good deal of the institutional structure of Palestinian society—illustrates how the rhetoric of 'terror' is a causal factor in generating even more terrorism. Pro-Israeli articles immediately appeared in major Israeli and American publications explicitly justifying the deaths of Palestinian civilians.[38] On one side, the bulk of the Israeli public and the American Congress were led to endorse the actions of the Israeli military. For example, when Amnesty International (AI) pointed out that the Israeli army violated human rights and international law in its crackdown in the West Bank, the House of Representatives rejected AI's findings by a vote of 352-21, declaring that 'Israeli military operations are an effort to defend itself...and are aimed only at dismantling the terrorist infrastructure in the Palestinian areas.'

The Senate echoed this sentiment in a 94-2 vote, referring to the Israeli assault as 'necessary steps to provide security to its people.' And after the attack on the Jenin refugee camp during which Israel fired missiles into houses where no fighters were present, used Palestinian civilians as shields, and leveled entire residential districts with armored bulldozers, President George W. Bush was able to speak of Israel's Prime Minister, Ariel Sharon, as a 'man of peace' without being laughed off the editorial pages of the country's newspapers, and prominent senators could urge the country to 'stand with Israel against Arab tyranny and terror.' On the other side, the flames of outrage and revenge were fanned, once again, among Palestinians and their sympathizers, and a rash of suicide bombings took the lives of scores of Israeli civilians in the aftermath. Once again, the skewed portrayal of cause and effect cleared the road for continued violence against noncombatants on both sides, hence, to more terrorism, not less.

The attack on the Jenin refugee camp, like that on Sabra and Shatilla 20 years earlier, are two examples of how the rhetoric of 'terror' has made it easier for the world to accept Israeli violence. The overwhelming impression conveyed is that Israel is reacting to Palestinian aggression and attempts to destroy the Jewish state. Little is said or understood about the historical origins of Palestinian grievances, about Palestinian support for peace talks and a two-state solution, or even about the fact that Israeli forces are occupying Palestinian territory. Lost in the media sensationalism over terrorist incidents is the subtle fact that successive Israeli governments, through a dual campaign of media manipulation and continual provocation, successfully perpetuated the image of Palestinians as violent rejectionists and paved the way for their own brand of state terrorism. In so doing, they have employed the rhetoric of 'terror' as an instrument of terror.

9. Can terrorism be justified?

In the current climate of opinion, attempts to justify terrorist actions on moral grounds are likely to be met with expressions of incredulity, at both the scholarly and the popular level. Robespierre's ominous 'virtue without terror is powerless' lost whatever credibility it might have appeared to have long ago, at least as a moral maxim. It is more common to hear sweeping denunciations of terrorism on the grounds that it is a brutal violation of the human rights, fails to treat people as 'moral persons' (Khatchadourian, 1998), does not differ from murder (French, 2003), indiscriminately attacks the innocent (Walzer, 1988,

p. 238), targets those who are innocent of the grievances from which it stems (Primoratz, 2004a, p. 21; Jaggar, 2005, p. 212), or, simply, is a violation of the *jus in bello* discrimination rule. Terrorism is also likely to generate disgust, hatred, and vengeance, not only within the targeted community, but also among the external audience with little understanding of the relevant history, rendering it a strategy that backfires by increasing the determination and volume of one's enemies. Michael Walzer contends that no sort of 'apologetic descriptions and explanations,' for example, that it is effective, a last resort, the only alternative, or not distinct from other forms of political struggle, provide an excuse for terrorism (Walzer, 1988, pp. 239–42). Recalling Kant's insistence that war can be justified only if it is expected to contribute to future peace, it is precisely because terrorism is capable of generating intense feelings of hatred and vengeance that it threatens to undermine trust and the possibility of future coexistence (Khatchadourian, 1998). As Kant realized, criminal stratagems raise the frightening possibility that genocidal annihilation of one or both parties might be the only way to end a conflict.[39]

Yet, it is not obvious that these considerations trump all others if terrorism is the only means available to secure an overridingly justifiable end, that is, when not committing terrorism would have morally worse consequences than engaging in terrorism. Can such a scenario ever exist? We have already noted that history is replete with defenses of terrorism as a necessary means of conquering territory, or, with Robespierre and Trotsky, as a mechanism for advancing the interests and safety of 'the people.' Apart from such dubious identifications of the public good or glorifications of territorial theft, some have justified state terrorism on defensive grounds, say, in the case of 'supreme emergency,' and others have added that terrorism by communities other than states might be justified in similar cases of self-defense.[40]

To investigate this issue, let us generalize the notion of a community to include any society of persons having some level of geographical and political unity and containing entire families that ensure its continued existence through the usual reproduction of individuals who *ipso facto* become members. States are communities possessing sovereignty over territory, but there are various levels of non-state communities as well, for example, those constituting political or regional divisions within a state, local municipalities, religious communities, ethnic minorities, and so on. Any community can be subjected to threats and attacks stemming from civil disorder, government oppression, foreign invasions, and occupations. Normally, the job of defending a community is vested in the sovereign power, but the sovereign might not deliver, especially if it is too weak, has been decimated or destroyed, or, is itself the aggressor. Just as individuals have a right of self-defense in the absence of police protection, so too, a community has the right to collective self-defense when state protection is unavailable—at least when it is legitimately constituted within the territory where the aggression occurs (see Chapter 1, Section 2 on legitimacy). If so, the constraints imposed by just war theory can be considered in relation to non-state agents (Valls, 2000).

Nowhere is the justice of collective self-defense more manifest than when a community faces an aggressive threat to its very existence. This can take different forms (Gilbert, 2003, p. 26), with attempted extermination of its members being the clearest threat warranting a community's recourse to self-defense. But even where extermination is not at issue, an aggressor might try to destroy a community in other ways, say, by enslavement or forced conversions of its members, destruction of its vital institutions (economic, agricultural, political, and cultural), appropriation of its natural resources, and seizure of its territory and dispersion of its members. Each of these threats to a community's survival is an *existential* threat and, typically, will be viewed as unjustifiable from that community's perspective. A right of collective self-defense need not be limited to existential threats to survival, for it can also arise when there are threats to a society's political independence, territory, resources, technological and military capabilities, or 'basic freedoms of its citizens and its constitutionally democratic political institutions' (Rawls, 1999a, p. 91).

Let us confine attention to existential threats and inquire how collective self-defense to be pursued. This depends upon the broader legal and political orders that the community exists under, but the following are what might be called the *standard measures* of self-defense that a community may take when threatened by an aggressor:

- Offers of direct negotiation with the aggressor to resolve the problem.
- Appeals to external agencies, institutions, and laws in order to arbitrate and work towards a peaceful solution of the problem.
- Appeals to a recognized sovereign, or to external powers to forcibly intervene to stop the aggression.
- Resort to non-violent resistance to halt or retard the aggression.

If these measures fail, then the community has the right to,

- Resort to military resistance, whether through conventional or guerrilla warfare, against the aggressor's military forces.

While this latter measure is usually accorded to organized states, if a community is not being protected by a state then it has the right to direct its members to take up arms in pursuit of collective self-defense. This is not a surprising allowance given that a state might persecute its own population or a segment thereof.

So far, so good. Now consider the situation from the standpoint of generalized just war theory, for we should not expect any community—state or non-state—to be justified in resorting to violence unless it has a just cause and uses violence as a last resort, through a competent authority, with expectations of success, and so on. Refusing to apply the considerations of *jus ad bellum* and *jus in bello* to violence waged by non-state agents would be to delegitimize any resistance to repression by a non-state community, including all revolutions, national liberation movements, and resistance to tyrannical government. That is an implausible conclusion.

Suppose now that members of a community faced with an existential threat have good reason to believe that the aggression is unjustifiable by widely accepted canons (say, applicable international conventions), thereby presupposing that their own community is worth preserving. Suppose further that the leadership of the community under threat has resorted to each of the standard measures for self-defense against the aggression. In particular, this leadership has appealed to the aggressor for direct negotiations, publicly argued its case by appeal to international law, requested assistance from international organizations (say, the United Nations), regional alliances, and major world powers, resorted to non-violent methods of protest, and confronted the aggressor's military within the standard *jus in bello* guidelines. Suppose, furthermore, that repeated efforts of these sorts have proved unsuccessful. In such circumstances, the targeted community faces a *radical* existential threat, namely, a situation when it is subject to an unjustifiable existential threat, and its recourse to the standard measures of self-defense have failed to end or abate that threat. A situation of radical existential threat qualifies as a 'supreme emergency' and a paradigmatic just cause—namely, to eliminate or reduce the threat—if anything does.

Would terrorism be a justifiable option when a community faces a radical existential threat? If so, then we allow that the *jus in bello* principle of discrimination can either be overridden or suitably refined. Accordingly, any defense of terrorism would either have to be conducted outside the bounds of generalized just war theory, or, be buttressed by a reasonable modification of the discrimination principle. The latter option is favored herein, but before articulating it, let us first observe how the other criteria of generalized just war theory can be satisfied by communities contemplating a campaign of terrorism.

In a situation of radical self-defense, the criterion of just cause is readily satisfied. Without a protective sovereign, the community is justified in taking self-defense into its own hands through strategies that it judges will best end or abate the threat, whether these involve acquiescence, surrender, flight, or resistance. The situation is similar to what we, as individuals, encounter when assaulted or threatened with assault in the absence of police protection; we have a right of active self-defense. However, for a community to justifiably defend itself, its chosen courses of action must also satisfy the requirement of competent authority, either through endorsement by the acknowledged leadership of the community or by the community itself through the best available means of determining consent. Moreover, if the goal of the agents of that contemplated action is to end or reduce the existential threat, then they act with right intent. Nothing prohibits satisfaction of these conditions.[41]

By the very way a radical existential threat is described, recourse to terrorism might also satisfy the requirements of proportionality and last resort given that the aggression is unjustified and that standard measures of self-defense have been tried and have failed. Terrorism would then be a *Machiavellian* course of action since it would violate widely shared standards for the sake of an overridingly just goal, namely, to reduce or end an unwarranted existential threat. Machiavelli's allowance for occasional cruelty was offered as a 'last resort' strategy for the sovereign, but, in a situation of radical existential threat a community is its own sovereign. In plain fact, communities have and still do face radical existential threats, and some have tried the standard measures of self-defense before resorting to terrorism. It is precisely because of gross disparities in economic and military resources between oppressor and oppressed, and because of the continual technological improvements in protection of military personnel, that terrorism might be the only means of resistance available. Suicide terrorism, in particular, is viewed by its agents as a strategy of last resort when embroiled in a 'zero-sum' conflict (Pape, 2005, pp. 89–94).

If a proposed act or campaign of terrorism is to satisfy the last resort condition, not only must it be assumed that terrorist acts can be carried out, its proponents must have evidence that there is a reasonable hope of success that they might enable the community to reach the goals related to the just cause. This is often the most difficult *jus ad bellum* condition to satisfy (Fotion, 2004, pp. 49–53), but a few points should be kept in mind. First, although some argue that terrorism never works to advance a group's ultimate goals (thus, Walzer, 1988, p. 240; Khatchadourian, 1998, p. 27; Carr, 2002), there are a number of counter-examples. For one thing, state terrorism has frequently achieved desired goals; the American 'manifest destiny' was partly achieved through terrorism against native Americans, and it has been argued that the terror bombing of Japanese cities in 1945 hastened the end of World War II. Non-state terrorism has also been effective (see Wilkins, 1992, p. 39; Pape, 2005, pp. 61–76). As argued above, terrorist tactics have been effective in achieving both short-term and long-term goals by non-state groups in the struggle over Palestine.

In the case of a radical existential threat, there are different ways in which a threatened community's resort to terrorism against powerful unwarranted aggression could be successful in advancing its goal of self-preservation.

1. The aggressor concludes that the price of its aggression is too high and, to avoid the effects of terrorism upon its own civilian population, decides to desist from that aggression.[42]
2. External states and alliances are caused to intervene to bring an end to the aggression.[43]
3. By retaliating against aggression, the threatened community gains credibility and recognition, both from external parties and from other members of their own community who might thereby become more confident, more hopeful, and more committed to joining a resistance whose likelihood of success is increased with greater participation and unity.[44]

The probability of success is enhanced if the aggressor has itself used terrorism in either its direct or structural modes. Such *parity of means* in the method of violence might strengthen the conviction in external parties, as well as in the aggressor's own population, either that it is appropriate to return terrorism for terrorism or that tit for tat violence has escalated out of proportion. An asymmetrical use of terrorism, by contrast, runs the risk of evoking contempt for the threatened community among external parties and in alienating members of the threatened community who would normally be opposed to such tactics.

Up to this point, the argument has been consequentialist; communities have a right to defend themselves against radical existential threats by terrorist means because the consequences of failing to act in this way are worse. Barring a pure utilitarian consequentialism, however, concern for a just distribution of the value of the expected consequences must also be factored in. And here we come to a direct challenge to any attempt to justify terrorism. If one party is innocent of an aggression against another, then the latter's violence against the former in pursuit of redress would be a gross violation of justice (Primoratz, 2004a, pp. 20–1). So, how could violence against civilians be justified if they are innocent of the terrorists' grievances?

Answer? Violence directed against an innocent person cannot be justified, but it is incorrect to suppose that civilians are automatically 'innocent' of their community's aggression against another community. They might be culpable of that aggression in a number of ways and in varying degrees (Holmes, 1989, p. 187). For one thing, civilians might participate by voluntarily paying taxes or by publicly supporting political, economic, or national policies and activities that generate and sustain that aggression. For another, the aggressor might have a representative political system that operates under the principle of popular sovereignty, namely, that ultimate political power is vested in the citizenry and exercised by the governing institutions through the consent of that citizenry. Popular sovereignty entails shared responsibility for the laws, policies, and actions of the state insofar as these represent the consent of the collective of which each individual is a member. Those who voluntarily join any association or institution share in responsibility for its actions, and citizenship in a representative system is voluntary since it can be renounced, even if there are dramatic consequences for so doing such as imprisonment or exile. Responsibility in a representative system is not avoided by belonging to the political opposition or having been critical of the government's policies and acts, even though, in such cases, one's culpability might be of a lesser degree. In sum, terrorism is justified only if a further *culpability condition* is satisfied, namely, that those who would direct violence against civilians within the aggressor community must have evidence that those civilians share in the responsibility for that aggression.[45]

While this might seem a brute tossing of the *jus in bello* rules to the wind, the departure is less dramatic than might appear. The *jus in bello* demand of proportionality can continue to be respected; not every imagined act of terrorism by the threatened community could be justified, and no more should be used than is necessary to end or reduce the existential threat. Furthermore, the prohibition on using illegitimate means can be respected; the weapons used by terrorists, bombs, guns, knives, and so on are more primitive forms of the weapons in the arsenals of state militaries; that some terrorism is justified does not imply that terrorism through any means, for example, nuclear weapons, nerve gas, and so on, would also be justified. Similarly, the requirement of treating prisoners of war humanely is satisfiable; even though the weaker parties in asymmetric conflicts usually do not have the resources to take prisoners of war, when they do, there is no reason they could not respect the standard conventions on prisoners of war. Finally, and perhaps most importantly, while the principle of noncombatant immunity is abandoned in the case of a radical existential threat, a modified principle of discrimination, remains: *in redressing a grievance, those innocent of that grievance are to be immune from harm.* In yet other words, there is no reason why terrorism cannot discriminate, targeting only those members of the aggressor community who are guilty of that aggression (Valls, 2000, p. 76). The truly non-culpable, for example, children, the mentally ill, and so forth, should be immune from attack.

Let me now bring this to a head. I have argued that where various conditions are met, then terrorism against an aggressor can be justified. More precisely, if the members of a community have adequate evidence that

- their community is subjected to an unjustifiable radical existential threat from an identifiable aggressor (hence, that the *jus ad bellum* just cause and last resort conditions are met);
- a projected campaign of terrorism would satisfy the *jus ad bellum* conditions of competent authority, proportionality, right intent, and reasonable hope of success;
- the aggressor is using terrorism against their community (parity of means condition);
- the adult civilians of the aggressor are culpable of the aggression that constitutes the existential threat (the culpability condition);
- the *jus in bello* demands of proportionality, legitimate means, humane treatment of captives, and discrimination (do not target innocents) are to be respected.

then their recourse to terrorism against the aggressor community for the purposes of ending or reducing that threat is morally justifiable.

10. Justified terrorism in the Israeli–Palestinian conflict

Terrorism in the Arab–Israeli conflict has been both a deliberate and an inevitable consequence of the aims of both parties. As described above, Zionist strategic terrorism in 1948 was an effective means of creating a Jewish state with a decisive Jewish majority in Palestine, and since 1967, the combination of Israeli structural and direct terrorism has been instrumental in extending Israeli control beyond the 1949 armistice lines. Palestinian terrorism, strategic and reactive, stems from a decided determination to resist the loss of a traditional homeland by any means possible. While it has not brought about Palestinian self-determination, it has achieved some of the desired objectives towards that ultimate goal, and, as with Zionist terrorism, it is likely that it was essential in so doing.

Has any of this terrorism been morally justified? No doubt, plenty of instances have not been. But we have seen that there are those on both sides of the Israeli–Palestinian conflict who have found terrorism to be a rational strategy for defending and ensuring the independence of their people. Given a conviction in the morality of their goals, they have also argued that their violence is completely justifiable. The real question is whether their respective ends of national self-preservation and self-determination—as conceived by each side—confers overriding moral significance upon the terrorism each has inflicted upon the other. Both the ends and the envisioned means must be examined more carefully.

There are the maximalists on both sides of the Israeli–Palestinian conflict who, believing that they are in a zero-sum game, take terrorism to be the only way to succeed in achieving an exclusive possession of the entire region under dispute. As far as their means-end thinking is concerned, they are absolutely correct; establishing either a completely Jewish or a completely Arab state throughout Palestine would necessitate violence against civilians. The more controversial issue is whether either maximalist goal is of such overriding importance as to justify terrorism. Here, it is very important to distinguish the inherent desirability of an end from the justifiability of pursuing that end given standing demographic and political realities. The vision of a nation-state established on a defensible and economically viable territory in which people are able to develop its culture without interference from outside is not in itself wrongful, even though the principle of self-determination does not grant any collective a right to such a state (as argued in Chapter 1). But since maximalist programs for implementing that vision in Palestine would entail massive violence against civilians who are legitimately living in the region of mandated Palestine, whether Arab or Jew, and pose a threat to peace throughout southern Asia, and since there are reasonable alternatives to solving the conflict that avoid these extremes, then there are moral grounds for holding that the maximalist ends on either side cannot justify terrorism.

Justifications in terms of maximalist ends are not the only arguments available for defending terrorism. Let us consider the major terrorist strategies in the Israeli–Palestinian conflict that are independent of maximalist assumptions.

10.1. Terrorism in establishing a Jewish state within Palestine

If the end of Zionism—the establishment of Jewish state in Palestine with a decisive Jewish majority—was of overriding importance, then the Jewish recourse for strategic terrorism against the Palestinians was justifiable. Given that the Palestinians were determined to retain and reside in their homeland, then achieving the end of Zionism required the use of violence against civilians in order to dismantle the Palestinian Arab community and remove as many Arabs as possible from the targeted area. However, this justification for terrorism against Palestinians cannot be anchored in the foregoing self-defense argument. The Palestinians were not the aggressors in the overall conflict, and since the importation of thousands of European Jews into Palestine during the Mandate period was against the will of the majority of Palestine's residents, then whatever existential threat the Palestinians posed to that Jewish community, it was not a threat to a community that was legitimately constituted in Palestine, hence, not an unjustifiable threat if a threat at all. Furthermore, as argued in Chapter 1, achieving the goal of Zionism was not itself justifiable since realizing it meant violating the principle of self-determination. Yet, even if the League of Nations Mandate and the UN-GA Resolution 181(II) justified the establishment of a Jewish state in Palestine, those decisions did not sanction removal of the resident Palestinian population. Such expulsion was the effect of explicit strategic decisions made by the Zionist leadership to create a Jewish state with a decisive Jewish majority in as much of mandated Palestine as could be captured. Since that end did not have overriding moral significance, then the terrorist strategy to secure it could not be morally justified.

10.2. Terrorism in expanding the Jewish state within Palestine

Assuming that recognized international law is a reliable guide to a sound international morality, then Israeli structural terrorism in the occupied territories has not been morally justified. The political end which this terrorism serves, namely, the expansion of Israel control in the West Bank, requires the acquisition of territory by force, forbidden under international law (Cattan, 1976, chap. VII; Quigley, 1990, part 4; Boyle, 2003, chap. 5) and constitutes a violation of the principle of self-determination. Moreover, the policies of the Israeli occupation violate both the Fourth Geneva Convention, which prohibits colonization of occupied territory, and the major conventions protecting the civil, political, economic, and cultural rights of the resident population. Despite the claims that Israel needs this territory to ensure its own survival (e.g., O'Brien, 1991, p. 230), the Palestinians in the occupied territories have never posed an existential threat to Israel given the gross asymmetry of power between Israelis and Palestinians and the massive imbalance in the terror inflicted. Israel is one of the world's strongest military powers, equipped with some of the most advanced weapons on the planet. Palestinians have no weaponry to compare with Israel's F-16 fighter planes, Apache helicopters, Merkava tanks, and the like. Although the Israeli Government has a right to defend its population against unwarranted aggression, its structural and direct terrorism in the occupied territories exists for the sole purpose of expanding the Jewish state and, hence, both are offensive and provocative rather than defensive. Israel has other alternatives for countering threats from Palestinians to its population, specifically, ending its occupation of the West Bank and seriously working with the Palestinian leadership towards achieving a just compromise of their long-standing conflict.

10.3. Palestinian strategic terrorism in self-defense

Using the argument from radical self-defense that has been developed in Section 9, there is a *prima facie* case for the legitimacy of both past and current Palestinian terrorism directed against Israelis. The proof is in the details.

First, the Palestinian community throughout Palestine, and the Palestinian communities in various regions within Palestine, have faced, and still face, an existential threat from Zionism. Palestinians have perceived this threat early on. In a letter to the British High Commissioner in Palestine in December 27, 1934, the Palestinian leader, Haj Amin El-Husseini, spoke of Arab fears that the 'inevitable result' of continued Jewish immigration 'would be the destruction of the Arab race in Palestine.' This threat has been demonstrated in many ways:

- Israel's expulsion of Palestinians in 1948 and again in 1967 and the refusal to repatriate Palestinian refugees.
- Israel's colonization, land confiscation, and other forms of structural terrorism in the occupied West Bank that began in 1967 and have continued until the present, including during the period of the Oslo Accords.
- Israel's systematic violation of Palestinians' human rights in the occupied territories.
- Israel's refusal to comply with international resolutions calling for its withdrawal from the territories occupied in the 1967 war.
- Israel's opposition to peace initiatives, for example, repeated calls for an international peace conference on the Middle East, the Rogers Plan of 1969–70, the Reagan Plan of 1982, Prince Fahd's peace plan of 1981–82, the PLO's offer of peace in 1988, and the Arab League's proposals of 2002.
- Israel's deliberate efforts to destroy the PLO's capacity to establish and maintain an independent state in the occupied territories (Yaniv, 1987, *passim*).
- Israel's deportation of Palestinian political leaders during the 1970s (Lesch, 1979).
- Israel's assassinations of Palestinian political leaders, extending from the 1970s to the present.
- The expressed intention by the dominant Israeli political parties to retain control of the West Bank or large segments thereof, as demonstrated by the Labor Party's early support of the Allon Plan and its subsequent expansion of the settlement network during the 1990s, the Likud's election platform vows to retain all of the West Bank and its rapid acceleration of settlement building when in power, and the publication of official Israeli maps showing the West Bank as part of Israel. The only difference between the leading political parties in Israel concerns how much of the West Bank is to be incorporated into the Jewish state (Reinhart, 2002, chap. ix).
- Israel's refusal to permit establishment of a viable Palestinian state in the occupied territories, as revealed by Moshe Sharett's agreements with Abdullah (Rogan & Shlaim, 2001), Ehud Barak's breaking off talks at Taba in January 2001 (Reinhart, 2002, chap. II), and Ariel Sharon's rejection of the Arab League's peace overtures in spring 2002, the 2002 Geneva Accords between moderate Israelis and Palestinians (Shuman, 2003; date of access: June 17, 2006), and the call for establishing a Palestinian state in the Bush Administration's 2002 'Road Map' for

peace (see *Journal of Palestine Studies* 32, 3, 121, for more on the reception of the Bush administration's Road Map).

- The virtually unquestioned support for Israeli policies by the government of the United States.[46]

That this existential threat is unjustifiable is due to its violation of the human rights of Palestinians, including the right of self-determination (see Chapters 1 and 2).

Second, in light of this threat, the Palestinians have a just cause for resorting to violence, not so much for achieving political independence as for survival of their community. A group's goal of self-determination is not always overriding and cannot, by itself, justify a campaign of terrorism, for not every impediment to a national group's quest for political independence poses a radical existential threat. The Palestinians' quest is for their survival as a community in their home territory, and in this sense their case is arguably different from the situation faced by Kurds, Tamils, Basques, Irish, and so on, however legitimate the demands for self-determination for these groups might be.

Third, the Palestinians have attempted the standard measures of self-defense noted above. (i) As early as 1913, Palestinian leaders sought accommodation with the Zionists (Hirst, 2003, p. 154). The major Palestinian political organization, the PLO, has tried diplomacy by entering into direct negotiations with representatives of the Israeli government and various Israeli groups and individuals (Shehadeh, 1997), and in 1988 the Palestine National Council ratified the two-state solution, thereby explicitly recognizing Israel's right to exist. The Palestinian Authority in the occupied territories has repeatedly stressed its acceptance of the two-state solution, yet Israel has not reciprocated, since it has steadfastly refused to negotiate any deal with the Palestinians that would grant them a viable state in Palestine. The claim that Israel's leadership is seriously interested in a meaningful compromise with the Palestinians is undermined Israel's actions, specifically, the direct and structural terrorism described in Sections 4–6, or in the persistent vilification and dehumanization of Palestinians noted in Section 8. (ii) The Palestinians have also appealed to external agencies for assistance (e.g., the League of Nations, the United Nations, and the Arab League) and to external powers, they have supported international resolutions calling for a two-state solution to the conflict (see the record summarized in Finkelstein, 2005, pp. 294–300), and in April 2003, they endorsed the Bush Administration's Road Map. (iii) Palestinians have repeatedly used techniques of non-violence in combating the Israeli occupation

[Holmes, 1995; Saleh, 2003 (date of access: November 11, 2006), Abunimah, 2006, pp. 49–51] and have sought and received the help of like-minded Israelis, but to no avail. (iv) The Palestinians have resisted established militaries, viz., the British military in 1936–39, the Zionist forces in 1947–48, and the Israeli military since the establishment of the Jewish state. None of these measures has been successful in ending or abating the existential threat they face, much less in securing their self-determination. In the atmosphere of ongoing hostilities accompanying the American occupation of the Middle East, there is even less likelihood that availing themselves of these standard measures of self-defense will be successful. By emasculating Palestinian diplomacy, intensifying the control over the West Bank, Israel has deprived young Palestinians of hope, leaving terrorism one of the few avenues of active resistance left. Thus, there is good reason to conclude that the Palestinians in the West Bank face a radical existential threat, in which case terrorism presents itself as a last resort strategy for that community.[47]

Fourth, there is evidence that recourse to terrorism has produced at least some desired results for the Palestinians, even though it has not yet secured Palestinian self-determination nor ended the existential threat posed by Israel. In plain fact, Palestinian terrorism has succeeded in perpetuating the cycle of violence that Israelis and Palestinian have been locked in for over 80 years. One result is that considerable attention is kept riveted upon the conflict and, thus, upon Palestinian suffering and Palestinian demands. As indicated in Section 4, the result is that not only have many people pressed for answers to questions about why this sort of violence is occurring, but many people throughout the world have become more sympathetic and supportive of the Palestinians. For over 80 years, beginning with the British commissions of the 1920s, extreme violence has caused external players to play a more active role in resolving the Israeli–Palestinian conflict. It has led some Israelis to question policies of the Israeli government in the occupied territories, and, in a few instances, it has caused the Israeli government to make some concessions to the Palestinians (Pape, 2005, chap. 5). Given the intentions of the Israeli leadership, quiet acquiescence on the part of Palestinians would have resulted in slow strangulation. Furthermore, striking back against their oppressors has also alleviated the Palestinians' sense of impotence against a powerful adversary and, thereby, strengthened the confidence, resolve, and unity among Palestinian communities.[48]

Fifth, the remaining conditions for justifying the Palestinian's campaign of terrorism appear to be satisfied. Palestinian militancy has received enough popular support from the Palestinian residents of the territories to sanction at least the general strategy of violence against Israeli civilians (see the figures reported in Finkelstein, 2005, pp. 298–9). This kind of support intensifies whenever the Israeli military increases the amount of terrorism it employs against the Palestinians (Sections 3–5). Not only is the parity of means condition satisfied, thereby, but since Israel is a representative democracy with large percentages of its adult citizens publicly supporting the measures that constitute the existential threat to the Palestinians, then the culpability condition is also met. The Israeli electorate has placed in power men with a record of violence against Palestinians civilians, including Menachem Begin and Yitzhak Shamir, terrorists from the 1940s, Yitzhak Rabin who directed the forced expulsion of Palestinian from their homes in 1948 and implemented the 'iron fist' policy in the Occupied territories in the 1980s, and Ariel Sharon with a record of 50 years of aggression against Palestinians. The Israeli public was not blind to the pasts and polices of these men, and this is concrete evidence that it supported terrorism against Palestinians (Steinhoff, 2004, pp. 103–5; Finkelstein, 2005, pp. 300–1). In 2004, despite the deaths of over 3000 Palestinians since September 2000, they returned the Likud party to power, doubling its number of seats in the Knesset. According to a March 2002 poll, 46 percent of Israelis favored expulsion of Palestinians from the occupied territories and 60 percent favored 'encouraging' Palestinian citizens of Israel to leave (Ammon Barzilai, 'More Israeli Jews Favor Transfer of Palestinians, Israeli Arabs, Poll Finds,' *Ha'aretz*, March 12, 2002). In a 2005 poll, 65 percent of Israelis expressed opposition to a full Israeli withdrawal to the 1949 armistice lines or abandoning the 'neighborhoods' that surround East Jerusalem—the very settlements that 'have destroyed the contiguity of the West Bank and cut Palestinians off from Jerusalem and each other' (Abunimah, 2006, p. 52).

These facts certainly do not justify every act of terrorism committed by Palestinians, but they constitute a strong *prima facie* case that the Palestinians have been justified in resorting to terrorism in some instances. Not all Palestinians agree. Since the recourse to terrorism has also damaged Palestinians' reputation, and provided the Israeli government with a pretext to tighten its control over the West Bank, to impose further restrictions upon its residents, and to intensify its own violence, many thoughtful Palestinians have condemned such actions on the following grounds:

> Suicide bombings deepen the hatred and widen the gap between the Palestinian and Israeli people. Also, the destroy they possibilities of peaceful co-existence between them in two neighboring states.... they strengthen the enemies of peace on the Israeli side and give Israel's aggressive government under Sharon the excuse to continue its harsh war against our people.... there is a need to re-evaluate these acts considering that pushing the area towards an existential war between the two people living on the holy land will lead to destruction for the whole region. ('Urgent Appeal to Stop Suicide Bombings,' *Al Quds*, June 20, 2002)

On the other side, there is no reason to assume that if the Palestinians had not responded to Israeli policies with violence the Israelis would have desisted from their plans to colonize the West Bank and undermine the Palestinian presence there through structural terrorism. The undeniable fact remains that the Israeli political leadership has always been determined to expand the Jewish state beyond the 1949 armistice lines, and the settlement program is an integral phase in this expansion. Not only are the settlements projected as irreversible facts on the ground, they are instrumental to the argument that the only way to end hostilities is by separating the two communities by either transferring the Palestinians out of the area or isolating them within increasingly infeasible 'bantustans' (Reinhart, 2002, chaps. V, IX). It is ludicrous to think that these settlements in occupied territory are driven by a desire for security; if anything, they multiply Israel's security concerns, for not only must the Israeli government continue to expend large amounts of money in protecting the settlements and their inhabitants, but Palestinian outrage and frustration will only intensify with every dunum confiscated and every Israeli house built. Unless there is a collective decision on the part of Palestinians to concede defeat and evacuate their ancestral homeland, these emotions will seek outlets.

11. Concluding remarks

No one should be sanguine about any attempt to defend terrorism. Given our massive uncertainty about the future, consequentialist justifications are always tenuous, and this should sober anyone who would advocate, pursue, or defend a campaign of terrorism. Yet, before making any final moral judgments about violence between Israelis and Palestinians, it is important to keep some final observations in mind.

The burden of ending this tragic violence lies primarily with the stronger party, Israel, especially since the Palestinian leadership and the Arab states have repeatedly expressed their willingness to accept a compromise by recognizing Israel in exchange for a Palestinian state in the occupied territories. Israel has a sufficiently strong military to defend itself against armed threats without itself engaging in terrorism. The Jewish desire for security is a powerful one, and fully understandable, in light of the prejudice, discrimination, and persecution that Jews have experienced throughout their remarkable history, but it is doubtful that long-term security can be achieved by antagonizing the rest of the Middle East. The ambitious arrogance, and perhaps, the short-sightedness, of Israeli leaders and their supporters in the United States and elsewhere, are chiefly to blame for the ongoing cycle of violence, even if they are triumphant in the short run. The gross asymmetry in military and economic power between the two sides fosters skepticism that the Palestinians can ever succeed in achieving self-determination in Palestine by any means. As such, the conclusion of the previous section is best viewed as conditional rather than categorical; if Palestinian recourse to terrorism is likely to defeat or even diminish a radical existential threat to their community, then given that the other conditions for justified political violence are met, some instances of Palestinian terrorism can be justified. Whether this antecedent is fulfilled is a deep and complex matter, for, as noted, there are powerful considerations on both sides.

If recourse to violence is likely not to be successful in ending an existential threat, can terrorism be justified by any other argument? In particular, could purely retaliatory terrorism (Section 2) be justified? Here, one must distinguish between there being no reasonable hope of ending or reducing an existential threat and there being no hope of successfully carrying out a punitive act against the aggressor. If the latter holds, a contemplated act of terrorism would be futile. But suppose there is a way of harming the aggressor, even if it would not succeed in ending or reducing the aggression? Would inflicting harm under such circumstances be morally justified as long as the other *jus ad bellum* and *jus in bello* conditions are observed? There are at least three reasons for claiming that it would be.

1. Under the assumption that every community, like every human being, has a moral right of self-defense against unjustified aggression, then allowing terrorism under a radical existential threat conveys the message to future governments and generations that existential aggression against others will generate violent responses, whether

from the victim or from those who sympathize with the victim. Concern for the safety and future of their own civilians may very well function as a deterrent that would stay the hand of the would-be aggressors, especially in an era of advanced weaponry when the actions of a disaffected group might obliterate an entire city. Rules permitting punitive retaliation for grievous wrongs have too great a deterrence value to warrant their suspension in the absence of a reasonable hope of success of ending or reducing a particular existential threat.

2. Denying the legitimacy of retaliation against powerful adversaries would give every society, every state, every political faction, a reason for the acquisition of overwhelming power. Suppose a society acquired enough power to make it very clear that any opposition to its aggression against another society would likely be unsuccessful. Suppose, further, that its military and leadership have nearly immunized themselves from retaliation, leaving only terrorism—violence against the more exposed, yet culpable civilians—as a means of retaliation. If the lack of a reasonable hope of success in ending the aggression is the only thing that keeps such proposed terrorism from being right, then a corollary of the might makes right formula would triumph under the guise of might makes wrong: acquire enough power so that your opposition cannot justifiably retaliate. Who could resist such immunization? Adherence to that precept would be a greater danger to the world, and a greater offense to human dignity, than adherence to any rule permitting retaliatory terrorism against an unjustified aggressor.
3. Few situations are worse than being faced with a humiliating unjustified annihilation of oneself and all that one holds dear without the power of retaliation. No human being should be morally required to passively submit to such a fate; each has a right to alleviate the suffering caused by such a condition and preserve one's dignity as a human being through the available means. Some might have the strength to preserve dignity through non-violent resistance, peaceful acquiescence to their fate, or even solitary stoical suicide, and no one can criticize their decision. But not everyone has had the philosophical luxury, religious and moral training, or the saintly strength of spirit to transform such ideals into viable practical alternatives capable of sustaining a course of action when threatened with humiliating extermination. The first impulse when attacked is to fight back, and when the attack is viewed as uncalled for then that impulse is strengthened. To most humans, the conviction that those guilty

> of a crime are to be punished is too compelling a practical maxim to abandon even when it is reasonable to expect that the crime will be committed regardless of what one does. The decision to strike back against overwhelming odds can be a valuable means for reducing misery and retaining dignity while enduring the threat of destruction, before the twilight falls.

On each of these grounds, then, retaliatory terrorism against those who pose a radical existential threat is morally justifiable. Neither individuals nor communities can be morally required to passively submit to their own future extermination without the right of resistance against those responsible. If an existential threat is so severe that it would be carried out in the absence of resistance, then, for the reasons given, terrorism against unjustified aggressors is better than the available alternatives.

Before passing final judgment on the Palestinian response to the threat they are facing, it is worth reflecting on the lives of young Palestinians brought up under Israeli military occupation. From birth, they have been subjected to the brutality of midnight searches, beatings, imprisonment, torture, restrictions on their movement, and to the ongoing spectacle of watching their parents, their relatives, their friends being humiliated on a daily basis.[49] According to a 2004 survey of 944 youths in Gaza, age 10–19, nearly half showed symptoms of severe post-traumatic stress disorder. Among them, the most prevalent types of trauma exposure were witnessing funerals (94.6 percent), witnessing shooting (83.2 percent), seeing injured or dead who were not relatives (66.9 percent), seeing family members injured or killed (61.6 percent), and witnessing their fathers being humiliated or beaten by Israeli soldiers (55 percent).[50] In many cases, the dead and injured were children, like themselves. Add to this the fact that they have continually been reminded that this land used to belong to them, the Palestinians, the Arabs, for centuries before the catastrophe of 1948, of how those distant fields belonged to their village, of how they had free access to the rest of the country, to the holy cities of Jerusalem (*Al-Quds*) and Hebron (*Al-Khalil*), to the Dead Sea, and to the hills of the Galilee. If, throughout their lives, this is what they have seen and heard, then it is understandable when they become young adults they would be consumed by four powerful emotions:

- *humiliation*, derived from a violation of dignity and honor;
- *outrage*, derived from a violation of a sense of justice;

- *despair,* derived from nearly four decades of life under the structural terrorism of the Israeli occupation and the failure of the world community to end it;
- *vengeance,* derived from humiliation, outrage, and despair.

Is it surprising that they should react with the desperation of suicidal terrorism where they fail to see their victims as innocent? When members of a society repeatedly resort to vengeance of this magnitude, we must not fall for the incredible suggestions that it is because of their cultural or religious beliefs, or, even more ludicrously, their 'hatred of freedom,' their 'desire to kill without cause,' or their 'disposition toward unbridled violence.' That large numbers of Palestinians are so consumed by humiliation, outrage, and despair that they find violence to be the only outlet, is a vivid testimony to the political failure of international diplomacy and the moral failure of the world community. Their final act is very likely a plea that the pain and horror they have endured throughout their lives ought not be tolerated by any human being or community.

Apart from the issue of justification, enough has been said to show that in the absence of a just peace, terrorism in the Israeli–Palestinian conflict will continue as long as both parties retain their current aims and passions, or, until one side is utterly crushed or eliminated (Gordon & Lopez, 2000, p. 112). The signs are ominous. Not only has the Israeli leadership consistently opposed a viable Palestinian state west of the Jordan River, but a sizeable segment of the Israeli public openly supports the idea of compulsory transfer. Wholly outgunned, the Palestinians will be unable to stop the expansion of the Jewish state without a significant change in either Israeli public opinion or the global political *status quo,* and their continual victimization will continue to have profound repercussions upon the future, even if the details cannot be presently ascertained. Throughout history, intense struggles have never ceased to produce astonishing outcomes. While Israeli Jews presently enjoy a strong vigorous state, it cannot yet be determined whether Zionism's victory and expansion by force at the expense of another people can long be tolerated or sustained. While Palestinian Arabs have gained recognition and a place at the negotiating table, it is too early to tell if either their diplomatic efforts or their resort to violence will secure their self-determination in Palestine or survival as a distinct people. One thing is certain from the past 90 years; combating terrorism with more terrorism will not stop the intercommunal violence so long as both parties are left standing and determined.

Notes

1. See the descriptions in Brown (1970), Churchill (1997), and Mann (2005). Holy scriptures were not far from the minds of those Americans who supported atrocities against native Americans. In 1794, George Henry Loskiel wrote that the American settlers 'represented the Indians as Canaanites who without mercy ought to be destroyed from the face of the earth, and considered America as the land of promise given to the Christians' (cited in Mann, 2005, p. 151).
2. The U.S. State Department (http://www.state.gov; date of access: January 18, 2005) takes its definition from Title 22 of the *United States Code*, Section 2656f(d): 'The term "terrorism" means premeditated, politically motivated violence perpetrated against noncombatant targets by sub-national groups or clandestine agents, usually intended to influence an audience. (The term "noncombatant" is interpreted to include, in addition to civilians, military personnel who at the time of the incident are unarmed or not on duty.)' The FBI (http://www.fbi.gov/publications/terror/terror2000_2001.htm; date of access: January 18, 2005) endorses a definition found in the U.S. *Code of Federal Regulations*: 'Terrorism is the unlawful use of force and violence against person or property to intimidate or coerce a government, the civilian population, or any segment thereof, in further of political or social objectives.' The U.S. Defense Department (http://www.dtic.mil/doctrine/jel/new_pubs/jp1_02.pdf; date of access: July 23, 2007) describes terrorism as 'the calculated use of unlawful violence or threat of unlawful violence to inculcate fear; intended to coerce or to intimidate governments or societies in the pursuit of goals that are generally political, religious, or ideological.'
3. Similar definitions can be found in several sources, for example, Garnor (2001, date of access: November 15, 2006), Coady (2004c), and Netanyahu (2001). Controversy has surrounded attempts to define 'terrorism' in the United Nations [Thalif Deen, 'Battle Rages Over UN Anti-Terror Treaty,' *Online Asia Times*, November 30, 2001 (http://www.atimes.com/front/CK30Aa02.html; date of access: November 15, 2006). In Article 2(b) of its *International Convention for the Suppression of the Financing of Terrorism* (May 5, 2004), the United Nations provided this definition of terrorism: 'any act intended to cause death or serious bodily harm to a civilian or non-combatants, or to any other person not taking an active part in the hostilities in a situation of armed conflict, when the purpose of such an act by its nature or context, is to intimidate a population, or to compel a government or an international organization to do or to abstain from doing any act.' An interesting list of definitions of 'terrorism' appears in Best and Nocella (2004, pp. 9–13).
4. The U.S. State Department employs a broad notion of noncombatant to include military personnel who are unarmed or who are not on duty. There is some rationale to this if we relativize the notions of *combatant* and *noncombatant* to specific courses of action. If a course of action is any action or plan of action that can be intentionally undertaken, whether throwing a particular hand grenade, planning an ambush, invading a country, and so on, then a combatant relative to an act of violence, say, a battle, is

an agent who plays some role in the conduct of that action, whether as fighter, director, or support staff. A combatant relative to given military campaign, for example, an occupation of a city, is one who takes part in that campaign. This allows that a person might be a combatant with respect to a given campaign but not relative to a particular battle within that campaign. Accordingly, if terrorism is violence against noncombatants, then this relativization of combatant affects what gets counted as terrorism as well. This understood, I will avoid the complications of such relativization in the text.

5. Several writers have pointed out that being random, indiscriminate, or irrational are not essential to politically motivated violence against civilians, see, for example, Valls (2000, p. 67), Coady (2004c, p. 7), and Young (2004, pp. 56–7). Those who describe terrorism in this manner, for example, Walzer (1988, pp. 238–40), typically do so with the intent to discredit terrorism.
6. The terms 'terroriste' and 'le terreur' were initially applied to the actions of the revolutionary Jacobin government in eradicating its enemies (Laqueur, 1987, p. 11). During Robespierre's Reign of Terror, it is estimated that some 400,000 men, women, and children were imprisoned by government authorities, and some estimates place the number executed as high as 40,000. By the late nineteenth century, 'terrorism' was used to signify anti-government activities, for example, the campaigns of Irish dissidents in the 1860s and of Russian revolutionaries of the 1880s (Laqueur, 1987, chap. 1). The United Nations, in its convention on terrorism, allows that states can be the agents of terrorism. Selden and So (2004) defines state terrorism as 'systematic state violence against civilians in violation of international norms, state edicts, and precedents established by international courts designed to protect the rights of civilians' (p. 3). See also Ashmore (1997), Primoratz (2004b), and Jaggar (2005).
7. See Glover (1991, pp. 257, 273), Gordon and Lopez (2000, pp. 110–1), Pilger (2004), and Jaggar (2005, p. 208). A contrary view is presented in Robert Pape's study of suicide terrorism (2005), which defines 'terrorism' as 'the use of violence by an organization other than a national government to intimidate or frighten a target audience' (p. 9). Pape does not restrict the targets of terrorism to noncombatants and argues that broadening the definition to include governments as agents of terrorism 'would distract attention from what policy makers would most like to know: how to combat the threat posed by non-state actors to the national security of the United States and our allies.' Also, because states and non-state actors have 'different levels of resources, face different kinds of incentives, and are susceptible to different types of pressures'...they 'require separate theoretical investigations' (2005, p. 280). Pape's qualification reflects a scholar's explicit decision to abide by the canons that enable him to comment on U.S. foreign policy. Without doubt, terrorism, as he defines it, exists. The drawback of his definition is that, apart from the considerations already raised, it classifies all political violence by non-state actors that might 'intimidate or frighten' as terrorist, including the actions of all revolutionary, resistance, and national liberation movements, no matter how justified.

8. In his diary, Herzl wrote: 'We shall try to spirit the penniless population across the border by procuring employment for it in the transit countries, while denying it any employment in our own country.... Both the process of expropriation and the removal of the poor must be carried out discreetly and circumspectly' (Patai, 1960, vol. I, p. 88).
9. See Flapan (1987, p. 103), Morris (1999, p. 659; 2001, p. 44). Tom Segev writes that despite attempts by Ben-Gurion's biographers to distance Ben-Gurion from the idea of forcible transfer, his 'stand on deportation, like that of other Zionist leaders is unambiguous and well-documented' (1999, p. 407). The expedient of forced transfer also entered into the recommendations of the 1937 Peel Commission Report which first recommended a partition of Palestine into separate Jewish and Arab states. The Commission stated that if the Arabs who lived in the area assigned to the Jews did not leave of their own accord, then their removal should be 'compulsory' (Morris, 1999, p. 138).
10. Hirst (2003, pp. 169–73). Subsequently, Ben-Gurion was more candid. In 1938, addressing the Mapai Political Committee, Ben Gurion said, 'When we say that the Arabs are the aggressors and we defend ourselves—that is only half the truth. As regards our security and life we defend ourselves... politically, we are the aggressors and they defend themselves' (Flapan, 1979, p. 141).
11. The exact number of Palestinian victims is disputed. The figure of 254 fatalities can be found in Hirst (2003, p. 250), while Morris (1987, p. 113) cites a figure of 250. The number 350 is suggested in De Reynier (1971, p. 764), whereas Morris (2002b, p. 127) concludes that the figure closer to 110, and Pappe (2006, p. 91) reports a figure of 93, explaining that 'dozens' of Palestinians killed in fighting were not included in the official list of massacre victims. Pappe describes other massacres that had larger numbers of Palestinian victims, for example, at Tantura and Dawaymeh (2006a, pp. 133–7, 195–7). Menachem Begin denied any massacre of Arab civilians had occurred at Deir Yassin, but he acknowledged that the story 'invented' about what happened there 'helped carve the way to our decisive victories on the battlefield' (Begin, 1977, p. 165).
12. In the years after the 1947–49 war, the story was perpetrated that Arabs left their homes at the behest of Arab leaders who pledged to cleanse the area of Zionist forces—see, for example, a speech by Abba Eban (Laqueur, 1976, pp. 151–64). This myth, perhaps initiated by the American Zionist, Joseph Schechtman (Khalidi, 2005, pp. 43–4), has long since been debunked (see Flapan, 1987; Morris, 1987; Khalidi, 2005; Pappe, 2006a; and much earlier, Childers, 1961). Before his assassination by members of the Jewish Lehi militia in September 1948, Count Folke Bernadotte, the UN Mediator in Palestine, wrote: 'The exodus of Palestinian Arabs resulted from panic created by fighting in their communities, "by rumors concerning real or alleged acts of terrorism, or expulsion... There have been numerous reports from reliable sources of large-scale looting, pillaging and plundering, and of instances of destruction of villages without apparent military necessity"' (UN document A/648, part I, chap. V).
13. See Alon (1980, pp. 68–81), which mentions that the Israeli policy of combating 'international terrorism' included the proviso that civilian

populations that 'shelter anti-Israeli terrorists' will not be immune from punitive action. See also Gal-Or (1994) for a discussion of Israeli policy, as well as the earlier study of Blechman (1971).

14. Morris (1993, pp. 136–7, p. 415). In 1979, Livia Rokach, the daughter of Moshe Sharett, Israel's first foreign minister and its second prime minister (1954–55), published excerpts from his diary that revealed more details of Israel's strategic terrorism [appearing in English in Rokach (1980)]. She notes how Israel's leaders were unhappy with the 1949 armistice borders and never seriously believed in an Arab threat to the existence of Israel. To expand,Israel had to provoke Arab states into confrontation, a campaign that 'inevitably presupposed the use of large scale, open violence' and the glorification of terrorism and revenge. In every case, whether against Qibya or other West Bank villages, for example, upon Nahalin in 1954, Israel portrayed its military actions as 'retaliation.' These facts, as well as others noted in this section, belie the contention in O'Brien (1991, pp. 24–5) that Israel has made 'serious efforts' to 'avoid civilian damage.'
15. Abou Iyad (1981, pp. 111–2) and see Hirst (2003, pp. 439–40) and O'Brien (1991, chap. 1). Not only did the Olympics Committee exclude the Palestinians, it refused to respond to letters from the Palestinians requesting that they be allowed representation in the Olympic Games, causing considerable indignation and rage among young Palestinian militants (Abou Iyad with Eric Rouleau, 1978, p. 106).
16. Khalidi (1989) summarizes the statistics compiled from several sources. He notes that the number of Israeli soldiers killed by Palestinians from 1965 to 1988 was 432 as against approximately 2824 Palestinian combatants killed by the IDF. Countering terrorism was the pretext for the Israeli invasion of Lebanon in 1982—dubbed 'Operation Peace for the Galilee'—as the Israeli Government claimed its security was threatened by PLO cross-border raids and shelling. However, the Lebanese–Israel border had been largely quiet for 11 months due to a cease-fire negotiated by the Reagan emissary Philip Habib. After the reelection of Menachem Begin in mid-1981 and the appointment of Ariel Sharon as Defense Minister, air raids on Lebanon occurred with greater frequency (Bleier, 2003; date of access: November 12, 2006). Israeli troops began massing at the border in the spring of 1982, days in advance of an attempted assassination of an Israeli diplomat in London that Israel used an excuse to launch an invasion. The purpose of this invasion was to crush the PLO politically and remove it from Lebanon (Chomsky, 1999, pp. 198–208; Hirst, 2003, pp. 528–53). Throughout the subsequent 22-year occupation of southern Lebanon, Israeli forces frequently shelled civilian centers. For example, Operation Accountability in July 1993 killed some 120 civilians and injured another 500, with an estimated 150,000–200,000 displaced from their homes. In April 1996, nearly 200 civilians were killed in Operation Grapes of Wrath, including 102 who had taken refuge in a United Nations center in town of Qana.
17. B'tselem's report on the use of human shields was posted at its website, www.btselem.org, on 8 March 2007. Figures on casualties are listed in various sources, including B'tselem's, the Israeli Ministry of Defense at http://www.israel-mfa.gov.il, the Palestine Monitor at http://www.palestinemonitor.org, and Miftah at http://www.miftah.org. In one instance,

a family of eight was killed by Israeli shelling as they were having a picnic on a Gazan beach (see the report issued by Human Rights Watch http://hrw.org/english/docs/2006/06/20/israb13595_txt.htm; date of access: July 3, 2006).

18. There is a vibrant strain of religious nationalism within Zionism, fueled by popular justifications for Zionism in terms of divine promise and the religious mission of the Jews. The Ashkenazi Chief Rabbi from 1921 to 1935 in Palestine, Avraham Kook, taught that redemption of the land is as important as redemption of the people, and he lauded the young Jews of Jabotinsky's Betar movement for being 'willing to sacrifice their lives in the cause of their Holy Place' (Smith, 2001, p. 89). 'The arousal of desire in the whole nation to return to its Land, to the essence of its spirit and character, reflects the glow of repentance. It is an inner return, despite the many veils that obscure it' (Shimoni, 1995, p. 148). His son, Zvi Yehuda Kook, inspired the messianic *Gush Emunim* (Bloc of the Faithful) movement which has been at the forefront of Israeli settlement in the West Bank. He declared that the *Halakha* forbids giving up any land that has been restored to Israel: 'There is no Arab land here, only the inheritance of our God – and the more the world gets used to this thought, the better it will be for them and for all of us' (Friedman, 1992, p. 19). Holding that Eretz Israel should be settled and defended at any cost, Kook's followers settled on the outskirts of Hebron in 1970 and in the center of the city in 1979. As settlers protested in the summer of 1995 against any withdrawal of Israeli troops from the territories, a group of rabbis (the Union of Rabbis for the Land of Israel) reiterated Kook's *Halakha* prohibition and urged soldiers to disobey evacuation orders, angering Prime Minister Yitzhak Rabin (*Chicago Tribune*, July 13, 1995). Yigal Amir, Rabin's assassin some months later, stated that he had been directed by God to prevent Rabin from endangering Israel by handing over land to Palestinian rule: 'Everything I did was for the God of Israel, the Torah of Israel, the people of Israel and the Land of Israel' (*New York Times*, March 28, 1996).
19. According to B'Tselem—the Israeli Information Center for Human Rights in the Occupied Territories—Israeli settlers killed at least 11 Palestinians between September 2000 and September 2001 and injured dozens more. The Palestine Monitor reported that settlers killed at least 54 Palestinians during 2000–5 (http://www.palestinemonitor.org; date of access: July 11, 2006). Settlers have also attacked Palestinian homes, destroyed stores, automobiles and other property, uprooted trees, prevented farmers from reaching their fields, blocked major roads, stoned Palestinian cars, including ambulances, and targeted humanitarian workers, diplomats, and journalists. The Israeli authorities rarely intervened to stop or prevent settler attacks against Palestinians or to investigate them. When they did, perpetrators received disproportionately light sentences if they were punished at all.
20. See, for example, Graff (1991, 1997) for discussions of deliberate killing of Palestinian children by the Israeli army. Finkelstein (1995, p. 47) cites a 'Save the Children' study that concluded that more than 50,000 Palestinian children required medical attention for injuries due to gunshots, teargas, and beatings inflicted by the Israeli military. Israeli actions are documented by numerous reports issued during this time by Physicians for Human Rights

USA, Amnesty International, Human Rights Watch (1993, 1994, 1996, and 2002), B'tselem, the Israeli League for Human and Civil Rights, and the Palestinian organization Al Haq. See also, numerous articles by Gideon Levy in *Ha'aretz*, for example, 'Twilight Zone' (February 7, 2002), 'Twilight Zone: Suffer the Little Children' (December 4, 2004), and 'Killing Children Is No Longer a Big Deal' (October 17, 2004).

21. Casualty estimates vary; see for example, reports by B'tselem http://www.btselem.org and the Palestine Monitor at http://www.palestinemonitor.org. Statistics for the first four years of the intifada can be found in the *Journal of Palestine Studies*, xxxiv, 2, Winter 2005. The Palestine Authority also reported that over 7000 private Palestinian houses were destroyed in this period, 4785 of them located in Gaza Strip alone, 645 buildings belongs to the public sector and the security facilities were completely or partially destroyed, over 76,867 dunums of land were razed, and hundreds of thousands of trees were uprooted.
22. See, for example, Halper (2002, pp. 36–7) and Roy (2007, chaps. 5, 10, 15). For reports on the effects of recent Israeli policies in the West Bank, see the websites of the Electronic Intifada, http://electronicintifada.net/new.shtml, and B'tselem, http://www.btselem.org/English/.
23. David Hirst claims that Goldstein's massacre was no mere isolated act of a madman. A follower of New York's Lubavitcher Rebbe, his act was praised by extremist rabbis who delicately called it an 'act,' 'event,' or 'occurrence.' 'Within two days the walls of Jerusalem's religious neighborhoods were covered with posters extolling Goldstein's virtues and lamenting that the toll of dead Palestinians had not been higher' (Hirst, 2004; date of access: June 7, 2006). Hirst reports that the view of extremists within the Gush Emunim is that 'force is the only way to deal with the Palestinians.' So long as they stay in the Land of Israel, they can only do so as 'resident aliens' without 'equality of human and civil rights,' those being 'a foreign democratic principle' that does not apply to them. But, in the end, they must leave. There are two ways in which that can happen. One is 'enforced emigration.' The other way is based on the biblical injunction to 'annihilate the memory of Amalek.' In an article on 'The Command of Genocide in the Bible,' Rabbi Israel Hess opined that 'the day will come when we shall all be called upon to wage this war for the annihilation of Amalek.' He advanced two reasons for this. One was the need to ensure 'racial purity.' The other lay in the antagonism between Israel and Amalek as an expression of the antagonism 'between light and darkness, the pure and the unclean' (Hirst, 2004; date of access: June 7, 2006) 'Amalek' is a term that Jewish religious extremists use in referring to Palestinians; see for example, Begon (2002, p. 47).
24. Despite its readiness to return violence with violence, Hamas has frequently declared a willingness to negotiate. For example, in early 2003, a Hamas official said, 'Hamas is sticking by its proposal formulated a year ago by recommending an end to attacks on civilians on both sides,' and pledged that, 'Hamas would stop attacking Israeli civilians without distinction for geographic boundaries if Israel stops attacking, killing and arresting Palestinian civilians and blockading their towns and villages' (Agence France Presse, January 19, 2003).

25. See Section 11 of this chapter and also Hoffman and Lieberman (2002) as well as Steven Erlanger, 'Years of Strife and Lost Hope Scar Young Palestinians,' *The New York Times*, March 12, 2007. Pape (2005) reports that the most active suicide terrorist group of the past 25 years has been the Tamil Tigers, whose ideology is Marxist, employing 143 suicide operations between 1987 and 2001. Pape's claim concerning that a quest for self-determination underlies suicide terrorism is confirmed by the campaign of suicide bombing in Iraq after the 2003 invasion by the United States. Prior to the American occupation, Iraq had never experienced a single suicide terrorist attack in its history (Pape, 2005, p. 246). Similarly, the Palestinian citizens of Israel have not engaged in suicide terrorism. Former Attorney General of Israel, Michael Ben Yair put it this way: 'The intifada is the Palestinian people's war of national liberation. Historical processes teach us that no nation is prepared to live under another's domination and that a suppressed people's war of national liberation will inevitably succeed. We understand this point but choose to ignore it. We are prepared to engage in confrontation to prevent an historical process, although we are well aware that this process is anchored in the moral justification behind every people's war of national liberation and behind its right to self-determination' ('The War's Seventh Day,' *Ha'aretz*, March 3, 2002).
26. The terms 'terrorist' and 'terrorism' have not always been associated with a negative connotation. The Jacobins used 'terror' with a positive connotation during their Reign of Terror, though after the fall of Robespierre their opponents associated a negative connation with the term, a connotation preserved in the writings of Edmund Burke (Laqueur, 1987, p. 11). Geoffrey Nunberg has noted that '...the word "terrorism" led a double life—a justified political strategy to some, an abomination to others' http://www.sfgate.com/cgi-bin/article.cgi?file=/chronicle/archive/2001/10/28/IN159328.DTL (date of access: November 22, 2005). The Russian revolutionaries who assassinated Tsar Alexander II in 1881 used the word proudly. As late as 1947, the Jewish Stern Gang in Palestine referred to themselves as 'terrorists,' and Ben Hecht wrote approvingly of the Jewish 'terrorists of Palestine' in their attacks upon British targets in Palestine and, in the *New York Herald Tribune*, promised that the Jews of America 'are working to help you' (Hirst, 2003, p. 243). On the other hand, Menachem Begin opposed labeling the acts of the Jewish underground as 'terrorist' (1977, pp. 100–1).
27. This has been known for some time among many scholars. In 1977, C. C. O'Brien wrote: 'The words "terrorism" and "terrorist" are not terms of scientific classification. They are imprecise and emotive. We do not apply them to all acts of politically motivated violence or to all people who commit such crimes. We reserve their use for politically motivated violence of which we disapprove' (O'Brien, 1977, p. 91). Noam Chomsky has repeatedly pointed out that there is a 'propangandistic usage' in which 'the term "terrorism" is used to refer to terrorist acts committed by enemies against us or our allies' (interview number 5 at http://www.znet.com; date of access: January 7, 2006). Similar points are made by Oliverio (1998, chap. 1). Robert Picard writes that it 'has become an axiom that terrorism describes acts of violence committed by others, and the similar violence committed by one's own nation or by those with whom one sympathizes, is legitimate'

(Picard, 1993, p. 3). See also Collins (2002, pp. 163–6), which argues that it is essential that the United States not define 'terrorism' at all, since otherwise the United States and its allies would be deemed guilty of terrorism as well. See Best and Nocella (2004, p. 3) and Held (2004b, p. 65), who make similar points. A study by Simmons (1991) confirms this egocentric usage of 'terrorism' in major American media, and Donald Wycliff, Public Editor of the *Chicago Tribune*, explicitly acknowledged an egocentric employment of 'terrorism' in a *Tribune* op-ed piece of March 21, 2002.

28. In January 2005, the Iraq Body Count Database website at http://www.iraqbodycount.net (date of access: January 13, 2006) reported that up to 31,676 Iraqi civilians were killed in the first two years of the American invasion, actions by the U.S. military forces accounting for a sizeable percentage of this total. John Pilger reports that in May 2004, American forces killed approximately 600 civilians in Fallujah, 'a figure far greater than the total number of civilians killed by the "insurgents" during the past year. The generals were candid; this futile slaughter was an act of revenge for the killing of three American mercenaries' (Pilger, 2004). See also, 'What is the Difference Between Their "Terrorism" and our "War"?' at http://www.axisoflogic.com/artman/publish/article_19213.shtml (date of access: January 13, 2006), which reports that after the American siege of Fallujah in November 2004, 60–70 percent of all buildings had been damaged enough to render them uninhabitable. The three main water treatment plants, the electrical grid and the sewage treatment plant were severely damaged, leaving Fallujans without any of the basic services they will need to return to a normal life. The full force of America's arsenal, including F-16s, C-130s, Abrams tanks, and Apache Helicopters were unleashed on a few thousand rebels in a civilian enclave that contained at least 50,000 residents according to Red Cross estimates at the time. Among the 1200 Iraqis killed in the first week of the siege, at least 800 were civilians were killed (Dahr Jamail, '800 Civilians Feared Dead in Fallujah,' Inter Press Service, November 17, 2004), and some estimate that the final total was Iraqis killed in Fallujah was 6000 (see http://www.dahrjamailiraq.com, and http://www.afsc.org/pwork/0412/041204.htm; date of access: January 13, 2006).
29. The failure to recognize such instances of state terrorism is pointed out in many places, for instance, in Chomsky (1988a,b), Herman (1982), and Falk (1991). See also the examples listed in Herman and O'Sullivan (1991) and George (1991). The truth about Chechnya is similarly suppressed. On February 4, 2000, Russian aircraft attacked the Chechen village of Katyr Yurt. They used 'vacuum bombs,' which release petrol vapor and suck people's lungs out and are banned under the Geneva Convention. The Russians bombed a convoy of survivors under a white flag, killing 363 men, women, and children. It was one of countless, little known acts of terrorism in Chechnya perpetrated by the Russian state (Pilger, 2004).
30. The 'terrorist' label is rarely used to describe the structural violence instituted by a government's policies. Besides the institutionalized repression of Palestinian civilians in the Israeli-occupied territories, there was the campaign against Iraq throughout the 1990s, including both the U.S. bombing of Iraqi technological infrastructure in 1991 and the subsequent

policy of UN sanctions that led to the deaths of over a million Iraqis. Documentation concerning both cases can be found on the websites of several human rights organizations, including, Human Rights Watch, Amnesty International, Voices in the Wilderness, the World Health Organization, B'tselem, and the Palestine Monitor. U.S. Secretary of State Madeleine Albright admitted that the sanctions were intended to serve a political purpose despite acknowledged harm to civilians. When asked what she felt about the deaths of 500,000 Iraqi children caused by the sanctions, Albright replied that it was 'a very hard choice,' but, all things considered, 'we think the price is worth it' (*60 Minutes* interview, aired May 12, 1996).

31. See for example, the State Department's *Patterns of Global Terrorism 2000* (Alexander & Musch, 2001, pp. 1–126). In it, one finds Hezbollah attacks on the Israeli targets described as 'terrorist' despite the fact that these attacks were directed upon the forces of a military occupation in southern Lebanon (p. 39). Actions by the Palestinian Hamas and Islamic Jihad are described as 'terrorist' even when directed against Israeli occupying forces, whereas Israel's undercover assassinations of Palestinian figures were not so described (pp. 41–5). The use of 'terrorism' to describe Palestinian violence against an occupying Israeli military is also a feature of academic studies, O'Brien (1991, p. 224), Pape (2005, *passim*), and Cordesman (2005, chap. 2). Prudently, Pape and Cordesman do not define 'terrorism,' whereas O'Brien's usage violates his own definition on page 15.
32. See Kapitan (2003, 2005). The strategy of discouraging inquiry into causes is typified in the following statement by Harvard professor Alan Dershowitz: 'We must commit ourselves never to try to understand or eliminate its alleged root causes, but rather to place it beyond the pale of dialogue and negotiation' (Dershowitz, 2003, p. 24). Israel and the Western Democracies adopted the use of rhetoric of 'terror' in the 1970s to describe those who opposed their policies (see Chomsky, 1991; Herman and O'Sullivan, 1991, pp. 43–6). During this period, terrorists were portrayed as anti-democratic forces supported by Soviet style communism. In the 1990s, after the fall of the Soviet Union, the pro-communist gloss was submerged and terrorists were seen as an expression of radical Islam. In 1999, during the second invasion of Chechnya, Russian authorities themselves began to use the label, calling the Chechnya rebels 'terrorists.' Previously, Moscow had identified the rebels as 'bandits' (*Chicago Tribune*, November 3, 2002).
33. A CBS/New York Times poll conducted a few days after September 11, 2001 and whose results were published in *The New York Times* on 16 September 2001, reported that of 1216 Americans polled, 60 percent responded affirmatively when asked that if U.S. military action against 'whoever is responsible' for the attacks of September 11 meant that 'many thousands of innocent civilians may be killed,' then should such action be taken? The 'terrorist' classification is used by the United States to circumvent the applicability of international humanitarian law to detainees in the 'war on terror' (see Hajjar, 2006, pp. 31–2, p. 41, Notes 31–2). Mike Donning reports the following: '...operating in the midst of a violent insurgency and on unfamiliar terrain, U.S. forces in Iraq often detain people without clear evidence that the prisoners are involved in guerrilla activity....The taint of association with terrorists can influence the way soldiers treat these prisoners,

said John Hutson, dean of Franklin Pierce Law Center in Concord, N. H. and former judge advocate general of the Navy, the service's top legal officer: "...These are terrorists and different rules apply"' ('Prisoner Abuse Poses Peril for Bush,' *Chicago Tribune*, July 12, 2004).

34. Rokach (1980, pp. 5–10) notes that the Israel government under Ben-Gurion and Sharett understood in the early 1950s that the Israeli public must be inundated with images portraying the Palestinians as monsters, even if this required provocations that endangered the lives of Jewish citizens.
35. Noam Chomsky wrote of this a decade before: 'The Palestinians are a particularly natural target for Western racism. They are weak and dispersed, hounded on every side, but they refuse to accept their fate and melt away, an affront to civilization—not unlike the Jews. They must be despised, or how are we to justify their fate?' (Chomsky, 1976; Said, 1988). The American media frequently portrays the Palestinians as initiating violence and the Israelis as retaliating. David Hirst has said that 'the figures were something like 100 to 8 times that the word "retaliation" referred to what the Israelis did, 100 times to Israelis 8 times to Palestinians, while in it became clearer and clearer as the intifada went on, it was more the other way around. The Israelis were initiating violence and the Palestinians were retaliating. And yet it persisted like this, so that is a very typical reflection on the way in which the American media has covered the intifada' (Maureen Murphy, 'The Media, Nuclear Power, and Failed Peace: An Interview with David Hirst,' http://www.electronicintifada.org, January 9, 2004; date of access: February 17, 2006). The BBC is no different. Pilger (2004) reports that 'the State of Israel has been able to convince many outsiders that it is merely a victim of terrorism when, in fact, its own unrelenting, planned terrorism is the cause of the infamous retaliation by Palestinian suicide bombers ... BBC reporters never report Israelis as terrorists: that term belongs exclusively to Palestinians imprisoned in their own land. It is not surprising, as the recent Glasgow University study concluded, that many television viewers in Britain believe that the Palestinians are the invaders and occupiers.'
36. Sharon's article appeared in *The New York Times*, September 20, 1986. Like Netanyahu's book, it is a deliberate attempt to align the United States in Israel's battle against Palestinian nationalism by demonizing it as an instance of Arab and Islamic radicalism (see Margalit, 1995; Beinin, 2003, p. 20). The rhetoric of 'terror' extends beyond the mainstream media and corporate 'think tanks.' Academics also employ it, for example, Alan Dershowitz, who calls for the organized destruction of a single Palestinian village in retaliation for every terrorist attack against Israel: 'It will be a morally acceptable trade-off even if the property of some innocent civilians must be sacrificed in the process' ('A New Way of Responding to Palestinian Terrorism,' *The Jerusalem Post*, March 18, 2002).
37. See the Human Rights Watch report on the IDF's siege of the Jenin camp at http://www.hrw.org/press/2002/05/jenin0503-prin (date of access: March 27, 2005). Amnesty International and B'tselem published similar reports. The director of the Palestinian Red Crescent Society in Jenin told Human Rights Watch of the difficulty of sending assistance into the camp during the siege. Whenever IDF tanks saw the ambulances, they blocked their way and

occasionally shot at them. They continued to be denied access to the refugee camp until April 15, so that almost no injured persons from the camp were brought to the hospitals by ambulance from April 5 to April 15. Human Rights Watch, Amnesty International, and B'tselem reported that the Israeli military used Palestinian civilians as shields during the fighting, one of the more horrific war crimes documented by these organizations in the first few weeks after the fighting had ceased. For first hand accounts of the fighting, see Baroud (2002). Israel refused to accept a delegation that the UN Security Council approved for a fact-finding mission to Jenin, and under threat of a U.S. veto the delegation was disbanded.

38. See the statement by Alan Dershowitz quoted in Note 36. Other examples include the columnist Michael Kelly, who urged Israelis to 'unleash an overwhelming force' against Palestinians and to 'go ahead and escalate the violence' and to 'destroy, capture, and expel' (*Washington Post*, August 15, 2001). Again, columnist Ralph Peters claimed that the killing of Palestinian civilians, including children, who 'shield' terrorists—'human monsters' who are enemies of Israel or the United States—is 'justifiable' ('Civilian Casualties: No Apology Needed,' *Wall Street Journal*, July 25, 2002). Israel manipulated the graphic images of suicide bombings to vilify the Palestinian resistance movement, overlooking the much superior and deadlier Israeli violence meted out to the Palestinians. Ilan Pappe, professor of political science at Haifa University, stated that Israeli state terror has effectively pushed the Palestinians to the edge. He told Aljazeera that Israel's 'harsh and criminal' response to the Palestinian uprising was 'deliberate and calculated' (Aljazeera.net, http://www.infoimagination.org/islamnm/second_intifada.html, July 5, 2004; date of access: January 11, 2005).
39. See Kant's sixth preliminary article in his 1795 essay, 'To Perpetual Peace' (Kant, 1983, pp. 109–10).
40. Walzer (1977, pp. 255–61) and Rawls (1999a, pp. 98–9, 1999b, p. 568) have defended a state's recourse to terrorism by means of this supreme emergency exemption to the discrimination rule. As for non-state terrorism, Hare (1979) suggests that the terrorism practiced by the European Resistance during World War II was morally justified, and Wilkins (1992, pp. 26–8) similarly argues that Jews would have been justified in using terrorism against the Germans at that time. More recent defenses can be found in Valls (2000), Honderich (2006), Young (2004), Held (2004a, 2005), and Dahbour (2005). Both C. A. J. Coady (2004b) and Christopher Toner (2004) point out that the justification Walzer and Rawls provide for state terrorism under supreme emergency implies that individuals and non-state groups may also engage in terrorism against 'innocents' in supreme emergencies, and for this reason, both reject the supreme emergency exemption.
41. Andrew Valls writes: 'if an organization claims to act on behalf of a people and is widely seen by that people as legitimately doing so, then the rest of us should look on that organization as the legitimate authority of the people for the purpose of assessing its entitlement to engage in violence on their behalf' (Valls, 2000, p. 71). Virginia Held (2005, pp. 185–8) points out that while democratic authorization of a leadership is not always possible when

democratic mechanisms are inhibited, this does not preclude the requirement of legitimate authority from being satisfied for acts of terrorism by non-state groups.

42. Pape (2005, chap. 5) addresses the issue whether suicide terrorists calculate the benefits of their policies. He says that groups such as Hamas, Islamic Jihad, Hezbollah, and the Tamil Tigers began with more conventional guerrilla operations, but after these operations proved ineffective, they resorted to suicide attacks with an initial confidence that they would yield more positive results. Governments have entered into negotiations with these groups after the suicide campaigns began (pp. 64–5), and in some cases, governments have been coerced, as with the United States and France in Lebanon in 1983, Israel in Lebanon in 2000, and Sri Lanka in 2001 (p. 55). Pape conjectures that the government of Israel was coerced by Hamas in 1994–5 (pp. 66–73).
43. The motivation of intervening parties can vary. Some might see intervention as a means of either harming or defeating the aggressor or as an opportunity to extend influence over the threatened community. Again, the intervener might be caused to act because it is alarmed that the violence between the two communities has reached such proportions and poses greater threats to future peace and stability. Such intervention has repeatedly taken place since World War II, especially in Africa. The intervention by Western powers in the Balkans in the 1990s was partly caused by a desire to halt the continued aggression and atrocities in Bosnia and Kosovo. It is likely that the PLO adopted this strategy by provoking Israel into an extreme reaction that would bring Israel into conflict with neighboring states and discredit it in the eyes of the world community (O'Brien, 1991, p. 13).
44. The positive effects of violence as a confidence building measure and as a means of unity among members of an oppressed community were argued for by Frantz Fanon (1963, 38). Pape (2005, chap. 6), provides further evidence in support for this strategy. Regarding the Palestinians, see Section 4.
45. Similar reasoning can be found in Wilkins (1992) who cites Karl Jaspers' distinction between the political guilt that people within a community harbor when their state commits crimes and the moral guilt of an individual who participates in, supports, or favors those crimes (Wilkins, 1992, pp. 21–2). Wilkins finds that political guilt is both collective and distributive, and only individuals who completely sever their ties to the political community are exempt from moral guilt (p. 25). On these grounds, he argues that terrorism is justified as a form of self-defense when all other political and legal remedies have been exhausted or are inapplicable and the terrorism is directed against guilty members of the aggressor (1992, p. 28). See also Virginia Held who writes that '*If* a government's policies are *unjustifiable* and *if* political violence to resist them is *justifiable* (these are very large "ifs," but not at all unimaginable), then it is not clear why the political violence should not be directed at those responsible for these policies' (2004b, p. 6; emphasis is in original.). Some writers are skeptical of using 'collective responsibility' as a way of widening the range of legitimate targets (e.g., Coady, 2004a, pp. 55–7; Miller, 2005, which argue that one shares in collective responsibility for a rights violation only if one 'intentionally contributed' to that violation, and, thus, where intention is lacking, so is the

responsibility). However, the 'consent' one gives through membership in a voluntary association is a general intention to abide by, and accept responsibilities for, that association's policies and acts, whatever these might be. Quite apart from this, it is doubtful that moral responsibility for a situation requires an intention to bring about or sustain that situation. Criminal law typically allows that one can be responsible for what one rationally foresees will happen as a result of one's action or inaction.

46. See Section 8. American support for Israel is well documented [see, e.g., Lilienthal, 1982; Christison, 1999; Chomsky, 1999; Aruri, 2003; Swisher, 2004; Mearsheimer & Walt, 2005 (date of access: September 23, 2006); Petras, 2006]. Opposition to Israeli settlements moved from 'illegal' under the Carter Administration, to 'obstacles' under Reagan, to 'unhelpful' under Clinton. A letter from President Bush to Ariel Sharon dated April 14, 2004, stated that 'it is unrealistic to expect that the outcome of the final status negotiations will be a full and complete return to the armistice lines' (http://www.whitehouse.gov; date of access: November 18, 2006), and in June 2004, the House of Representatives voted 407-9 to endorse the text of Bush's letter. The statements by some Congressional leaders have been truly astounding. For example, the House Majority Whip in 2002, Dick Armey, publicly advocated Israel's confiscation of the entire West Bank and the expulsion of the Palestinian population (Abunimah, 2006, p. 102). Again, Senator Hillary Clinton called for 'total U.S. support of Israeli policy' while visiting Israel in February 2002. When a reporter asked Clinton whether Palestinians also deserve U.S. sympathy, she replied: 'The United States' role is to support Israel's decisions' (*Chicago Tribune*, February 26, 2002).
47. See Section 6 and also Pape (2005, pp. 64–74). The Hamas leader, Dr. Abd al-Aziz Rantisi, assassinated by Israel in April of 2004, justified suicide bombings against Israel saying they were the 'weapons of last resort' because 'Israel is offering us two choices, either to die a meek lamb's death at the slaughter house or as martyr-bombers' http://www.infoimagination.org/islamnm/second_intifada.html (date of access: November 11, 2005). Smilansky (2004, pp. 794–5) claims that the Palestinians have not availed themselves of viable alternatives to terrorism. However, he gives a historically skewed summary of the choices Palestinians made and did not make, for example, that they could have had a state in 1948 alongside Israel, that they did not attempt a campaign of nonviolent resistance in the territories, that they, rather than Israel, derailed the progress towards a Palestinian state called for in the Oslo Accords, and that they rejected a 'generous offer' by Prime Minister Barak in the summer of 2000. These claims are addressed in the main text above as well as in Chapter 1.
48. Igor Primoratz (2006), while acknowledging that the Palestinian community faces a 'true moral disaster' (p. 37), argues that terrorism 'does not seem to have brought the Palestinians any closer to liberation, self-determination, and repatriation' and, therefore, cannot be justified since it fails to meet the condition of effectiveness (p. 40). This judgment seems premature. He underestimates Fanon's emphasis on the role of violence in strengthening determination to combat a much more powerful adversary. The Palestinian cause is at the forefront of ever-widening Islamic resistance to U.S.-Israeli hegemony over the Middle East. The so-called war on terrorism may well strengthen

the willingness of Muslims to support the Palestinians and confront this hegemony as they see their own fate as increasingly linked to the Israeli–Palestinian conflict, something that would likely not have happened had not tensions between Israelis and Palestinians been kept before the public eye.

49. Pape (2005) notes that many suicide terrorists have had friends or family members killed by occupying forces, for example, the 'black widows' in Chechnya (p. 211). He also writes of Dhanu, a member of the Tamil's Black Tigresses, who killed Rajiv Gandhi in a suicide bombing. Previously, her home in Jaffna had been looted, her four brothers killed, and she had been gang-raped by Indian soldiers. Being a victim of rape is a stigma that destroys prospects for marriage (pp. 226–30). Among Palestinian suicide bombers, Saed Hotari killed 21 Israelis on June 1, 2001. His father said that 'he was radicalized by the anger, by the humiliation. Look before your eyes. We are living in a jail. I would be a liar to say I feel sorry for the people who are oppressing us day by day' (p. 233).
50. The survey was carried out by the Gaza Community Mental Health Program, founded by Dr. Eyad El-Sarraj, whose reports on this and other related studies can be found at its website, http://www.gcmhp.net (date of access: March 12, 2007).

4
The One-State Solution

Raja Halwani

In this chapter, I discuss the merits of various solutions to the Israeli–Palestinian conflict, and I defend the claim that creating a secular, democratic state for all its citizens is the morally optimal solution, a secular state that does not define itself as the exclusive state of an ethnic, religious, or national group. A morally optimal solution satisfies the following three criteria: (i) it respects and does not infringe or violate the properly delineated moral rights of either group, Palestinians and Jewish Israelis; (ii) it satisfies both parties' morally permissible desires; and (iii) it protects the individual human rights of all the state's citizens.

Unlike some popular arguments to the effect that the two-state solution is no longer possible and so we are 'pushed' into accepting the one-state option, my argument for the one-state solution is based on moral grounds and proceeds by elimination. After scrutinizing the relevant, possible solutions for the conflict, it concludes that a single, secular, democratic state for all its citizens is the only morally optimal one.

The first section lists and explains the options and quickly eliminates those whose dismissal as immoral is easy. The second section argues that the standard two-state solution is not morally optimal and that the two-state solution that is actually taking place—based mostly on Israel's vision—is immoral. The third section argues that another variant of the two-state solution, the Jordan option, is also immoral. The fourth section explains past proposals of the one-state solution. The fifth argues that a bi-nationalist state is not morally optimal and that a democratic, secular state for all its citizens is morally better. It also enumerates some important features of the secular, democratic single state and argues why such a one-state solution is morally optimal. The sixth and final section addresses some objections to the solution of a secular, single state.

1. The options

Generally speaking, there are seven relevant options for solving the I-P conflict:

1. Maintaining the *status quo*, including Israel's occupation of the West Bank and the Gaza Strip and all that this entails in terms of violence.
2. A two-state solution comprising the state of Israel and of Palestine on the territory of historic Palestine.
3. The Jordan option (a two-state solution not solely within historic Palestine, most notably, a Palestinian state in Jordan and, possibly, in parts of historic Palestine).
4. A single Jewish state (containing only or mostly Jews) in all historic Palestine.
5. A single Palestinian state (containing only or mostly Palestinians) in all historic Palestine.
6. A single bi-national state in all historic Palestine, with Jews and Palestinians constituting the two main ethnic groups of the state.
7. A single, secular, democratic state in all historic Palestine.

Maintaining the *status quo* is a live option: continuing the Israeli occupation of the West Bank and the Gaza Strip, continuing to deny the general Palestinian population self-determination, and continuing to deny the right of return of Palestinian refugees could very well be strategies to exhaust the Palestinians, wear them down, and eventually get them to lower their expectations and demands, if not to altogether leave the region. But this list of what continuing the *status quo* amounts to—and adding the predictable resulting violence on both sides—is actually a list of the reasons why the first option is immoral. Occupying a population, appropriating its lands, targeting its civilians, and so on are examples of immoral actions, actions that would remain immoral even if some good came out of them. Thus, maintaining the *status quo* should be ruled out as an option for solving the conflict.

Currently, the most politically accepted solution to the I-P conflict is the two-state solution: two states, Israel and a future Palestine, existing in historic Palestine. But depending on how one understands the notions of 'state' and 'sovereignty' and how one carves up the borders, 'two states' could mean different things. For example, the ex-prime minister of Israel, Ariel Sharon (now in a coma), although having recently accepted the idea of a Palestinian state in what is left of historic Palestine, does not seek a fully sovereign and independent one, opting instead for, in addition to the Gaza Strip, barely geographically contiguous Palestinian enclaves in the West Bank that would serve as the Palestinian state, but having no sovereignty over vital state functions such as having a viable army and controlling borders, foreign relations, airspace, and the principal natural resources (Chris McGreal, 'No Independent Palestine, Note that Sharon Insists,' *The Guardian*, March 17, 2003). Note that Sharon is not the only Israeli prime minister to seek an enfeebled Palestinian state.

By contrast, the Palestinians desire their state to have full sovereignty, be made up of all the Gaza Strip and the West Bank, with the latter including East Jerusalem and being geographically contiguous (but possibly involving land swaps of equal size and value to allow major Jewish settlements to be annexed to Israel). I refer to this solution as the standard one, because there is international consensus that it is, indeed, what the Palestinian state should be. Thus, both these are two-state solutions, even though they differ in various ways.

Another variation of the two-state solution—the 'Jordan option'—is for the Palestinian state to be in Jordan. Sharon had endorsed this solution, and it is still accepted by many right wing Israelis and their supporters,[1] such as the Israeli ex-cabinet minister Binyamin Elon (Tilley, 2005, p. 7). Although the 'Jordan option' would probably also include some parts of the West Bank as parts of the Palestinian state, as a solution to the conflict it is utterly rejected by both Jordan and the Palestinians (Tilley, 2005, p. 8). [Yet another variation is dividing Palestine along the 1947 United Nations Partition Plan (see Map A and Map B); no one today proposes this version, and I will not discuss it.]

Like the two-state one, there are different variations of the one-state solution. One extreme form is of an ethnically pure Jewish state in historic Palestine, and another extreme form is of an ethnically pure Palestinian one. Some Jewish maximalists—for example, the Moledet Party—call for the expulsion (or 'voluntary transfer,' as the euphemism goes) of the Palestinians (including the approximately 1.2 million Israeli Palestinians with Israeli citizenship) to somewhere outside historic Palestine. The latter ethnically pure state is possible, though I know of no Palestinian group that calls for the expulsion of Israeli Jews, let alone all of them. Hamas's charter famously calls for the destruction of Israel. However, this is not the same as Jewish expulsion, but as getting rid of Zionism. At best, the charter is ambiguous: in some places, it allows for coexistence between Jews and Muslims (Article 31), but in other places, for example, Article 32, it equates the struggle against Zionism with that against Jews (Mishal & Sela, 2006, pp. 175–99; see also Hroub 2006b, pp. 31–41). Similarly for the Palestine Liberation Organization (PLO) charter: even this defunct document allowed for what it dubbed 'Palestinian Jews' to remain in the country (see Section 4).

Each of these one-state solutions is morally unacceptable. First, the means to bring them about are immoral. Unless the population not belonging to the right ethnicity is genuinely willing to leave historic Palestine—a logical but neither a political nor psychological possibility—implementing each solution requires forcibly removing one or the other population, a morally wrong method. Indeed, because establishing a purely Palestinian or a purely Jewish state is not a powerful enough good (if purely ethnic states are good to begin with), this goal does not even redeem or permit the immoral means of forcibly removing either population. Second, the end result is also unacceptable, because the uprooting of people from their lands, homes, and ways of lives, with all the suffering and hardship this usually implies is immoral, rendering the members of the uprooted population unable to lead their lives as they see fit in areas in which they are historically rooted. Hence, as with the option of maintaining the *status quo*, I set these two aside.

There are, however, morally acceptable versions of the one-state idea that are currently debated, mostly by intellectuals and academics from both sides of the conflict.[2] The Palestinian leadership also recently, for a brief period only, floated the idea, although it is not clear whether it has done so out of genuine commitment or as a way of exerting pressure on Israel to withdraw from the occupied territories by playing on its demographic fears.[3] The idea is that both people, Israeli Jews and Palestinians, should form and live in one state in historic Palestine. The state can be bi-nationalist, a state for Jews and Palestinians, or a state for all its citizens, regardless of whether they are Jews or Palestinians, even though these two peoples would probably constitute the state's largest populations.

To sum up, I have argued that of the seven relevant solutions to the I-P conflict, the maintenance of the *status quo* and the two maximalist one-state solutions are morally unacceptable. I set them aside.

2. Two-state solutions

The two-state solution admits of many versions, depending on how one draws the boundaries and defines central terms. However, there is general international consensus on the standard two-state solution, namely, that the Palestinian state would comprise the West Bank, the Gaza Strip, and East Jerusalem, and that Israel would be within the 1967 borders or green lines. This solution is morally acceptable: it ends the Israeli occupation of Palestinian territories, and it allows many Palestinians genuine self-determination. However, in Section 2.1.1., I will raise some moral difficulties with this standard solution, showing that it is not morally optimal. In Section 2.1.2., I point to some Israeli-created 'facts on the ground' that, I argue, show two things: that the standard two-state solution faces some practical problems, and that the Israeli vision of the Palestinian state, a vision that differs considerably from the standard one, is morally untenable.

2.1. Problems with the standard two-state solution

2.1.1. Moral problems

Let us assume that the standard two-state solution comes into existence, that a viable, fully sovereign Palestinian state exists in all the West Bank, the Gaza Strip, and East Jerusalem. This solution would be morally acceptable because it ends the Israeli occupation of the West Bank and the Gaza Strip, thus allowing many Palestinians (but possibly not the refugees) to exercise self-determination in a viable state. Nevertheless, I argue that it suffers from three moral shortcomings stemming from the treatment of the Jewish settlers, the right of return of Palestinian refugees, and issues of self-determination, thus rendering it non-morally optimal.

2.1.1.1. The Jewish settlers. Despite the morally bad behavior of the Jewish settlers (especially the ideological ones, those who believe that all historic Palestine is for Jews and Jews only) towards the Palestinians, it remains morally desirable for Jews, due to religious, historic, and other reasons, to able to live in non-Israeli areas (e.g., the West Bank) in historic Palestine. A two-state solution might disallow this, depending on how the fate of the Jewish settlers (and other Jews) is decided. There are basically two types of arrangement for Jews who wish to live in the West Bank and other areas of a future Palestinian state. Either they would reside in the Palestinian state but not under Palestinian sovereignty (they would be Israeli citizens subject to Israeli law), or they would be subject to Palestinian sovereignty in a number of ways (they would be, say, Palestinian citizens or legal aliens, or might even have an autonomous status to some degree). The first option violates the sovereignty of the Palestinian state because it allows a number of its residents to not be subject to its rule of law. There is, indeed, no genuinely sovereign state in the world that has a chunk of its residents complying only with another state's laws.[4]

The second option, and regardless of the actual desires of the Jewish settlers, most of whom would reject this option,[5] is also problematic because of the standard two-state solution's purpose to separate the two populations from each other, to have Jews live in Israel and Palestinians (though not Israel's Palestinian citizens) in a Palestinian state. Since allowing Jews to live wherever they like in historic Palestine is morally desirable, and since the two-state solutison is meant to secure a Jewish state and a Palestinian state, it would not allow for this moral desideratum. Indeed, in not doing so, it encounters a further moral obstacle: to be implemented, the two-state solution requires relocating—forcibly, if the removal of the Gaza settlers in 2005 is evidence for what might transpire—first and even second-generation Jewish settlers from the West Bank. It might be wrong to uproot the settlers rather than find a better arrangement for them to equitably co-exist with the Palestinians. So it seems that the two-state solution requires an immoral way of bringing it about, and it does not fulfill the moral desideratum of allowing Israeli Jews to live where they please in historic Palestine.

2.1.1.2. The right of return of Palestinian refugees. In Chapter 2, I concluded that the refugees have this right and that it should be implemented. The standard two-state solution is related to this issue in one of two ways: it either denies the right (or, at least, its implementation) or it fully recognizes the right.

Under the second possibility, there would be a Palestinian state in the West Bank and the Gaza Strip, and a separate Israeli state, with the refugees allowed to return to their original village sites in Israel proper.[6] Assuming that the refugees are treated as full, equal citizens of Israel and that the birth rates of Jews and Palestinians remain more or less constant, the Palestinian citizens of the state of Israel—now made up of the returning refugees and the original citizens (those who remained since 1948)—would soon constitute a majority. But then, the two-state solution becomes moot, because one of its purposes—if not the only purpose—is for each people to have its own state, governing it, and living in it as a majority. So if the right of return is allowed, the one crucial motive for a two-state solution is undercut. We might as well argue that the Palestinian and Israeli states should merge. Morally speaking, this merger would be better, as it would allow both populations to fully exercise their self-determination (see Section 2.1.1.3.).

Under the first possibility, the two-state solution implies the denial of the right of return (as we have seen in Chapter 2, the Geneva Accords and the People's Voice initiatives have this repercussion). Indeed, since the two-state solution is meant to secure a Jewish state and a Palestinian state, it would have to deny at least the implementation of the right of return. But this would constitute an injustice to the refugees, who constitute a large segment of the Palestinian population. Thus, the two-state solution is, in this respect, morally lacking in serious ways.

One might argue that not implementing the right of return could be part of an overall morally desirable arrangement, and so in this respect the standard two-state solution would be morally good. But as I argued in Chapter 2, for this to render the standard two-state solution morally optimal, denying the right cannot be done against the refugees' wishes, because the solution would be unjust and so not morally optimal. If the refugees willingly waived the right, the standard two-state solution would not be unjust but it would still not be morally optimal, as it would still face the moral problems explained in the previous and next subsections.

2.1.1.3. Self-determination. Adopting Kapitan's regional interpretation of the principle of self-determination (Chapter 1), the standard two-state solution does not satisfy what the right to self-determination entitles both Palestinians and Israelis (Jewish and non-Jewish), and that, assuming the territory in question covers all historic Palestine (present-day Israel, the West Bank, and the Gaza Strip)—an assumption defended below—both Palestinians and Israelis are legitimate residents of that territory. 'Legitimate residents of region X' means that the inhabitants are entitled to full moral and political rights, including the right to self-determination, in and over X. Moreover, the expression is normative, not descriptive: to say that A is a legitimate resident of X is not necessarily to say that A actually lives in X or is considered by X's actual laws to be a citizen of X, but that A ought to be a citizen of X.

First, as far as issues of self-determination are concerned, what are the Palestinian and Israeli peoples entitled to?[7] Granting that self-determination entitles them to decide on their own political and social institutions (subject to the rightful claims of others), the issue is what territory the Palestinians and Israelis are entitled to politically govern (also subject to the rightful claims of others). Is it, respectively, the West Bank and the Gaza Strip, and Israel? Or is it all historic Palestine? In other words, what territory are the Palestinians legitimate residents of, such that, given their causal, historic, and cultural roots to that territory, over which they would be entitled to regional self-determination? Similarly, is the territory to which self-determination entitles the Israelis to govern only Israel? Or is it all historic Palestine?

Obviously, the non-refugee Palestinian inhabitants of the West Bank and the Gaza Strip are legitimate residents of this region since they already belong to it. The people of Gaza, East Jerusalem, Jenin, Jericho, Ramallah, Hebron, Bethlehem, and other cities, towns, and villages in the west Bank and the Gaza Strip are descendents of Palestinian families who have lived there for centuries without interruption. Indeed, few contest this history (even many right-wing Jewish Israelis, those calling for the Palestinians' 'transfer,' admit that these Palestinians are legitimate residents of the area, but argue that their removal will achieve peace). So non-refugee Palestinians are legitimate residents of the West Bank and the Gaza Strip. Since these two territories are parts of historic Palestine, the non-refugee Palestinians are legitimate residents of historic Palestine. They are, therefore, entitled to self-determination over it.

Similar reasoning applies to Israelis. First, Israeli Palestinians are also descendents of Palestinians whose families continuously lived for centuries in Haifa, Jaffa, the Galilee, the Negev, and other cities, towns, villages, and areas in Israel. Second, the majority of Israeli Jews are also descendents of Jews who lived in historic Palestine for decades, many prior to the establishment of Israel in 1948. Both groups of Israelis are then legitimate residents of Israel. Since Israel is part of historic Palestine, Israelis would be legitimate residents of historic Palestine. They, too, are therefore entitled to self-determination over it. (Although this argument does not cover the comparatively few Jews who recently immigrated to Israel, an argument for their legitimate residency can be made on the grounds of Jewish cultural, religious, and historic ties to Israel and historic Palestine. I will not pursue this argument here.)

The Palestinian refugees present the difficult case. At the time of the United Nations Partition Plan in 1947, the Palestinians constituted a majority of all the people and owned most of the land of historic Palestine (Smith, 2001, pp. 190–1). Because they were forced or feared war, many Palestinians fled or became refugees. In Chapter 2, I argued that the refugees retain residential and territorial rights over lands in what is today Israel, even though they have not been actually residing there. In fact, despite their relocation, the refugees continue to have historic and other causal (emotional, religious, historic, etc.) ties to historic Palestine. All the above suggests that they, too, are legitimate residents of that territory and so would have the right to self-determination over the entire region of historic Palestine.

But do they have this right? Consider first how from the fact that the Palestinian refugees have residency and territorial rights to lands in Israel it follows that they have some political rights in that territory. Residency and territorial rights to particular territories are not 'thin,' constituting narrowly defined rights to, say, simply till the soil and inhabit particular swaths of land. Rather, they are 'thick,' entitling their bearers to some political participation in the governing processes of their lives, because if they were understood only as 'thin,' they would be almost meaningless. For one cannot lead one's life in such a constricted way: owning a house, for instance, means very little if the owner has no say in how the government can legislate laws regarding his neighborhood, the education of his children, the conduct of his personal life, and so on. This is why, for example, some countries allow their non-citizen, legal residents to vote in either municipal or general elections or both. Thus, the Palestinian refugees have 'thick' residency and territorial rights to lands in Israel, including rights such as rights to vote in municipal elections, to be gainfully employed and employ others, to worship freely, to decide on how their children should be educated, to some form of cultural expression, and to free movement, at least within the areas they inhabit.

However, although these 'thick' residential rights entail some political rights, it is not clear that they entail rights to full self-determination. For if the legitimacy of the Palestinian refugees is basically residential, education- and employment-related, and if whatever political rights they have stem from the need to have their residential, educational, and employment rights be meaningful, it is possible that no further political rights are necessary to make these former rights meaningful. Thus, they might have no larger political rights having to do with how, say, the entire country is to be governed or what foreign policies it should adopt. If so, then the Palestinian refugees might have no rights to self-determination over historic Palestine, as they would not be legitimate residents of that territory, given my characterization of this notion.

This might be true were it not for the fact that the Palestinian refugees have cultural, historic, and causal ties to the territory of Israel. They are the descendents of Palestinians who have uninterruptedly lived for centuries in cities, towns, and villages in Palestine. Because the refugees have historic, cultural, and other types of causal ties to these lands, and because they also have residential and other types of rights to Israel, they are legitimate residents of Israel. Since Israel is part of historic Palestine, the Palestinian refugees are its legitimate residents. They, too, are therefore entitled to self-determination over it.

To illustrate, imagine a country, C, that offers some of its residents, Rs, a legal status allowing them to be employed, to be employers, to have businesses, to own real estate, and so on. If we assume that such 'residential rights' are not merely legal but also moral, that is, that Rs are fully justified in having such residential rights (as is the case with the Palestinian refugees' residency rights in Israel), then Rs would also be justified in having more robust political rights, such as the right to vote in municipal elections, the right to some form of cultural expression, and even rights specific to their own protection as a minority, were they to be one. If they did not have such additional political rights, the very justification of the residential rights would be undercut. But now suppose that Rs are not, say, immigrants from a place with no cultural ties to C, and that they are not in C owing to economic hardships or to pursue a better education. Suppose instead that they have strong historical and other types of ties to C (as in the case with the Palestinian refugees and Israel). If so, in addition to recognizing their entitlement to residential and some political rights, we also recognize their entitlement to full-blooded political rights to C. This is because we recognize that they belong to C. So although the Palestinian refugees' residential and territorial rights entitle them to live in Israel, their cultural and other ties convert them to full citizens. Thus, the Palestinian refugees are legitimate residents of Israel and so of historic Palestine, and therefore have full-blooded political rights, including the right to self-determination.

Thus, Palestinians (refugees and non-refugees) and Israelis (Jewish and non-Jewish) have political rights in and to historic Palestine, including the right to self-determination. If this is correct, then the standard two-state solution confines Palestinians and Israelis to territorial fragments of the entire territory of historic Palestine, and so grants them less than full self-determination. This is the problem with the standard two-state solution as far as self-determination is concerned.

I have so far relied on the assumption that the troubled region in question is all historic Palestine. But supporters of the standard two-state solution might object to including all historic Palestine, because the whole point is to divide the land into two states. Israel already exists, and since the Israeli occupation of the West Bank and the Gaza Strip is viewed as the main, if not the only, obstacle to implementing the standard two-state solution, why not consider instead the West Bank and the Gaza Strip to be the troubled regions?

However both the standard two-state and the one-state solutions provide competing ways to solve the I-P conflict. The former recommends dividing historic Palestine, the latter sharing it. Indeed, both these solutions must take historic Palestine as one territorial unit because the conflict arises from two people competing for sovereignty over that unit. So my argument does not beg any questions against the two-state solution in focusing on historic Palestine as a single region.

There are additional reasons for believing that 'troubled region' is all historic Palestine, rather than just the West Bank and the Gaza Strip. First, since the Palestinian refugees' rights to territories in Israel are one aspect of the Israeli–Palestinian conflict, the conflict engulfs all historic Palestine, not just the West Bank and the Gaza Strip. Second, there are concerns about the legitimacy of Israel's coming into being and about Israel's legitimacy as a state, especially given its treatment of its own Palestinians citizens (For a Fuller discussion, see Chapter 1).

To summarize, there are three moral strikes against the standard two-state solution, showing it to be morally non-optimal, albeit morally acceptable. First, it denies Jews the ability to reside in the non-Israeli areas of historic Palestine. In this respect, it violates the second criterion for a morally optimal solution, namely, the satisfaction of the morally permissible desires of both parties. Second, it either does not deny the right of return, in which case it undermines its very purpose, or it denies the right, in which case it violates the first criterion for a morally optimal solution, and possibly the second criterion to the extent the refugees desire to return to their village sites. Third, it falls short of giving the Palestinians and Israelis their due as far as self-determination goes, thus violating the first criterion for a morally optimal solution.

2.1.2. Practical problems

In this section, I argue that the 'facts on the ground'—how political, economic, and other decisions and actions are actually shaping the potential Palestinian state—constitute a serious obstacle to the standard two-state solution. In presenting these facts and arguing that they are obstacles to the standard two-state solution, I will be brief, since much has been ably written on both issues (e.g., Tilley, 2005).

Expanded East Jerusalem. Israel annexed East Jerusalem right after the 1967 war (which was under Jordanian control until then), declaring it part of the whole city of Jerusalem, its 'eternal, undivided' capital. Soon after, Israel proceeded to build large Jewish settlement blocs around it and to make them part of the city, thus enlarging the boundaries of Jerusalem and taking land from the West Bank (about 60 square kilometers) to do so. As a result, Jerusalem almost doubled in geographical size. Today, there are about 200,000 Jewish settlers in the area of East Jerusalem. Israel continuously proposes to, and does, build thousands of new homes in this area. From what we can gather, both Likud and Labor Israeli leaders, and for the foreseeable future at least, refuse to relinquish any part of the city, while defining its boundaries in such a way that they expropriate quite a bit of West Bank land. Under these conditions, a Palestinian future state would have to be content with an area that excludes these expropriated parts (unless, again, equal land in terms of quality and quantity is compensated).[8]

Original, Non-Expanded East Jerusalem. Israel has also added Jewish settlers to Palestinian neighborhoods within the original city limits of East Jerusalem, while making it as difficult as possible for Palestinian residents to continue to comfortably live there (e.g., neglecting Palestinian neighborhoods and demolishing, on grounds of illegality, Palestinian homes, even though it is virtually impossible for Palestinians to obtain building permits from the Israeli authorities). If this continues and Jerusalem becomes a predominantly Jewish city, East Jerusalem will probably not be the capital of a Palestinian state.[9]

Jewish Settlements in the West Bank. Since its victory in the 1967 war, Israel has actively relocated many Jewish citizens to compounds in the West Bank and the Gaza Strip (the 8000 or so settlers in Gaza were evacuated in August 2005). There are currently over 260,000 settlers in the West Bank (in 125 official settlements), excluding those in East Jerusalem. The Labor Party justified the settlements on grounds of security, the Likud on grounds of Jewish rights to 'Greater Israel.' Today, these Jewish-only settlements—some quite large—dot the region of the West Bank (see Map E), are often located on hilltops overlooking Palestinian villages, and are connected to each other and to Israel by a network of Jewish-only roads that bypass Palestinian towns, resulting in the literal fragmentation of the West Bank. If we also consider the other lands (including so-called safety zones and roads) allotted to the settlements or expropriated by Israel for military and other purposes, then about 42 percent of the West Bank is taken up Israel's expropriation. If Israel retains all or most of these settlements, a future Palestinian state would have to be content with even smaller territory.[10]

Israel's Concessions Prior to Sharon's Withdrawals. What has Israel been willing to give up of the West Bank and the Gaza Strip as part of a future peace deal? Under the Oslo Accords, Israel withdrew its troops from the main Palestinian urban centers while maintaining control over the majority of the West Bank, including the settlements, the Jewish-only roads, and much of the land between them. Subsequently, the Israeli government erected military checkpoints between the Palestinian urban centers, resulting in Israel's military and economic control over all the land in and borders of the West Bank and the Gaza Strip. A decade later, this temporary arrangement continues until the resolution of the final status issues: Jerusalem, the borders of the future Palestinian state, the Palestinian refugees, and the Jewish settlements. During the Camp David Summit in 2000, Israel proposed the Gaza Strip and about 80 percent of the West Bank for a Palestinian state. Israel would have retained control of the settlements, their infrastructure, and some other aspects of the Palestinian state, such as some highways, its air space, and its external borders. These figures again indicate Israel's rejection of a fully sovereign Palestinian state.[11]

Sharon's and Olmert's Convergence Plan. Ariel Sharon's plan, announced on February 3, 2004, was to first withdraw the Israeli army and evacuate the Jewish-only settlements from the Gaza Strip, which Israel has done, while reserving the right for its army to renter the Strip at any time, which Israel has also done on numerous occasions. Israel also refused to allow Palestinian control over Gaza's borders, airspace, and water resources. In withdrawing from the Gaza Strip, Sharon aimed to free Israel of jurisdiction over a sizeable non-Jewish population, thus avoiding a future settlement that renders Gaza Palestinians citizens of Israel or under its jurisdiction in another way.

Regarding the West Bank, Sharon intended a different approach. On this land, Israel would retain large settlement blocks and other aspects of a future Palestinian state, as evidenced by the unabated building of settlements, by interviews he gave, and by pronouncements by his aides. Sharon's successor, Ehud Olmert, seems to be moving in the same direction. Calling Sharon's plan 'convergence' (or 'realignment'), Olmert seeks to evacuate about 70,000 settlers from some far-flung settlements in the West Bank, annex the rest of the settlements (especially the large ones), retain Jerusalem, and maintain a military presence in the area, including the Jordan Valley. Olmert appears prepared to declare Israel's borders by 2010 with or without agreement from the Palestinians. Again, this plan leads to a shrunken Palestinian state with limited sovereignty.[12] However, the 'convergence' plan seems to have been shelved or at least temporarily suspended since the July 2006 Lebanon war ('Olmert Suspends Withdrawal Plan,' BBC News, August 18, 2006; Doug Struck, 'Israel Shelves Plan to Pull Out of Settlements in West Bank,' *The Washington Post*, August 23, 2006).

The Jewish Settlers. The Jewish settlers are roughly divided into two types, the 'economic' settlers, comprising about 80 percent of the settler population and living in the Palestinian territories due to economic incentives, and the 'ideological' settlers, who live in the territories out of ideological commitments to the 'Greater Land of Israel.' The former are open to relocating to inside Israel's green line if given adequate compensation and a comparable way of life, but the latter are typically not, because they believe that they should be there, and that Jews and Jews alone are entitled to the land. They have become a powerful force in Israel's political landscape even though they are numerically a minority. Getting them to leave will be difficult because they are ideologically motivated and have the backing of powerful parties and political movements in and outside Israel (e.g., Christian Zionists). The resistance to Sharon's plan of disengaging from the Gaza Strip testifies to the power and influence of the ideological settlers. Indeed, it seems that Sharon was able to successfully pull off the evacuation mainly because no large-scale abandonment of the West Bank is in the offing.[13]

The Wall. The barrier—mostly a wall but in some parts consisting of wire fences—that Israel is building on the western West Bank does not follow the green line border and seems to be designed to include as many Jewish settlements and Palestinian land as possible, while excluding as many Palestinians as possible (see Map G). The International Court of Justice found the wall to violate international law and required Israel to dismantle it (which Israel did not and likely will not). The point is not so much whether the barrier is easy to dismantle, but that the intentions behind it do not bode well for a future, viable Palestinian state. It is also not clear whether Israel will build another wall on the eastern West Bank, although rumors that it will abound. However, it may not need to do so. Currently, Israel has 21 Jewish settlements in the Jordan Valley, containing some 2500 settlers. According to Jerusalem's Orient House mapping and survey specialist Khalil Tufakji, Israel plans to expand and annex these settlements as part of any final agreement with the Palestinians. This allows Israel to create 'a human barrier between the future Palestinian state and Jordan,' thus not needing a wall. Although the Knesset has not yet approved such plans, they do not augur well for a future Palestinian state ('Israel's Jordan Valley Plan: An Interview with Khalil Tufakji,' *Palestine Report*, June 29, 2005). The completion of one or both of these walls implies, again, a shrunken Palestinian state.[14]

The above facts point to two conclusions. First, Israel does not intend the Palestinians to have a full-fledged state in all the West Bank and the Gaza Strip, and it has created a large physical infrastructure to ensure its ability to keep those territories of the West Bank it wishes to. This constitutes a serious—without downplaying the moral repercussions—practical obstacle to implementing the standard two-state solution. Indeed, many have argued (e.g., Tilley, 2005) that because of these facts, the standard two-state solution is effectively dead.

Second, and a corollary to the first conclusion, recent Israeli governments, especially those of Sharon and Olmert, have a particular vision of what the Palestinian state should look like: a state in all the Gaza Strip but in only parts of the West Bank, with much of its sovereignty under Israeli control. Moreover, the Sharon-Olmert vision might actually come to fruition, even if temporarily, because, first, much actual work for it has already been done, in terms of settlements and infrastructure, and, second, there seems to be no other contending trajectory. Politically, militarily, and diplomatically, the Palestinians have proven to be by far the weaker party, while Israel has proven to be the much stronger one, especially given the U.S. financial, political, diplomatic, and military backing. If we add the general lack of willingness or effort on behalf of the European Union and other relevant parties (such as the Arab nations and the Arab League) to effect important changes in the way things are going, the Sharon-Olmert plan is really the only option. As Yoav Peled puts it, 'The real reason the [standard] two-state solution is dead is... [that] the Palestinians who fought for it, with the help of some Jews, were defeated' (Peled, 2006, p. 26).

The Sharon-Olmert Palestinian state would not be viable. Its rulers, lacking proper sovereignty, would not be able to properly serve their people. This is the first reason why this two-state solution would be immoral. Second, it would have much less territory than the Palestinians are minimally entitled to (all the West Bank). Thus, this *de facto* two-state solution would be unjust, and so immoral. Third, since Israel does not intend to fulfill the right of return of Palestinian refugees, allowing them, at best, to 'return' to a future Palestinian state, this solution would also be unjust, and so immoral, for this reason.

To summarize, the standard two-state solution must overcome a variety of difficult practical problems owing to Israel's expansion beyond its 1967 'borders' and its subsequent entrenchment in these lands. More important, perhaps, it also suffers from some moral problems. Although they do not render it morally unacceptable, they certainly prevent it from being a morally optimal solution.

3. The Jordan option

It is not entirely clear how the idea that Palestine is Jordan has become popular in some circles. One possible explanation is the (possibly racist) belief that all Arabs are more or less the same and so if a Palestinian state were to be erected in nearby Jordan, not much is lost. Another explanation is Jordan's geographical proximity. A third is that in 1920, the

League of Nations mandated a Jewish home in Palestine, which then included both Palestine and Jordan, fostering the idea that an equitable partition solution would give the Israelis historic Palestine and would give the Palestinians Jordan.[15] A fourth explanation is that Jordan had annexed the West Bank after the 1948 war and maintained close ties with its inhabitants since then. A fifth is that many Palestinian refugees left to Jordan and most of them have become naturalized Jordanian citizens. A combination of some or all of these facts probably leads some to believe that Jordan as a Palestinian state is a 'natural' way to solve the conflict.

A number of right-wing Israeli Jews accept this solution today, and Ariel Sharon has advocated it in the past (according to Gary Sussman [2005], he never abandoned it, though he eventually thought of it as a federation between Jordan and whatever West Bank lands the Palestinians get to keep. On the other side, while Palestinians are not averse to having strong ties with Jordan, they, along with Jordan, reject the idea that Jordan should be the Palestinian state or should be part of that state.

Regardless, however, of what the parties think, the Jordan option is morally unacceptable. First, since the disputed region is historic Palestine, most Palestinians are not entitled to self-determination over Jordan's territory because they are not its legitimate residents. Thus, the Jordan option would, on the one hand, give the Palestinians the ability to exercise self-determination over areas to which they are not entitled, while, on the other, prohibiting them from exercising self-determination over areas to which they are. In this way, it is an unjust solution. (If we consider the disputed region to be both banks of the Jordan River, then Jordanians, Israelis, and Palestinians would be entitled to self-determination over the entire area—not quite what the Jordan option is supposed to be.)

Second, if the Jordan option denies the right of return of Palestinian refugees by allowing them to return only to the projected Palestinian state (Jordan alone or Jordan-and-West Bank), not to their village and home sites, it would be unjust in this way also. (Logically, the Jordan option does not entail the denial of the right of return, but does so in fact, since, like other two-state solutions, it is meant to solve the problem by securing Israel's Jewishness along numerical lines.)

Thus, the Jordan option is morally compromised and so is not optimal. It violates the first criterion of what a morally optimal solution should be, and, insofar as Palestinians have no desire to have a state in Jordan, violates the second criterion also.

4. Historic precedents for the one-state solution

The idea of a single state for both Jews and Palestinians is not new. I focus on three of its forms proposed by Palestinians, Jews, and the international community to emphasize that the idea was not alien to the parties most relevant to the conflict.

It was only in November 1988 that the Palestine National Council (PNC) formally accepted negotiations with Israel based on the two-state solution, implicitly recognizing its existence as a state. In 1993, the late Palestinian president Yasser Arafat recognized 'the right of the State of Israel to exist in peace and security' in his letter to Yitzhak Rabin, then prime minister of Israel (Smith, 2001, p. 458). This letter was part of the Letters of Mutual Recognition that formed one aspect of the 1993 Oslo Accords.[16]

But prior to these events, the PLO was against the idea of a two-state solution and advocated, instead, a single state. For example, Resolution 19 of the Palestine National Council of July 1–17, 1968 (the entirety of these resolutions constitute the Palestinian National Charter) considers illegal both the 1947 partition of Palestine and the establishment of Israel, while Resolution 15 states that 'The liberation of Palestine... is a national duty and it attempts to repel the Zionist and imperialist aggression against the Arab homeland, and aims at the elimination of Zionism in Palestine' (Smith, 2001, p. 344). The aim is to get rid of Israel as a state and to replace it with a Palestinian national entity of some sort (Resolution 9 claims that the only way to 'liberate Palestine' is through armed struggle, that the Palestinian people are determined to return to Palestine, and that they have the right to exercise self-determination and sovereignty over it [Smith, 2001, p. 344]). As to the Jews in Israel, Resolution 6 claims, 'The Jews who had normally resided in Palestine until the beginning of the Zionist invasion will be considered Palestinians' (Smith, 2001, p. 343).

However, a later book published under PLO auspices considers all Jews living in Israel as members of this single state, provided they forego Zionism (Rasheed, 1970, p. 35). Moreover, in 1970, the PNC formally adopted Fatah's (the largest group in the PLO) vision of the future 'Democratic State of Palestine' (Hirst, 2003, p. 422). Although the total liberation of Palestine was still the goal, Fatah nonetheless acknowledged the 'physical Jewish presence in Palestine.' Specifically, 'All Jews now in

Palestine, not just those who were already there before 1917, 1948, or whenever the Palestinians deemed the "Zionist invasion" to have begun, would be entitled to stay there. Naturally they would have to foreswear their Zionist beliefs' (Hirst, 2003, p. 421). The envisioned state was to be democratic and secular, in which Muslims, Jews, and Christians will have equal rights and will worship freely (Laqueur & Rubin, 2001, pp. 130–31). Both Fatah and the PLO also distinguished between a bi-national state and a state for all its citizens, explicitly rejecting the former because it would enhance sectarian loyalties rather than help the people from different religions and ethnicities to peacefully co-exist (Rasheed, 1970, p. 38; Hirst, 2003, p. 421).

So the Palestinians advocated a single state about 30 years prior to current discussions of the one-state solution. Moreover, in being a democratic, secular state rather than bi-nationalist, the envisioned state seems to be morally ideal, based mainly on individual citizens' interests rather than those of ethnic groups.

On the Jewish side, the mainstream Zionist movement, from Theodore Herzl, to the resolutions of the Zionist Biltmore Conference in New York City in May 1942, to Ben Gurion, never accepted the idea of a secular, democratic state, and sought to establish as Jewish a state in Palestine as possible (Masalha, 1992; Smith, 2001, chap. 5; Pappe, 2006a, chap. 2). Although this reflected the majority of Zionist opinion, some Zionist sympathizers did propose the idea of a single state, though their views never gained currency. During the 1920s, 1930s, and early 1940s, a number of Jewish organizations called for a peaceful coexistence in Palestine between Arabs and Jews. The goal of Brit Shalom (the Covenant of Peace), founded in Jerusalem in 1925 from the 'conviction that the Zionist leadership was misguidedly overlooking the crucial importance of relations with the Arab population of Palestine,' was to find a way in which Arabs and Jews are to form their 'mutual relations in Palestine on the basis of absolute political equality of two culturally autonomous peoples' (Shimoni, 1995, p. 372). Arab–Jewish cooperation 'was the vital prerequisite for the fulfillment of Zionism.' Adopting the goal of creating a bi-national state in Palestine, Brit Shalom also declared that establishing a Jewish community in Palestine is to be done regardless of whether the Jews formed a minority or a majority (Shimoni, 1995, pp. 372–3).

Dissolved in 1933, Brit Shalom's main ideas were adopted by successive groups, such as Kedma Mizraha (Forward to the East), the League for Jewish–Arab Rapprochement and Cooperation, and the Ihud (the Union Association) (Shimoni, 1995, p. 373). The last, formed in 1942 and having both Martin Buber and Judah Magnes as members, 'advocated an Arab-Jewish binational state in a self-governing and undivided Palestine, based on equal political rights for the two peoples of Palestine' (Shimoni, 1995, pp. 373–4). Magnes, an American-born Reform rabbi, insisted on the distinction between nation and state, claiming that Zionism's importance lay in maintaining a Jewish cultural and ethnic community in Palestine, not in establishing a Jewish state (Shimoni, 1995, pp. 374–5).

According to Buber, the Jewish people's need for Palestine was not so much physical as it was spiritual, for Judaism's mission is to form a community that 'aspired to the optimal human relationship between man and man' that would 'consummate the divinely inspired covenant' of the Bible (Shimoni, 1995, p. 346). Buber was also convinced that Palestine would have enough room for both Arabs and Jews, and that its soil, if cultivated well and efficiently, would sustain both (Shimoni, 1995, p. 347). Like Magnes, Buber also believed that a bi-national co-existence in historic Palestine was not only possible but also the genuine fulfillment of Zionism in its moral form.

These positions did not develop beyond the idea that both Arabs and Jews would have equal political rights in Palestine. Moreover, the groups advocating bi-nationalism were always 'politically peripheral' and the idea among Jews of bi-nationalism fizzled away soon after Israel was created in 1948 (Shimoni, 1995, p. 372). Still, ideas regarding a bi-nationalist state in historic Palestine have had their Jewish supporters.

At the international level, the idea of a single state was one of the recommendations made by the United Nations Special Committee on Palestine (UNSCOP)—a United Nations General Assembly special committee, established in May 1947 to offer possible solutions to the conflict in Palestine. Although seven members endorsed partition, the remaining three members (India, Iran, and Yugoslavia) favored a federated state in historic Palestine. After receiving these reports, the General Assembly formed two subcommittees, one to discuss the partition option and one to discuss other options. The second subcommittee, whose members were Afghanistan, Colombia, Egypt, Iraq, Lebanon, Pakistan, Saudi Arabia, Syria, and Yemen, offered three draft resolutions, one of which called for a democratic state in Palestine.[17] Noteworthy is that, with the exception of Colombia, these states, predominantly Arab or Muslim, favored a democratic state for both Jews and Arabs. Contrary to popular beliefs, they were not hostile to a Jewish presence as such in Palestine.[18]

5. The one-state solution

5.1. Bi-nationalism

A single state for both people can take many morally acceptable forms, two of which have dominated the literature: a bi-national state and a secular, democratic state for all its citizens (other forms, including a consociational democracy and a federalist state, are variations on the specific political arrangement that a bi-nationalist or a secular state could take, so I set them aside). Relying on general moral considerations, we should investigate which of the two is morally better than the other.

A bi-national state tends to the interests of the members of the nations of which it is a state. Its primary task is to ensure the well-being and rights of its national (or ethnic) populations, individually and collectively—in our case, Palestinians and Jews. The state's symbols, moreover, would reflect the histories, aspirations, and cultures of both these populations because nationalist states, whether uni-nationalist, bi-nationalist, or multi-nationalist, are supposed to attend to their citizens as members of national groups. When a state organizes itself to be the state of its, say, two ethnic groups, X and Y, it is, theoretically at least, committing itself to promoting the interests and the well-being of its citizens as members of X and Y. Also, the rulers of this state would belong to, or be from, X and Y, and they would also govern in the name of X and Y.

Since almost all ethnic states today contain members who do not belong to the ethnic majority (or ethnic majorities), bi-nationalist and multi-nationalist states face the question—both theoretical and practical—of how to treat such members. Nationalist states might be unable to eliminate the possibility that non-nation members will be treated in ways inequitable and inferior to those of the nation members. Although many such states do treat their non-ethnic members in equitable ways, it is not obvious how they would do so while still defining themselves as nationalist states. Their practices, in other words, might be different from, perhaps even better than, their theoretical bases. Moreover, the repercussions go beyond issues of fair treatment of non-ethnic members. For a system of unfair treatment could harm the non-ethnic members, or at least lead them to experience less prosperity than they otherwise would. Thus, nationalist states are morally inferior—though not morally bad—to secular, democratic ones.[19]

A bi-nationalist state in historic Palestine would inherit the above moral problem. In treating inequitably some of its population—those who are neither Palestinian nor Jewish—it acts unjustly and so immorally. For example, (i) it might instigate strict citizenship laws such that only Jews, Palestinians, and their descendents are entitled to citizenship. (ii) It might distinguish between different types of citizenship, such that only individuals (Palestinians and Jews) holding a particular type of citizenship are allowed state benefits. (iii) Palestinians and Jews, collectively and individually, might be the state's primary and first choice in its allocation of resources, possibly depriving others of these. (iv) The governance of the state might be undertaken in such a way that only the two groups have power. (v) Finally, unfair laws might be enacted to force non-Palestinians and non-Jews to socially and culturally conform to the predominant cultures (as some European countries have done to their Muslim constituents).

Such a treatment might be justified in the short run, since the new state would need some time to organize, to get its institutions running, and to calm fears and allay worries its Palestinian and Jewish populations would potentially have. So temporarily, it might have to set aside issues dealing with members not belonging to these two groups. But in the long run, the bi-nationalist state would have to confront the moral justification of treating non-Jewish and non-Palestinian citizens inequitably. If, in actual practice, it does provide equitable treatment, it needs to tackle the issue of how this squares with its bi-nationalism.

Moreover, given the historical enmity between Israeli Jews and Palestinians, there is bound to be lingering tensions between them. Theoretically speaking, a state based on the claims and needs of each group, as a bi-nationalist state would be, could end up maintaining, and even exacerbating, these tensions. A state for all its citizens, however, could lessen this mistrust simply because it is based on individual rights and needs (whether this would actually happen is, of course, a different issue). Thus, in the case of Palestine and Israel, there are both general and particular reasons why a secular state is morally better than a bi-nationalist one.

A secular, democratic state for all its citizens would respect the rights of its individual members regardless of their ethnic, cultural, historic, or religious membership. Although this need not preclude the protection and fostering of different cultural, ethnic, and religious groups, it would have to be done equitably. For example, the state would allow for communal (and, of course, individual) religious or cultural freedom and would offer state funding to different groups to help them flourish and thrive. To do so equitably, it need not allocate the same amount of resources to all groups, but proportionately and depending on need. The state would of course have to negotiate different, often competing, claims by the different groups and would have to sometimes make hard decisions regarding the allocation of limited state resources, but this is a fact of all such states. Democratic states would, and do, have the institutional processes to adjudicate such issues properly and fairly.

One important factor is immigration. A state, even a democratic, secular one, would have to pay attention to and carefully devise its immigration policies. We live in a world comprised of states, each with its own borders and immigration controls, regardless of what we think of the fairness of such a global 'system.' Sometimes such states, while fair to their citizens, are unfair to immigrants and to outsiders wishing to attain immigrant status. A state aspiring to moral goodness on all fronts must devise fair immigration policies. This does not preclude giving priority to individuals belonging to particular groups, when other individuals are not in crucial need to immigrate to that state, or when the state is not in need of a particular type of immigrants (e.g., scientists). For example, suppose that in a particular year the state of Israel-Palestine has only ten slots for new immigrants. Suppose there are only 20 applications, ten from Jewish-Americans and Palestinian-Americans and ten from applicants who are neither. Were Israel-Palestine to favor the former over the latter ten if the latter ten have no crucial need to immigrate to the new state, it would not violate requirements of justice. The favoritism, moreover, would not be arbitrary, because both Jews and Palestinians have historic, religious, and other connections to the region. Moreover, if particular Diaspora Jewish communities face, at some point, a resurgence in anti-Semitism, they would have a demonstrable need to immigrate to Israel/Palestine, and the immigration laws of the sate should allow this. Thus, Israel-Palestine could continue to be a state for both people in this respect.[20]

I consider the issue of the moral superiority of the secular, democratic state over the bi-nationalist one to be settled. Henceforth, I use the phrases 'the one-state solution (idea)' and 'a single state' to refer to a secular, democratic state for all its citizens.

5.2. Basic features of the secular state

What crucial features would a single state for both Jews and Palestinians have? I propose seven. They are crucial to any single state if it is to succeed and be just to Jews, Palestinians, and others. They are neither exhaustive nor detailed—they should not be, since it is ultimately up to both peoples to design their own state—but merely form a framework for the state to genuinely be for its people.[21]

First, the state should have a proper, functional constitution, which includes the delineation of the rights of individual citizens and groups, and the declaration of the borders of the state. It should stress the equality of all the citizens before the law, regardless of religious, ethnic, or cultural background. To address the protection of minority rights, the constitution could mandate that any constitutional change affecting these rights would require the approval of the majority of the minority group in question (Tilley, 2005, pp. 223–4).

Second, the state should maintain a system of checks and balances; its governing institutions should have executive, legislative, and judicial branches. Membership in these government branches should not be along religious or ethnic lines, as in the Lebanese confessional system. The legislative branch should be democratically elected; its laws should not violate any basic human rights or the rights of minority groups. The judiciary system should include a supreme court, whose judges are appointed or elected by the legislative branch and whose terms of service are decided by the constitution. The prime minister or president should head the executive power, with each of his or her powers carefully delineated in the constitution. Initially, the cabinet should include a minister (or two or more) for a truth and conciliation cabinet position, whereby past injustices on both sides are addressed.

Third, state symbols should reflect the cultural, historical, or religious aspects of its major population groups, but such that none alienates members of other populations. Ideally, the symbols would dip into and reflect those aspects of both Jewish and Palestinian (or Muslim or Christian or Arab) culture and identity that are universal, with which an individual not belonging to one of these groups can identify.

Fourth, the state school curricula should include a proper understanding of universal human values, the history of both Jews and Palestinians, including the parts of each that intersect, with their good and ugly chapters, the dominant spoken languages of the state (e.g., Arabic and Hebrew) and other languages crucial for an individual to function properly in an increasingly global world (e.g., English). The state should not prohibit private schools that cater to specific religious or ethnic groups.

Fifth, the state should maintain a strict separation between state and religion. No individual or group should be given favoritism in public office, employment, housing, and so on, based on religious affiliation. However, the state should also maintain the freedom of its citizens to worship and practice their religions as they choose. The state may also foster and protect its diverse religious, ethnic, and cultural groups, but without violating the rights of other groups or individuals.

Sixth, the state should enact carefully thought-out and fair immigration laws. Within the bounds of justice, it may give priority to Jews, Palestinians, or people of Jewish or Palestinian descent in its selection of new immigrants.

Seventh, the state should be especially vigilant in combating forms of racism and of hatred motivated by race, ethnicity, religion, and so on and in prosecuting those who are bent on ensuring its failure. The institutions of the state should reflect a sincere commitment to the new state and to its ability to prosper.

These are the minimum aspects of the single state of Israel-Palestine. They are meant to put in place basic regulative standards by which a minimally decent state, especially in the context of the I-P conflict, can and should function.

5.3. Arguments for the secular state solution

It might seem that because all the other options for solving the I-P conflict are either morally unacceptable or suboptimal, the one-state solution emerges as the only optimal one. However, this does not follow, for this solution itself might also be morally unacceptable or suboptimal. That is, it just might be that no solution to the I-P conflict is morally optimal. Thus, we need to show how the one-state solution satisfies the three criteria for what a morally optimal solution is, which, to recapitulate, are as follows. The solution (i) does not infringe or violate either party's properly formulated basic rights, (ii) satisfies both parties' morally permissible desires, and (iii) protects the individual human rights of the residents of the territory of historic Palestine.

Let us start with the third, and easiest, criterion. A secular, democratic state for all its citizens is designed (among other things) to protect the individual rights of its residents, regardless of their religious or ethnic affiliation. Moreover, since the Palestinian refugees are legitimate residents of historic Palestine, and since the right of return is primarily an individual right, the one-state solution respects this right by allowing for its recognition and implementation. For, according to the one-state solution, historic Palestine is the state for both Palestinians and Israeli Jews, and there is no principled reason why it would block the recognition or the implementation of the right of the Palestinian refugees to return.

Moreover, the state of Israel-Palestine can preserve the individual right to the public expression of one's cultural identity—assuming, that is, and as some have argued (Tamir, 1993), that there is such a right (much depends on what 'identity,' 'cultural,' 'public,' and 'expression' mean). There is no reason why this state would prohibit individuals from expressing their religion openly, from wearing traditional garb to express (one aspect of) their culture, from engaging in religious and non-religious cultural rituals, from engaging in open debates about the future of the country as seen from the particular perspective of different groups, and from a host of other things.

Note two things. First, although there are on-going debates about whether the state can interfere in the public expression of one's culture, even if such expression harms no one (e.g., France's prohibition on wearing religious symbols in public work places), they are not of any special relevance to the one-state solution. While some of the issues might take on special urgency given the history of the conflict, the theoretical issues are general. Second, in addition to allowing for the individual public expression of one's cultural identity, the one-state allows for the individual public expression of one's dissension from one's cultural identity. This is, after all, part of what it means for a state to secure individual human rights.

The first criterion for a morally optimal solution is that the solution does not infringe or violate either group's properly delineated basic rights. 'Properly delineated' means 'non-spurious rights that each group might claim for itself'—a qualification needed to ensure that the rights in question are genuine, not claims masquerading as rights.

One crucial group right is that to self-determination. If, as Kapitan argues, a right to self-determination is best understood in a regional, not nationalist, sense, both Israeli Jews and Palestinians (including Israeli Palestinians) collectively, as legitimate residents of the region of historic Palestine, would have the right in question. Thus, neither group, *qua* Jews or *qua* Palestinians, has the right to self-determination. All the segments of the entire population (e.g., Palestinians, Palestinian Christians, Palestinian Muslims, Israeli Orthodox Jews, and Israeli secular Jews) share in the right to self-determination.[22] The one-state solution satisfies this right by allowing members of both groups to exercise determination over historic Palestine.

Another crucial group right is that of groups to chart and express their cultural and religious ways of life as they see fit. The one-state solution does not deny this right. Beyond calling for a single state, it does not specify any internal arrangement that the state should enact with respect to the ways of life of its various cultural, ethnic, and religious groups. Indeed, it is perfectly compatible with the idea of a secular, democratic state that the state foster and protect its diverse cultural, ethnic, and religious groups.

The first criterion for a morally optimal solution is also relevant to the right of return of Palestinian refugees. If, in addition to its being an individual right, the right of return is a collective right that the Palestinian refugees, as a group, have, the one-state solution clearly does not deny this right. Since it calls for both Palestinians and Israeli Jews to share the land, it allows for both the recognition and implementation of the right of return.

The one-state solution, then, does not deny the fulfillment of three crucial group rights: of self-determination, cultural autonomy and expression, and return.

Let us now turn to the second criterion for a morally optimal solution: that it satisfies the morally permissible desires of both parties ('morally permissible' is another needed qualification to ensure that morally impermissible desires are discounted, such as the desire by either group to have Palestine exclusively). Since the list of such desires could be open-ended, I confine the discussion to the two obvious ones.

The principal morally permissible desire that each group (generally) has is for its members to lead their lives as they see fit in historic Palestine, a territory to which members of both groups are attached. The one-state solution satisfies this desire by allowing current Jewish and Palestinian residents, and their descendents, to continue to reside anywhere they wish on this land, to travel freely in it, and, in general, to lead their individual and communal lives as they see fit (abiding by, of course, equitable governing institutions). The one-state solution would also allow, under properly formulated immigration laws, Jews, Palestinians, and their descendents living outside to relocate to historic Palestine if they desire.

Another group desire might be for each group to have its culture and way of life secure and perpetuated down the generations. Again, the one-state solution can satisfy this desire by taking measures to protect either group's cultural, religious, and other forms of ethnic expression.

One might object that this discussion neglects the actual desires that people have. For example, Israeli Jews do not simply desire to live their lives as they see fit in historic Palestine, but to do so in a Jewish state in historic Palestine. But if this specific desire leads to something morally unacceptable, such as a state designed to be ethnically pure or that treats its non-Jewish residents and citizens in inequitable ways, the desire in question would be morally impermissible and should not be satisfied, just as any other morally impermissible desire should not be satisfied. If, however, 'Jewish state' refers to something else, such as a state with Jewish cultural aspects, the one-state solution could satisfy this desire since it allows for the protection of ethnic and religious groups, and even for prioritizing Jewish (and Palestinian) immigration (within moral limits).

I cannot survey every potential desire that each party might have, but any objection based on the immoral wishes or desires of any group will not do precisely owing to the immorality of the desires. Whether there are morally permissible desires not satisfied by the one-state solution remains to be seen. I cannot think of any.

6. Replies to possible objections[23]

Although the two-state solution falls short of being morally optimal, the one-state solution does not. However, it still faces some objections, to which I now turn.

6.1. The historical rejection of the one-state solution

The Arabs rejected bi-nationalism in the past, and there is no indication that they would (sincerely) accept it now. So it is a pointless proposition today.[24]

However, historically and philosophically things are more nuanced. First, although bi-nationalism had some support among Jewish and non-Jewish Zionists, it was never the official Zionist position on the issue of the Jewish presence in historic Palestine. So it is not the case that rejection eliminated bi-nationalism while Zionists were clamoring for it. Moreover, the Arab leadership naturally reacted to the official, majority-backed political efforts to establish a Jewish presence in historic Palestine,[25] and rejected the conversion of historic Palestine or parts of it into a Jewish state. Because the Zionist leadership never seriously advocated bi-nationalism, it is hard to gauge what the Arab reaction to it would have been.

Second, actual historical evidence supports the claim that Arab resistance, by both the leadership and the people, was not to Jewish presence in Palestine as such, but to the erection of a Jewish state on Palestinian or Arab land. For example, Resolution 7 of the General Syrian Congress of July 2, 1919, rejected both Zionism and its sponsorship of Jewish immigration to Palestine, but gave full political equality to 'our Jewish fellow-citizens' (Smith, 2001, p. 104). Another example is the testimony of Jamal al-Husayni, the leader of the Arab High Committee, before the United Nations Ad Hoc Committee on the Palestinian Question (September 29, 1947), which conveys the same attitude in Resolution 7 above (Smith, 2001, p. 216).

Among the general population, the evidence also indicates that the Palestinians, especially the peasants and the farmers, became hostile towards Jews after fearing the loss of their livelihoods owing to Jewish control of the lands (Smith, 2001, chap. 3; Hirst, 2003, pp. 141–53). Indeed, after the Palestinian riots of August 1929, in which many Jews, especially Orthodox, were killed in Jerusalem, Hebron, and other towns, the British Shaw Commission concluded that the main cause of the riots was the 'Arab feeling of animosity and hostility towards the Jews...based on the two-fold fear...that by Jewish immigration and land purchases [the Arabs] may be deprived of their livelihood and placed under the economic domination of the Jews,' a conclusion later bolstered by the British Hope-Simpson Committee (Smith, 2001, pp. 131–2). The evidence, then, demonstrates that the Palestinians' hostility was directed not at the Jews as Jews, but as the founders of a new state on Palestinian land and what that entailed concerning their rights and ways of life. How the Palestinians' would have reacted to a genuine bi-nationalist state is difficult to gauge.

Assuming, however, that Palestinians would have been hostile to the Jewish presence even if part of a bi-nationalist scheme, we should not conclude that raising the idea of a one-state solution today is pointless because the Palestinians, or, for that matter, mainstream Zionists, rejected it then. Moral solutions to present problems need to take into account historical changes. Whatever the actions and intentions of the parties were, the morally optimal solution needs to take into account current facts, without riding roughshod over history. Thus, even if Palestinians rejected, and Jews accepted, a single state, it does not follow that it should not be accepted today. So the argument that we should not propose the one-state idea because it was rejected in the past is invalid.

6.2. The one-state solution destroys Israel

Another common objection attributes vicious motives to those who advocate a one-state solution, especially of wanting to destroy Israel. For example, Leon Wieseltier writes, 'The Palestinians who espouse binationalism are acting on their fondest and most uncompromising dreams. It is their device for defeating Zionism and gaining dominion over the entirety of the land, the shrewdest form of the Palestinian rejection of the idea of partition' (2003, p. 22). And Frederick Krantz states, 'For if achieved, what [the one-state solution] would, in fact, mean – and, indeed, what it is *intended* to mean – would be politicide, the destruction of Israel as a sovereign Jewish state' (*Montreal Gazette*, November 14, 2003; my emphasis; see also David Saks, 'For Israelis, Option of Binationalism Would Be Foolhardy Recipe,' *Cape Times*, December 3, 2003). Although this objection concerns motives, it also points to another concerning results: the one-state solution, in effect, destroys Israel as a state.

Perhaps some of those supporting the one-state solution do so out of the motive of wanting to destroy Israel. But this, of course, cannot be an objection to the one-state solution itself, because some people also support the one-state solution out of good motives, out of having the interests of both Israeli Jews and Palestinians at heart. Furthermore, the one-state solution ought to be addressed on its own grounds, attending to its merits and demerits, rather than to the motives of those advocating it. Moreover, those who raise this objection rarely properly defend the underlying assumption that Israel is a legitimate state, an assumption I consider further below.

Given the tenor of the usual discussion of this topic, the idea that the one-state solution leads in effect to the destruction of Israel bears explanation. If the concern is that the one-state solution will destroy the people of Israel, then the claim is false. The one-state solution does not and is not meant to kill or eliminate anyone. What is true is that if the one-state solution is implemented, then Israel, as a state, with its current 'borders,' laws, educational curricula, and so on, will no longer exist. This is part of what it means to implement the one-state solution. So to object to it on these grounds is in effect to say, 'The one-state solution is bad because it is the one-state solution'—not much of a substantive claim.

However, the real charge of the objection might be that the one-state solution leads to the elimination of Israel as the Jewish state. The underlying idea here is that it is good that Israel remain as the (or a) Jewish state understood in terms of Jewish numerical majority, with the state's symbols being exclusively Jewish (otherwise, there is no problem, for the single state could be Jewish in ways explained already). Coupled with this particular claim, there is also puzzlement why those who support the one-state solution do not also propose something similar for other regions in the world, such as uniting India and Pakistan, and uniting the Balkans (Wieseltier, 2003, p. 21; see also Omer Bartov and Michael Walzer's letters in *The New York Review of Books*,

December 4, 2003, 57–8). Given the current make-up of our world, nation-peoples are expected, if not entitled, to have their own states. So why treat Israel differently? Why start with or 'pick on' it?

Those who support the one-state solution for Israelis and Palestinians need not be against the idea of reunifying other regions in the world as a matter of principle, but such proposals should be discussed on a case-by-case basis. In the case of Israelis and Palestinians, the one-state solution is the most appropriate. If Israel were established on uninhabited land, if Israel did not create a Palestinian refugee crisis, if the Palestinian refugees did not have the right of return, if Israel did not go on to occupy more Palestinian land, if Israel did not make this occupation almost impossible to reverse, and if only one people, rather than two, had and continue to have claims to historic Palestine, few would support the one-state solution and so 'pick on' Israel. The fact of the matter is that the one-state solution is optimal because of what the conflict and the history of the region morally dictate.

Moreover, the objection that the one-state solution destroys Israel relies on two important assumptions that need to be honestly faced. The first is that Israel is good for the Jews, and any proposal that implies its destruction cannot but be bad for them. The second is the mainstream Zionist assumption that, much like France is a French state, Israel is a Jewish state. So any proposal that implies its destruction should, consistently, imply the elimination of other nation-states.

In many respects, Israel is, and has been, good for its citizens, Jewish ones especially. But, when large numbers of Jews are safe and thriving outside Israel, it is clear that Israel is not the only good arrangement for Jews. If so, then a single state for two people need not threaten Jewish culture, religion, and ways of life. As argued in Chapters 2 and 3, given the history of Israel, it exists in a hostile environment not because of rabid Arab anti-Semitism, but because of its record of injustices. If Israel continues to refuse to acknowledge and rectify its past injustices, it is difficult to see how it can offer safety to its Jewish citizens. Moreover, Israel was not built on uninhabited land. No matter how safe and good it is for Jews, Palestinians have rights to that same land, and so a morally optimal solution would be for both people to share it. These points are connected: when Israel denies Palestinian rights, it puts itself in the path of anger and potential violence. The one-state solution is meant to provide security, prosperity, and a lasting, just settlement to all the parties involved by properly rectifying the past.

Considering the second assumption, I will confine myself to two points, since much has been written on Judaism, Israel, and Zionism (e.g., Beit-Hallahmi, 1992; Cook, 2006; Nathan, 2005; Neumann, 2005, part I; Rabkin, 2006; Rose, 2005; Tilley, 2005). First, when discussing Israel's status, people often assert a claim amply stated by Abraham Foxman, National Director of the Anti-Defamation League, '[Israel's] identity as a Jewish state is comparable to France's identity as a state of the French and Italy's identity as a state of the Italians' ('An Alternative Future: An Exchange,' *The New York Review of Books*, 2003, 50 (19): 57). On reflection, this claim is problematic. France does not make a distinction between French nationality and some other type of citizenship. But Israel does make a distinction between Jewish nationality and Israeli citizenship. Although someone who is Muslim or Druze or Christian or Jewish can be an Israeli citizen, only a Jew can be of Jewish nationality. Coupling this idea with Israel's claim that it is the state of the Jewish people gives us the first difference between Israel, on the one hand, and France and Italy, on the other: there are no French and Italian nationals outside France and Italy, respectively, who are also not French or Italian citizens (though there are, of course, people of French or Italian descent). In declaring itself the state of the Jewish people, Israel actually lays claim to all Jews who are not actual Israeli citizens as potential ones.[26] This is very different from every other nation-state in the world. As Virginia Tilley puts it, 'Israel is not a nation-state in the sense understood in all other countries – that is, the state of its citizens, who are nationals by virtue of that citizenship' (2005, p. 147). Becoming an Israeli citizen does not make one a Jewish national, as one becomes a French national on becoming a French citizen.

Moreover, because Israel is the state of the Jewish people, 'only the Jewish nation has juridical status, and a great body of civil rights and privileges are consigned to that nation... No non-Jewish nationality can gain comparable national rights and privileges, because no other nationality is admitted to hold legal rights within the country' (Tilley, 2005, p. 147). This is far indeed from usual conceptions of democracy.

Second, mainstream Zionism has sought to establish a state for the Jewish people. As a by-product of its political program, it has required the more or less cleansing of historic Palestine of non-Jews. As Tilley (again) eloquently puts it, the hostility between Palestinians and Israeli Jews is not between the two people: 'Rather, antipathy toward Arabs is an accidental outgrowth of Zionists' fundamental nationalist premise, which is exclusive Jewish control over the land' (2005, p. 144). Indeed, Israel's disengagement from the Gaza Strip and its desire to retain large swaths of the West Bank are meant to retain its demographic majority to maintain itself as a Jewish state.[27]

The point is that Israel's Zionist foundations and what they imply for the treatment of non-Jews (including the way in which Israel came into existence) are ultimately undemocratic and allow it to treat its non-Jewish residents and citizens inequitably. As Milton Fisk puts it, 'the Zionist state cannot, without ceasing to be Zionist, avoid subordinating the Palestinians' (1997, p. 309). Hence, since the one-state solution need not endanger Jews and could allow them to prosper in a region resolved of past hostilities, to object to the one-state solution on the grounds that it eliminates Israel can only mean that it eliminates the state of Israel as it currently exists. But, and regardless of what good this state has done for the majority of its citizens, it is ultimately an anti-democratic state catering to only a segment of them. Thus, that the one-state solution leads to the removal of this kind of state is not a decisive objection against it after all.

6.3. Multiethnic states do not work

Another objection is that that 'Binational or multinational states do not work. All such instances... clearly show this' because there 'seems to be a deep-seated need for a one-to-one relationship between the ethnic/national entity and state sovereignty. Each ethnic/national entity wants its own state on the analogy of each family wanting its own home. And when two or more families must share the same house (the same kitchen and bathroom), a state of continual irritation and tension leading, sooner or later, to fighting and eventually to separation will almost inevitably ensue, and this will also happen when two or more ethnic/national entities are to share one and the same state' (Vogel, 1997, p. 249). Note that this objection by Manfred Vogel is not (only) about states that define themselves as bi- or multi-ethnic, but about any state that contains more than one national people or ethnic group.

First, the house analogy is defective, for we need not assume that the house must have only one bathroom or that the house is small (perhaps a building analogy is better). Regarding a single state for Israelis and Palestinians, there is no reason to believe, nor are there empirical data to support, the claim that it will be overcrowded. Moreover, even if future projections point to over-crowdedness, this problem can be dealt with in ways other than insisting that the two people live apart. Issues over water shortages and distribution are regional concerns, involving also Lebanon, Syria, and Jordan. An equitable solution would have little, if anything, to do with how Israelis and Palestinians share their area of this larger region.

Second, in claiming that there is a need for a relationship between an ethnic/national group, on the one hand, and its own state, on the other, Vogel commits himself to a distinction between the two. But then his claim that bi-national and multinational states do not work would be false, because there are many such states that seem to work just fine (e.g., Australia, the United States, Canada, France, and Russia); their ethnic groups are not clamoring to secede (assuming this to be the relevant criterion of functionality). These states are not problem-free—few states, multi-ethnic or not, are—but surely the criterion for a state's functioning cannot be so high as to require that the state be free of problems.

Many well-functioning multi-ethnic states demonstrate that Vogel's 'deep-seated need' for each ethnic/national group to have its own state is a false claim. Indeed, there are other reasons to believe that this 'need' is dubious. Given that the emergence of nation-states is a more or less modern phenomenon (Anderson, 1983), how deep seated can this need be? Furthermore, vast empires containing large numbers of ethnic groups (e.g., the Greek, Roman, Arab, British, and Ottoman empires) functioned for long periods during which different groups lived in relative harmony and did not desire to secede. Vogel also ignores the fact that different regions in the world have troubles for causes specific to their own history. The Catalans' reason, for example, for wanting to secede is different from the French Quebecans.' Reducing these reasons to a mystical, deep-seated need rides roughshod over important historical, geographical, and political details that might prove crucial in explaining why particular groups of people desire to form their own states. Moreover, these reasons cannot simply be divorced from the political and cultural atmosphere from which they arise. Currently, ideas of nation-states and nationalism are common and popular. The political debates occurring in some European countries, such as Holland, France and Germany, are at their core about how to reconcile the idea of having a specific (e.g., French) culture with the commitment to universal norms of equal treatment and individualism. Because the idea of the nation-state remains popular, we expect political leaders, the media, and other institutions (e.g., the Olympic Games) to support it, often directly helping to shape people's desires. It is hard for the majority of people not to support and even agitate for nation-states when the entire political and cultural atmosphere supports these.[28] So alternative, more plausible reasons than Vogel's 'deep-seated need' explain why some ethnic groups desire their own states. Locating the desire for statehood in an unexplainable ahistorical need is intellectually irresponsible.

Finally, if Vogel's objection applies only to states that define themselves as bi- or multi-nationalist, then it would be irrelevant to the one-state solution defended in this chapter, since the single state is secular and for all its citizens.

6.4. Why stop at the borders of historic Palestine?

This objection attempts to reduce the idea of a one-state solution to an absurdity by arguing that there is no principled reason to stop at the boundaries of that proposed state and not include other geo-political entities, such as Syria, Jordan, and Lebanon. Elias Baumgarten implies that the argument for the one-state solution based on the idea that both peoples are attached to the land is unsound, for 'if Jews and Palestinians have separate "common lives" and two such different common lives are to coexist in one country, why not include Jordan, Lebanon, and Egypt as well? Why not the whole Middle East or even Europe? Why divide the land of the world into separate nations unless doing so is judged to be efficient or administratively convenient as a way of distributing responsibility?' (2000, p. 84). If Jews and Palestinians have different ways of life, and if we discount dividing states simply on the basis of administrative convenience, 'there seems no good reason to group Palestinians with Jews rather than with Jordanians and no basis for grouping Jewish Israelis with Arabs rather than Americans' (Baumgarten, 2000, p. 84).

Baumgarten is correct that it is difficult, if not impossible, to justify the division of land into states based simply on concepts such as 'attachment to the land' or 'different ways of life.' The only way to do this would be based on pragmatic considerations, such as ease of administration. Yet this is not an objection to the one-state solution as such, for if Baumgarten is correct, his would be an argument of throwing out the baby with the bathwater, because it shows that none of the boundaries of current states is justified. Both Jews and Palestinians have ties to the historic land of Palestine, and our world is divided into states, justified or not. Since the solution to the I-P conflict falls within these parameters, the territory that Jews and Palestinians would have to share is that of historic Palestine. So although there is no principled reason why a state that includes Syria, Jordan, and so on should not be formed, the historical, current political, and pragmatic facts imply that we operate in a world divided into states, and the one-state solution is housed within this framework.

Moreover, one premise in Baumgarten's argument is suspect: Israeli and Palestinian lives are not that different from each other. After all, Israeli Jewish society contains segments culturally close to non-Israeli Palestinians (Israeli Oriental Jews and Israeli Palestinians).

6.5. The rise of Islamic parties endangers a secular state

In 2006, the Palestinians voted Hamas (the Islamic Resistance Movement) into power. Even without official rule, Hamas was, and continues to be, very popular among the Palestinians. Since Hamas is an Islamic party, and insofar as its political platform reflects the desires of the Palestinians, this might spell doom for a secular state in historic Palestine: if most Palestinians desire some form of Islamic rule, then, because Islamic rule goes against a secular form of governance, this would be a serious obstacle facing a secular state, especially given the fact that the one-state solution is intended for all the inhabitants of historic Palestine, not just Muslims.

The objection, however, is built on misconceptions.[29] First, Palestinian society has traditionally been one of the most secular societies in the Arab world. The popularity of Hamas and other Islamic parties is relatively recent, reflecting the increasing frustration of the Palestinians with the Israeli occupation and with the ineffective Palestinian leadership. In this respect, the Palestinian situation mirrors that of many Arabs in both Arab and non-Arab countries who have increasingly supported Islamic parties owing to (i) the failure of secular Arab regimes and of Western democracies to attend to their rights, (ii) the injustices of Israel's occupation and policies, and (iii) the American political and military interference in the Middle East.

Second, its popularity among the Palestinians stems not so much from Hamas's Islamic political platform as from four interrelated reasons that also explain why many Palestinian Christians voted for Hamas in 2006. First, Palestinians generally perceive Hamas's officials and leaders to be honest and not corrupt, in contrast with the Palestinian Authority's officials. Second, Hamas has been very successful in instituting, even prior to its coming to power, wide-ranging social and economic organizations that have helped thousands of Palestinians during a time when Palestinian Authority officials were seen as doing virtually nothing. Third, Hamas's political insistence on refusing to recognize Israel, on ending the Israeli occupation, and on recognizing the Palestinian refugees' right of return, has had wide resonance with the Palestinian public, especially in contrast with the perceived Palestinian Authority's defeatist and quisling attitude towards Israeli leaders and demands. Fourth, Hamas has been at the forefront in dispatching suicide bombers and, more recently, in firing the homemade and mostly ineffectual

Qassam rockets from the Gaza Strip into Israel. Many Palestinians see this as a form of legitimate resistance, given that all else has failed. Hence Hamas's Palestinian popularity.

Note the absence of any religious causes. Recent polls indicate that the Palestinian vote for Hamas does not reflect a refusal of a negotiated settlement with Israel (indeed, Hamas leaders themselves have insisted on negotiations; see, e.g., 'Palestinian PM Accepts State in 1967 Borders in Exchange for Truce,' Agence France Presse, September 22, 2006, and Khaled Mish'al, 'Our Unity Can Now Pave the Way for Peace and Justice,' *The Guardian*, February 13, 2007). Moreover, other polls also indicate that support for an Islamic state has hovered at most around three percent (Abunimah, 2006, pp. 164–8), for although many Palestinians are religiously observant, they do not necessarily favor a religious state (as in many countries whose populations tend to be socially, but not politically, religious, such as Italy, Spain, and Greece).

In short, Hamas's popularity has little to do with Palestinian support for an Islamic religious state, but much with the Palestinian's despair owing to their crumbling lives and to the lack of any foreseeable settlement of their conflict with Israel. Were they to believe that an equitable, single state might actually come to exist, few Palestinians would choose instead an Islamic state. Of course, were such a secular, single state to exist, Hamas would probably not cease to function. But it would take its place among other political parties, thus participating in the democratic processes of the secular state, while also rethinking the role its religious platform would play in this state.

6.6. The one-state solution is unrealistic

Finally, one might object that the one-state solution is unrealistic. Before discussing this objection, a commentary on the current popularity of the solution is important, for any settlement of the I-P conflict that goes against the wishes and desires of the people involved would be, for obvious reasons, disastrous. Also, if the one-state is morally better than a two-state solution, that the majority of the people involved opposes it raises a pressing question: What is to be done when the people involved in a conflict reject the morally optimal solution to that conflict?

From what can be gathered, the one-state solution is not very popular. Polls reveal that many Israeli Jews have negative attitudes towards Palestinian Israelis (who make up about 19 percent of the population), some even wanting the state to encourage them to leave; many Israeli leaders are also blunt about this.[30] Since these attitudes are towards the

Palestinian citizens of Israel, one can only infer that the attitudes would be even more hostile to the one-state idea.

The attitudes of the Palestinians of the West Bank, the Gaza Strip, and East Jerusalem, are difficult to gauge.[31] Indeed, gauging the attitude of the general Palestinian population is more complex than gauging that of Jewish Israelis for three reasons. First, many Palestinians reject the one-state idea because they fear second-class status were they to live with Israeli Jews, indicating that their rejection stems from the kind of life they fear they would lead, not from the idea itself.[32] Second, the Palestinian refugees who insist on the right of return usually do so knowing that the return is to Israel, not a future Palestinian state. To them, the idea of living in a single state with Israeli Jews would not be objectionable. Third, as the consistently weaker party, the Palestinians have not had the luxury throughout this conflict to form autonomous desires; many of their actual desires are in reaction to political realities. Hence, what they often desire as far as statehood is concerned might reflect their perception of the limits to what they can realistically desire. As Daniel Gavron puts it, 'Many Palestinians have told me that they would prefer a single state but accept a two-state solution because that is what the Jews want' (2004, p. 235).

Moreover, things might be slowly changing in favor of the one-state idea among both Israelis and Palestinians. For example, the 'Olga Document' (named after the Giva't Olga resort in Israel), signed by more than one hundred Israeli Jews, calls for a single state in historic Palestine (Abunimah, 2006, pp. 171–82). Ali Abunimah also argues that the one-state idea is gaining popularity among Palestinians because they now recognize that the two-state solution is effectively dead, and because the Israeli occupation has slowly eroded Palestinian nationalism by reducing the Palestinians to such a low state that they now have individual aspirations (e.g., survival and security), not national ones (2006, pp. 161–4). Indeed, a very recent poll claims that 70 percent of the Palestinians are in favor of a single state (Near East Consulting; http://www.neareastconsulting.com, February 2007; date of access: March 26, 2007).

With this in mind, I turn to the objection that the one-state solution is unrealistic, addressing the version of the veteran Israeli peace activist Uri Avnery (2003; date of access: April 4, 2004).[33] Avnery claims that if the one-state solution has any chance of materializing, it will not happen for 'another two or three generations.' First, there is 'no chance at all that the present, post-holocaust, Israeli generation, or its successor, will accept this solution, which conflicts absolutely with the myth and the ethos of Israel... The Jews would return to the traumatic experience of a people without a state throughout the world, with all that that implies. And not as a result of a crushing military defeat, but as a free choice. Not very likely.' Avnery adds that 'the great majority of the Palestinian people want to live, at last, in a national state of their own, a state that expresses their national identity, under their flag and their government, like other peoples.'

Second, 'in order to function properly, one of two conditions must be fulfilled: either all sides cede their national identity or they must have equal economic and political power.' Since neither Israelis nor Palestinians are likely to cede their national identities, Avnery claims that if a single state came to pass, 'the Jews would dominate the economy and most other aspects of the state, and try very hard to preserve that situation. At this point in time, a bi-national state would be an occupation regime in a new form that would thinly disguise a reality of exploitation and economic, cultural, and probably political repression. The situation of the Arab citizens in Israel, after 55 years, is not very encouraging.' Avnery concludes that the one-state solution would not end the conflict but only 'set it on a different track, perhaps even more severe and more violent.'

Avnery offers two compelling reasons for the one-state solution's irrealism, and, it seems to me, there are no decisive replies to these reasons, for they rely on facts with which any attempt to implement the one-state idea must grapple. 'Implement' is intentional, for Avnery's objection is really against the one-state solution's implementation, not its moral, theoretical cogency.

To start with the second reason, Avnery is correct that the current economic, political, and cultural balance favors Israel. Thus, he predicts that the imbalance will exist in a single state. History supports this. Today, the blacks of South Africa are still economically disadvantaged in comparison with the whites, despite the fact that apartheid ended. But South Africa's leadership is committed to ending the imbalance. Once both populations, blacks and whites, accepted the fact that apartheid is over, they were committed to make things better for all concerned. This is the core of the reply to Avnery's second reason: once a single state is accepted and implemented, all sorts of issues, including economic ones, will have to be addressed. Indeed, no one is so naïve as to believe that implementing the one-state solution will be easy. But it will solve the basic parameters of the conflict.[34]

Moreover, the Palestinians' current economic situation is sub par by all measures, and it is not obvious that a two-state solution will improve it in any substantial way, for the economic, political, military, and other restrictions that Israel plans to impose on a Palestinian state do not augur well for its economic health. Thus, Avnery's second reason is not decisive.[35]

Regarding the first reason, Avnery is correct that the ethos of the Israeli public accepts the idea of a Palestinian state next to Israel, but rejects a single state for both people. Given that it is the Israeli public—not merely the leadership—that is against it, we have a serious obstacle facing the one-state solution. The issue here is not theoretical—it is not, say, whether the one-state solution violates Israeli Jews' rights, an issue with which I have already dealt—but practical: How does one propose, let alone implement, the one-state solution against the Israeli (Jewish) public's wishes?

Although true, proclaiming, 'No one said it would be easy,' is not of much force. But what is puzzling about objections such as Avnery's is their assumption that people's views are set in stone, forgetting that they are shaped by many factors, including leaders' pronouncements, media promptings, and the very cultural climate. If the one-state solution were the morally right solution to the I-P conflict, then, since people's views do change, one would do much better to campaign for it, rather than surrender to the prevailing political ethos of this or that public. Imagine saying the following about civil rights: 'It is pointless to advocate for these rights for black people, because the ethos of the Southern white population is against it.' This is an unconvincing argument, especially from a moral standpoint. Although some struggles are uphill battles and so are practically difficult to implement, it is wrongheaded—indeed, immoral—to suggest that they ought not to be engaged in because there is, even severe, resistance to them. Advocating for the one-state solution should not be on the basis of its ease or difficulty of implementation, but, first and foremost, on moral grounds. Moreover, moral considerations are not idle; they have normative force, motivating people to act. This, coupled with the point about people's attitudes potentially changing owing to convincing campaigning and education, blunts the force of Avnery's first reason.[36]

Nonetheless, since the one-state solution is not on the international 'table,' since both Israelis and Palestinians generally reject it, how does one go about implementing it? There is no clear, obvious, or easy answer, but we have two options. We can advocate for a single state either directly or indirectly. Let us consider each in turn.

To advocate for it indirectly is to advocate for a two-state solution as a preamble to a single state. This approach, however, is fraught with difficulties. First, in advocating for a two-state solution, should we—the supporters of the single state—be honest that it is the first step to a single state? If yes, then we are likely to be met with as much hostility as if we were directly advocating for the single state. If no, then we would be employing a deceptive, and so immoral, strategy. There is also the question of what will happen when the two states exist and we reveal that they are but a step to a single state. Will the hostility be any less then? Perhaps, though this is hard to predict. It might be just as vociferous (if not more, since people will justifiably feel cheated).

Additionally, what would happen to the right of return of Palestinian refugees as we struggle for the two-state idea? Should we simply drop it from the moral map? If yes, that would be unjust. Should we then support its recognition but not its implementation? If yes, then, aside from a partial moral victory in getting Israel to recognize it, the advocacy would be moot. If we advocate for both its recognition and the implementation, what would be the point of also advocating for a two-state solution, given that the main reason for doing the latter is the idea, reflected in international opinion and *realpolitik*, that each people, Jews and Palestinians, should have its own state?

I submit, however, that the right of return is not an insurmountable obstacle for the strategy of advocating a two-state as a first step to a one-state solution, because we can advocate for both the recognition and implementation of the right, yet defer actual implementation until a single state begins to emerge. Nonetheless, the questions I raised about the right of return need to be carefully thought through, especially in connection with the idea of supporting two states as a preamble to a single state.

Lastly, if the current direction in which the two-state solution is heading will not yield a viable Palestinian state, advocating for two states as a first step for a single one will simply not work, since there would be nothing, really, for which to advocate, unless, of course, we do so in the knowledge that a weak Palestinian state is likely to exist but that this situation would end up actually helping a single state to emerge. This might be a feasible strategy, but its drawback is that it consists in waiting for dire conditions to obtain before calling for a single state. Thus, it will face more or less the same hostility in the future as advocating for a single state does now.

Consider now direct advocacy for the one-state solution. To state the obvious, this will not be easy. A number of steps can be taken, but none ensures the success of the campaign. First, a massive and wide-spread educational campaign, targeting especially the populations and the leaders of the countries most relevant to the conflict (Israel, the Arab world, the United States, Europe, and Russia), and which must include historical, political, and moral facts about the I-P conflict, must be launched. The campaign would need to be tailored to suit its specific audiences and to include a highly convincing blueprint of what the single state would look like, one that would address the relevant parties' obvious potential worries. In this vein, given Israelis' fears about Palestinian terrorism and anti-Semitism, Palestinians must, as Abunimah rightly emphasizes (2006, pp. 157–60), present Israelis with a blueprint of how the two people are to coexist.

Second, specific campaigns targeting relevant political players will also be needed. For example, U.S. congressmen and women should be approached with the proper views on the conflict and how it should be resolved. Third, the media must be targeted, its skewed reporting corrected, and encouraged to air debates about views currently deemed anathema, such as the place and morality of Zionism, especially as it has been implemented in historic Palestine, the right of return of Palestinian refugees, and the one-state solution.

Given that the current political climate is generally hostile to any idea of a single state, the above schematic strategies will require massive effort, time, and money, and it is difficult to see where they will come from. More importantly, it is difficult to see who will be engaging in these efforts, especially since a large number of people will be needed to conduct such a currently unpopular campaign. Because there are crises in this world other than the I-P conflict, and because campaigning for the single state will not, initially at least, be popular, the needed numbers will be hard to come by. Thus, it is difficult to see both how to directly campaign for the one-state solution and how the campaign can even get off the ground.

There is a dilemma here. On the one hand, the one-state solution should be pursued because it is morally optimal. On the other, it is difficult to see how campaigning for it can get off the ground.

I conclude with a prediction. There will, eventually, be a Palestinian state. But given current politics, Israel will have no difficulty imposing its own terms on how this state will come into being and what it will 'look like.' It will be made up of enclaves, with no worthwhile sovereignty, economically stagnant and dependent on continuous aide, and with many a military incursion by Israel's army. The Palestinians will refuse to live under such conditions and will rise up (again), in which case one of three things will happen. Either they will more or less be obliterated through war ('We gave them a state but all they want is to kill us,' will run the excuse, leading to a much bloodier version of post-Camp David 2000), or they will demand a truly independent viable state, or they will demand integration with Israel (one person, one vote). Let us hope that the first option does not happen. If the second does, we will be back to 'square one,' but this time it will be extremely difficult to see how the Palestinians will get a viable state and from which territories: if the world consents to the initial arrangement and Israel consolidates its borders, how likely will it be that it will cede needed territory to the Palestinians? The chances of such a state seeing the light will not be highly improbable, as it is now, but virtually impossible. If the third option occurs, it will be a popular call among the Palestinians for a single state. It might or might not succeed. But, for the sake of Palestinians, Israeli Jews, and all those who have been badly affected by this protracted and far-reaching conflict, we are better off trying to save ourselves much bloodshed and deepening enmity by advocating for a single state now, despite the difficulties. Doing so will probably not make it happen, but it will put the idea in the public domain, more so than it is now, so that by the time the Palestinians rise up (again), the world might be a bit more ready to accept a single state.

There is hope, but its light is dim. Achieving a single state will be arduous. But what options do we really have? The one-state solution is the only morally optimal solution. And when morality calls, we must heed it.

Notes

1. Gary Sussman (2005; date of access: July 13, 2005) argues that Sharon had never given up on the Jordan option. It is not clear whether Sharon's successor, Ehud Olmert, shares this view.
2. Abunimah (2006), Gavron (2004), Judt (2003b) (and the exchange on Judt's essay [*New York Review of Books*, December 4, 2003, 57–62]), Tilley (2003, 2005), and Yiftachel (2006, chap. 12). See also Ignatiev (2004) (date of access: April 20, 2005); May (2004, date of access: April 20, 2005); and Ari Shavit, 'Cry, The Beloved Two-State Solution,' *Ha'aretz*, August 7, 2003. See also Meron Benvenesti's articles on this issue, all in *Ha'aretz* (for example, 'The Binational Option,' November 7, 2002; 'Which Kind of Binational State?' November 20, 2003; and 'Founding a Binational State,' April 22, 2004). The Web site, http://www.one-state.org, contains almost all the essays printed on the issue.
3. Ahmad Qureia, the Palestinian ex-Prime Minister, called for a one state in 2004 (Wafa Amr, 'Palestinian PM Says Two-State Solution in Danger,' Reuters, January 8, 2004).
4. So my claim is not relevant to the usual case in which the laws of both their host and original states apply to legal and illegal visitors and immigrants.

5. See Goldberg (2004), Harvey Morris ('Jews Could Live in a Palestinian State,' *Financial Times*, May 17, 2005), and Jonathan Saul ('Jewish Settler Seeks to Become Palestinian,' Reuters, July 18, 2005) for the few examples of Jewish settlers willing to become Palestinian citizens.
6. This is a nightmare scenario to many Israelis and their leaders. Here's Sharon: 'There cannot be a situation where there are two states for one people. Let's make the issue clear' (Chris McGreal, *The Guardian*, May 14, 2003).
7. Note that there is a distinction between what the principle of self-determination entitles the Palestinians to (a normative issue) and what they actually self-determine or aspire to. Investigating the gap between the two allows us to home in on the morally relevant reasons for the one-state solution.
8. Dan Williams, 'Israel's New Jerusalem Plan Angers Palestinians,' Reuters, March 21, 2005; 'Israeli Cabinet OKs Jerusalem Barrier,' Associated Press, July 10, 2005; Mark Lavie, 'Barrier Meant to Ensure Jewish Majority,' Associated Press, July 11, 2005; 'Sharon Defiant on Jerusalem as Clashes Flare at Mosque Compound,' Agence France Presse, June 6, 2005; Aluf Benn and Shlomo Shamir, 'PM to U.S. Jewish Leaders: I Won't Compromise on Jerusalem,' *Ha'aretz*, May 23, 2005; 'Olmert: Settler Blocs to Be Part of Israel Forever,' *Ha'aretz*, May 4, 2006.
9. Jeff Halper (2005, date of access: June 3, 2005); Scott Wilson, 'Jewish Inroads in Muslim Quarter,' *Washington Post*, February 11, 2007. On the history of Judaizing East Jerusalem, see Cheshin, Hutman, and Melamed (1999) and Tsemel (1999).
10. For figures on the settlements and settlers, see http://www.peacenow.org. See also Molly Moore, 'Israel Is Funding Outposts: "Blatant Violation" of Law Alleged,' *The Washington Post*, March 9, 2005; Amy Teibel, 'Settler Leaders Contradict Israel Claims,' Associated Press, March 8, 2005; James Sturcke, 'Call to Prosecute Sharon Over Settlements,' *The Guardian*, March 9, 2005. See also Tilley (2003). For some very recent settlement expansion, see Corinne Heller, 'Israel Starts Work on Settlement Expansion: Source,' Reuters, March 13, 2006; Amos Harel, 'Peretz Approves Expansion of Four West Bank Settlements,' *Ha'aretz*, May 22, 2006; Laurie Copans, 'Israel Beefs Up Settlements Even While It Talks of West Bank Withdrawal,' Associated Press, June 2, 2006; 'Israel Plans New Homes in West Bank Settlement,' Reuters, June 12, 2006; Nadav Shragai, 'Peace Now: Building in Illegal Outposts Stepped-Up During War,' *Ha'aretz*, October 3, 2006; Amos Harel, 'Settlements Grow on Arab Land, Despite Promises Made to U.S.,' *Ha'aretz*, October 24, 2006; Nadav Shragai, Yoav Stern, and Akiva Eldar, 'Tenders Issued for Hundreds of Homes in W. Bank Settlements,' *Ha'aretz*, September 4, 2006; 'Government Issues Tenders for 164 New Homes in the West Bank,' *Ha'aretz*, September 21, 2006; Nadav Shragai, Nir Hasson, and Yair Ettinger, 'New Settlement Planned for Former Gaza Settlers,' *Ha'aretz*, December 26, 2006; Yair Shragai, 'State Releases New Tender for 44 Housing Units in Ma'aleh Adumim,' *Ha'aretz*, January 15, 2007; 'Israel Building 3,000 New Settler Homes,' Reuters, February 22, 2007.
11. See Bennis (2002), Kimmerling (2003), Malley and Agha (2001), Reinhart (2002, 2006), and Swisher (2004).
12. Yoel Marcus, 'Sharon's Plan,' *Ha'aretz*, February 3, 2004; Akiva Eldar, 'Sharon's Palestinian "State," ' *The Daily Star*, June 21, 2004; 'Special UN

Rapporteur: Israel will Remain Occupier After Disengagement,' *The Electronic Intifada*, January 27, 2005 (http://www.electronicintifada.net; date of access January 27, 2005); Alan Johnston, 'Israel's "Invisible Hand" in Gaza,' BBC News, January 17, 2007. For a list of the evacuated settlements, see Bradley Burston, 'Sharon's List: The Doomed Settlements, A Guide,' *Ha'aretz*, February 24, 2005. On Gaza, see Sara Roy, 'Erasing the "Optics" of Gaza,' *The Daily Star*, February 14, 2004, and David Newman, 'Boxing in Palestinians,' *Los Angeles Times*, August 4, 2004. On the repercussions of Sharon's plan for Gaza, see Jonathan Freedland, 'A Gift of Dust and Bones,' *The Guardian*, June 2, 2004. See also Ilil Shahar, 'Government Reneges on Undertaking to US,' *Maariv*, August 1, 2004; 'Israel Gears Up for New Settlement Masterplan,' Agence France Presse, September 1, 2005; 'Israel Plans to Double Number of Settlers in Jordan Valley,' Agence France Presse, June 24, 2005; Nadav Shragai and Gideon Alon, 'Government Issues Two Construction Tenders for West Bank Settlement,' *Ha'aretz*, August 4, 2005; Amos Harel and Nadav Shragai, 'Livnat Says Pullout Is a "Window" to Build W. Bank, Even Over U.S. Ire,' *Ha'aretz*, September 6, 2005; John Ward Anderson, 'Sharon Aide Says Goal of Gaza Plan Is to Halt Road Map,' *The Washington Post*, October 7, 2004; Ori Nir, 'West Bank Settlements to Stay,' *Forward*, July 1, 2005; Sussman, 2005; Aluf Benn, 'Olmert: We Must Pull Out from Parts of the West Bank,' *Ha'aretz*, January 25, 2006; Chris McGreal, 'Israel Unveils Plan to Encircle Palestinian State,' *The Guardian*, February 8, 2006; Richard Galpin, 'Israel Tightens Grip on Jordan Valley,' BBC News, March 16, 2006; Akiva Eldar, 'Some 2,000 Palestinians Banned from Entering Jordan Valley,' *Ha'aretz*, March 14, 2006; Laurie Copans, 'Israel Intent on Keeping Jordan Valley,' Associated Press, May 8, 2006; 'Olmert: Settler Blocs to Be Part of Israel Forever,' *Ha'aretz*, May 4, 2006; Mahmoud Habboush, '"Tell Aviv Not Committed to Pull Out of 1967 Land,"' *The Jordan Times*, June 23, 2006.

13. For updates on the settlements, see http://www.peacenow.org.il. On the settlers, see Goldberg (2004), Hirst (2003, pp. 79–89, 508–15), and Margalit (2001).
14. For maps and further explanations, see http://stopthewall.org. See also Weizman (2004), Rubin (2005, date of access: July 9, 2005); Matthew Tempest, 'UN Calls for Israel to Tear Down the Wall,' *The Guardian*, July 21, 2004; Greg Myre, 'UN Study: Wall to Absorb Almost 15% of West Bank,' *Chicago Tribune*, November 12, 2003; Yuval Yoaz, 'State to High Court: Fence Route Determined Not Only by Security Considerations,' *Ha'aretz*, July 4, 2004; Virginia Tilley, 'The Deeper Meaning of the Wall,' *Counterpunch*, February 26, 2004; Yuval Yoaz, 'Justice Minister: West Bank Fence Is Israel's Future Border,' *Ha'aretz*, December 1, 2005; Meron Rapoport, 'PM Approves Eastward Move of Section of Separation Barrier,' *Ha'aretz*, January 31, 2007.
15. By 1922, when the mandate was ratified, the League had separated Jordan and Palestine into two different areas, its mandate applying only to Palestine.
16. In his letter, Rabin recognized the PLO as the representative of the Palestinians, not the Palestinians' right to a state.
17. The relevant text is excerpted in Tilley (2005) as Appendix A.II. A detailed discussion of UN deliberations is found in Pappe (1992, chap. 1).

18. Other international endorsements of a single state for both people include the resolutions of the Syrian Congress of 1919, especially Resolution 7 (Smith, 2001, p. 104), and the British 1939 White Paper (Smith, 2001, p. 164).
19. The general issues involved here are complex. For a survey, see Benhabib (2004), Hampton (1997, chap. 6), and Schwartz (1995).
20. Thus, this avoids the objection that a secular, democratic state 'gives no status to peoples' (Young, 2005, p. 153). Moreover, continuing to have the Law of Return, perhaps even broadening it to include Palestinians in the Diaspora, would help maintain both a Jewish and a Palestinian character to Israel-Palestine. However, the law must be just; at minimum, the state should not admit Jews and Palestinians at the expense of others who demonstrate a need to immigrate to the new state.
21. Many of the features are found in Qumsiyeh (2004, pp. 217–9), from whom I have borrowed and adjusted. For a similar list, see Abunimah (2006, pp. 110–11). Recently, Adalah ('Justice' in Arabic), the Israeli Arab group that advocates for the recognition of the rights of Israel's Palestinians, proposed a constitution for Israel that characterizes the state as a multicultural rather than a Jewish one (Yoav Stern, 'Israeli Arab Group Proposes New "Multi-Cultural" Constitution,' *Ha'aretz*, February 28, 2007). However, the constitution is for Israel, not a single state in historic Palestine.
22. Even if we accept a national right to self-determination, it would still need to be properly delineated in such a way that it is not a *carte blanche* for each nation to act as it pleases. Thus, if both Palestinians and Jews have rights of national self-determination, they might have to share the territory, in which case we are back to the one-state solution.
23. I do not repeat those objections, and their replies, also raised against the right of return: the preservation of Israeli Jewish culture, the history of enmity between Palestinians and Israeli Jews, the desire to maintain the Jewishness of Israel, and the need for Jews to have their own state.
24. Leon Hadar, 'Two Peoples, Two States,' *The American Conservative*, January 19, 2004; Frederick Krantz, 'One-State Idea Would Mean the Liquidation of Israel,' *Montreal Gazette*, November 14, 2003.
25. Naguib Azoury, the Arab nationalist and founder of the League of the Arab Fatherland, wrote in 1905 that 'the latent effort of the Jews to reconstitute on a very large scale the ancient kingdom of Israel' is fated to clash with Arab nationalism 'until one of them wins' (Smith, 2001, p. 57). Ghada Karmi claims that the 'vast majority' of Palestinians, prior to 1948, was 'opposed to bi-nationalism in any form' (1999a, p. 249) but gives no evidence for this claim. See also Muslih (1988, chap. 3).
26. Jonthan Cook writes, 'Israel has never assigned an "Israeli" nationality to its citizens. This is because it refuses to recognize Israel as a nation apart from the Jewish nation. In 1970 the Supreme Court backed the government in ruling that there was no such thing as Israeli nationality. Instead the Interior Ministry assigns its citizens one of 137 possible statuses: from Jew, Georgian, Russian and Hebrew through to Arab, Druze, Abkhazi, Assyrian, and Samaritan' ['"Democratic" Racism (2),' *Al-Ahram Weekly*, July 15–21, 2004].
27. For a brief but good article on the current research conducted in Israel on demographics, see Yair Sheleg, 'The Demographics Point to a Binational State,' *Ha'aretz*, May 27, 2004.

28. A good discussion focusing on Great Britain of how the media and the politicians fanned the flames of xenophobia, racism, and bigoted nationalism is Dummett (2001, part II).
29. In what follows, I rely on Abunimah (2006, chap. 6), Agha and Malley (2006), Hilal (2006), Hiro (2002, pp. 263–79), Hroub (2004, 2006a, 2006b), Milton-Edwards and Crooke (2004), Mishal and Sela (2006), Pape (2005, pp. 47–51, 191–3), and Usher (2006).
30. Yulie Khromchenco, '64% of Israeli Jews Support Encouraging Arabs to Leave,' *Ha'aretz*, June 21, 2004; Jonathan Cook, ' "Democratic" Racism (2),' *Al-Ahram Weekly*, July 15–21, 2004; Yoav Stern, 'Most Israeli Jews Say Israeli Arabs Should Emigrate,' *Ha'aretz*, April 4, 2005; Ferry Biedermann, 'Israelis Resist the Arabs in Their Midst,' Inter Press Service, April 28, 2005; Amiram Barkat, 'More Than Half of Israelis Want Government to Help Arabs Emigrate,' *Ha'aretz*, May 9, 2006.
31. Some commentators cite a poll that concludes that about 25 percent of Palestinians favor a single-state. It is not clear, however, who the Palestinians polled are (native West Bankers? Refugees?); see Cynthia Johnston, 'The Democratic State of Israel-Palestine?' Reuters, July 8, 2004, and Michael Tarazi, 'Two Peoples, One State,' *New York Times*, October 4, 2004. Tilley cites a poll conducted by the Jerusalem Media and Communication Centre that puts the Palestinian approval rating of a bi-national state somewhere around 20 to 30 percent (depending on the month). But, as Tilley warns, the poll should be taken cautiously because among Palestinians there is no proper discussion of and consensus about what the central terms of the debate mean (Tilley, 2005, Appendix B, and 2006, pp. 41–2). Things might be changing, however, as a recent poll by Near East Consulting states that 70 percent of Palestinians are in favor of a single state (see discussion in the next paragraph).
32. Palestinians' fear of second-class citizenship is well founded (see Cook, 2006). Israelis also fear living with Palestinians. But their majority also rejects the very idea of a single state because it implies the rejection of Zionism.
33. For another version of the objection, see the interview with Noam Chomsky on Znet, March 30, 2004, one reply by Noah Cohen, and Chomsky's response, August 26, 2004 (http://www.zmag.org; date of access April 20, 2005).
34. Aware of this reply, Avnery counters that unlike the white racists in South Africa, Israeli Jews have strong support by American Jews; with the latter's influence, it will be difficult to pressure Israeli Jews to relinquish their economic and political power. But Avnery is too quick to predict the ease with which American Jews will maneuver once the international community accepts the idea of a single state.
35. In relying on what the Palestinian state would actually, rather than ideally, be under a two-state solution, my reply is in line with Avnery's actual-based, rather than ideal, reasons against the one-state solution.
36. Chomsky's objection to the one-state idea is that 'There has never been a legitimate proposal for a democratic secular state from any significant Palestinian (or of course Israeli) group. One can debate, abstractly, whether it is "desirable." But it is completely unrealistic. There is no meaningful international support for it, and within Israel, opposition to it is close to

universal . . . Those who are now calling for a democratic secular state are . . . in effect providing weapons to the most extreme and violent elements in Israel and the US' ('Justice for Palestine?' http://www.zmag.org, March 30, 2004; date of access April 20, 2005). But, first, no sane person would advocate imposing a single-state on both people; this would be disastrous, as Chomsky rightly claims. Hence, part of advocating for a single state must be an effort to change public opinion and create international consensus. Second, although Chomsky is right that there is consensus on it, little has been done to actually implement an equitable two-state solution. What might emerge is a truncated, non-viable Palestinian state, a result that will perpetuate the conflict. The international consensus of which Chomsky writes is pure rhetoric; so what role it effectively plays in his rejection of the one-state idea is unclear.

References

Abou Iyad, with Eric Rouleau. 1981. *My Home, My Land: A Narrative of the Palestinian Struggle*. New York: Times Books.

Abraham, Daniel. 2006. *Peace is Possible*. New York: Newmarket Press.

Abu Shakrah, Jan. 2001. 'Deconstructing the Link: Palestinian Refugees and Jewish Immigrants from Arab Countries.', In Aruri 2001.

Abu Sitta, Salman. 1999. 'The Feasibility of the Right of Return.' In *The Palestinian Exodus, 1948–1998*, edited by G. Karmi and E. Cotran. Reading, UK: Ithaca Press.

_____. 2001a. *The End of the Palestinian-Israeli Conflict: From Refugees to Citizens at Home*. London: Palestine Land Society and Palestinian Return Centre.

_____. 2001b. 'The Implementation of the Right of Return.' In Carey 2001.

_____. 2001c. 'The Right of Return: Sacred, Legal and Possible.' In Aruri 2001.

Abunimah, Ali. 2006. *One Country: A Bold Proposal to End the Israeli-Palestinian Impasse*. New York: Metropolitan Books.

Abunimah, Ali, and Hussein Ibish. 2001. *The Palestinian Right of Return*. Washington, D.C.: The American-Arab Anti-Discrimination Committee Research Institute.

Acton, Lord J. E. E. 1967. *The Liberal Interpretation of History*. Chicago: University of Chicago Press.

Agha, Hussein, and Robert Malley. 2006. 'Hamas: The Perils of Power.' *The New York Review of Books* 53 (4): 22–24.

Akram, Susan. 2001. 'Reinterpreting Palestinian Refugee Rights under International Law.' In Aruri 2001.

Alexander, Yonah. 2002. *Palestinian Religious Terrorism: Hamas and Islamic Jihad*. Ardsley, N.Y.: Transnational Publishers.

Alexander, Yonah, and Donald Musch, eds. 2001. *Terrorism: Documents of International and Local Control*, Volume 26. Dobbs Ferry, N.Y.: Oceana Publications.

Almond, Brenda. 1991. 'Rights.' In *A Companion to Ethics*, edited by P. Singer. Oxford: Blackwell Publishers.

Alon, Hanan. 1980. *Countering Palestinian Terrorism in Israel: Toward a Policy Analysis* Santa Monica, Calif.: Rand Corporation.

Al-Qasem, Anis. 1999. 'The Right of Return in International Law.' In *The Palestinian Exodus, 1948–1998*, edited by G. Karmi and E. Cotran. Reading, UK: Ithaca Press.

Al-Rayyes, Nasser. 2000. *The Israeli Settlements from the Perspective of International Law*. Ramallah, Palestine: Al-Haq Institute.

Amstutz, Mark R. 1999. *International Ethics*. New York: Rowman & Littlefield.

Anderson, Benedict. 1983. *Imagined Communities: Reflections on the Origin and Spread of Nationalism*. London: Verso.

Antonious, George. 1965. *The Arab Awakening*. New York: Capicorn Books.

Arab Higher Committee. 1948. *Why the Arab States Entered Palestine*. New York: Memorandum to the United Nations Delegations.

Arendt, Hannah. 1978. *The Jew as Pariah: Jewish Identity and Politics in the Modern Age*, edited by R. H. Feldman. New York: Grove Press.

Aruri, Naseer, ed. 2001. *Palestinian Refugees: The Right of Return*. London: Pluto Press.
_____. 2003. *Dishonest Broker: The U.S. Role in Israel and Palestine*. Cambridge, Mass.: South End Press.
Arzt, Donna. 1997. *Refugees into Citizens: Palestinians and the End of the Arab-Israeli Conflict*. New York: Council on Foreign Relations.
Ashmore, Robert. 1997. 'State Terrorism and Its Sponsors.' In Tomis Kapitan 1997.
Avineri, Shlomo. 1981. *The Making of Modern Zionism: The Intellectual Origins of the Jewish State*. New York: Basic Books.
Avnery, Uri. 2003. 'The Bi-national State: The Wolf Shall Dwell with the Lamb.' http://www.counterpunch.org, July 15, 2003.
Bachi, Roberto. 1974. *The Population of Israel*. Jerusalem: Institute of Contemporary Jewry, Hebrew University.
Ball, George W. and Douglas B. Ball. 1992. *The Passionate Attachment*. New York: Norton.
Baroud, Ramzi, ed. 2002. *Searching Jenin: Eyewitness Accounts of the Israeli Invasion*. Seattle: Cune Press.
Bassiouni, Cherif. 1978. 'The Palestinians' Right to Self-Determination and National Independence.' Arab-American University Graduates Information Paper No. 22 (December).
Baumgarten, Elias. 2000. 'Zionism, Nationalism, and Morality.' In *Nationalism and Ethnic Conflict: Philosophical Perspectives*, edited by N. Miscevic. Chicago and La Salle, IL: Open Court.
Begin, Menachem. 1977. *The Revolt*. Revised Edition. New York: Nash Publishing.
Begon, Dov. 2002. 'Canaanites and Amalekites: As Then so Today.' *Jewish Press*, June 21, 2002: 47.
Beiner, Ronald, ed. 1999. *Theorizing Nationalism*. Albany, N.Y.: SUNY Press.
Beinin, Joel. 2003. 'Is Terrorism a Useful Term in Understanding the Middle East and the Palestinian-Israeli Conflict?' *Radical History Review* 85: 12–23.
Beit-Hallahmi, Benjamin. 1992. *Original Sins: Reflections on the History of Zionism and Israel*. New York: Olive Branch Press.
Ben-Ami, Shlomo. 2006. *Scars of War, Wounds of Peace: The Israeli-Arab Tragedy*. Oxford: Oxford University Press.
Benhabib, Seyla. 2004. *The Rights of Others: Aliens, Residents, and Citizens*. Cambridge: Cambridge University Press.
Bennis, Phyllis. 2002. *Understanding the Palestinian-Israeli Conflict*. Orlando, Florida: TARI Publications.
Benvenisti, Meron. 2000. *Sacred Landscape: The Buried History of the Holy Land Since 1948*. Translated by M. Kaufman-Lacusta. Berkeley and Los Angeles: University of California Press.
Berg, J. 1991. 'The Right to Self-Determination.' *Public Affairs Quarterly* 5: 211–226.
Best, Steven, and Anthony J. Nocella II. 2004. 'Defining Terrorism.' *Animal Liberation Philosophy and Policy Journal* 2: 1–18.
Bhalla, R. S. 1989. 'The Right of Self-Determination in International Law.' In *Issues of Self-Determination*, edited by William Twining. Aberdeen: Aberdeen University Press.
Black, Ian, and Benny, Morris. 1991. *Israel's Secret Wars: A History of Israel's Intelligence Services*. New York: Grove Weidenfeld.
Blechman, Barry. 1971. *The Consequences of Israeli Reprisals: An Assessment*. Ph.D. Dissertation: Georgetown University.

Bleier, Ronald. 2003. 'In the Beginning There was Terror.' *The Link* 36 (3), www.ameu.org/printer.asp?iid=249&aid=358.
Bowersock, G. W. 1988. 'Palestine: Ancient History and Modern Politics.' In Said and Hitchens 1988.
Boyle, Francis. 2003. *Palestine, Palestinians, and International Law*. Atlanta: Clarity Press.
Brenner, Lenni. 1984. *The Iron Wall: Zionist Revisionism from Jabotinsky to Shamir*. London: Zed Books.
Brown, Dee. 1970. *Bury My Heart at Wounded Knee*. New York: Bantam Books.
Brownlie, Ian. 1990. *Principles of Public International Law*. 4th edition. Oxford: Clarendon Press.
Buchanan, Allen. 1991. *Secession: The Morality of Political Divorce from Fort Sumter to Lithuania and Quebec*. Boulder, Colo.: Westview.
_____. 1997a. 'Self-Determination, Secession, and the Rule of Law.' In McKim and McMahan 1997.
_____. 1997b. 'Theories of Secession.' *Philosophy and Public Affairs* 26: 31–61.
Burrows, Paul. 2004. 'Geneva Accord: Analysis of the Bankruptcy.' *Electronic Intifada*; electronicintifada.net; January 3, 2004.
Butler, Judith. 2003. 'No, it's Not Anti-Semitic.' *London Review of Books* 25 (16): 19–21.
Campbell, Tom. 2006. *Rights: A Critical Introduction*. Milton Park, UK: Routldge.
Carey, Roane, ed. 2001. *The New Intifada: Resisting Israel's Apartheid*. London and New York: Verso.
Carr, Caleb. 2002. *The Lessons of Terror: A History of Warfare against Civilians: Why it has Always Failed and Why it Will Fail Again*. New York: Random House.
Carter, Jimmy. 2006. *Palestine: Peace, Not Apartheid*. New York: Simon and Schuster.
Cattan, Henry. 1969. *Palestine, the Arabs, and Israel: The Search for Justice*. London: Longman.
_____. 1976. *Palestine and International Law*. 2nd edition. London: Longman.
_____. 2000. *The Palestine Question*. London: Al-Saqi Books.
Chen, Lung-chu. 1976. 'Self-Determination as a Human Right.' In *Toward World Order and Human Dignity*, edited by M. Reisman and B. Weston. New York: Free Press.
Cheshin, Amir, Bill Hutman, and Avi Melamed. 1999. *Separate and Unequal: The Inside Story of Israeli Rule in East Jerusalem*. Cambridge, Mass.: Harvard University Press.
Chiha, Michel. 1969. *Palestine*. Beirut: Trident Publications.
Childers, Erskine. 1961. 'The Other Exodus.' *The Spectator*, May 12, 1961, 672–675
Chomsky, Noam. 1976. 'Civilized Terrorism.' *Sevendays*, July 26, 1976.
_____. 1988a. *The Culture of Terrorism*. Boston: South End Press.
_____. 1988b. 'Middle East Terrorism and the American Ideological System.' In Said and Hitchens 1988.
_____. 1991. 'International Terrorism: Image and Reality.' In *Western State Terrorism*. New York: Routledge.
_____. 1999. *The Fateful Triangle: The United States, Israel, and the Palestinians*. Cambridge, Mass.: South End Press.

_____. 2003. *Middle East Illusions*. Lanham, Md.: Rowman and Littlefield.
Christison, Kathleen. 1999. *Perceptions of Palestine: Their Influence on U.S. Middle East Policy*. Berkeley: University of California Press.
Churchill, Ward. 1997. *A Little Matter of Genocide: Holocaust and Denial in the Americas, 1492 to the Present*. San Francisco: City Lights Books.
Clarke, Thurston. 1981. *By Blood and Fire*. London: Hutchinson.
Coady, C. A. J. 2004a. 'Terrorism and Innocence.' *The Journal of Ethics* 8: 37–58.
_____. 2004b. 'Terrorism, Morality, and Supreme Emergency.' *Ethics* 114: 772–789.
_____. 2004c. 'Defining Terrorism.' In *Terrorism: The Philosophical Issues*. Houndmills, edited by Igar Primoratz. UK: Palgrave Macmillan.
Cobban, Alfred. 1945. *National Self-Determination*. London: Oxford University Press.
Cohen, Avner. 1998. *Israel and the Bomb*. New York: Columbia University Press.
Cohen, Michael. 1982. *Palestine and the Great Powers, 1945–1948*. Princeton, N.J.: Princeton University Press.
Collins, John. 2002. 'Terrorism.' In *Collateral Language*, edited by J. Collins and R. Glover. New York: New York University Press.
Cook, Jonathan. 2006. *Blood and Religion: The Unmasking of the Jewish and Democratic State*. London: Pluto Press.
Copp, David. 1997. 'Democracy and Communal Self-Determination.' In McKim and McMahan 1997.
_____. 1999. 'The Idea of a Legitimate State.' *Philosophy and Public Affairs* 28: 3–45.
Cordesman, Anthony. 2005. *The Israeli-Palestinian War: Escalating to Nowhere*. Westport, Conn.: Praeger Security International.
Corlett, J. Angelo. 2002. 'Wrongdoing, Reparations, and Native Americans.' In *Injustice and Rectification*, edited by R. C. Roberts. New York: Peter Lang.
Crawford, J. 1979. *The Creation of States in International Law*. Oxford: Oxford University Press.
Cunningham, Alan. 1948. 'The Last Days of the Mandate.' *International Affairs* 28: 481–90.
Dahbour, Omar. 2003. *The Illusion of Peoples: A Critique of National Self-Determination*. Lanham, Md.: Lexington Books.
_____. 2005. 'The Response to Terrorism: Moral Condemnation or Ethical Judgment?' *The Philosophical Forum* 36: 87–95.
Dahbour, Omar, and Micheline Ishay, eds. 1995. *The Nationalism Reader*. New York: Humanities Press.
Davis, Uri. 2004. *Apartheid Israel: Possibilities for the Struggle within*. London: Zed Books.
De George, Richard. 1990. 'The Myth of the Right of Collective Self-Determination.' In *Issues of Self-Determination*, edited by William Twining. Aberdeen: Aberdeen University Press.
De Reynier, Jacques. 1971. 'Deir Yasin, April 10, 1948.' In Khalidi 1971.
Dershowitz, Alan. 2003. *Why Terrorism Works: Understanding the Threat, Responding to the Challenge*. New Haven, Conn.: Yale University Press.
Dummett, Michael. 2001. *On Immigration and Refugees*. New York: Routledge.
Dworkin, Ronald. 1977. *Taking Rights Seriously*. Cambridge, Mass.: Harvard University Press.
_____. 2003. 'Terror and the Attack on Civil Liberties.' *The New York Review of Books* 50 (17): 37–41.

Eban, Abba. 1956. 'The Toynbee Heresy.' In *Toynbee and History*, edited by M. F. A. Montagu. Boston: Porter Sargent.

_____. 1972. *My Country*. New York: Random House.

El Sarraj, Eyad. 2002. 'Suicide Bombers: Dignity, Despair, and the Need for Hope: An Interview with Eyad El Sarraj' by Linda Butler. *Journal of Palestine Studies* 31 (4): 71–76.

Emerson, Rupert. 1971. 'Self-Determination.' *American Journal of International Law* 65: 459–471.

Esco Foundation for Palestine, Inc. 1947. *Palestine: A Study of Jewish, Arab, and British Policies*. New Have: Yale University Press.

Espiell, Hector Gross. 1980. *The Right to Self-Determination: Implementation of United Nations Resolutions*. New York: United Nations.

Etzioni, Amitai. 1992–93. 'The Evils of Self-Determination.' *Foreign Policy* 89: 21–25.

Fackenheim, Emil. 1988. *A Political Philosophy for the State of Israel*. Jerusalem: Jerusalem Center for Public Affairs.

Falk, Richard. 1991. 'The Terrorist Foundations of Recent U.S. Policy.' In *Western State Terrorism*. New York: Routledge.

Fanon, Franz. 1963. *The Wretched of the Earth*. New York: Grove Press.

Farley, Lawrence T. 1986. *Plebiscites and Sovereignty*. Boulder, Colo.: Westview Press.

Feinberg, Joel. 1970. 'The Nature and Value of Rights.' *The Journal of Value Inquiry* 4: 243–257.

Feinberg, Nathan. 1970. *The Arab-Israeli Conflict in International Law*. Jerusalem: Magnes Press.

_____. 1974. 'The Recognition of the Jewish People in International Law.' In *The Arab-Israeli Conflict, Readings and Documents*, edited by J. N. Moore. Volume 1. Princeton: Princeton University Press, pp. 59–87.

_____. 1979. *Studies in International Law*. Jerusalem: Magnes Press.

Finkelstein, Norman. 1995. *Image and Reality of the Israel-Palestine Conflict*. London and New York: Verso.

_____. 2005. *Beyond Chutzpah: On the Misuse of Anti-Semitism and the Abuse of History*. Berkeley: University of California Press.

Fischbach, Michael. 2003. *Records of Dispossession: Palestinian Refugee Property and the Arab-Israeli Conflict*. New York: Columbia University press.

Fisk, Milton. 1997. 'Zionism, Liberalism, and the State.' In Kapitan 1997.

Flapan, Simha. 1979. *Zionism and the Palestinians*. London: Croom Helm.

_____. 1987. *The Birth of Israel*. New York: Pantheon.

Fotion, Nick. 2004. 'The Burdens of Terrorism.' In *Terrorism: The Philosophical Issues*, edited by Igor Primoratz. Houndmills, UK: Palgrave Macmillan.

French, Shannon. 2003. 'Murderers, Not Warriors: The Moral Distinction between Terrorists and Legitimate Fighters in Asymmetric Conflicts.' In *Terrorism and International Justice*, edited by James Sterba. New York: Oxford University Press.

Friedman, Robert. 1992. *Zealots for Zion*. New York: Random House.

Frum, David, and Richard Perle. 2003. *An End to Evil: How to Win the War on Terror*. New York: Random House.

Gal, Allon. 1991. *David Ben-Gurion and the American Alignment for a Jewish State*. Bloomington IN: Indiana University Press.

Gal-Or, Noemi. 1994. 'Countering Terrorism in Israel.' In *The Deadly Sin of Terrorism*, edited by D. Charters. Westport, Conn.: Greenwood Press.

Garnor, Boaz. 2001. 'Defining Terrorism: Is One Man's Terrorist Another Man's Freedom Fighter?' Institute for Counter-Terrorism; http://www.ict.org.il; June 25, 2001.

Gavron, Daniel. 2004. *The Other Side of Despair: Jews and Arabs in the Promised Land*. Lanham, Md.: Rowman and Littlefield.

Gellner, Ernest. 1983. *Nations and Nationalism*. Oxford: Blackwell.

Genet, Jean. 1986. *Prisoner of Love*. Translated by B. Bray. New York: New York Review of Books.

George, Alexander, ed. 1991. *Western State Terrorism*. New York: Routledge.

Gewirth, Alan. 1978. *Reason and Morality*. Chicago: The University of Chicago Press.

Gilbert, Paul. 2003. *New Terror, New Wars*. Washington, D.C.: Georgetown University Press.

Gill, Kathleen. 2002. 'The Moral Functions of an Apology.' In *Injustice and Rectification*, edited by R. C. Roberts. New York: Peter Lang.

Glover, Jonathan. 1991. 'State Terrorism.' In *Violence, Terrorism, and Justice*, edited by Raymond Frey and Christopher Morris. Cambridge: Cambridge University Press.

Goldberg, Jeffrey. 2004. 'Among the Settlers.' *The New Yorker*, May 31, 46–69.

Gordon, Neve, and George Lopez 2000. 'Terrorism in the Arab-Israeli Conflict.' In *Ethics in International Affairs*, edited by Andrew Valls. Lanham Md.: Rowman and Littlefield.

Gorny, Yosef. 1987. *Zionism and the Arabs*. Oxford: Clarendon Press.

Graff, James. 1991. *Palestinian Children and Israeli State Violence*. Toronto: Near East Cultural and Educational Foundation of Canada.

_____. 1997. 'Targeting Children: Right versus *Realpolitik*.' In Kapitan 1997.

Hajjar, Lisa. 2006. 'International Humanitarian Law and "Wars on Terror": Comparing Israeli and American Doctrines and Policies.' *Journal of Palestine Studies* 36 (1): 21–42.

Halberstam, Malvina. 1994. 'Nationalism and the Right to Self-Determination: The Arab-Israeli Conflict.' *New York University Journal of International Law and Politics* 26: 573–584.

Halper, Jeff. 2002. 'The Key to Peace: Dismantling the Matrix of Control.' In *The Other Israel: Voices of Refusal and Dissent*, edited by R. Carey and J. Shainin. New York: The New Press.

_____. 2005. 'The Process of Transfer Continues.' *The Electronic Intifada*, June 3, 2005; http://www.electronicintifada.net.

Hampton, Jean. 1997. *Political Philosophy*. Boulder, Colo.: Westview Press.

Hare, R. M. 1979. 'On Terrorism.' *Journal of Value Inquiry* 13: 240–249.

Hass, Amira. 1999. *Drinking the Sea at Gaza: Days and Nights in a Land Under Siege*. Translated by E. Wesley and M. Kaufman-Lacusta. New York: Henry Holt.

_____. 2003. *Reporting from Ramallah: An Israeli Journalist in an Occupied Land*. Translated by R. L. Jones. Los Angeles: Semiotext(e) Active Agents Series.

Heckscher, A. 1991. *Woodrow Wilson*. New York: Scribner's.

Held, Virginia. 2004a. 'Terrorism, Rights, and Political Goals.' In *Terrorism: The Philosophical Issues*, edited by Igor Primoratz. Houndmills, UK: Palgrave Macmillan.

_____. 2004b. 'Terrorism and War.' *The Journal of Ethics* 8: 59–75.

_____. 2005. 'Legitimate Authority in Non-state Groups Using Violence.' *Journal of Social Philosophy* 36: 175–193.

Herman, Edward. 1982. *The Real Terror Network: Terrorism in Fact and Propaganda.* Boston: South End Press.

Herman, Edward, and Gerry O'Sullivan. 1989. *The Terrorism Industry.* New York: Pantheon Books.

_____. 1991. ' "Terrorism" as Ideology and Cultural Identity.' In George 1991.

Hertzberg, Arthur, ed. 1977. *The Zionist Idea: A Historical Analysis and Reader.* New York: Atheneum Press.

Herzl, Theodor. 1970. *The Jewish State.* New York: Herzl Press.

Hilal, Jamil. 2006. 'Hamas's Rise as Charted in the Polls, 1994–2005.' *Journal of Palestine Studies* 35 (3): 6–19.

Hiro, Dilip. 2002. *Sharing the Promised Land: A Tale of Israelis and Palestinians.* New York: Olive Branch Press.

Hirst, David. 2003. *The Gun and the Olive Branch: The Roots of Violence in the Middle East.* 3rd edition. New York: Thunder's Mouth Press/Nation Books.

_____. 2004. 'Pursuing the Millenium: Jewish Fundamentalism in Israel.' http://www.thenation.com/doc.mhtml?i=20040216&s=hirst; February 2, 2004.

Hocking, William Ernest. 1945. 'Arab Nationalism and Political Zionism.' *The Moslem World* 35: 216–223.

Hoffman, Michael. 2002. 'State Sponsored Assassinations by Agents of the Israeli Government.' http://www.revisionisthistory.org/palestine7.html.

Hoffman, Michael, and Moshe Lieberman. 2002. *The Israeli Holocaust against the Palestinians.* Coeur d'Alene, Idaho: The Independent History and Research Co.

Hohfeld, Wesley Newcomb. 1964. *Fundamental Legal Conceptions* (1919). London and New Haven: Greenwood Press.

Holmes, Robert. 1989. *On War and Morality.* Princeton, N.J.: Princeton University Press.

_____. 1995. 'Nonviolence and the Intifada.' In *From the Eye of the Storm,* edited by L. F. Bove and L. D. Kaplan. Amsterdam: Rodopi.

Honderich, Ted. 2006. *Right and Wrong, and Palestine, 9-11, Iraq, 7-7.* Boston: Seven Stories Press.

Hroub, Khaled. 2000. *Hamas: Political Thought and Practice.* Beirut: Institute for Palestine Studies.

_____. 2004. 'Hamas after Shaykh Yasin and Rantisi.' *Journal of Palestine Studies* 33 (4): 21–38.

_____. 2006a. 'A "New Hamas" through its New Documents.' *Journal of Palestine Studies* 35 (4): 6–27.

_____. 2006b. *Hamas: A Beginner's Guide.* London: Pluto Press.

Human Rights Watch. 1993. *A License to Kill: Israeli Undercover Operations against 'Wanted' and Masked Palestinians.* Washington, D.C.: Human Rights Watch.

_____. 1994. *Israel's Interrogation of Palestinians from the Occupied Territories.* Washington, D.C.: Human Rights Watch.

_____. 1996. *Civilian Pawns: Laws of War Violations and the Use of Weapons on the Israel-Lebanon Border.* Washington, D.C.: Human Rights Watch.

_____. 2002. *World Report 2002.* http://www.hrw.org/wr2k2/mena.html.

Hunter, F. Robert. 1991. *The Palestinian Uprising: A War by Other Means.* Berkeley and Los Angeles: University of California Press.

Ignatiev, Noel. 2004. 'Zionism, Anti-Semitism and the People of Palestine.' *Counterpunch,* June 17, 2004; http://www.counterpunch.com.

Jaggar, Alison. 2005. 'What is Terrorism, Why is it Wrong, and Could it Ever be Morally Permissible?' *Journal of Social Philosophy* 36: 202–217.
Jeffries, J. M. N. 1971. 'Analysis of the Balfour Declaration.' In Khalidi 1971, pp. 173–188.
Jewish Agency for Palestine. 1947. *The Jewish Plan for Palestine*. Jerusalem: The Jerusalem Press.
Jiryis, Sabri. 1976. *The Arabs in Israel*. New York: Monthly Review Press.
_____. 1981. 'Domination by Law.' *Journal of Palestine Studies* 11 (1): 67–92.
Johnson, Harold. 1967. *Self-Determination within the Community of Nations*. Leiden, the Netherlands: A. W. Sijtoff.
Judt, Tony. 2003a. 'Anti-Americans Abroad.' *The New York Review of Books* 50 (7): 24–27.
_____. 2003b. 'Israel: The Alternative.' *The New York Review of Books* 50 (16): 8–10.
Kagan, Shelly. 1998. *Normative Ethics*. Boulder, Colo.: Westview Press.
Kant, Immanuel. 1983 [1795]. 'To Perpetual Peace: A Philosophical Sketch.' In *Perpetual Peace and Other Essays*. Translated by T. Humphrey. Indianaopolis, Ind.: Hackett.
Kapeliouk, Amnon. 1982. *Sabra and Chatila, Enquete sur un Massacre*. Paris: Seuil.
Kapitan, Tomis. 1995. 'Self-Determination and the Israeli-Palestinian Conflict.' In *From the Eye of the Storm*, edited by L. Bove and L. Kaplan. Amsterdam: Rodopi.
_____. ed. 1997. *Philosophical Perspectives on the Israeli-Palestinian Conflict*. Armonk, N.Y.: M. E. Sharpe.
_____. 2003. 'The Terrorism of "Terrorism."' In *Terrorism and International Justice*, edited by James Sterba. New York: Oxford University Press.
_____. 2005. ' "Terrorism" as a Method of Terrorism.' In *Ethics of Terrorism and Counter-Terrorism*, edited by Georg Meggle. Frankfurt: Ontos Verlag.
Karmi, Ghada. 1999a. 'Concluding Vision: A Return to Israel/Palestine?' In *The Palestinian Exodus, 1948–1998*, edited by G. Karmi and E. Cotran. Reading, UK: Ithaca Press.
_____. 1999b. 'The Question of Compensation and Reparations.' In *The Palestinian Exodus, 1948–1998*, edited by G. Karmi and E. Cotran. Reading, UK: Ithaca Press.
Khalaf. Issa. 1991. *Politics in Palestine: Arab Factionalism and Social Disintegration 1939–1948*. Albany: SUNY Press.
Khalidi, Muhammad Ali. 1997. 'Formulating the Right of National Self-Determination.' In Kapitan 1997.
Khalidi, Rashid. 1988. 'Palestinian Peasant Resistance to Zionism before World War I.' In Said and Hitchens 1988.
_____. *et al.*, eds. 1991. *The Origins of Arab Nationalism*. New York: Columbia University Press.
_____. 1997. *Palestinian Identity: The Construction of Modern National Consciousness*. New York: Columbia University Press.
_____. 1999. 'Truth, Justice and Reconciliation: Elements of a Solution to the Palestinian Refugee Issue.' In *The Palestinian Exodus, 1948–1998*, edited by G. Karmi and E. Cotran. Reading, UK: Ithaca Press.
_____. 2006. *The Iron Cage: The Story of the Palestinian Struggle for Statehood*. Boston: Beacon Press.
Khalidi, Walid, ed. 1971. *From Haven to Conquest: Readings in Zionism and the Palestine Problem Until 1948*. Beirut: Institute of Palestine Studies.

_____. 1984. *Before Their Diaspora*. Washington, D.C.: Institute for Palestine Studies.

_____. ed. 1987. *From Haven to Conquest: Readings in Zionism and the Palestine Problem Until 1948*. 2nd Printing. Washington, D.C.: Institute for Palestine Studies.

_____. 1988. 'Plan Dalet: Master Plan for the Conquest of Palestine.' *Journal of Palestine Studies* 38 (1): 4–20.

_____. 1989. *At a Critical Juncture: The United States and the Palestinian People*. Washington, D.C.: Center for Contemporary Arab Studies.

_____. ed. 1992. *All that Remains: The Palestinian Villages Occupied and Depopulated by Israel in 1948*. Washington, D.C.: Institute for Palestine Studies.

_____. 1997. 'Revisiting the UNGA Partition Resolution.' *Journal of Palestine Studies* 27 (1): 5–21.

_____. 2005. 'Why did the Palestinians Leave?' *Journal of Palestine Studies* 34 (2): 42–54.

Khatchadourian, Haig. 1998. *The Morality of Terrorism*. New York: Peter Lang.

_____. 2000. *The Quest for Peace between Israel and the Palestinians*. New York: Peter Lang.

Khouri, Fred. 1976. *The Arab-Israeli Dilemma*, 2nd edition. Syracuse, New York: Syracuse University Press.

Kimmerling, Baruch. 2003. *Politicide: Ariel Sharon's War against the Palestinians*. New York: Verso.

Klug, Brian. 2004. 'The Myth of the New Anti-Semitism: Reflections on Anti-Semitism, Anti-Zionism and the Importance of Making Distinctions.' *The Nation*, February 2, 23–29.

Kollatt, Israel. 1971. 'The Chances for Peace and the Right to a Homeland.' In *Israel and the Palestinians*, edited by S. Avineri. New York: St. Martin's Press.

Kubursi, Atif. 2001. 'Valuing Palestinian Losses in Today's Dollars.' In Aruri 2001.

Kushner, Tony, and Alisa Solomon, eds. 2003. *Wrestling with Zion: Progressive Jewish-American Responses to the Israeli-Palestinian Conflict*. New York: Grove Press.

Kymlicka, Will. 1989. *Liberalism, Community and Culture*. Oxford: Clarendon Press.

Lansing, R. 1921. *The Peace Negotiations*. Boston: Houghton-Mifflin.

Laqueur, Walter, ed. 1976. *The Israel-Arab Reader*. 3rd edition. New York: Bantam Books.

_____. 1987. *The Age of Terrorism*. Boston: Little, Brown, and Company.

Laqueur, Walter, and Barry Rubin, eds. 2001. *The Israel-Arab Reader: A Documentary History of the Middle East Conflict*. 6th edition. New York: Penguin.

Lesch, Ann. 1979. 'Israel's Deportation of Palestinians from the West Bank and Gaza Strip, 1967–1978.' *Journal of Palestine Studies* 8 (2): 101–131 and (3): 81–112.

Lichtenberg, Judith. 1997. 'Nationalism, For and (Mainly) Against.' In McKim and McMahan 1997.

Lilienthal, Alfred. 1982. *The Zionist Connection II*. New Brunswick, N.J.: North American Publishers.

Lloyd-George, David. 1939. *Memoirs of the Peace Conference*. New Haven, Conn.: Yale University Press.

Lustick, Ian. 1980. *Arabs in the Jewish State: Israel's Control of a National Minority*. Austin, Tex.: University of Texas Press.
_____. 1993. *Unsettled States, Disputed Lands: Britain and Ireland, France and Algeria, Israel and the West Bank-Gaza*. Ithaca, N.Y.: Cornell University Press.
Lynk, Michael. 2005. 'Down by Law: The High Court of Israel, International Law, and the Separation Wall.' *Journal of Palestine Studies* 35 (1): 6–24.
MacCallum, Gerald. 1987. *Political Philosophy*. Englewood Cliffs, N.J.: Prentice-Hall.
MacIntyre, Alasdair. 1984. *After Virtue*. 2nd edition. Notre Dame, Ind.: University of Notre Dame Press.
Malley, Robert, and Hussein Agha. 2001. 'Camp David: The Tragedy of Errors.' *The New York Review of Books* 48 (13): 59–65.
Mallison, W. Thomas and Sally V. Mallison. 1980. 'The Right of Return.' *Journal of Palestine Studies* 9 (125): 125–136.
_____. 1986. *The Palestine Problem in International Law and World Order*. Essex: Longman.
Mann, Barbara. 2005. *George Washington's War against Native Americans*. Westport, Conn.: Praeger.
Manuel, Frank E. 1971. 'Judge Brandeis and the Framing of the Balfour Declaration.' In Khalidi 1971, pp. 165–172.
Margalit, Avishai. 1995. 'The Terror Master.' *The New York Review of Books* 42 (15): 17–22.
_____. 1997. 'The Moral Psychology of Nationalism.' In McKim and McMahan 1997.
_____. 2001. 'Settling Scores.' *The New York Review of Books* 48 (14): 20–24.
Margalit, Avishai, and Moshe Halbertal. 1994. 'Liberalism and the Right to Culture.' *Social Research* 61: 491–510.
Margalit, Avishai, and Joseph Raz. 1990. 'National Self-Determination.' *Journal of Philosophy* 87: 439–461.
Masalha, Nur. 1992. *Expulsion of the Palestinians: The Concept of 'Transfer' in Zionist Political Thought, 1882–1948*. Washington, D.C.: Institute for Palestine Studies.
_____. 1997. *A Land without a People: Israel, Transfer, and the Palestinians, 1949–96*. London: Faber and Faber.
_____. 2001. 'The Historical Roots of the Palestinian Refugee Question.' In Aruri 2001.
_____. 2003. *The Politics of Denial: Israel and the Palestinian Refugee Problem*. London: Pluto Press.
Massad, Joseph. 2001. 'Return or Permanent Exile?' In Aruri 2001.
May, Todd. 2004. 'The Emerging Case for a Single-State Solution.' *Counterpunch*, September 9, 2004; http://www.counterpunch.com.
McCarthy, Justin. 1990. *Palestine's Population During the Ottoman and the British Mandate Periods*. New York: Columbia University Press.
McDonald, James. 1952. *My Mission to Israel*. New York: Simon and Schuster.
McKim, Robert, and Jeff McMahan, eds. 1997. *The Morality of Nationalism*. Oxford: Oxford University Press.
Mearsheimer, John, and Stephen Walt. 2005. 'The Israel Lobby.' The John F. Kennedy School of Government, *Faculty Research Working Paper* Series, http://ksgnotes1.harvard.edu/Research/wpaper.nsf/rwp/RWP06-011/$File/rwp_06_011_walt.pdf.

Michalska, Anna. 1990. 'Rights of Peoples to Self-Determination in International Law.' In *Issues of Self-Determination*, edited by William Twining. Aberdeen: Aberdeen University Press.

Miller, David. 1995. *On Nationality*. Oxford: Oxford University Press.

Miller, Seumas. 2005. 'Terrorism and Collective Responsibility.' In *Ethics of Terrorism and Counter-Terrorism*, edited by George Meggle. Frankfurt: Ontos Verlag.

Milton-Edwards, Beverley and Alastair Crooke. 2004. 'Elusive Ingredient: Hamas and the Peace Process.' *Journal of Palestine Studies* 33 (4): 39–52.

Mishal, Shaul, and Avraham Sela. 2006. *The Palestinian Hamas: Vision, Violence, and Coexistence*. New York: Columbia University Press.

Moaz, Zeev. 2006. *Defending the Holy Land*. Ann Arbor, Mich.: University of Michigan Press.

Montague, Phillip. 1984. 'Rights and Duties of Compensation.' *Philosophy and Public Affairs* 13: 79–88.

Moore, Margaret. 2001. *The Ethics of Nationalism*. Oxford: Oxford University Press.

Moratinos, Miguel. 2001. 'Taba Negotiations: The Moratinos Non-Paper.' European Union. http://www.mideastweb.org/moratinos.htm.

Morris, Benny. 1987. *The Birth of the Palestinian Refugee Problem, 1947–1949*. Cambridge: Cambridge University Press.

_____. 1993. *Israel's Border Wars, 1949–1956*. Oxford: Oxford University Press.

_____. 1994. *1948 and after: Israel and the Palestinians*. Oxford: Clarendon Press.

_____. 1999. *Righteous Victims: A History of the Zionist-Arab Conflict, 1881–2001*. New York: Vintage Books.

_____. 2001. 'Revisiting the Palestinian Exodus of 1948.' In Rogan and Shlaim 2001.

_____. 2002a. 'An Interview with Ehud Barak.' *The New York Review of Books* 49 (10): 42–45.

_____. 2002b. *The Road to Jerusalem*. London: I. B. Tauris.

Muslih, Muhammad. 1988. *The Origins of Palestinian Nationalism*. New York: Columbia University Press.

Najjar, Orayb. 2003. '*Falastin* Editorial Writers, the Allies, World War II, and the Palestine Question in the 21st Century.' *Studies in Media and Information Literacy Education* 3 (4): www.utpjournals.com/jour.ihtml?1p=simile/issue12/najjarfulltext.html.

Nathan, Susan. 2005. *The Other Side of Israel: My Journey Across the Jewish-Arab Divide*. New York: Doubleday.

Netanyahu, Benjamin, ed. 1986. *Terrorism: How the West Can Win*. New York: Farrar, Strauss, and Giroux.

_____. 2000. *A Durable Peace: Israel and its Place Among the Nations*. New York: Warner Books.

_____. 2001. *Fighting Terrorism: How the West Can Defeat the International Terrorist Network*. New York: Farrar, Strauss, and Giroux.

Neumann, Michael. 2005. *The Case against Israel*. Petrolia, Calif.: Counterpunch.

Norman, W. 1998. 'The Ethics of Secession as the Regulation of Secessionist Politics.' In *National Self-Determination and Secession*, edited by Margaret Moore. Oxford: Oxford University Press.

Notter, Harley A. 1965. *The Origins of the Foreign Policy of Woodrow Wilson*. New York: Russell & Russell.

O'Brien, Conor Cruise. 1977. 'Liberty and Terrorism.' *International Security* 2: 56–57.
O'Brien, William. 1991. *Law and Morality in Israel's War with the PLO*. New York: Routledge.
Ofuatey-Kodjoe, W. 1977. *The Principle of Self-Determination in International Law*. New York: Nellen.
Oliverio, Annemarie. 1998. *The State of Terror*. Albany, N.Y.: SUNY Press.
Palumbo, Michael. 1987. *The Palestinian Catastrophe: The 1948 Expulsion of a People from their Homeland*. London and New York: Quartet Books.
Pape, Robert. 2003. 'The Strategic Logic of Suicide Terrorism.' *American Political Science Review* 97: 343–61.
_____. 2005. *Dying to Win: The Strategic Logic of Suicide Terrorism*. New York: Random House.
Pappe, Ilan. 1992. *The Making of the Arab-Israeli Conflict, 1947–1951*. London and New York: I. B. Tauris.
_____. ed. 1999. *The Israel/Palestine Question: Rewriting Histories*. London and New York: Routledge.
_____. 2004. *A History of Modern Palestine*. Cambridge: Cambridge University Press.
_____. 2006a. *The Ethnic Cleansing of Palestine*. Oxford: Oneworld.
_____. 2006b. 'The 1948 Ethnic Cleansing of Palestine.' *Journal of Palestine Studies* 36 (1): 6–20.
_____. 2007. 'Palestine 2007: Genocide in Gaza, Ethnic Cleansing in the West Bank.' *The Electronic Intifada*; http://electronicintifada.net.
Parekh, B. 1999. 'The Incoherence of Nationalism.' In Beiner 1999.
Patai, Raphael, ed. 1960. *The Complete Diaries of Theodor Herzl*. New York: Herzl Press and Thomas Yoseloff.
Pearlman, Wendy. 2003. *Occupied Voices: Stories of Everyday Life from the Second Intifada*. New York: Thunder's Mouth Press/Nation Books.
Peled, Yoav. 2006. 'Zionist Realities.' *New Left Review*, vol. 38, March/April, 21–36.
Peters, Joan. 1984. *From Time Immemorial: The Origins of the Arab-Jewish Conflict over Palestine*. New York: Harper and Row.
Petras, James. 2006. *The Power of Israel in the United States*. Atlanta: Clarity Press.
Petrovic, Drazen. 1994. 'Ethnic Cleansing: An Attempt at Methodology.' *European Journal of International Law* 5: 342–359.
Philpott, Daniel. 1995. 'In Defense of Self-Determination.' *Ethics* 105: 352–385.
Picard, Robert. 1993. *Media Portrayals of Terrorism*. Ames, Iowa: Iowa State University Press.
Pilger, John. 2004. 'The Most Important Terrorism is Ours.' *The New Statesman*, September 16, 2004.
Pogrebin, Letty Cottin. 2003. 'In Defense of the Law of Return.' In Kushner and Solomon 2003.
Pomerance, M. 1976. 'The United States and Self-Determination: Perspectives on the Wilsonian Conception.' *American Journal of International Law* 70: 1–27.
_____. 1984. 'Self-Determination Today: The Metamorphosis of an Ideal.' *Israel Law Review* 23: 310–339.
Porath, Yehoshua. 1974. *The Emergence of the Palestinian-Arab National Movement 1918–1929*. London: Frank Cass.
Primoratz, Igor. 2004a. 'What Is Terrorism?' In *Terrorism: The Philosophical Issues*. Houndmills, edited by Igor Primoratz. UK: Palgrave Macmillan.

_____. 2004b. 'State Terrorism and Counter-terrorism.' In *Terrorism: The Philosophical Issues*, edited by Igor Primoratz. Houndmills, UK: Palgrave Macmillan.
_____. 2006. 'Terrorism in the Israeli-Palestinian Conflict.' *Iyyun: The Jerusalem Philosophical Quarterly* 55: 27–48.
Quigley, John. 1990. *Palestine and Israel: A Challenge to Justice*. Durham NC: Duke University Press.
_____. 1999. 'The Right of Displaced Palestinians to Return to Home Areas in Israel.' In *The Palestinian Exodus, 1948–1998*, edited by G. Karmi and E. Cotran. Reading, UK: Ithaca Press.
_____. 2005. *The Case for Palestine: An International Law Perspective*. Durham, N.C.: Duke University Press.
Qumsiyeh, Mazen. 2004. *Sharing the Land of Canaan: Human Rights and the Israeli-Palestinian Struggle*. London: Pluto Press.
Rabkin, Yakov. 2006. *A Threat from Within: A Century of Jewish Opposition to Zionism*. London: Zed Books.
Rasheed, Mohammad. 1970. *Towards a Democratic State in Palestine*. Beirut: Palestine Liberation Organization Research Center.
Rawls, John. 1993. *Political Liberalism*. New York: Columbia University Press.
_____. 1999a. *The Law of Peoples*. Cambridge, Mass.: Harvard University Press.
_____. 1999b. 'Fifty Years after Hiroshima.' In *Collected Papers*, edited by S. Freeman. Cambridge, Mass.: Harvard University Press.
Reinhart, Tanya. 2002. *Israel/Palestine: How to End the War of 1948*. New York: Seven Stories Press.
_____. 2006. *The Road Map to Nowhere: Israel/Palestine since 2003*. New York: Verso.
Reporters Without Borders, eds. 2002. *Israel/Palestine: The Black Book*. London: Pluto Press.
Rice, Michael. 1994. *False Inheritance: Israel in Palestine and the Search for a Solution*. London: Kegan and Paul International.
Roberts, Adam. 1990. 'Prolonged Military Occupation: The Israeli-Occupied Territories Since 1967.' *American Journal of International Law* 84: 44–103.
Robinson, Jacob. [1947]. 1971. *Palestine and the United Nations*. Westport, Conn.: Greenwood Press.
Rogan, Eugene L., and Avi Shlaim, eds. 2001. *The War for Palestine: Rewriting the History of 1948*. Cambridge: Cambridge University Press.
Rokach, Livia. 1980. *Israel's Sacred Terrorism: A Study Based on Moshe Sharett's Personal Diary and Other Documents*. Belmont, Mass.: Association of Arab-American University Graduates.
Rose, Jaqueline. 2005. *The Question of Zion*. Princeton, N.J.: Princeton University Press.
Ross, Dennis. 2004. *The Missing Peace*. New York: Farrar, Straus and Giroux.
Rostow, Eugene. 1990. 'Bricks and Stones.' *The New Republic*. (April 23): 19–23.
Roy, Sara. 2007. *Failing Peace: Gaza and the Palestinian-Israeli Conflict*. London: Pluto Press.
Rubin, Andrew. 2005. 'One Year On: We are No Longer Able to See the Sun Set.' *The Electronic Intifada*, July 9, 2005; http://www.electronicintifada.net.
Sachar, Howard. 1989. *A History of Israel*. New York: Alfred A. Knopf.
Said, Edward. 1988. 'The Essential Terrorist.' In Said and Hitchens 1988.
_____. 1992. *The Question of Palestine*. New York: Vintage Books.

_____. 2000. *The End of the Peace Process: Oslo and After*. New York: Vintage Books.

Said, Wadie. 2001. 'The Obligations of Host Countries to Refugees under International Law: The Case of Lebanon.' In Aruri 2001.

Said, Edward, and Christopher Hitchens. 1988. *Blaming the Victims: Spurious Scholarship and the Palestinian Question*. London: Verso.

Saleh, Abdul Jawad. 2003. 'The Palestinian Non-Violent Resistance Movement.' *Alternative Palestinian Agenda*, http://www.ap-agenda.org/11-02/overview.htm

Schechtman, Joseph. 1961. *Fighter and Prophet: The Last Years*. New York: Yoseloff.

Schwartz, Warren (ed.). 1995. *Justice in Immigration*. Cambridge: Cambridge University Press.

Segev, Tom. 1986. *1949: The First Israelis*. New York: Henry Holt.

_____. 2000. *One Palestine, Complete*. Translated by H. Watzman. New York: Metropolitan Books.

_____. 2001. *Elvis in Jerusalem: Post-Zionism and the Americanization of Israel*. Translated by H. Watzman. New York: Henry Holt.

Selden, Mark, and Alvin Y. So, eds. 2004. *War and State Terrorism: The United States, Japan, and the Asia-Pacific in the Long Twentieth Century*. Lanham, Md.: Rowman and Littlefield.

Shaw, J. V. W. 1991. *A Survey of Palestine: Prepared in December 1945 and January 1946 for the Information of the Anglo-American Commission of Inquiry*, Vol. 1. Reprint. Washington D.C.: Institute for Palestine Studies.

Shehadeh, Raja. 1997. *From Occupation to Interim Accords: Israel and the Palestinian Territories*. Leiden, the Netherlands: Brill Academic Publishers.

Sher, George. 1980. 'Ancient Wrongs and Modern Rights.' *Philosophy and Public Affairs* 10: 3–17.

Shimoni, Gideon. 1995. *The Zionist Ideology*. Hanover and London: University Press of New England.

Shlaim, Avi. 2000. *The Iron Wall: Israel and the Arab World*. London and New York: W. W. Norton.

_____. 2001. 'Israel and the Arab Coalition in 1948.' In Rogan and Shlaim 2001.

Shohat, Ella Habiba. 2003. 'Dislocated Identities: Reflections of an Arab-Jews.' In Kushner and Solomon 2003.

Shuman, Ellis. 2003. 'Sharon: "Geneva Accord" Is Most Historic, Tragic Mistake Since Oslo.' *Israelinsider*, October 12, 2003. http://www.israelinsider.com.

Silberman, Neil Asher. 1989. *Between Past and Present: Archaeology, Ideology, and Nationalism in the Modern Middle East*. New York: Anchor Books.

Simmons, Brian. 1991. 'U.S. News Magazines' Labeling of Terrorists.' In *Media Coverage of Terrorism*, edited by A. O. Alali and K. K. Eke. London: Sage.

Simmons, A. John. 2001 'On the Territorial Rights of States.' *Philosophical Issues* 11: 300–326.

Smilansky, Saul. 2004. 'Terrorism, Justification, and Illusion.' *Ethics* 114: 790–805.

Smith Charles D. 1996. *Palestine and the Arab-Israeli Conflict: A History with Documents*. 3rd edition. Boston and New York: Bedford/St. Martin's.

_____. 2001. *Palestine and the Arab-Israeli Conflict: A History with Documents*. 4th edition. Boston and New York: Bedford/St. Martin's.

_____. 2004. *Palestine and the Arab-Israeli Conflict: A History with Documents*. 5th edition. New York: Bedford/St. Martin's.

Stace, W. T. 1947. 'The Zionist Illusion.' *The Atlantic Monthly*, 179: 82–86.

Stein, Kenneth W. 1984. *The Land Question in Palestine, 1917–1939*. Chapel Hill: University of North Carolina Press.

Steinhoff, Uwe. 2004. 'How Can Terrorism Be Justified?' In *Terrorism: The Philosophical Issues*, edited by Igor Primoratz. Houndmills, UK: Palgrave Macmillan.

Stone, Julius. 1981. *Israel and Palestine*. Baltimore: Johns Hopkins University Press.

Sturgis, Matthew. 2003. *It Ain't Necessarily So: Investigating the Truth of the Biblical Past*. Leicester: Charnwood.

Sumner, L. W. 1987. *The Moral Foundation of Rights*. Oxford: Clarendon Press.

_____. 2000. 'Rights.' In *The Blackwell Guide to Ethical Theory*, edited by H. LaFollette. Malden, Mass.: Blackwell Publishers.

Sussman, Gary. 2005. 'Ariel Sharon and the Jordan Option.' *Middle East Report Online*, March 2005.

Swisher, Clayton. 2004. *The Truth about Camp David: The Untold Story about the Collapse of the Middle East Peace Process*. New York: Nation Books.

Tadmor, Yoav. 1994. 'The Palestinian Refugees of 1948: The Right to Compensation and Return.' *Temple International and Comparative Law Journal* 8: 403–434.

Takkenberg, Lex. 1998. *The Status of Palestinian Refugees in International Law*. Oxford: Clarendon Press.

Talhami, Ghada Hashem. 2003. *Palestinian Refugees: Pawns to Political Actors*. New York: Nova Science Publishers.

Tamir, Yael. 1991. 'The Right to National Self-Determination.' *Social Research* 58: 565–590.

_____. 1993. *Liberal Nationalism*. Princeton: Princeton University Press.

Taylor, Alan. 1974. *The Zionist Mind*. Beirut: The Institute for Palestine Studies.

Thompson, Janna. 2001. 'Historical Injustice and Reparation: Justifying Claims of Descendents.' *Ethics* 112: 114–135.

Thomson, Judith Jarvis. 1986. *Rights, Restitution, and Risk: Essays in Moral Theory*, edited by W. Parent. Cambridge, Mass.: Harvard University Press.

_____. 1990. *The Realm of Rights*. Cambridge, Mass.: Harvard University Press.

Tilley, Virginia. 2003. 'The One-State Solution.' *London Review of Books* 25 (21): 13–16.

_____. 2005. *The One-State Solution: A Breakthrough for Peace in the Israeli-Palestinian Deadlock*. Ann Arbor, Mich.: University of Michigan Press.

_____. 2006. 'The Secular Solution.' *New Left Review*, vol. 38, March/April, 37–57.

Toner, Christopher. 2004. 'Just War and Graduated Discrimination.' *The American Catholic Philosophical Quarterly* 78: 649–665.

Toynbee, Arnold. 1954. *A Study of History*, vol. 8. Oxford: Oxford University Press.

_____. 1961–62. 'Jewish Rights in Palestine.' *The Jewish Quarterly Review* 52: 1–11.

_____. 1971. 'Samson Shakes the Pillar.' New York: Arab Information Center.

Tsemel, Leah. 1999. 'The Continuing Exodus – the Ongoing Expulsion of Palestinians from Jerusalem.' In *The Palestinian Exodus, 1948–1998*, edited by G. Karmi and E. Cotran. Reading, UK: Ithaca Press.

Umozurike, U. O. 1972. *Self-Determination in International Law*. Hamden, Conn.: Archon Books.

Usher, Graham. 1995. *Palestine in Crisis: The Struggle for Peace and Political Independence After Oslo*. London: Pluto Press.

_____. 2006. 'Hamas Risen.' *Middle East Report* Spring, 238: 2–11.

U.S. State Department. 2001. 'Patterns of Global Terrorism 2000.' In *Terrorism: Documents of International and Local Control*, Volume 26. Dobbs Ferry, N.Y.: Oceana Publications.

Valls, Andrew. 2000. 'Can Terrorism be Justified?' In *Ethics in International Affairs*, edited by Andrew Valls. Lanham, Md.: Rowman and Littlefield.

Vereté, Mayir. 1982. 'The Balfour Declaration and Its Makers.' In *Palestine and Israel in the 19th and 20th Centuries*, edited by E. Kedourie and S. G. Haim. London: Frank Cass.

Vogel, Manfred. 1997. 'The Ethical Dimension of the Jewish-Arab Conflict.' In Kapitan 1997.

Wagner, Donald. 2003. *Dying in the Land of Promise: Palestine and Palestinian Christianity from Pentacost to 2000*. London: Melisende.

Waldron, Jeremy. 1992. 'Superseding Historical Injustice.' *Ethics* 103: 4–28.

Walker, Margaret Urban. 2006. *Moral Repair: Reconstructing Moral Relations after Wrongdoing*. New York: Cambridge University Press.

Walzer, Michael. 1977. *Just and Unjust Wars: A Moral Argument with Historical Illustrations*. New York: Basic Books.

_____. 1983. *Spheres of Justice: A Defense of Pluralism and Equality*. New York: Basic Books.

_____. 1988. 'Terrorism: A Critique of Excuses.' In *Problems of International Justice*, edited by S. Luper-Foy. Boulder, Colo.: Westview Press.

Weizman, Eyal. 2004. 'Strategic Points, Flexible Lines, Tense Surfaces, Political Volumes: Ariel Sharon and the Geometry of Occupation.' *The Philosophical Forum* 35: 221–244.

Weizmann, Chaim. 1966. *Trial and Error: The Autobiography of Chaim Weizmann*. New York: Schocken.

Wellman, Carl. 1979. 'On Terrorism Itself.' *Journal of Value Inquiry* 13: 248–262.

Wexler, Paul. 1996. *The Non-Jewish Origins of the Sephardic Jews*. Albany, N.Y.: SUNY Press.

Whitehead, Alfred North. 1939. 'An Appeal to Sanity.' *The Atlantic Monthly* 158: 309–320.

Whitelam, Keith W. 1996. *The Invention of Ancient Israel: The Silencing of Palestinian History*. London and New York: Routledge.

Wieseltier, Leon. 2003. 'What is not to be Done: Israel, Palestine, and the Return of the Bi-national Fantasy.' *The New Republic*, 27 October, 20–23.

Wilkins, Burleigh Taylor. 1992. *Terrorism and Collective Responsibility*. New York: Routledge.

Wilkinson, Paul. 1986. *Terrorism and the Liberal State*. 2nd edition. New York: New York University Press.

Wilson, Woodrow. 1927. *War and Peace: Presidential Messages, Addresses, and Public Papers (1917–1924)* (two volumes), edited by R. S. Baker and W. E. Dodd. New York: Harper.

Yaniv, Avner. 1987. *Dilemmas of Security: Politics, Strategy, and the Israeli Experience in Lebanon*. Oxford: Oxford University Press.

Yiftachel, Oren. 2006. *Ethnocracy: Land and Identity Politics in Israel/Palestine*. Philadelphia: University of Pennsylvania Press.

Young, Iris Marion. 2005. 'Self-Determination as Non-Domination: Ideals Applied to Palestine/Israel.' *Ethnicities* 5: 139–159.

Young, Robert. 2004. 'Political Terrorism as a Weapon of the Politically Powerless.' In *Terrorism: The Philosophical Issues*. Houndmills, edited by Igor Primoratz. UK: Palgrave Macmillan.
Zuaiter, Akram. 1994. *For the Sake of My Nation*. Beirut: Alasriyya.
Zunes, Stephen. 2003. *Tinderbox*. Monroe, Maine: Common Courage Press.
Zureik, Elia. 1996. *Palestinian Refugees and the Peace Process*. Washington, D.C.: Institute for Palestine Studies.

Index